# Invitation to Midrash

## The Workings of Rabbinic Bible Interpretation

*A Teaching Book*

JACOB NEUSNER

HarperSanFrancisco

*A Division of* HarperCollins*Publishers*

For
William Scott Green
and
Rebecca MacMillan Fox
on the occasion of
their seventh wedding anniversary
August 2, 1988

and for
Noah
and
Ethan

Grateful acknowledgement is made to Stephen A. Kaufman and Michael Arsers for their work in providing the Hebrew selections.

**Library of Congress Cataloging-in-Publication Data**

Neusner, Jacob, 1932–
    Invitation to Midrash.

    Includes index.
    1. Midrash—History and criticism.    2. Bible. O.T.—
Criticism, interpretation, etc., Jewish.    I. Title.
BM514.N47    1989    296.1'4061    88-45695
ISBN 0-06-066107-0

91  92  93  HC  10  9  8  7  6  5  4  3  2

# Contents

# Preface

The three major trends in rabbinic Bible interpretation—exegetical, propositional, and narrative—show us how Midrash works in Judaism. Midrash in Hebrew means investigation, and, when applied to Scripture, Midrash means investigation of the meaning of Scripture, hence, interpretation. Here we follow three successive trends of rabbinic Bible interpretation worked out in the first seven centuries of the Common Era (=A.D.). In the first, the focus of interest is on individual verses of Scripture, and interpreting those verses in the sequence in which they appear forms the organizing principle of sustained discourse. In the second, the center of interest attends to the testing and validating of large-scale propositions, which, through the reading of individual verses, an authorship wishes to test and validate. In that rather philosophical trend in rabbinic Bible interpretation, the interpretation of individual verses takes a subordinate position, the appeal to facts of Scripture in the service of the syllogism at hand. The third approach directs attention not to concrete statements of Scripture, whether in sequences of verses or merely individual verses or even words or phrases, but to entire compositions of Scripture: biblical themes, stories. This investigation of Scripture's meaning generates Midrash as narrative: the imaginative recasting of Scripture's stories in such a way as to make new and urgent points through the retelling.

The first of the three trends is represented here by Sifra and Sifré to Numbers, in Part Two, which match medium to message, making their points in an eloquent and powerful way both by how and also by what is said. In my concluding theological proposition, I claim that out of the rather arid materials of Sifra and Sifré to Numbers we come across majestic con-

ceptions of the power of the human intellect. The second trend
we follow in Part Three through Genesis Rabbah, Leviticus
Rabbah, and Pesiqta deRab Kahana. This trend leaves us no
doubt as to the overriding themes and recurrent tensions that
precipitated Bible interpretation among their authorships. In
my concluding propositions on Midrash and culture, I invoke
the detailed rereading of biblical genealogies and family stories
to explain how Midrash mediates from age to age, sustaining a
connection between the received and the given of a later time.
The third trend, that of narrative, carries its new message and
medium, as we see in Part Four. Here too the remarkable authority of Midrash to form in a single plane of being the diverse ages of remote and late antique Israel comes to the fore,
once more showing how Midrash works so as to hold together
in a single paradigmatic moment the detritus of diverse times
and places.

Through the concrete texts at hand, therefore, we consider
Midrash from its detailed interpretation of a given verse to its
larger uses in setting forth principal positions of the Judaic religious system worked out by the sages at hand, those Judaic
masters who, from the first to the seventh centuries, defined
the Judaism of the dual Torah, the paramount Judaism from
their time to ours. Then, at the end, I explain my understanding of what Midrash teaches us in particular, offering cultural
and theological propositions, both negative and constructive,
that address an important message to our own time. Everything the English reader requires is here. (I provide at the back
selections from the Hebrew texts for those who wish to follow
the Midrash-compilations in the original.) As we walk together through the samples of the interpretation of verses of Scripture accomplished by the Judaic sages and then follow the uses
to which they put Scripture through their interpretation, we
shall come to a clear understanding of the power to define the
history of Judaism imparted to Scripture by the hands of these,
the Scripture's great exegetes. We shall further see how those
processes of ongoing civilization exemplified in the workings

of Midrash as they unfold in the major trends of rabbinic Bible interpretation show us the underpinnings of the civilization of the West: the power to see one thing in many things and to hear many messages out of a single word.

It is important to identify the particular Judaism, the exegesis of which stretches forth in this teaching book. It is the Judaism of the dual Torah, oral and written, terms I shall presently explain. We hear, in particular, from the sages, who bore the honorific title *rabbi*, meaning "my lord," and so gave to their Judaism the title *rabbinic*. The Judaic sages who produced the ancient Midrash-compilations did not stand alone in their interest in Scripture. In ancient times there were many groups of Judaic masters, each addressing its own circle of "Israel," that is, its world of Jews, each developing its world view and way of life and theory of who Israel is into a religious system, into a Judaism distinctive to itself. Late antiquity knew many such Judaisms, each with its world view, way of life, account of Israel, and, consequently, its distinctive and characteristic method and mode of reading in detail and in the aggregate the received writings of ancient Israel, the Hebrew Bible. Of these diverse groups we can immediately think of two—the Judaic sages or rabbis who form the focus of this book, and the Christian evangelists who interpreted scriptural themes in such writings as Matthew, with its rich and systematic exegesis of verses of prophecy, and the Letter to the Hebrews, with its powerful and imaginative interpretation of sacrifice, priesthood, and Temple. Both of these groups of Judaic thinkers turned to Scripture and interpreted it, each in light of the profound concerns that brought Scripture into the center of discourse and discussion. Other such Judaic groups include the Essene community of Qumran, which has left us sizable Midrash-compilations of Midrash-exegeses following its principles of Midrash-interpretation; the synagogue community at Dura Europos, which, in the painted walls, in ca. 250 C.E., created a systematic exegesis of scriptural themes and topics as these were to be mediated to their life and circumstance; and many others.

Many interpreters of Scripture, both Judaic and Christian, produced their Midrash, and here we follow principal trends in only one type of Judaism. In a quite separate venture, *What Is Midrash?*, my colleagues and I present a brief survey of a much broader segment of Judaic Bible interpretation than that most influential one deriving from "our sages of blessed memory," the rabbis of the Midrash-compilations and the two Talmuds we examine here.* Since there was no single "Judaism," nothing to correspond to orthodoxy, there also was no such thing as a single Midrash, one Jewish way of reading ancient Scripture. Accordingly, just as we cannot imagine homogenizing all Judaisms into one, so we may not present all approaches to scriptural exegesis as a single ubiquitous "Jewish hermeneutics." It would be an error to try to combine all these diverse and distinctive approaches to Scripture, with their various interpretations, selections of, and imputations of particular meaning to distinct verses.

Each group's mode of Midrash (if the word applied to them all) took shape within its large Judaic system, asking the questions important to that system, finding self-evidently valid answers in Scripture as that system dictated those answers, whether in detail or in large and encompassing character, were to be found. In this book, therefore, we consider only a single Judaic system, its singular world view, way of life, and identification of Israel, as these took shape in and came to rich expression in Midrash-exegesis, compiled in Midrash-documents, following a well-defined program of Midrash-principles of interpretation.

All Judaisms and all Christianities read the same Scripture and revered the same books. But each selected those portions of Scripture that mattered to it. So while everything was true, not everything was equally relevant. A system—a Christianity, a Judaism—defined for itself an urgent, ineluctable question, answering that question in a self-evidently valid response,

---

*Jacob Neusner (with Ernest S. Frerichs, Gary G. Porton, William Scott Green, and Paul Flesher), *What Is Midrash?* (Philadelphia: Fortress Press, 1987).

which took the form of the way of life and world view for Israel that, for that system, constituted (in our language, not theirs) "Judaism," or with the necessary changes of detail, "Christianity." In consequence, in no way may we speak of "Jewish exegesis of Scripture," meaning a single Midrash-exegesis or Midrash-compilation or Midrash-process or even a common set of encompassing rules everywhere held authoritative by Jewry. The relationship between the Midrash-system of one distinct group of Jews to that governing some other varied. True, certain practices characterized all interpreters of Scripture. For example, it was routine to cite a verse of Scripture and to say in a few words what it meant. That simple procedure characterizes most documents that collect and present exegeses of verses of Scripture, documents that originated in diverse Judaisms.

But that merely adventitious fact by itself hardly validates the commonplace, and wrong, premise that such a thing as a single, unitary, linear, and incremental "Jewish exegesis of Scripture" operated pretty much everywhere. All documentary evidence of diverse Jews' exegesis of Scripture points in the opposite direction. In general, comparing one group's treatment of Scripture with that of another shows different people using different rhetorical forms and appealing to distinct logical categories to address a singular topical program; thus we find different people talking in different ways about different things to different people. Even within a single Judaism, such as the Judaism of the dual Torah that we shall investigate, diverse documents used distinctive rhetorical plans, logical modes of making intelligible statements, and topical programs. The few exegeses of Scripture that intersect among the writings produced a number of diverse Judaic contexts ("Judaisms"). And these prove so commonplace or so fragmentary as to yield no trace of a single, systematic, and comprehensive exegesis of Scripture. So there was no common exegesis among all Jews.

It therefore would be misleading to speak of "*the* Midrash," meaning a single and uniform system of exegesis of Scripture operative among all Jews in general. It is still more confusing to treat as fragments of a single system of biblical interpretation all the bits and pieces of information deriving from various communities scattered throughout the territories of the Near and Middle East and covering a span of hundreds of years. When, therefore, we wish to investigate Jews' exegeses of Scripture, we must follow the course of distinct bodies of sources. Each system of exegesis of Scripture emerges from its distinct historical setting, addresses its own social entity, and tells us, usually only in bits and pieces of detailed information, about itself alone. Whether whole or fragmentary, systems of Jewish exegesis of Scripture do not coalesce into one ideal system.

True, one might seek a lowest common denominator among all systems of exegesis of Scripture followed by all Jewish groups. That, then, would be deemed "the Midrash," or "the (particularly) Jewish exegesis of Scripture." But details, even when shared among a variety of Judaisms, make full and complete sense only in their respective contexts. Each, on its own, matters in the system in which it makes its appearance and plays its role. So if we wish to consider the development of "the Midrash," we have first to decide whose Midrash we propose to describe and to analyze. Systematic studies of the Midrash of the Jews in Alexandria, the Jews in Elephantine, the Jews in the Essene community of Qumran, and, of course, the Jews who stand behind the exegesis of Scripture now presented in the Mishnah and its successor documents all present appropriate foci of inquiry. Among these and other Judaic systems, including their respective modes of exegesis of Scripture, produced by Jews, the one of greatest importance is that commencing with the Mishnah, ca. 200 C.E. And it is the working of the Midrash of the sages, or rabbis, who created that Judaic system, that I illustrate and explain here.

In this book, which forms a sequel to my *Invitation to the Talmud: A Teaching Book,* 2d ed. (San Francisco: Harper & Row, 1985), I lead the reader through particular Midrash-texts, line by line, and so through concrete texts I illustrate Midrash-exegesis. I further show the reader the character of the documents at hand and therefore display Midrash-compilations as works of literature and interpretation. This display, specifically, allows us to see how through discrete interpretation of individual verses, sages found it possible to make cogent statements, to argue in behalf of large and important propositions. Finally, I trace the unfolding of the compilations and their contents in their broader canonical setting and thus present a clear picture of Midrash-hermeneutics. In this way we see Midrash as part of the larger history of Judaism in its formative age.

Let me briefly lay out the program of this book. I begin by stating for the Judaism studied here—the one that produced the documents of Midrash we shall read—the large and critical question concerning the Hebrew Scriptures: What precisely motivated attention to Scripture? Why did the Judaism we address find it necessary to approach Scripture in the way it did, and for the purposes that defined the traits of that approach? In this book I answer that question within the limits of the canon of the Judaism of the dual Torah, its logic and inner tensions.* In Part One I lay out the issue of Scripture as it would reach definition in the setting of the Judaism of the dual Torah, oral and written. That requires us to turn to Midrash where it is not present, not only where it plays a role. For while the authorship of the Mishnah only occasionally introduced a text of Scripture to prove a proposition at hand and still more rarely took up the verse-by-verse exegesis of Scripture, for that authorship, Scripture constituted a complete and exhaustive

---

*In a separate work, I place the same question into its context in the debate with Christianity. I refer to my *Judaism in the Matrix of Christianity* (Philadelphia: Fortress Press, 1986). In yet another work, *Midrash in Context: Exegesis in Formative Judaism* (Philadelphia: Fortress Press, 1983), I spell out the basic theory taken for granted here on the Mishnah as the precipitant for sages' formation of Midrash-compilations. I further show that the same taxonomic scheme that serves the exegetical modes applying to the Mishnah in the Talmud of the Land of Israel encompasses the exegetical modes applying to the book of Genesis in Genesis Rabbah. These are two quite distinct contexts in which Midrash-compilations are to be seen, and I am inclined to see these as two among more than three dimensions such as I have studied here and in the other two books.

statement of God's will and word for Israel. Consequently, where we do not find Midrash as exegesis of Scripture, even more than where we do, we have to ask about the workings of Midrash and discover what we can about the rabbinic interpretation of the Hebrew Bible.

In Parts Two and Three we take up the two types of Midrash-compilations of Midrash-exegeses of Scripture. In the former, and I think chronologically earlier, of the two, Midrash-exegesis produces propositions; in the latter, propositions yield Midrash-exegesis. These two types of Midrash-compilations differ in rhetorical, logical, and, of course, topical aspects. In Part Four we turn to yet another meaning of Bible interpretation, and that is a large-scale reworking of biblical stories, another form of Midrash besides the form of exegetical and propositional or syllogistic discourse. In Part Four I set forth a clear picture of how Midrash-interpretation functions through narrative, storytelling of a very particular order. I show that the Scripture story and the sage story differ in narrative character, and I explain how the Scripture story constitutes a fresh mode of Midrash-exegesis of biblical topics or themes. In Part Five I turn from the Midrash-compilations to the two Talmuds and show the ways in which they assemble compositions parallel to those found in the Midrash-compilations. At the end, in the concluding theological chapter, I address contemporary issues of theology and theology of culture as these pertain to Midrash. I discuss specific statements on the character of Judaism and of Midrash and test them against the evidence we have reviewed. I then offer two alternative propositions of a theological character concerning the nature of human culture and the character and definition of humanity "in our image, after our likeness," as our study of Midrash in its principal trends in rabbinic Bible interpretation permits us to frame such propositions.

In this brief account I mean also to open up for the world today the workings of Midrash. I think contemporary generations—faithful Jews and Christians alike— may not only derive insight from the Midrash-exegesis and Midrash-compilations we have received; we may also enter into that process of ersation with Scripture that, for the history of the West, has sustained our common life, our society, our culture, our hope. For Western civilization rests upon the foundations of the Hebrew Bible, and if we propose to build toward the twenty-first century, we shall have to learn how to regain access to that long-ago age in which, through Israel, God addressed to the world those principles of culture and theology that would sustain the life of humanity on this earth.

Jacob Neusner

July 28, 1988
My fifty-sixth birthday

Program in Judaic Studies
Brown University
Providence, Rhode Island

Prologue  # FROM SCRIPTURE TO TORAH:
THE PROBLEMATIC
OF MIDRASH

# Prologue

The rabbis' interpretation of Scripture teaches us how, through scriptural exegesis, the Judaism of the dual Torah, oral and written, formulated and presented its fundamental truth. Specifically, rabbis turned to Scripture in the way in which Greek philosophers turned to nature and to logic—as a means of testing and verifying their principal propositions about reality. These were syllogisms concerning the rules and character of Israel's sacred life in the here and now and the condition of Israel's salvation at the end of time. When we understand that world of cogent, sustained, and rigorous discourse of biblical interpretation, we regain access to modes of thought and interpretation with which we in our time may enter into conversation.

Rabbinic Bible interpretation read the Hebrew Scriptures as one-half, the written half, of the whole Torah, that is, the dual Torah in two media, writing and memory, revealed by God to Moses at Sinai. The other half of that same Torah, the oral part, derives from oral formulation and oral transmission of God's word, finally preserved in the teachings of the Judaic sages themselves. Midrash so works as to lead us into the world of the Hebrew Bible as that Scripture entered into Judaism. For the Holy Scriptures were transformed by the Judaic sages or rabbis in the first through seventh centuries, the formative centuries of Western civilization. *Through the workings of Midrash the Hebrew Bible became the written half of the one whole Torah, oral and written, revealed by God to Moses our Rabbi at Mount Sinai.*

Midrash works in three dimensions: first, as explanation of meaning imputed to particular verses of Scripture; second, as a mode of stating important propositions, syllogisms of thought, in conversation with verses or sustained passages of Scripture;

and, third, as a way of retelling scriptural stories that imparts new immediacy to those stories. In this book we shall learn how to read samples of all three ways in which Midrash works, and we shall further gain access to the lessons that Scripture has to teach us, for the sake of our own encounter with the Hebrew Bible.

When we understand how Midrash works, we learn two things. The first is how Judaism took shape and became the enduring religious system that has so long sustained Israel, the Jewish people, wherever they lived in the history of Western civilization. The second lesson places before us one of the important ways in which the Hebrew Bible has given shape and meaning to the civilization of the West, as Judaism, along with Christianity and Islam, made its profound imprint upon the West. For when we know how the Hebrew Bible lent structure and significance to societies and cultures, we understand the process of meaning that has made us what we are—and are not. The particular lesson of Midrash as the rabbis framed biblical interpretation centers upon how an ancient text retains perpetual relevance and gains renewal in succeeding ages. For by bringing their profound concerns to Scripture in the assumption that Scripture spoke to them, even to them, sages invested Scripture with perpetual contemporaneity. And by reading Scripture in the assumption that they, even they, might state authoritatively the meaning and message of Scripture, sages imparted to Scripture the structure of their own minds, the sensibility of their own intellects. They therefore formed a bridge to mediate between one age and another and, of still greater consequence, to mediate between one mind and another: the intellect of God, speaking through the Torah in two media, and the intellect of humanity, participating through Midrash in conversation with God about issues of shared intelligibility.

By the word *Midrash,* the Hebrew word for investigation, people commonly mean one of three things. First comes the sense of Midrash as the explanation, by Judaic interpreters, of the meaning of individual verses of Scripture. The result of the interpretation of a verse of Scripture is called a Midrash-exegesis. The result of the interpretation of Scripture is collected, second, in Midrash-compilations, or what I call a Midrash-document. Third, the process of interpretation, for instance, the principles that guide the interpreter, is called Midrash-method.

So when people speak of Midrash, they may refer—moving up the scale—to the method by which meaning is gained in Scripture, individual verses, or sustained passages; they may mean the collection of interpretations, formed into a composition on its own; they may mean the reading and explanation of the components of a single verse. How one important and influential group of Jews—the sages or rabbis who formed Judaism as we know it—read the Hebrew Scriptures, or Old Testament, is the subject of this book. We speak, specifically, of the sages of Judaism, called by the title of respect, *rabbi,* meaning "my lord," who between the first and the seventh centuries of the Common Era (=A.D.) so interpreted the Hebrew Scriptures as to define Judaism as it has flourished from their time to ours. Thus describing the process of interpretation of Scripture, or Midrash, allows us to follow the formation of Judaism.

The process of interpretation used by ancient rabbis and the consequent formation of Judaism become topics of general interest for several reasons. First, Midrash understood as a particular Judaic group's interpretation of Scripture provides us with a picture of one systematic and important result of the encounter with the Hebrew Bible. It is a part of the record of how the Hebrew Scripture shaped the civilization, including the religions, therefore also the religion, of the West.

Midrash, second, presents us with a case study of how in the formation of a religion, the received Scripture contributes where and when its contribution is welcome and does so in such a way as to give more than the recipients have asked for. That is to say, we see how, through the labor of Midrash-exegesis and Midrash-compilation, the Judaic sages mediated between the authoritative Scriptures of the past and the world they proposed to create.

Midrash understood as a distinctive process of the reading of Scripture, third, presents us with a sustained and sizable sample of the process of interpretation, by one group in a distinctive context, of a received text created by another, earlier group in a different circumstance. As such, Midrash provides us with insight into the continuity of culture over a changing era, a striking and interesting example of the general hermeneutical possibilities of accommodating change through exegesis of the received in light of the givens of a new age. Midrash gives us an example of cultural continuity read in universal terms but illustrated in detail by the interpretive process before us, seen in very particular terms. For the history of religion—therefore also of culture—is the story of the ongoing exegesis of the inherited imperatives in response to the fresh possibilities of Scripture across the ages.

Why should the framers of a Judaic system have turned to Scripture at all? The answer scarcely requires exposition. From the late sixth and fifth centuries B.C.E., when the Five Books of Moses were formed out of ancient stories and traditions, Scripture, that is, the Pentateuch made up of Genesis, Exodus, Leviticus, Numbers, and Deuteronomy, was received as God's revelation. With the later completion of the canon through the Prophetic books, which are Joshua, Judges, Samuel, Kings, Isaiah, Jeremiah, Ezekiel; the twelve smaller prophetic books; and the Writings—Psalms, Proverbs, Job, Song of Songs, Ruth, Lamentations, Qohelet, Esther, Daniel, Ezra, Nehemiah, and Chronicles—no Judaism challenged the authority of Scripture, and every Judaism took shape in response to it.

Accordingly, the question that demands attention is not why Scripture at all, but what *particular* problem, in respect to Scripture, sages had to work out. When we know the answer to that question, we may understand the workings of Midrash as the Judaic sages produced a literature of biblical interpretation. It is the question that sages brought to Scripture that tells us why they found what they located there, how their attention was drawn to one passage, rather than some other, and the way in which they, for their part, knew right from wrong, truth from error, in their reading of Scripture. Scripture formed the problem, and the question addressed to sages by the character of their own system defined the problematic that guided their address to that problem.

For why should Scripture have formed a problem at all? The answer to that question draws us to sages' Judaism seen whole, complete, and final. For it is only by viewing their Judaism at the end, a finished building in its complete and final architectural statement, that we gain perspective on the architectonics, the proportions and structure of the parts. And, moreover, we ask a question not of history, finding out which came first and which followed, but of inner structure and logic.* The unfolding of logic, order, proportion, and cogency follows an inner dynamic, an implicit discipline that we discern only after the fact, therefore at the end of the process.

Now if we see the Judaism of the dual Torah at the end, the first question we must confront is the obvious one: how can this Judaism, which posits the existence of two Torahs—one formulated and handed on in writing, the other formulated and transmitted orally, through processes of memorization—explain the one Torah, the oral, in relationship to the other, the written? That question covers the entire canon of the Judaism of the dual Torah and also reaches into the depths of acute detail at every point; it is the problematic. When sages turned to Scripture, they saw Scripture as one part of the dual Torah, and at every point discourse demanded detailed attention to the interplay of the two Torahs, the one Torah in two media.

---

*As said above, that question of history—why in the particular circumstance in which sages produced Midrash-compilations did they undertake that work, then, not earlier—is addressed in *Judaism in the Matrix of Christianity*. In that setting I argue that Midrash-compilations constitute one of the important ways in which sages met the crisis of the Christian challenge to Judaism after Constantine's Christianization of the empire.

One document forms the pivot around which all else turned, and that is tractate Avot, The Fathers or Founders, produced as an account of the origins and authority of the Mishnah about a generation after the closure of the Mishnah. When we consider the place and uses of Scripture, the written Torah, in the account of the origin and meaning of the Torah of Sinai, we shall realize in a clear and cogent statement the entirety of the issue of Midrash, that is, the tasks of biblical interpretation as these confronted the rabbis of the Judaism of the dual Torah.

Here are the first two chapters of tractate Avot. What is important in Chapter One is the sequence of authorities, who they are and what they say.

## THE SAYINGS OF THE FATHERS

### CHAPTER ONE

1:1.   Moses received the Torah at Sinai and handed it on to Joshua, Joshua to elders, and elders to prophets. And prophets handed it on to the men of the great assembly. They said three things, "Be prudent in judgment. Raise up many disciples. Make a fence for the Torah."

If Judaism has in one sentence a Declaration of Independence, Constitution, and Bill of Rights all together, it is in this simple statement: *Moses received the Torah and handed it on.* For what follows is so jarring as to lead us to see all things in a new way. The chain of *receiving* and *handing on*—that is, of tradition—encompasses not (merely) biblical figures, such as Joshua and the prophets, but also figures we do not know in Scripture, such as the men of the great assembly (whoever they were, whenever they lived). That simple detail prepares us to see the tradition of the Torah in a new way, for it asserts that, within the processes of tradition of the Torah, existed not only figures known in the Hebrew Scriptures, which, we realize, to the system of Judaism constituted the written half of the Torah, but also others found outside of the written Torah. Not only so, but the sequence of sayings leads us far from Scripture. It follows that the opening statement in its elaboration denies that all that Moses received as Torah was the Scripture everyone knew; in other words, it affirms that Torah contains another component in addition to the written one. To find out who these others were and what importance was imputed to them, we proceed through the list.

1:2.   Simeon the Righteous was one of the last survivors of the great assembly. He would say: On three things does the world stand: On the Torah, and on the Temple service, and on deeds of lovingkindness.

1:3.   Antigonus of Sokho received [the Torah] from Simeon the Righteous. He would say: Do not be like servants who serve the master on condition of receiving a reward, but [be] like servants who serve the master not on condition of receiving a reward. And let the fear of Heaven be upon you.

Once more we find the Torah moving on through the names of authorities not located in the Scriptures. Consequently, the chain of tradition implicitly differentiates between the whole Torah and a part of the Torah, the part that is contained within the Hebrew Bible. It is a statement not made explicitly, but it is eloquent and powerful for people who know how to listen to detail: the mere variation in names from the names of biblical heroes, such as Joshua and the prophets, tells the tale. We now proceed through a set of five paired names, and the second message of the list will resonate when we understand the identities of those who are now listed.

1:4.   Yosé b. Yoezer of Zeredah and Yosé b. Yohanan of Jerusalem received [the Torah] from them. Yosé ben Yoezer says: Let your house be a gathering place for sages. And wallow in the dust of their feet, and drink in their words with gusto.

1:5.   Yosé ben Yohanan of Jerusalem says: Let your house be open wide. And seat the poor at your table ["make the poor members of your household"]. And don't talk too much with women. (He referred to a man's wife, all the more so is the rule to be applied to the wife of one's fellow. In this regard did sages say: So long as a man talks too much with a woman, he brings trouble on himself, wastes time better spent on studying the Torah, and ends up an heir of Gehenna.)

1:6.  Joshua ben Perahyah and Nittai the Arbelite received [the Torah] from them. Joshua ben Perahyah says: Set up a master for yourself. And get yourself a companion-disciple. And give everybody the benefit of the doubt.

1:7.  Nittai the Arbelite says: Keep away from a bad neighbor. And don't get involved with a bad person. And don't give up hope of retribution.

1:8A.  Judah ben Tabbai and Simeon ben Shetah received [the Torah] from them.

1:8B.  Judah ben Tabbai says: Don't make yourself like one of those who advocate before judges [while you yourself are judging a case]. And when the litigants stand before you, regard them as guilty. But when they leave you, regard them as acquitted [when they have accepted your judgment].

1:9.  Simeon ben Shetah says: Examine the witnesses with great care. And watch what you say, lest they learn from what you say how to lie.

1:10.  Shemaiah and Avtalyon received [the Torah] from them. Shemaiah says: Love work. Hate authority. Don't get friendly with the government.

1:11.  Avtalyon says: Sages, watch what you say, lest you become liable to the punishment of exile, and go into exile to a place of bad water, and disciples who follow you drink bad water and die, and the name of Heaven be thereby profaned.

1:12.  Hillel and Shammai received [the Torah] from them. Hillel says: Be disciples of Aaron, loving peace and pursuing grace, loving people and drawing them near to the Torah.

1:13A.  He would say [in Aramaic]: A name made great is a name destroyed, and one who does not add, subtracts.

1:13B.  And who does not learn is liable to death. And the one who uses the crown, passes away.

1:14.  He would say: If I am not for myself, who is for me? And when I am for myself, what am I? And if not now, when?

1:15.  Shammai says: Make your learning of the Torah a fixed obligation. Say little and do much. Greet everybody cheerfully.

The power of the list is shown in two aspects. First, no one cites the written Scripture—yet the list contains authoritative Torah-teachings. Second, the names themselves give remarkable testimony. The importance of the five pairs of names derives from an unstated fact. All of those ten authori-

ties occur in the Mishnah, and two of them, Hillel and Shammai, together with their schools of houses, prove paramount
figures in the Mishnah, cited many hundreds of times. Consequently, in the set of five paired names we find a stunning statement as to the Mishnah's standing and authority within the
Torah. The authorities of the Mishnah—and therefore also the
lessons that they teach, what they say—fall within the realm of
the Torah. It follows that what they say has the same standing
as what Scripture says, *because what these authorities say is from
Sinai,* as much as what we find in the written Torah is part of
the same Torah received by Moses from God at Sinai.

Let us complete the picture and note where, in concrete historical terms, it has led us.

1:16.   Rabban Gamaliel says: Set up a master for yourself. Avoid doubt.
Don't tithe by too much guesswork.

1:17.   Simeon his son says: All my life I grew up among the sages, and I
found nothing better for a person [the body] than silence. And not the learning is the thing, but the doing. And whoever talks too much causes sin.

1:18.   Rabban Simeon ben Gamaliel says: On three things does the world
stand: on justice, on truth, and on peace. As it is said, *Execute the judgment of
truth and peace in your gates* (Zech. 8:16).

Only at the end do we have a prooftext, a remarkable con-
cession given the character of what has gone before. The
named figures, Gamaliel and his son, Simeon b. Gamaliel, are
known to have lived in the first century of the Common Era.
The former is mentioned in the New Testament as a Pharisee,
the latter in the writings of Josephus as a leading figure in the
Jewish government, also as a Pharisee. It follows that the line
of tradition from Sinai has carried us through the entire epoch
of the life of ancient Israel and down into the first century of
the Common Era.

We have neglected, for the moment, to pay attention to the
Torah-teachings of the sages of our list. For that purpose, we
take up the second chapter of the same document, because it
contains powerful testimony concerning not only the author-

ity but also the message and teachings of that one whole Torah of Moses, revealed by God at Sinai. Specifically, we shall now see what the sages' half, the oral part, of the Torah teaches. And what we learn is that the oral Torah stands separate and alone as much in its message as in its masters. The authorities are not those named in Scripture, and what they say rarely cites a verse of Scripture. What that means is that the Torah in its oral sector does not simply restate or interpret or apply the Torah of the written sector. It is, as I just said, distinct and majestically independent in message as much as in master. When we have reviewed the substance of the Torah-teachings that lie before us, we shall realize the full task that confronted the masters of Midrash: building a bridge between the two Torahs, so showing the propositions of the one through the proofs supplied by the other.

## CHAPTER TWO

2:1.  Rabbi says: What is the straight path which a person should choose for himself? Whatever is an ornament to the one who follows it, and an ornament in the view of others. Be meticulous in a small religious duty as in a large one, for you do not know what sort of reward is coming for any of the various religious duties. And reckon with the loss [required] in carrying out a religious duty against the reward for doing it; and the reward for committing a transgression against the loss for doing it. And keep your eye on three things, so you will not come into the clutches of transgression. Know what is above you. An eye which sees, and an ear which hears, and all your actions are written down in a book.

2:2.  Rabban Gamaliel, a son of Rabbi Judah the Patriarch says: Fitting is learning in the Torah along with a craft, for the labor put into the two of them makes one forget sin. And all learning of the Torah which is not joined with labor is destined to be null and causes sin. And all who work with the community—let them work with them [the community] for the sake of Heaven. For the merit of the fathers strengthens them, and the righteousness which they do stands forever. And, as for you, I credit you with a great reward, as if you had done [all the work required by the community].

2:3.  Be wary of the government, for they get friendly with a person only for their own convenience. They look like friends when it is to their benefit, but they do not stand by a person when he is in need.

2:4.   He would say: Make His wishes into your own wishes, so that He will make your wishes into His wishes. Put aside your wishes on account of His wishes, so that He will put aside the wishes of other people in favor of your wishes. Hillel says: Do not walk out on the community. And do not have confidence in yourself until the day you die. And do not judge your companion until you are in his place. And do not say anything which cannot be heard, for in the end it will be heard. And do not say: When I have time, I shall study, for you may never have time.

2:5.   He would say: A coarse person will never fear sin, nor will an *am ha-Aretz* [one who does not master the Torah] ever be pious, nor will a shy person learn, nor will an ignorant person teach, nor will anyone too occupied in business get wise. In a place where there are none of worth, try to be a person of worth.

2:6.   Also, he saw a skull floating on the water and said to it [in Aramaic]: Because you drowned others, they drowned you, and in the end those who drowned you will be drowned.

2:7.   He would say: Lots of meat, lots of worms; lots of property, lots of worries; lots of women, lots of witchcraft; lots of slave girls, lots of lust; lots of slave boys, lots of robbery. Lots of the Torah, lots of life; lots of discipleship, lots of wisdom; lots of counsel, lots of understanding; lots of righteousness, lots of peace. [If] one has gotten a good name, he has gotten it for himself. [If] he has gotten teachings of the Torah, he has gotten himself life eternal.

2:8A.   Rabban Yohanan ben Zakkai received [the Torah] from Hillel and Shammai. He would say: If you have learned much Torah, do not puff yourself up on that account, for it was for that purpose that you were created. He had five disciples, and these are they: Rabbi Eliezer ben Hyrcanus, Rabbi Joshua ben Hananiah, Rabbi Yosé the Priest, Rabbi Simeon ben Nethanel, and Rabbi Eleazar ben Arakh.

2:8B.   He would list their good qualities: Rabbi Eliezer ben Hyrcanus—a plastered well, which does not lose a drop of water. Rabbi Joshua—happy is the one who gave birth to him. Rabbi Yosé— a pious man. Rabbi Simeon ben Nethanel—a man who fears sin, and Rabbi Eleazar ben Arakh—a surging spring.

2:8C.   He would say: If all the sages of Israel were on one side of the scale, and Rabbi Eliezer ben Hyrcanus were on the other, he would outweigh all of them.

2:8D.   Abba Saul says in his name: If all of the sages of Israel were on one side of the scale, and Rabbi Eliezer ben Hyrcanus were also with them, and Rabbi Eleazar [ben Arakh] were on the other side, he would outweigh all of them.

2:9A.   He said to them: Go and see what is the straight path to which some-one should stick.

2:9B.   Rabbi Eliezer says: A generous spirit. Rabbi Joshua says: A good friend. Rabbi Yosé says: A good neighbor. Rabbi Simeon says: Foresight. Rabbi Eleazar says: Goodwill.

2:9C.   He said to them: I prefer the opinion of Rabbi Eleazar ben Arakh, because in what he says is included everything you say.

2:9D.   He said to them: Go out and see what is the bad road, which some-one should avoid. Rabbi Eliezer says: Envy. Rabbi Joshua says: A bad friend. Rabbi Yosé says: A bad neighbor. Rabbi Simeon says: A loan. All the same is a loan owed to a human being and a loan owed to the Omnipresent, the blessed, as it is said, The wicked borrows and does not pay back, but the righ-teous person deals graciously and hands over [what is owed].

2:9E.   Rabbi Eleazar says: Ill will.

2:9F.   He said to them: I prefer the opinion of Rabbi Eleazar ben Arakh, because in what he says is included everything you say.

2:10A.   They [each] said three things.

2:10B.   Rabbi Eliezer says: Let the respect owing to your companion be as precious to you as the respect owing to yourself. And don't be easy to anger. And repent one day before you die. And warm yourself by the fire of the sages, but be careful of their coals, so you don't get burned—for their bite is the bite of a fox, and their sting is the sting of a scorpion, and their hiss is like the hiss of a snake, and everything they say is like fiery coals.

2:11.   Rabbi Joshua says: Envy, desire of bad things, and hatred for people push a person out of the world.

2:12.   Rabbi Yosé says: Let your companion's money be as precious to you as your own. And get yourself ready to learn the Torah, for it does not come as an inheritance to you. And may everything you do be for the sake of Heaven.

2:13.   Rabbi Simeon says: Be meticulous about the recitation of the Shema and the Prayer. And when you pray, don't treat your praying as a matter of routine; but let it be a [plea for] mercy and supplication before the Omnipresent, the blessed, as it is said, *For he is gracious and full of compassion, slow to anger and full of mercy, and repents of the evil* (Joel 2:13). And never be evil in your own eyes.

2:14. Rabbi Eleazar says: Be constant in learning of the Torah. And know what to reply to an Epicurean. And know before whom you work, for your employer can be depended upon to pay your wages for what you do.

2:15. Rabbi Tarfon says: The day is short, the work formidable, the workers lazy, the wages high, the employer impatient.

2:16. He would say: It's not your job to finish the work, but you are not free to walk away from it. If you have learned much Torah, they will give you a good reward. And your employer can be depended upon to pay your wages for what you do. And know what sort of reward is going to be given to the righteous in the coming time.

Judah the Patriarch stands for the Jews' government, the rule of the *nasi,* or patriarch, and Yohanan ben Zakkai stands for the Jews' sages, the rabbis who served in the government and taught Torah to the community. So the continuity of the original list from Sinai draws us deep in to the institutions of Israel in the centuries beyond the destruction of the Temple in 70 C.E., the patriarchate on the one side, the sages' movement on the other. Both stand in direct connection to Moses at Sinai—a remarkable statement in a political document that accounts for the Mishnah and the rule of those who, in the third century, execute those of its laws that applied.

Now the one question we have before us is whether the Torah-lessons of Rabbi Judah the Patriarch, with whom we begin, correspond to the Torah-lessons of Scripture, and whether those of Yohanan ben Zakkai, who commences the second component of the chapter, have derived from Scripture—or whether Scripture has played any part at all in the matter. The key passages are these:

What is the straight path which a person should choose for himself?

Go and see what is the straight path to which someone should stick. Rabbi Eliezer says: A generous spirit. Rabbi Joshua says: A good friend. Rabbi Yosé says: A good neighbor. Rabbi Simeon says: Foresight. Rabbi Eleazar says: Goodwill.

One question will show us what is at stake: does Scripture not give answers to these questions? Of course it does. Whether in the Pentateuch, the Prophetic Books, or the Writings, Scripture is rich in reflection on these questions, in both general terms and detail. The framers of tractate Avot have not cited Scripture. It appears not as a source for their thought (though we know, in fact, that in the wisdom literature, for example, Proverbs, much that they say here is commonplace) nor as a proof for the correctness of their propositions, that is, as a source of prooftexts. Whether or not the beliefs or values of components of Scripture play a role in the framing of sages' viewpoints is not pertinent. What we do ask is whether or not the written part of the Torah begun at Sinai has provided the sages at hand with their program. The answer is that, on the surface, it has not. And yet, that superficial answer contradicts the character of Scripture, with its claim to stand for God's word, and also the convictions of that large sector of Israel, the Jewish people, that recognized God's word in Scripture but knew no other source of revelation that encompassed the teachings or authority of the sages in that chain with which we began.

So through the formal qualities and propositional program of the opening chapters of tractate Avot, we are drawn to a clear picture of the problematic of Midrash. It is how to move *from* the Torah, encompassing (as we shall see in the next chapter) the Mishnah, *to* Scripture. And, given the priority and standing of Scripture, it is also how to move *from* Scripture *to* the Torah. It is a bridge that carries traffic in two directions. For it is clear that Scripture will play a principal role in the Judaism of the dual Torah. But precisely how that role will work itself out is much less clear. As we shall see, like philosophers who tested syllogisms against the facts of nature and reason, the Judaic sages developed propositions to be tested against the facts of society and history. For them Scripture formed the source of those facts of society and history, as much as, for the Greeks, nature and thought itself formed the source of facts against which all allegations as to truth required testing. The near absence of Scripture from the programmatic statements of tractate Avot, the curious indifference to the forms and patterns of the language of Scripture, the indifference to the names of scriptural authorities—these indicative traits do not deceive us. Nor were they meant to: they stated the premise of the system viewed whole, which is that Scripture forms one part of the heart divided into two, and one-half of the whole Torah of Judaism unfolding from the Mishnah forward. To repeat the critical proposition of this prologue to the rabbinic reading of Scripture: *Through the workings of Midrash the Hebrew Bible became the written half of the one whole Torah, oral and written, revealed by God to Moses our Rabbi at Mount Sinai.*

# 1. FROM SYSTEM TO SELECTION: THE MISHNAH AND SCRIPTURE

# 1. Defining the Torah in the Aftermath of the Mishnah: Program, Detail, and Exegesis

The Mishnah is an encompassing code of laws, some applicable at the time of publication, many not. Brought to closure in ca. 200 C.E. under the sponsorship of Judah the Patriarch, ethnarch or ruler of the Jewish communities of the Land of Israel ("Palestine"), the Mishnah's topical program is laid forth in six divisions. These take up the sanctity of the land and its use in accord with God's law ("Seeds" or agriculture), the differentiation and passage of sacred time and its impact upon the cult and the village ("Appointed Times"), the sacred aspects of the relationship between woman and man ("Women" or family), civil law ("Damages"), the maintenance of the Temple building and conduct of the cult in appropriate regularity and order ("Holy Things"), and the protection from cultic contamination of food prepared under the rules of cultic purity ("Purities"). The laws consistently stress the sanctification of Israel's life in the natural world through conformity to the rules governing the supernatural world. So the Mishnah presents a very particular construction, one proposing to form Israel into a holy community in accord with God's holy exegesis of Scripture, revealed in the Torah given to Moses at Mount Sinai. In this very broad and general sense, the Mishnah's system forms an exegesis on the Priestly Code of the Pentateuch—but only in this sense. For the Mishnah's system works out its own issues in its distinctive way, and only after the fact does it bring to Scripture a program of inquiry into specific verses and their rules.

## I. THE PROGRAM OF THE MISHNAH IN RELATIONSHIP TO SCRIPTURE

What makes the Mishnah important after its own time in the history of Judaism is a simple fact. The exegesis of the Mishnah yielding two Talmuds—one in the Land of Israel, the other in Babylonia—became the center, after Scripture, of the articulation of Judaism in law and theology. In the next three hundred years, parts of its system, vastly articulated and reworked, would form the jurisprudential and theological foundations of the practical law, administration, world view, and way of life of Israel's inner affairs, both in the Holy Land and in the diaspora. Accordingly, the Mishnah contributed some of its tractates to what became the normative Jewish exegesis of Scripture and theology. For nearly all Jews everywhere, for a long time, would live under a single law code and theological system. What makes the exegesis of the Mishnah consequential in the study of rabbinic Midrash is that the modes of exegesis developed in the new document guided the development of modes of exegesis applied to the received Scripture.* Since the Mishnah constituted the first document of the oral Torah, exegetical methods found appropriate for it came to bear upon the written Torah as well, with the result that a single system of Midrash encompassed both components of the one whole Torah of Moses, our Rabbi. But, from the perspective of 200, that development was long in coming, since, to begin with, the exegesis of the Mishnah had to unfold in its own terms.

Once the Mishnah had reached closure, four documents would in succession take up the task of apologia and articulation: tractate Avot, The Fathers; the Tosefta; the Talmud of the Land of Israel, or Yerushalmi; and the Talmud of Babylonia, or Bavli. We have already encountered the first, tractate Avot, ca. 250, a generation or two beyond the Mishnah. The authorship of that document explained the origin and authority of the

---

*I demonstrate that fact in *Midrash in Context.*

Mishnah by attributing to its sages positions in the chain of the tradition extending from Mount Sinai onward. When, as the text states, "Moses received Torah at Sinai" (Avot 1:1), he thus stood at the head of a chain of sages, which ended among the just-deceased authorities of the Mishnah itself. So the new code, in its first and principal apologia, found its place in the setting of the revealed Torah of Moses.

The second, third, and fourth compositions dealt in detail with the connections between laws in the Mishnah and counterpart rules or statements in Scripture. The premise was simple but would have astonished the authorship of Avot. The statements of the oral Torah (beginning with the Mishnah) rested on foundations in the written Torah. Each of the successor documents therefore supplied to the rules of the Mishnah texts of Scripture serving as proof of the validity or evidence of the source, in God's written Torah, of those rules.

The second document beyond the tractate Avot was the Tosefta, a composite of supplements to the Mishnah's rules, covering nearly the whole of the Mishnah's rules, item by item. The Tosefta was the only successor document to the Mishnah that accepted the Mishnah's topical program as it was received; the others picked and chose. The Tosefta is generally supposed to have reached closure in the later third or earlier fourth centuries, ca. 300 to 400. Its exegesis of the Mishnah consisted in amplification of its statements, supplementing its rules with further rules on the same topics, and, especially, adding prooftexts, that is, citations of verses of Scripture, to statements of the Mishnah that lack such prooftexts.

The third, the Talmud of the Land of Israel, also known as the Yerushalmi, took up thirty-nine of the Mishnah's sixty-two tractates (omitting Avot from the count) and supplied them with paragraph-by-paragraph exegeses. The framers of these exegetical exercises contributed amplifications in one of three classifications. First, they took up and explained phrases and sentences of the Mishnah-paragraph at hand. Second, they brought the Tosefta's supplementary formulations to bear upon those of the Mishnah, comparing and contrasting them. Third, they composed large-scale theoretical inquiries into the principles of the exegesis of Scripture, so joining one rule of the Mishnah to several others in search for the deeper line of order and structure of the exegesis of Scripture as a whole.

The fourth document, the Talmud of Babylonia or Bavli, ca. 600, contributed the same exegetical exercises to parts of the Mishnah, thirty-seven tractates in all (but not all of the same ones of interest to the compositors of the Talmud of the Land of Israel). While treating the fifth division, on Holy Things, the redactors extensively dealt with the three most practical parts of the Mishnah—the second, third, and fourth divisions—and so they created a complete and encompassing legal system, superimposed on the Mishnah, dealing with everyday religious life, affairs of the individual and the family, and all aspects of civil exegesis of Scripture. They treated the Mishnah much as did the authorship of the Yerushalmi.

But long before the time of the formation of the Bavli, as we shall see in Parts Two and Three, a second type of document, in addition to the one that organized their materials around the Mishnah and provided exegeses of its statements, had come into being. It was a composition that organized materials around verses or books of Scripture and amplified the sense or proposition of statements of Scripture. Taking cognizance of this second kind of composition, the authors of the Talmud of Babylonia, as we shall see in the penultimate chapter, organized vast stretches of discourse not around the Mishnah-tractate but around a biblical book. In doing so, they moved beyond the pattern established by authors of the Talmud of the Land of Israe!. Accordingly, for the purposes of large-scale organization of discourse, they used not only the Mishnah but also Scripture. Authors of the Talmud of the Land of Israel had relied for order and sequence mainly upon the Mishnah's structure. Authors of the other, later Talmud referred also to passages of Scripture. These they subjected to systematic exegesis along exactly those lines that guided their reading of the

Mishnah. So the Talmud of Babylonia joined together extensive explanations of the Mishnah's paragraphs with sizable and quite orderly explanations of verses of Scripture. Since the sages by that time regarded the Mishnah as the oral, or memorized, Torah, and Scripture as the written Torah, we may define the intent of the framers of the Talmud of Babylonia: to join important components of the Torah that had come from Sinai in two media, writing and memorization. So the framers presented as one whole and complete Torah this final and encompassing system of exegesis of Scripture and theology. The importance of the Mishnah in the history of Judaism derives from its position alongside Scripture as one of the two principal structures of organization and legal principles upon which the Talmud of Babylonia created its structure to contain and present systematically the exegesis of both Mishnah and Scripture for the authoritative state of Jewish law and theology.

This initiative of approaching the study of Midrash or exegesis of Scripture by asking about the treatment of the Mishnah is required by the importance of the Mishnah in the unfolding of the Judaism of the dual Torah. But that extrinsic consideration is not the only reason. At the same time, the Mishnah itself in its intrinsic traits stands at the beginning of the encounter with Scripture, on account of both what it says and its silences. So let us now ask about the role and authority of Scripture in the Mishnah, which is the first step in investigating the meanings imputed to Scripture by diverse Midrash-exegeses in various Midrash-compilations over the next four hundred years. Specifically, we take up two types of Mishnah-chapter. In one, Scripture plays no apparent role. In the other, Scripture provides important proofs for the truth of the Mishnah's authors' propositions. And the evidence of both proves only partial for a full picture of how the framers of the Mishnah defined their program of Bible interpretation and effected it, where and when they did, in their remarkable and independent document.

## II. A PASSAGE OF THE MISHNAH INDEPENDENT OF SCRIPTURE

Since in *Invitation to the Talmud* I supplied a detailed picture of Mishnah-tractate Berakhot Chapter Eight and then followed the treatment of that chapter in the Tosefta, Talmud of the Land of Israel, and Talmud of Babylonia, that chapter is readily accessible. We review the role of Scripture in its statements. I have divided the chapter by Roman numerals into its large-scale components, distinguished by their traits of rhetorical formalization. In the opening unit we have a perfect balance between two conflicting opinions on a single proposition, with the view of each party set up in such a way as to form a mirror image of its opposition.

### MISHNAH-TRACTATE BERAKHOT

#### CHAPTER EIGHT

**I.**

8:1A.  These are the things which are between the House of Shammai and the House of Hillel in [regard to] the meal:

—The meal in question is the Sabbath meal, and at issue is the blessing said over wine to be drunk in that connection. The other rules apply to ordinary meals as well as the Sabbath meal.

8:1B.  The House of Shammai say, "One blesses over the day, and afterward one blesses over the wine."

8:1C.  And the House of Hillel say, "One blesses over the wine, and afterward one blesses over the day."

The match is *day/wine* versus *wine/day*. It is a memory aid or mnemonic to arrange opinions in such a way that all one has to know is the topic, the possible answers, and the fixed order of the houses. We shall now proceed through the remainder of the opening composition, with its five disputes in the same rhetorical pattern.

8:2A. The House of Shammai say, "They wash the hands and afterward mix the cup."

8:2B. And the House of Hillel say, "They mix the cup and afterward wash the hands."

8:3A. The House of Shammai say, "He dries his hands on the cloth and lays it on the table."

8:3B. And the House of Hillel say, "On the pillow."

8:4A. The House of Shammai say, "They clean the house, and afterward they wash the hands."

8:4B. And the House of Hillel say, "They wash the hands, and afterward they clean the house."

8:5A. The House of Shammai say, "Light, and food, and spices, and *Havdalah*."

8:5B. And the House of Hillel say, "Light, and spices, and food, and *Havdalah*."

8:5C. The House of Shammai say, "Who created the light of the fire."

8:5D. And the House of Hillel say, "Who creates the lights of the fire."

M. 8:2–5

The exposition of the details at hand need not detain us, since I have already explained them in *Invitation to the Talmud*. Furthermore, our interest is in one set of questions alone. Do the framers of the Mishnah-passage before us refer to Scripture? Do they provide an exegesis of a detail of scriptural law, and do they propose to link their topical program to Scripture? The answers to these questions are negative. What has Scripture contributed? On the one side, it is in Scripture that the obligation to observe the Sabbath is set forth. On the other, the details of Sabbath observance at hand, for example, sanctification of the cup of wine, recitation of prayers at the end of the Sabbath (**M. 8:5**), derive not from Scripture but from some other source, presumably common practice. Scripture, therefore, stands entirely aside from the present passage, forming at most an undifferentiated backdrop against which the discursive action takes place.

**II.**

8:6A.   They do not bless over the light or the spices of gentiles, nor the light or the spices of the dead, nor the light or the spices which are before an idol.

8:6B.   And they do not bless over the light until they make use of its illumination.

M. 8:6

What has been said above applies here as well. The detail concerns the materials used in the recitation of the prayer marking the conclusion of the Sabbath.

**III.**

8:7A.   He who ate and forgot and did not bless [say Grace]—

8:7B.   The House of Shammai say, "He should go back to his place and bless."

8:7C.   And the House of Hillel say, "He should bless in the place in which he remembered."

8:7D.   Until when does he bless? Until the food has been digested in his bowels.

8:8A.   Wine came to them after the meal, and there is only that cup—

8:8B.   The House of Shammai say, "He blesses the wine, and afterward he blesses the food."

8:8C.   And the House of Hillel say, "He blesses the food, and afterward he blesses the wine."

8:8D.   They respond *Amen* after an Israelite who blesses, and they do not respond *Amen* after a Samaritan who blesses, until hearing the entire blessing.

M. 8:7–8

The recitation of the Grace after Meals concludes the account of the meal provided in the present chapter of the Mishnah. If we did not know that Scripture—the written Torah—

formed the foundation of the world of the authorship of the Mishnah, that authorship would not have suggested to us that any authoritative document beyond their own played any role in their thought. But that impression is far from the fact, as we shall now see.

## III. A PASSAGE OF THE MISHNAH DEPENDENT UPON SCRIPTURE

We now shall see the workings of Midrash-exegesis in the Mishnah in a Mishnah-chapter in which Scripture is cited verbatim. But if we were to assume that Scripture is present only when it is cited verbatim and then adduced as proof for a proposition, we should misunderstand the true importance of Scripture in the Mishnah, or of the written Torah in the first document of the oral one. For we should treat as trivial the important role of Scripture and sages' response to Scripture—a phenomenon we shall now observe.

Scripture supplies more than authoritative texts that people may cite for their own purpose. Scripture defines the very categories and metaphors to which people appeal and by which they make sense of the world. Accordingly, Scripture is present when it is not cited at least as palpably as when it is cited. The interplay between the written Torah and the Mishnah takes place at many levels. The one is at the surface, in the prooftext of Scripture. The other is more profound, in the interchange of metaphor and in the conflict of concern and emphasis. And that is to be expected in the encounter of an authorship of ancient Israel, facing its world and working out its concerns, with an authorship of Greco-Roman civilization, framing a way of life and a world view in the mediation of the two ages and the two conflicted worlds of what to them were antiquity and modern times. When we at the end ask how Midrash builds a bridge between the ancient times of Israel at Sinai and the modern times of Jewry under Rome, we shall recall how, at every point, each reference to Scripture, explicit or implicit, constituted a firm road across the abyss of centuries. And every citation of Scripture as proof for a contemporary proposition conveyed the fundamental proposition of Midrash: God's word is everywhere present as paradigm, at the surface or in the depths of reality.

In the passage at hand the Mishnah's authorship works out what appears to be an antiquarian interest in the rules governing the Israelite throne. The interest was antiquarian in that Israel, the Jewish people, had not had a king of its own for centuries. But the polemic should not be missed, and it was anything but antiquarian. In appealing to the house of David as the metaphor of the king, sages laid down their judgment on who really ruled Israel—and who enjoyed no legitimacy at all. Since sages did not accord recognition to either the Herodian dynasty or the Hasmonean one, they would have to reach back in their imagination to the last of the Davidic house—and, of course, legislate forward for the first of the renewed Davidic house of messianic time to come. The issue being merely theoretical, discourse could range hither and yon in reflection on the ideal ruler. So the utopian exercise distinguishes the officials of a government no one then knew or had known in concrete time and dictates the rules affecting the personal conduct of people who had never lived and—we now know—would never come into being. In this fantasy world, Scripture plays its part.

What we learn about Midrash from this encounter of Mishnah's sages with Scripture is simply stated: Midrash-exegesis explains one thing in terms of something else, and this metynomic and metaphorical mode of thought, treating palpable reality as merely suggestive and appealing to a deeper layer of being, characterizes the reading of both literature—Scripture—and also the workaday world. Generated within the one, the attitude of mind dictated the meaning to be imputed to the other. When we come to Genesis Rabbah and Leviticus Rabbah, we shall see still more wide-ranging exegeses in the metaphorical reading of contemporary reality in the model of the true being of scriptural Israel, with Abraham, Isaac, and Jacob defining the reference point against which Jewry of the current age would take its bearings.

## MISHNAH TRACTATE SANHEDRIN

### CHAPTER TWO

2:1A.    A high priest judges, and [others] judge him;

2:1B.    gives testimony, and [others] give testimony about him;

2:1C.    performs the rite of removing the shoe [Deut. 25:7–9], and [others] perform the rite of removing the shoe with his wife.

2:1D.    [Others] enter levirate marriage with his wife, but he does not enter into levirate marriage,

2:1E.    because he is prohibited to marry a widow.

2:1F.    [If] he suffers a death [in his family], he does not follow the bier.

2:1G.    "But when [the bearers of the bier] are not visible, he is visible; when they are visible, he is not.

2:1H.    "And he goes with them to the city gate," the words of R. Meir.

2:1I.    R. Judah says, "He never leaves the sanctuary,

2:1J.    "since it says, *Nor shall he go out of the sanctuary* (Lev. 21:12)."

2:1K.    And when he gives comfort to others

2:1L.    the accepted practice is for all the people to pass one after another, and the appointed [prefect of the priests] stands between him and the people.

2:1M.    And when he receives consolation from others,

2:1N.    all the people say to him, "Let us be your atonement."

2:1O.    And he says to them, "May you be blessed by Heaven."

2:1P.    And when they provide him with the funeral meal,

2:1Q.    all the people sit on the ground, while he sits on a stool.

**M. 2:1**

The basic proposition, an implicit syllogism that some rules govern the high priest and not the king, while others govern the king and not the high priest, will be exposed in full in the secondary expansion of what is before us. The specific rules then form the proof of the syllogism. Self-evidently, Scripture does not provide the framework through which discourse unfolds. Nor does Scripture address the issue at all. This is an example of the way in which the Mishnah's system begins within its own program and concerns and addresses Scripture on its terms and at its own due time. That is why we begin with the Mishnah's own program, laid out at **2:1A–I.** We need not dwell on the fact that the mode of discourse is syllogistic; a proposition is laid forth, which rests on facts, some of them explicit in Scripture (as Judah maintains), many of them not. The invocation of Scripture at **2:1I** serves only for a detail. Judah tests his proposition by reference to the facts supplied by Scripture.

2:2A.   The king does not judge, and [others] do not judge him;

2:2B.   does not give testimony, and [others] do not give testimony about him;

2:2C.   does not perform the rite of removing the shoe, and others do not perform the rite of removing the shoe with his wife;

2:2D.   does not enter into levirate marriage, nor [do his brothers] enter levirate marriage with his wife.

2:2E.   R. Judah says, "If he wanted to perform the rite of removing the shoe or to enter into levirate marriage, his memory is a blessing."

2:2F.   They said to him, "They pay no attention to him [if he expressed the wish to do so]."

2:2G.   [Others] do not marry his widow.

2:2H.   R. Judah says, "A king may marry the widow of a king."

2:2I.   "For so we find in the case of David, that he married the widow of Saul,

2:2J.   "for it is said, *And I gave you your master's house and your master's wives into your embrace* (2 Sam. 12:8)."

**M. 2:2**

The counterpart statement now completes the fundamental syllogism, implicit in the whole, effected through the matched contrast of the two statements, **M. 2:1** as against **M. 2:2**. We note the presence of yet another appeal to Scripture. But this one proves more suggestive than its role as a mere factual proof indicates. For the appeal is to David, and what we have is the invocation of the metaphor of the Davidic household—David, then Solomon—as the model for the true Israelite monarch. The detail that Scripture provides is secondary, the invocation of the metaphor, primary.

2:3A.  [If] [the king] suffers a death in his family, he does not leave the gate of his palace.

2:3B.  R. Judah says, "If he wants to go out after the bier, he goes out,

2:3C.  "for thus we find in the case of David, that he went out after the bier of Abner,

2:3D.  "since it is said, *And King David followed the bier* (2 Sam 3:31)."

2:3E.  They said to him, "This action was only to appease the people."

2:3F.  And when they provide him with the funeral meal, all the people sit on the ground, while he sits on a couch.

**M. 2:3**

The role of Midrash proves dual. First, Scripture contributes the governing metaphor, as I said. Second, and of much less consequence, Scripture also provides concrete cases, facts that sustain or contradict a proposed hypothesis, as much as facts of nature test propositions or facts of logic test syllogisms. The mode of thought is profoundly philosophical, in the model of Greco-Roman philosophy, and the workings of Midrash in the present passage comprise an idiomatic means of expressing a universal philosophical intelligence and intellect.

2:4A.  [The king] calls out [the army to wage] a war fought by choice on the instructions of a court of seventy-one.

2:4B.  He [may exercise the right to] open a road for himself, and [others] may not stop him.

2:4C.  The royal road has no required measure.

2:4D.  All the people plunder and lay before him [what they have grabbed], and he takes the first portion.

2:4E.  *He should not multiply wives to himself* (Deut. 17:17)—only eighteen.

2:4F.  R. Judah says, "He may have as many as he wants, so long as they *do not entice him* [to abandon the Lord (Deut. 7:4)]."

2:4G.  R. Simeon says, "Even if there is only one who entices him [to abandon the Lord], lo, this one should not marry her."

2:4H.  If so, why is it said, *He should not multiply wives to himself?*

2:4I.  Even though they should be like Abigail [1 Sam. 25:3].

2:4J.  *He should not multiply horses to himself* (Deut. 17:16)—only enough for his chariot.

2:4K.  *Neither shall he greatly multiply to himself silver and gold* (Deut. 17:16)— only enough to pay his army.

2:4L.  *And he writes out a scroll of the Torah for himself* (Deut. 17:17).

2:4M.  When he goes to war, he takes it out with him; when he comes back, he brings it back with him; when he is in session in court, it is with him; when he is reclining, it is before him,

2:4N.  as it is said, *And it shall be with him, and he shall read in it all the days of his life* (Deut. 17:19).

**2:4**

2:5A.  [Others may] not ride on his horse, sit on his throne, handle his scepter.

2:5B.  And [others may] not watch him while he is getting a haircut, or while he is nude, or in the bathhouse,

2:5C.  since it is said, *You shall surely set him as king over you* (Deut. 17:15)— that reverence for him will be upon you.

**2:5**

At **M. 2:4**E we encounter a quite different kind of Midrash. What is worked out now is not an autonomous proposition, tested against Scripture, but a systematic exegesis of the program of a verse of Scripture, translated into a set of rules that follow the topical order dictated by Scripture's statement. This quite different exegetical exercise centers, therefore, on Scripture's program, as laid out in the verse under investigation, rather than on the Mishnah's program, as laid out along topical-systematic lines dictated by the inner structure of a given theme: first this issue, then that issue. This exegetical mode of discourse is most elegantly portrayed at J–L: phrase, generalization of the sense of the phrase or statement in different words of the rule of that scriptural clause.

On the surface, therefore, Scripture stands in two relationships to the Mishnah. First, when the Mishnah's authorship has chosen a subject and on the basis of a lucid analysis of the components of the subject determined its inner composition, proportion, and order, Scripture may be asked to provide some facts pertinent to some component of the topic. That is a mode of thought determined by the subject at hand and the requirements of its exegesis, and to that issue Scripture proves tangential. Second, the Mishnah's authorship may—in the course of its topical-propositional discourse—light upon a given verse of Scripture and present a clause-by-clause exposition of the sense of that verse within that verse's own order, in accord with *its* composition and proportion. Then Scripture and its exegesis, rather than a topic and its inner structure, dictate discourse. The former mode of thought we call propositional or syllogistic, the latter, exegetical. For what makes the former cogent is the proposition at hand, and that is what holds things together, while what makes the latter intelligible is the verse of Scripture, which is what imparts such cogency as the sustained discourse may exhibit. As we shall see, these two distinct modes of thought and discourse will turn out to define both the rhetoric and logic of intelligible discourse of individual components of Midrash-exegesis and of Midrash-documents alike. Indeed, we shall find it possible to classify all Midrash-documents within one or the other of the two types of discourse —Sifra and Sifré to Numbers being essentially exegetical, while Genesis Rabbah, Leviticus Rabbah, and Pesiqta deRab Kahana are basically propositional—and all principles of rhetorical composition between the two. We shall discover that principles of differentiation between one Midrash-document and another emerge solely within the topical programs of the respective documents. But these too merge and form a complete and cogent statement—a set of coherent topical propositions—of their own.

## IV. TOPIC AND PROPOSITION: THE USES OF SCRIPTURE IN THE MISHNAH

As we move from the specific to the general, we observe that the authors of the Mishnah read Scripture, as they read much else, in terms of the system and structure they proposed to construct. We may say that first came the Judaism of the dual Torah, then the address to the written component of the dual Torah in light of the oral part. Their goals and conceptions told them what in Scripture they would borrow, expand, and articulate; acknowledge but neglect; or simply ignore. The Mishnah's authors took from Scripture what they chose in accord with the criterion of the one thing they wished to accomplish. This was the construction of their system. In order to show the preeminence, in the encounter with Scripture, of the perspective and purpose of the authors of the Mishnah, we simply review the Mishnah's tractates and ask how, overall, we may characterize their relationships to Scripture.

Let me review the choices. Were the relationships of Mishnah-tractates to Scripture (1) wholly dependent, (2) wholly autonomous, or (3) somewhere in between? That is, at the foundations in fact and generative problematic of a given tractate, we may discover nothing more than facts and interests of Scripture's law. The tractate's authors then simply articulate the data of Scripture. Or, second, when we reach the bedrock of a tractate, the point at which the articulation of the structure of the tractate rests, we may find no point of contact with facts, let alone interests, of Scripture's laws. And, third, we may discover facts shared by Scripture but developed in ways distinctive to the purposes of the framers of the Mishnah-tractate at hand. These three relationships, in theory, encompass all possibilities. Let us turn to the facts.

First, some tractates simply repeat in their own words precisely what Scripture has to say, and at best they amplify and complete the basic ideas of Scripture. For example, all of the cultic tractates of the Second Division, on Appointed Times, which tell what one is supposed to do in the Temple on the various special days of the year, and the bulk of the cultic tractates of the Fifth Division, which deals with Holy Things, simply restate facts of Scripture. In addition, all of the tractates of the Sixth Division, on Purities, which specify sources of uncleanness, depend completely on information supplied by Scripture. Every important statement in Mishnah-tractate Niddah, on menstrual uncleanness, and the most fundamental notions of Mishnah-tractate Zabim, on the uncleanness of the person with flux referred to in Leviticus 15, as well as every detail in Mishnah-tractate Negaim, on the uncleanness of the person or house suffering the uncleanness described at Leviticus 13 and 14, simply restate the basic facts of Scripture and complement those facts with other important ones.

Second, some tractates take up facts of Scripture but work them out in a way in which those scriptural facts cannot have led us to predict. A supposition concerning what is important about the facts, utterly remote from the supposition of Scripture, will explain why the Mishnah-tractates under discussion say the original things they say in confronting those scripturally provided facts. For example, Scripture takes for granted that the red cow will be burned in a state of uncleanness, because it is burned outside the camp, meaning the Temple. The priestly writers could not have imagined that a state of cultic cleanness was to be attained outside of the cult. The absolute datum of Mishnah-tractate Parah, by contrast, is that cultic cleanness can be attained outside of the "tent of meeting." In fact, the red cow was to be burned in a state of cleanness exceeding even that cultic cleanness required in the Temple itself. The problematic that generates the intellectual agendum of Parah, therefore, is how to work out the conduct of the rite of burning the cow in relationship to the Temple: is it to be done in exactly the same way or in exactly the opposite way? This mode of contrastive and analogical thinking helps us to understand the generative problematic of such Mishnah-tractates as Erubin and Besah, to mention only two.

Third, there are, predictably, many tractates that either take up problems in no way suggested by Scripture or begin from premises at best merely relevant to facts of Scripture. In the former category are Mishnah-tractate Tohorot, on the cleanness of foods, with its companion, Mishnah-tractate Uqsin; Mishnah-tractate Demai, on doubtfully tithed produce; Mishnah-tractate Tamid, on the conduct of the daily whole offering; and Mishnah-tractate Baba Batra, on rules of real estate transactions and certain other commercial and property relationships. Also dealing with property are Mishnah-tractate Ohalot, which spins out its strange problems using the theory that a tent and a utensil are to be compared to one another (!); Mishnah-tractate Kelim, on the susceptibility to uncleanness of various sorts of utensils; Mishnah-tractate Miqvaot, on the sorts of water that effect purification from uncleanness, and many others. These tractates draw on facts of Scripture, but the problems they confront in no way respond to problems important to Scripture. What we have here is a prior program of inquiry, which makes ample provision for facts of Scripture in an inquiry that begins essentially outside the framework of Scripture.

Some tractates merely repeat what we find in Scripture. Some are totally independent of Scripture. Some fall in between. True, Scripture confronts the framers of the Mishnah as revelation, not merely as a source of facts. But the framers of the Mishnah had to deal with their own world. They made statements in the framework and fellowship of their own age and generation. They were bound, therefore, to come to Scripture with a set of questions generated elsewhere than in Scripture. They brought their own ideas about what was going to be important in Scripture. This is perfectly natural. Their inquiry began outside Scripture, and that explains why some tractates merely repeat what Scripture says, some stand totally independent of Scripture, and some fall in between. The Mishnah is not so remote from Scripture as its formal omission of citations of Scripture verse suggests. But in no way can the Mishnah be described as contingent upon Scripture, for instance, as the result of teasing out secondary and dependent conceptions from verses of Scripture.

## V. EXEGESIS AND IMITATION

From the formation of ancient Israelite Scripture into a holy book in Judaism, beginning with the aftermath of the return to Zion and the creation of the Torah-book in Ezra's time (ca. 450 B.C.E.), the established canon of revelation (whatever its contents) presented a considerable problem to coming generations. As new writers came along, what they wrote had to be set into relationship with the established, authoritative Scripture. Otherwise, in the setting of Israelite culture, the new writings could find no ready hearing. Over the next six hundred years, from ca. 400 B.C.E. to ca. 200 C.E., four conventional ways to accommodate new writings—tradition—to the established canon of received Scripture came to the fore. First and simplest, a writer would sign a famous name to his book, attributing his ideas to Enoch, Adam, Jacob's sons, Jeremiah, Baruch, and any number of others, down to Ezra. Second, he might also imitate the style of biblical Hebrew and so try to creep into the canon by adopting the rhetorical cloak of Scripture. Third, he would surely claim his work was inspired by God, a new revelation for an open canon. Fourth, at the very least, a writer would link his opinions to biblical verses through the exegesis of the latter in line with the former so Scripture would validate his views.

The authors of the pseudepigraphic books of the Old Testament took the first route; the writers of the Dead Sea Psalms and other compositions, the second; some of the pseudepi-graphs, the third; the school of Matthew, the fourth. From the time of Ezra to the second century C.E., every book claiming religious sanction, clearly standing as a holy book and author-ity over Israel, the Jewish nation, conformed to one or more of these conventions. In these ways the new found its place in the framework of the old. Accordingly, we may describe how Is-raelite culture over the period of six hundred years dealt with the intimidating authority and presence of Scripture. We find essentially two modes of accommodation: imitation and aug-mentation. The newcomers either imitated the old or linked the new to the established. The Mishnah did neither, and the authorships of Midrash-compilations formed a link in their own way.

When in the case of the Mishnah we come across an excep-tion to the rule established by the literary conventions by which ancient writers made their way into the canon of Juda-ism, we must find the case remarkable. The Mishnah was the one document among all the canonical writings of all the Juda-isms of antiquity in which all of the established modes of say-ing the new in the guise of the old proved useless. The Mish-nah's authorship rarely cites Scripture and, furthermore, admits to no antecedents except Scripture itself. The work at hand claims no point of contact with a single book written by a Jew from its own day backward for nearly seven hundred years, to the time of Ezra (as we should say), or to the time of Moses (as its framers would allege). Further, from the Mishnah, over the next eighteen hundred years to the present day, all impor-tant expressions of Judaism would flow forth. The Mishnah followed no models but itself served as a model for many. So all roads lead back to the Mishnah, but the authorship of the Mishnah, ignoring all other Judaic writing prior to its own day, leaps back to Sinai alone. If we want to know the excep-tion to the iron rule of how in Judaism people say fresh and new ideas, we have to confront the one document that violated all the rules and therefore established a whole new set of rules.

In one important way, the framers of the Mishnah established a convention of discourse that remained firm throughout the unfolding of the Midrash-documents. Exegesis did not take the form of imitation. Consequently, the line between Scripture and the oral Torah, first as the Mishnah laid out matters, then as the Midrash-documents spelled things out, remained firm and palpable. *There is never a confusion between text and exegesis, Scripture and interpretation, in any document of the oral Torah, whether exegetical of the Mishnah or exegetical of Scripture.* The rigid differentiation is effected not only through explicit and self-conscious citation of Scripture as separate from discourse, for example, by saying "as it is written," but also through the use of language. The Mishnah's framers and all their successors developed their own language and never pretended to write more Scripture. The verb in this new language, for instance, provides not only for completed and continuing action, but also for past and future times, subjunctive and indicative voices, and much else. The syntax is Indo-European, in that we can translate the word order of the Mishnah into any Indo-European language and come up with perfect sense. None of that crabbed imitation of biblical Hebrew, which makes the Dead Sea Scrolls an embarrassment to read, characterizes the Hebrew of the Mishnah. Mishnaic style is elegant, subtle, exquisite in its sensitivity to word order and repetition, balance and pattern. When Scripture's verses are invoked, it is always with joining language, for example, "as it is said . . . ," "as it is written. . . ." More consequentially, no Mishnaic author ever continued the paraphrasing of a biblical passage in the style of that passage but instead always stated the exegetical message in language clearly different from the language of Scripture. Midrash-exegesis in language and style never entered into the text that was subject to interpretation or violated the lines of structure that differentiated the one from the other. The framers of the Mishnah and of the later compilations of exegesis of the Mishnah and of Scripture alike avoided imitating the documents they proposed to interpret and explain.

The authorship of the Mishnah took slight interest in linking up to Scripture. They eschewed imitating the style of Scripture. The authorities in the Mishnah also did not sign biblical names, for sayings in the Mishnah bear mainly the names of sages of the late first and second century C.E. Accordingly, we find not the slightest pretense of claiming antiquity for the documents' allegations. More to the point, as I have emphasized, the Hebrew of the Mishnah is totally different from the Hebrew of the Hebrew Scriptures. Exegesis imputed through composition in the pseudepigraphic mode and imitative style, common enough in other Judaisms of the age, proved the opposite of Midrash-exegesis as the rabbis worked it out.

## VI. THE AUTHORITY OF SCRIPTURE IN THE MISHNAH

The Mishnah contains no allegation that any of its statements derives from God. Nor are the authors of the document alleged to have received revelation. To be sure, as we noted, the rather odd and singular tractate, Avot, different from all other tractates of the Mishnah, begins with the allegation that Moses received Torah at Sinai. The implication may be that part of the Torah— the Mishnah—was handed on orally, not in writing alone. But even here there is no explicit claim that the Mishnah, in particular, is that oral Torah of Moses at Sinai to which reference is made. Perhaps that is what is meant. Many scholars suppose so. But it is not said—as we have just noticed—in the way in which, for example, writers of Old Testament pseudepigrapha say God spoke to them. Finally and most striking, unlike the splendid exegetical composition of the school of Matthew, the Mishnah contains remarkably little exegesis of the antecedent biblical writings, of the sort we noticed in Mishnah-tractate Sanhedrin. We discern no systematic effort to link laws and statements in the Mishnah with biblical verses.

The absence of such explicit links to Scripture as well as failure to provide some sort of myth of the origin of the law of the document together present a truly astonishing fact. The standing and authority of the Mishnah, the sanctions attending enforcement of the law, the reasons people ought to keep it and listen to the sages who enforced it—these questions are denied explicit attention. Perhaps the framers of the document, rather subtle philosophical lawyers, never imagined they should have to explain why people should obey the laws they made up because they never imagined people would do so. Perhaps the founders conceived their book as a kind of theoretical and speculative collection. Every paragraph of the Mishnah bears its share of contradictory opinions, framed as disputes about a common point, and that may mean the framers had not the slightest expectation that their book would serve as a law code. Arranging contradictory possibilities—*sic et non,* so to speak—may have served to turn abstract thought into concrete problems for future reflection. Accordingly, why invoke the authority and inspiration of Heaven for discourse on philosophical possibilities? In any event, the Mishnah enjoyed the political sponsorship of the head of that government, Judah, patriarch of the Jewish nation in its Land and recognized by the Roman government as ethnarch of the Jews of the Holy Land. It became the constitution and by-laws of the Jewish nation. So the intrinsic evidence of the document hardly suggests that the authorship of the Mishnah intended to appeal to Scripture for authority or proposed to constitute their law code as a Midrash on biblical law.

What lies on the surface should not obscure the implicit truth: the philosophers of the Mishnah conceded to Scripture the highest authority. At the same time, what they chose to hear, within the authoritative statements of Scripture, in the end formed a statement of its own. To state matters simply: *All of Scripture is authoritative. But only some passages of Scripture are relevant.* And what happened is that the framers and philosophers of the tradition of the Mishnah came to Scripture when they had reason to. They brought to Scripture a program of questions and inquiries framed essentially among themselves.

So they were highly selective. Their program itself constituted a statement upon the meaning of Scripture. Once more we recognize that the system—the Judaism at hand—forms prior to its canon and chooses the documents that form its canon. The Judaism of the dual Torah comes first, and after it, the Torah in two media that proves its characteristic trait. So too, in the principal propositional compilations, the proposition takes priority over the exegesis of verses that validate the proposition. But even the exegetical compilations such as Sifra and Sifré to Numbers contain implicit syllogisms of an original and profound character. In all, exegesis of the written part of the Torah, the Hebrew Scriptures, serves the one whole Torah of Moses, our Rabbi. That is why, paradoxically, Midrash is present even where, as in the Mishnah, Scripture is not cited and interpreted.

The authority of Scripture for the Mishnah, therefore, is simply stated. Scripture provided indisputable facts. It was wholly authoritative—once the authors made our choice of which part of Scripture they read. Scripture generated important and authoritative structures of the community, including disciplinary and doctrinal statements, decisions, and interpretations—once people had determined which part of Scripture to ask to provide those statements and decisions. Community structures envisaged by the Mishnah were wholly based on Scripture—when Scripture had anything to lay down. But Scripture was not wholly and exhaustively expressed in the structures that the Mishnah did borrow. Scripture dictated the character of formative structures of the Mishnah, but the Mishnah's system was not the result of the dictation of close exegesis of Scripture, except after the fact. Once the pertinent passage of Scripture had been selected, then and only then did Midrash-exegesis begin. But Midrash as a fundamental process of encounter with Scripture, not merely as a technique of teasing out meaning from particular verses of Scripture, encompassed above all even—especially—the Mishnah itself.

Scripture generated important and authoritative structures of the community, including disciplinary and doctrinal statements, decisions, and interpretations—once people had determined which part of Scripture to address in the search for statements and decisions. Community structures envisaged by the authorship of the Mishnah wholly depended upon Scripture—when Scripture had something to contribute. But Scripture is not wholly and exhaustively expressed in the structures that the Mishnah does borrow. Scripture has dictated the character of formative structures of the Mishnah. But the Mishnah's system, whole and complete, cogént and remarkably rich in integrity, is not the result of the dictation of close exegesis of Scripture—except after the fact. And the later program of the Midrash-compilations would cohere to this same mode of response to Scripture. Each would serve the cause of its implicit syllogisms and propositions. Scripture would provide a testing ground and therefore a source of validation for the propositions subject to investigation. *Midrash as investigation of propositions stated in sustained and rigorous statements—whole documents—therefore would take priority over Midrash as exegesis of particular verses of Scripture.*

## VII. BIBLICAL INTERPRETATION AND THEOLOGICAL IMAGINATION: TOWARD THE WORKING OF MIDRASH AS EXEGESIS OF DETAIL

Let us now turn from the particular example to the general problem of relating the Mishnah to Scripture. The Mishnah defined that problem and set the pattern for coming work on the Midrash-exegesis of Scripture. We dwell on why the Mishnah presents so stunning a literary anomaly and then raise the question of how the document was received by its continuators and brought into relationship with Scripture. When these two questions have been worked out, we shall have a fair picture of how the Hebrew Bible was received and mediated by Midrash into the religion of the Judaism of the dual Torah.

Whatever the original, theoretical character intended by the authors, the Mishnah almost immediately demanded what its framers through their original rhetoric and their autonomous program of topics denied it: a place within the canon of Judaism. In the nature of things, there were only two possibilities. Since no one now could credibly claim to sign the name of Ezra or Adam to a book of this kind, and since biblical Hebrew had provided no apologetic aesthetics whatever, the only options lay elsewhere. Authors could, first, provide a myth of the origin of the contents of the Mishnah, and, second, link each allegation of the Mishnah, through processes of biblical (not Mishnaic) exegesis, to verses of the Scriptures. These two procedures, together, would establish for the Mishnah the standing that the uses to which the document was to be put demanded for it: a place in the canon of Israel, a legitimate relationship to the Torah of Moses.

Work on winning for the Mishnah a place in the canon went forward in several ways, represented by diverse documents that succeeded and dealt with the Mishnah. In reviewing these possibilities, we shall locate the place in which the Midrash-compilations are to be found. The three principal positions are as follows: (1) the Mishnah requires no systematic support through exegesis of Scripture in light of Mishnaic laws; (2) the Mishnah by itself provides no reliable information and all of its propositions demand linkage to Scripture, to which the Mishnah must be shown to be subordinate and secondary; (3) the Mishnah is an autonomous document, but closely correlated with Scripture.

The first extreme is represented by tractate Avot, The Fathers, with its extreme claim of origination at Sinai even for teachings of Mishnah-authorities, and by the Tosefta, a corpus of supplementary information about the Mishnah, a small part of it deriving, indeed, from the same period as the Mishnah's own composition.

The second extreme is taken by the Sifra, a post-Mishnaic compilation of exegeses on Leviticus, and Sifré to Numbers. The Sifra and Sifré to Numbers systematically challenge reason (that is, the Mishnah), unaided by revelation (that is, exegesis of Scripture), to sustain positions taken by the Mishnah, which is cited verbatim. The authorships demonstrated the insufficiency of reason.*

The third, and mediating, view is that of the Talmud of the Land of Israel, among the various documents produced by the Jewish sages of the Land of Israel between the end of the second century and the sixth. The Talmud of the Land of Israel (also known as the Palestinian Talmud, Yerushalmi), like the one made up in Babylonia at the same period, in the third and fourth centuries, was organized around the Mishnah. It provided a line-by-line or paragraph-by-paragraph exegesis and amplification of the Mishnah. Produced in schools in Tiberias, Sepphoris, Lud (Lydda), and Caesarea, the Talmud of the Land of Israel developed a well-crafted theory of the Mishnah and its relationship to Scripture.

The process by which the sages of the Talmud of the Land of Israel received the Mishnah and naturalized it into the framework of Scripture forms the model for the development of the Midrash-exegesis and Midrash-documents that were to come. These later collections, beginning in the fifth century with Genesis Rabbah, at the outset carried out with reference to Scripture precisely those procedures of exegesis and amplification established with regard to the Mishnah in the pages of the Talmud of the Land of Israel. They constitute, therefore, a literary echo of the controversies of the third and fourth centuries, debates precipitated by the peculiar character of the Mishnah, on the one side, and necessitated by its powerful political status and capital historical importance, on the other.

The proper interpretation of the Mishnah in relationship to Scripture served as the ultimate guarantee of certainty. We

---

*In my *Uniting the Dual Torah: Sifra and the Problem of the Mishnah* (Cambridge and New York: Cambridge University Press, 1990), I refine this point.

therefore should anticipate a splendid myth of the origin and authority of the Mishnah, on which, for sages, all else rests. Yet, so far as I can see, neither the Talmud nor any Midrash-compilation presents an explicit theory of the Mishnah as part of the Torah, the revelation of Sinai. We have already seen that tractate Avot presents the theory that the authorities of the Mishnah stand in a direct line of tradition from Sinai. For its part, the Yerushalmi knows full well the theory that there is a tradition separate from, and in addition to, the written Torah. But this tradition it knows as "the teachings of scribes." The Mishnah is not identified as the collection of those teachings. An ample instantiation of the Yerushalmi's recognition of this other, separate tradition is contained in the following unit of discourse. What is interesting is that, if these discussions take for granted the availability to Israel of authoritative teachings in addition to those of Scripture, they do not then claim those teachings are contained, uniquely or even partially, in the Mishnah in particular. Indeed, the discussion is remarkable in its supposition that extrascriptural teachings are associated with the views of "scribes," perhaps legitimately called sages, but not in a book to be venerated or memorized as a deed of ritual learning.

### YERUSHALMI ABODAH ZARAH 2:7

III. A.    Associates in the name of R. Yohanan: "The words of scribes are more beloved than the words of Torah and more cherished than words of Torah: *Your palate is like the best wine* (Song 7:9)."

     B.    Simeon bar Ba in the name of R. Yohanan: "The words of scribes are more beloved than the words of Torah and more cherished than words of Torah: *For your love is better than wine* (Song 1:2)."

What is important in the foregoing is the distinction between teachings contained in the Torah and teachings in the name or authority of "scribes." These latter teachings are associated with quite specific details of the law and are indicated in the Mishnah's rule itself. The commonplace view, maintained in diverse forms of ancient Judaism, that Israel had access to a tradition beyond Scripture, clearly was well known to the framers of the Yerushalmi. The question of how, in that context, these framers viewed the Mishnah, however, is not to be settled by that fact. I cannot point to a single passage in which explicit judgment upon the character and status of the Mishnah as a complete document is laid down. Nor is the Mishnah treated as a symbol or called "the oral Torah." But there is ample evidence, once again implicit in what happens to the Mishnah in the Talmud, to allow a reliable description of how the Talmud's founders view the Mishnah.

That view may be stated very simply. The Mishnah rarely cites verses of Scripture in support of its propositions; the Talmud of the Land of Israel routinely adduces scriptural bases for the Mishnah's laws. The Mishnah seldom undertakes the exegesis of verses of Scripture for any purpose; the Talmud of the Land of Israel consistently investigates the meaning of verses of Scripture and does so for a variety of purposes. Accordingly, the Talmud of the Land of Israel, subordinate as it is to the Mishnah, regards the Mishnah as subordinate to, and contingent upon, Scripture. That is why, in the Talmud of the Land of Israel's view, the Mishnah requires the support of prooftexts of Scripture. That fact can mean only that, by itself, the Mishnah exercises no autonomous authority and enjoys no independent standing or norm-setting status. The task of the framers of the Talmud of the Land of Israel is not only to explain Mishnah-law but to prove from Scripture the facticity of rules of the Mishnah. Accordingly, so far as the Talmud of the Land of Israel has a theory about the Mishnah as such, as distinct from a theory about the work to be done in the exposition and amplification and application to the court system of various laws in the Mishnah, it is quite clear. To state matters negatively (and the absence of articulate statements makes this the wiser choice), the Mishnah does not enjoy autonomous and uncontingent authority as part of the one whole Torah of Moses revealed by God at Sinai. That conclusion is made ineluctable by the simple fact that one principal task facing sages, as I just said, is to adduce prooftexts for the Mishnah's laws. It follows that, without such texts, those laws stand on infirm foundations. We now turn to the ways in which the Yerushalmi does this work of founding upon the secure basis of the written Torah the fundamental propositions of the Mishnah's laws, taken up one by one.

The Mishnah in the exegesis of the Yerushalmi, which was aimed at relating the Mishnah to Scripture, was treated only as a collection of rules, each to be faithfully read by itself as a detail. That is why scriptural prooftexts were cited to support one rule after another, without any large-scale thesis about the status of the document containing those discrete rules. Just as the sages of the Talmud of the Land of Israel read the Mishnah bit by bit, so they adduced evidence from Scripture for its rules, bit by bit. There can then have been no consideration whatsoever of the proposition that the Mishnah stood alongside of, and next to, the written Torah, as the oral part of "the one whole Torah of Moses, our Rabbi." If that version of the Torah myth found its way into the Yerushalmi at all, it played no considerable role in the approach of the Yerushalmi to the question of the authority and certainty of the principal document, the Mishnah itself. The Talmud of the Land of Israel's fragmented vision of the Mishnah accounts for the character of the Yerushalmi's approach, through passages of the Mishnah, to verses of Scripture.

Let me give an instance in which a passage of the Mishnah is cited, then linked directly to a verse of Scripture, deemed to constitute self-evident proof for what has been said. The Mishnah's rule is given in italics.

### Y. ABODAH ZARAH 4:4

III. A.   [citing M.A.Z. 4:4:] **An idol belonging to a gentile is prohibited forthwith,** in line with the following verse of Scripture: *You shall surely destroy [all places where the nations whom you shall dispossess served their gods]* (Deut. 12:2)— forthwith.

B. And one belonging to an Israelite is prohibited only after it will have been worshipped, in line with the following verse of Scripture: *Cursed be the man who makes a graven or molten image, an abomination to the Lord, a thing made by the hands of a craftsman, and sets it up in secret* (Deut. 27:15)—when he will set it up.

C. There are those who reverse the matter:

D. An idol belonging to an Israelite is prohibited forthwith, as it is written, *Cursed be the man who makes a graven or molten image.*

E. And one belonging to a gentile is prohibited only after it will have been worshipped, as it is written, *You shall surely destroy all the places where the nations whom you shall dispossess served their gods.*

The instance shows the convention. A statement of the Mishnah is given, followed by a verse of Scripture regarded as proof of the antecedent conception. All we have are sentences from the one document, the Mishnah, juxtaposed with sentences from the other, the Scripture.

We proceed to an instance in which a disputed point of the Mishnah is linked to a dispute on the interpretation of the pertinent verses of Scripture. What is important now is that the dispute in the Mishnah is made to depend not upon principles of law, but upon readings of the same pertinent verses of Scripture. Once again the net effect is to turn the Mishnah into a set of generalizations of what already is explicit in Scripture, a kind of restating in other language of what is quite familiar—therefore well founded.

### YERUSHALMI MAKKOT 2:2

A. [If] the iron flew from the heft and killed someone,

B. Rabbi says, "He does not go into exile."

C. And sages say, "He goes into exile."

D. [If] it flew from the wood which is being split,

E. Rabbi says, "He goes into exile."

F. And sages say, "He does not go into exile."

A. What is the scriptural basis for the position of Rabbi [at M. 2:2D–E]?

B. Here it is stated, [*And the head*] slips [*from the handle and strikes his neighbor so that he dies*](Deut. 19:5).

C. And later on, the same verb root is used: [*For your olives*] *shall drop off* . . . (Deut. 28:40).

D. Just as the verb root used later means "dropping off," so here it means "dropping off."

E. What is the scriptural basis for the position of the rabbis [at **M. 2:2F**]?

F. Here the verb root "slipping" is used.

G. And later on elsewhere we have the following: *And clears away many nations before you* (Deut. 7:1).

H. Just as the verb root "clearing away" refers to an [active] blow there, so here too it speaks of an [active] blow [by an object which strikes something, for example, the ax, not chips of wood].

We see that both parties to the Mishnah's dispute read the same verse. The difference, then, depends upon their prior disagreement abut the meaning of the verse. The underlying supposition is that the Mishnah simply restates in general language the results of the exegesis of biblical law.

We consider, finally, an instance in which the discussion of the Talmud of the Land of Israel consists wholly in the analysis of the verses of Scripture deemed to prove the point of the Mishnah-passage at hand. The upshot is that we deal not with a mere formality but with a protracted, sustained inquiry. That is to say, the discussion of the Talmud of the Land of Israel transcends the limits of the Mishnah and becomes a well-developed discourse upon not the Mishnah's rule but Scripture's sense. What is important in the next item is that the search for prooftexts in Scripture sustains not only propositions of the Mishnah, but also those of the Tosefta as well as those of the Talmud of the Land of Israel's own sages. This is a stunning fact. It indicates that the search of Scriptures is primary, and the source of propositions or texts to be supported by those Scriptures is secondary. There is no limit, indeed, to the purposes for which scriptural texts will be found relevant.

## Y. SANHEDRIN 10:4

II. A. **The party of Korach has no portion in the world to come and will not live in the word to come [M. San. 10:4].**

B. **What is the scriptural basis for this view?**

C. *[So they and all that belonged to them went down alive into Sheol;] and the earth closed over them, and they perished from the midst of the assembly* (Num. 16:33).

D. *The earth closed over them*—in this world.

E. *And they perished from the midst of the assembly*—in the world to come [M. San. 10:4D–F].

F. **It was taught: R. Judah b. Batera says, "[The contrary view] is to be derived from the implication of the following verse:**

G. **"I have gone astray like a lost sheep: seek thy servant [and do not forget thy commandments]** (Ps. 119:176).

H. **"Just as the lost object which is mentioned later on in the end is going to be searched for, so the lost object which is stated herein is destined to be searched for"** [T. San. 13:9].

I. Who will pray for them?

J. R. Samuel bar Nahman said, "Moses will pray for them:

K. "*Let Reuben live, and not die, [nor let his men be few]* (Deut. 33:6)."

L. R. Joshua b. Levi said, "Hannah will pray for them."

M. This is the view of R. Joshua b. Levi, for R. Joshua b. Levi said, "Thus did the party of Korach sink ever downward, until Hannah went and prayed for them and said, *The Lord kills and brings to life; he brings down to Sheol and raises up* (1 Sam. 2:6)."

(We shall see this passage in another connection later on.) We have a striking sequence of prooftexts, serving, one by one, the cited statement of the Mishnah, A–C, then an opinion of a rabbi in the Tosefta, F–H, then the position of a Talmudic rabbi, J–K, L–M. The process of providing the prooftexts therefore is central, and the differentiation among the passages requiring the prooftexts is a matter of indifference.

We began with the interest in showing how the Scripture is made to supply prooftexts for propositions of the Mishnah, with consequences for the Talmud of the Land of Israel's theory of the Mishnah requiring no repetition. But we see at the end that the search for appropriate verses of Scripture vastly transcended the purpose of study of the Mishnah, exegesis of its rules, and provision of adequate authority for the document and its laws. In fact, any proposition to be taken seriously— whether one in the Mishnah, in the Tosefta, or in the mouth of a Talmudic sage himself—elicited interest in scriptural support. So the main thing is that the Scripture is at the center and focus. A verse of Scripture settles all pertinent questions, wherever they are located, whatever their source. That is the Talmud of the Land of Israel's position. We know full well that it is not the Mishnah's position.

Now that we understand how the lines of structure and order followed by the canon of the Judaism of the dual Torah stretched forth from the Mishnah, we turn to the Midrash-exegeses as these are collected and laid forth in the Midrash-compilations. The scriptural exegesis of the Mishnah's authorities has shown us the two operative choices. A third would take shape later on. In the next three sections we see how three quite different types of Midrash-exegesis come to expression. In that way we encounter, through detailed example, the working of Midrash in the three major trends of rabbinic Bible interpretation.

First, a particular verse of Scripture may form the foundation of sustained discourse, following the lines of topic and proposition suggested within the verse under discussion. This former mode of organizing thought shows us the working of Midrash as exegesis of detail. We see how the exposition of verses of a book of Scripture, read in sequence, dictates the order of discussion, and how the reading of the components of those verses permits the exegetes to say whatever in that context they wish to contribute. In this way, we see *Midrash-interpretation as exegesis yielding proposition.* This kind of Midrash is discussed in Part Two.

Second, a proposition or even a syllogism may be brought into relationship with Scripture. In this case we see *interpretation as proposition yielding exegesis,* that is, directing us to a particular verse, rather than to some other, and telling us what, in that verse, we wish to find out. It is the exposition of a topic in its inner structure that dictates the order of discussion, and by the way tells us which verses of Scripture may be invited to give their testimony. The workings of this kind of Midrash are illustrated in Part Three.

There is yet a third mode of Midrash-exegesis that yields Midrash-compilations. It is *Midrash through narrative*. It involves the formation of stories generated through the sustained reading of scriptural stories or working through of scriptural themes. In this way, we see Midrash-interpretation not as Midrash-exegesis of particular verses or even as Midrash-compilations of collections of exegesis of such verses. Nor do we encounter Midrash-exegesis as part of a larger syllogistic proposition. What we have, instead, is the Midrash-story, in which scriptural interpretation takes the form of a narrative of a very particular order. This engaging world of rabbinic Bible interpretation opens to us in Part Four. In Part Five we discover that each of the three principal trends in Midrash-exegesis and Midrash-compilation finds a counterpart in the Talmud of the Land of Israel. The building of documents on the organizing principle of Midrash-compilation, finally, comes to rich fruition in the Talmud of Babylonia, itself made up of large compositions of systematic exegesis of the Mishnah alongside large compositions of systematic exegesis of verses or themes of Scripture: two Torahs in one, oral and written, now make the one whole Torah of Moses, our Rabbi.

# 2. MIDRASH AS EXEGESIS: (1) INTERPRETATION AS EXEGESIS YIELDING PROPOSITION

# 2. Sifra and Sifré to Numbers

Sifra presents a verse-by-verse interpretation of the book of Leviticus, and Sifré to Numbers, as its name indicates, does the same for the book of Numbers. (Another compilation of exegeses, also called Sifré, serves the book of Deuteronomy.) The documents organize and convey whatever propositions their compilers wish to convey through the available structure of the verses of the books on which they comment. Within those books, discourse follows the orderly exposition of the components of the respective verses. That inductive presentation of inductively achieved results allows us to characterize the present mode of Midrash-exegesis-as interpretation in terms of *exegesis yielding proposition*. For, as is clear, the exposition of thought begins with the interpretation of the verse in its principal parts and only then moves upward to the display of evidence in behalf of a given proposition through the cumulative effect of numerous such interpretations of verses—a profoundly inductive procedure. The message therefore reaches us not only bit by bit, however, but also all at once, when sufficient data have repeated the same point and so sustained the same implicit premise or proved the desired implicit syllogism.

## I. THE DOCUMENTS

The two documents make numerous points. But, so far as the Midrash-exegesis at hand yields a single sustained proposition, it is the one that the crisis precipitated by the Mishnah has led us to expect: truth derives from Scripture, not from reason unaided by revelation. But a further proposition will attract our attention. By the very labor of explaining the meaning of verses of Scripture, the rabbinic exegetes laid claim to participate in the work of revelation. And by distinguishing their contribution from the received text of the Torah, they furthermore announced their presence within the process of revelation. In these two ways the exegetes who made up Sifra and Sifré to Numbers presented not one but two fundamental propositions. The first is that God's revelation in the written Torah takes priority. The second is that human reason in the exegesis of the written Torah enjoys full and legitimate place in the unfolding of the lessons of Sinai. When, at the end, we seek the theological meaning of Midrash, we shall find ourselves back in the initial documents with their subtle and understated propositions. For when we realize what stake the framers of Sifra and Sifré to Numbers defined for themselves, we recognize the power of their claim for the mind of the human person: "in our image, after our likeness," is now clearly identified with the human mind.

The rhetorical form of both documents underlines the topical program contained in the first of the two propositions. For if I want to underline over and over again the priority of not proposition—hence reason—but process—hence the exegesis of Scripture—my best choice is an obvious one. Begin at all points with a verse of Scripture and demonstrate that only by starting with the word choices and propositions of that verse of Scripture can all further interpretation proceed. But the second proposition, that man (we should now say, humanity) has a place in the process of revealing the Torah of Sinai, comes to expression in the careful separation of the cited verse of the written Torah from the contribution of the contemporary exegete. In that formal preference too, the authorship made a major point and established—if implicitly—a central syllogism: God's will follows the rules of reason. Humanity can investigate the consequences of reason as expressed in God's will. Therefore humanity can join in the labor of exploring God's will in the Torah.

Consequently, the authorships of both Midrash-compilations make their powerful case by their rhetorical program, which relies first and foremost on the citation and gloss of a

verse of Scripture, as much as by their proposition and syllogism: only by Scripture does truth gain certainty. The appeal to
Scripture, however, comes once the proposition is established,
and that appeal then dictates the rhetoric and topic alike. Only
when we know what question we bring to Scripture may we
devise appropriate formal and programmatic policies for our
Midrash-exegesis and Midrash-compilation alike. A second
formal preference in both documents, in addition to the exegetical form, makes the same point. That other form involves citation of a passage of the Mishnah followed by an extensive
discourse on how the verse of Scripture that pertains to the
topic of that Mishnah-passage must contribute its facts, revealed at Sinai, if we wish to know the truth. Reason alone,
which is systematically tested through a sequence of propositions shown to fail, will not serve.

Let me dwell on this matter of the exegesis aimed at proving
the fallacy of logic uncorrected by exegesis of Scripture. The
pattern at hand is not centered upon the exegesis of a verse,
though exegesis plays a role in the pattern. Rather, the focus is
upon an issue that applies to all exegeses: is exegesis necessary
at all, or can logic, independent of the evidence of scriptural
verses, reach firm and reliable conclusions? Formally, we deal
with a moving, or dialectical, exegetical form, but while the
basic trait is familiar—a sequence of shifts and turns in the possibility of interpretation, all of them subjected to close logical
scrutiny—the purpose is different. And the purpose comes to
expression not in content, which always is particular to diverse
passages, but in form. The formal indicator is the presence of
the question, in one of several versions: is it not a matter of
logic? That is the never-failing formal indicator. From that
clause we invariably move on to a set of arguments of a highly
formalized character on taxonomic classification: what is like,
or unlike? What is like follows a given rule, what is unlike follows the opposite rule, and it is for us to see whether the like-
nesses or unlikenesses prevail. The argument is formalized to
an extreme, and there are very few variations among our document's exempla of this form, though one—the matter of

length—should not be missed. The exegesis of the verse at hand plays no substantial role beyond its initial introduction. What is critical is the issue of the reliability of logic. The base verse before us contributes virtually nothing and in no way serves as the foundation for the composition at hand. An important example is given at Sifré to Numbers **CVII:III.3**. Let us quickly review a fine example of the form.

**CVII:III.**

3. A. Issi b. Aqabia says, "*To the Lord from the herd or from the flock . . . to make a pleasing odor to the Lord* means, from this species by itself or from that species by itself.

   B. "You say that it means, from this species by itself or from that species by itself.

   C. "But perhaps one may bring both simultaneously?

   D. "For there is an argument *a fortiori*: Now if the lambs brought for the Pentecost offering, which are brought in pairs, are valid if they come from a single species, a burnt offering, which is not brought in a pair [but is brought all by itself], surely they should be valid if it is of the same species as [the species of the other beast which accompanies it]!

   E. "No, if you have stated that rule in the case of the two lambs brought for Pentecost, concerning which Scripture imposed fewer requirements in connection with bringing them, and so validated them even if they come from a single species, will you say the same of the burnt offering, in which case Scripture has imposed more requirements in connection with the offering? Therefore it should not be valid unless it [and the beast accompanying it] derive from two different species.

   F. "Now the goats brought on the Day of Atonement and those brought on the New Month should prove the contrary. For Scripture has imposed on those offerings multiple requirements and yet they are valid if they all come of a single species. So they should provide a valid analogy for the burnt offering, so that, even though it comes along with numerous requirements, it too should be valid if it [and the beasts accompanying it] come from a single species.

   G. "No, if you have stated that rule concerning the goats brought on the Day of Atonement and those brought on the New Month, for even though Scripture has imposed on those offerings multiple requirements, they are not brought on every day of the year [but only on specified occasions], and therefore they all may derive from a single species. But will you say the same of the burnt offering, for, even though it comes along with numerous requirements, it may be offered on every day of the year? Therefore it should be valid only if it is accompanied by beasts of other species.

H. "Lo, a sin offering will prove to the contrary. For in its regard Scripture has imposed numerous requirements, and it may be offered on every day of the year, and it may come only if it is from a single species. So that should prove the rule for the burnt offering, in which case, even though Scripture has imposed numerous requirements, and even though it is brought every day of the year, it should be valid only if it derives from a single species.

I. "No, if you have stated that rule concerning the sin offering, on which Scripture has imposed limitations, since it may not be brought by reason of a vow or a freewill offering, and therefore it is valid only if it derives from a single species, will you say the same of the burnt offering, which is available for a variety of purposes, since it may be brought in fulfillment of a vow or as a freewill offering? Therefore it should be valid only if it derives from a single species.

J. "Why then is it necessary for Scripture to specify, *To the Lord from the herd or from the flock . . . to make a pleasing odor to the Lord,* meaning, from this species by itself or from that species by itself?"

Issi's proof is that only Scripture can give reliable guidance as to the law. The issue is whether the beasts for the specified offerings encompass both sheep and goats, or whether one may bring two sheep or two goats. The exercise presents the usual frustrations, since each analogy is shown to be inadequate. In consequence, argument by analogy alone does not suffice, and only a clear exegesis of Scripture settles the question. As we see, there is no interest only in the explanation of the cited verses or even of their topic. The real issue—the generative and precipitating intellectual program of the pericope—lies elsewhere. It is whether or not logic alone suffices. That issue is extrinsic to the passage at hand. But it occurs throughout both documents and forms one of both authorships' recurrent formal choices.

Further literary traits of the two documents deserve attention before we turn to our abstracts. Dealing first with Sifra, we shall see that in the main Sifra tends not to attribute its materials to specific authorities, and most of the pericopae containing attributions are shared with Mishnah and Tosefta. Further, as we should expect, Sifra contains a fair sample of pericopae that do not make use of the forms common in the exegesis of specific scriptural verses and, mostly, do not pretend to explain the meaning of verses, but rather resort to forms typical of Mishnah and Tosefta. When Sifra uses forms other than those in which its exegeses are routinely phrased, it commonly, though not always, draws upon materials also found in Mishnah and Tosefta. It is uncommon for Sifra to make use of nonexegetical forms for materials peculiar to its compilation. As we realize, rhetorical patterning of language appears in two forms in Sifra. First is the simple, in which a verse, or an element of a verse, is cited, and then a very few words explain the meaning of that verse. Second is the complex, in which a simple exegesis is augmented in some important way, commonly by questions and answers, so that we have more than simply a verse and a brief exposition of its elements or of its meaning as a whole.

Every example of a complex form, that is, a passage in which we have more than a cited verse and a brief exposition of its meaning, may be called "dialectical," that is, moving or developing an idea through questions and answers, sometimes implicit, but commonly explicit. What "moves" is the argument, the flow of thought, from problem to problem. The movement is generated by the raising of contrary questions and theses. There are several subdivisions of the dialectical exegesis, so distinctive as to be treated by themselves. But all exhibit a flow of logical argument, unfolding in questions and answers, characteristic, in the later literature, of the Talmud. One important subdivision of the stated form consists of those items, somewhat few in number but all rather large in size and articulation, intended to prove that logic alone is insufficient, and that only through revealed law will a reliable view of what is required be attained. The polemic in these items is pointed and obvious; logic (DYN) never wins the argument, though at a few points flaws in the text seem to suggest disjunctures in the flow of logic.

Since Sifra is a composite document, with what I think is an early stratum of simple exegeses and a later, and much larger, stratum of dialectical ones, the purposes of the ultimate formulators of the dialectical materials and of the final redactors is revealed in particular in these dialectical constructions. It is to apply rigorous logic to the exegesis of Scripture and to demonstrate that revelation, not logic alone, is necessary for the discovery of the law. In doing so, the formulators and redactors of the late second and early third century probably made use of the inherited, simple form, spinning out their theses by presenting ideas in that uncomplicated form and then challenging those ideas in various ways but in equally simple, disciplined forms and formulaic usages. The final redaction also drew abundant materials from completed, free-floating pericopae also utilized in the redaction of Mishnah and Tosefta. So far as we now can discern, these shared materials are prior to ultimate redaction to the work of compiling both Sifra and Mishnah and Tosefta. But they are, normally though not always, primary to the editorial and redactional purposes of Mishnah and Tosefta and secondary to those of Sifra.

The rhetorical plan of Sifra leads us to recognize that the exegetes, while working verse by verse, in fact have brought a considerable program to their reading of the book of Leviticus. It concerns the interplay of the oral Torah, represented by the Mishnah, with the written Torah, represented by the book of Leviticus. That question demanded, in their view, not an answer comprising mere generalities. They wished to show their results through details, masses of details, and, like the rigorous philosophers that they were, they furthermore argued essentially through an inductive procedure, amassing evidence that in its accumulation made the point at hand. The syllogism I have identified about the priority of the revelation of the written Torah in the search for truth is nowhere expressed in so many words, because the philosopher-exegetes of the rabbinic world, beginning with the philosopher-poets who composed the Mishnah as a mass of details implicitly demonstrating large but unstated generalizations, preferred to address an implicit syllogism and to pursue or to test that syllogism solely in a sequence of small-scale experiments. Sifra's authorship therefore finds in the Mishnah and Tosefta a sizable laboratory for the testing of propositions. We therefore have to ask, at what points do Sifra and Mishnah and Tosefta share a common agenda of interests, and at what points does one compilation introduce problems, themes, or questions unknown to the other? The answer to these questions is that Sifra and Mishnah and Tosefta form two large concentric circles, sharing a considerable area in common. Sifra, however, exhibits interests peculiar to itself. On the criterion of common themes and interests, Mishnah and Tosefta and Sifra overall exhibit a remarkable unity.

The authorship of Sifré to Numbers, for its part, took up a pentateuchal book that in no way focuses upon the topics paramount, also, in the Mishnah and the Tosefta, in the way in which the book of Leviticus covers subjects that take a prominent position in the later law codes. Consequently, we cannot find in Sifré to Numbers a counterpart to the stress of the matters we have located in Sifra. Still, the established polemic about the priority of Scripture over unaided reason does take its place. But it does not predominate as it does in Sifra. Sifré to Numbers bears its own points of interest. Let us begin with the formal traits of the exegetical unit of thought.

There are two types of exegetical constructions in Sifré to Numbers, external and internal. The distinction between extrinsic and intrinsic exegesis emerges from a simple formal trait: do verses *other* than the base verse, that is, the verse of the book of Numbers under discussion, play a considerable part? Are there many such verses besides the base one, or only a few? Do those many verses deal with the topic of the base verse or other topics? If the former, then they may serve to illuminate the verse under discussion; if the latter, then all the verses together, including the one chosen from the book of Numbers, may serve to demonstrate a given proposition external to all of the prooftexts. These questions find answers not in impressions but in simple facts: number of verses other than the base verse, origins of those other verses. The focus upon the verse other than that in the book of Numbers invokes a verse from some other book of Scripture to illuminate the one in Numbers and to demonstrate the unity of all Scripture for the case at hand— another powerful polemic. The focus upon the verse at hand in the book of Numbers follows a different program altogether, one in which the explanation of the components of what we may call the base verse defines the program of inquiry. We shall see this same pattern of rhetorical forms—intersecting verse, base verse, or exposition of the base verse—time and again as we follow the unfolding of the Midrash-compilations. Assuming that Sifré to Numbers came to closure early on, we may assign to its authorship responsibility for discovering the two principal rhetorical choices of the whole of the Midrash-compilations, down through the Talmud of Babylonia. But we have gotten ahead of our story. Let us go back to the formal choices of rhetoric executed by the authorship at hand.

Sifré to Numbers involves these formal patterns. First comes the extrinsic exegetical form, which consists of the citation of an opening verse, followed by an issue stated in terms extrinsic to the cited verse. The formal traits are these: (1) citation of a base verse from Numbers, (2) a generalization ignoring clauses or words in the base verse, (3) a further observation without clear interest in the verse at hand. The form yields a syllogism proved by a list of facts beyond all doubt.

Second is the intrinsic exegetical form, in which the verse itself is clarified. The focus is on the base verse and not on a broader issue. There are diverse versions of this exercise, some consisting only of a verse or a clause and a statement articulating the sense of the matter, others rather elaborate. But the result is always the same. The framers of Sifra would have found this form entirely familiar.

Third is what I call the form of *dialectical* exegesis that focuses on an *intrinsic* aspect of a verse. In *intrinsic* dialectical exegesis a sequence of arguments about the meaning of a passage focuses upon the meaning of the base verse. This is the internal-exegetical counterpart to the ongoing argument on whether logic works. Now logic pursues the sense of a verse, but the results of logic are tested, forthwith and one by one, against the language at hand. The question is asked, why is this stated? Or: you say it means X but why not Y? Or, if X, then what about Y? If Y, then what about Z? All of these rather nicely articulated exegetical programs impose a scriptural test upon the proposals of logic. The engaging exercise in practical reason has counterparts in both Talmuds.

Fourth is the counterpart, that is, the *extrinsic* dialectical exegesis, not centered upon a component of the verse at hand but aimed at proving the fallacy of logic uncorrected by exegesis of Scripture. The formal indicator is the presence of the question, in one of several versions: is it not a matter of logic? The exegesis of the verse at hand plays no substantial role. We have already noted an example of that rhetorical pattern.

The fifth form is a simpler statement of the same proposition as animates the fourth, namely, the specification of the scriptural basis for a passage of the Mishnah. What we have is simply a citation of the verse plus a law in prior writing (Mishnah, Tosefta), which the verse is supposed to sustain. The Mishnah's or the Tosefta's rule then cannot stand as originally set forth, that is, without any exegetical foundation. On the contrary, the rule, verbatim, rests on a verse of Scripture, given with slight secondary articulation: verse, then Mishnah-sentence. That suffices, the point is made.

Let us now characterize as a whole the formal traits of both Sifra and also Sifré to Numbers as a commentary. These, as I have already hinted, may be reduced to two classifications, based on the point of origin of the verses that are catalogued or subjected to exegesis: exegesis of a verse in the book of Numbers in terms of the theme or problems of that verse, hence, intrinsic exegesis; exegesis of a verse in Numbers in terms of a theme or polemic not particular to that verse, hence, extrinsic exegesis.

In all the forms of *extrinsic* exegesis, the implicit message of the external category proves simple to define, since the several extrinsic classifications turn out to form a cogent polemic. Let me state the recurrent polemic of external exegesis.

1. The syllogistic composition: Scripture supplies hard facts, which, properly classified, generate syllogisms. By collecting and classifying facts of Scripture, therefore, we may produce firm laws of history, society, and Israel's everyday life. The diverse compositions in which verses from various books of the Scriptures are compiled in a list of evidence for a given proposition—whatever the character or purpose of that proposition—make that one point. And given their power and cogency, they make the point stick.

2. The fallability of reason unguided by scriptural exegesis: Scripture alone supplies reliable basis for speculation. Laws cannot be generated by reason or logic unguided by Scripture. Efforts at classification and contrastive-analogical exegesis, in which Scripture does not supply the solution to all problems, prove few and far between (and always in Ishmael's name, for whatever that is worth). This polemic forms the obverse of the point above.

Once we have taken up our abstracts of both documents, we shall return to these two forms and ask about the fundamental proposition that they lay forth. For, as we shall now see, both documents present us with instances of Midrash as exegesis, in which interpretation in the form of exegesis yields propositions. Once we have seen the way in which the Midrash does its work, we shall ask about the consequent propositions that emerge out of the inductive examination of discrete data and form into a profound syllogism, capable of generating further propositions.

## II. SIFRA

Our samples will illustrate the workings of Midrash as verse-by-verse exegesis. We deal for Sifra* with *Parashat Ne-gaim*, corresponding to Leviticus 13:1ff., the passage on *saraat*, a skin ailment wrongly identified with Hanson's disease ("leprosy"). We shall see how the exegetes work their way through the opening verses of the chapter. I cite the verses, as usual, in italics, and where passages from the Mishnah or Tosefta occur, I give them in boldface type.

### SIFRA

#### PARASHAT NEGAIM PEREQ 1

A. *And the Lord spoke to Moses and to Aaron saying, "A man (Adam) when there will be on the skin of his body"* (Lev. 13:1–2):

B. Why does Scripture say so [speaking of Adam + will be]?

C. Because it is said, *And a man or a woman, when there will be on the skin of his flesh bright spots [the priest shall make an examination, and if the spots on the skin of his body are of a dull white, it is tetter that has broken out in the skin; he is clean]* (Lev. 13:38–39)—

D. [This refers to] clean bright spots.

E. It is hardly necessary to speak [in Lev. 13:2] of bright spots which do not exhibit the colors of plagues and which have not come into the category [of uncleanness, for Lev. 13:38–39 includes them].

F. But [there are, in accord with Lev. 13:2, clean] bright spots which do [nonetheless] exhibit the colors of plagues [namely]:

G. **Which were on him and he converted—**

H. **on the infant and he was born,**

I. **on the crease [of the flesh] and it was unfolded,**

J. **on the head and on the beard,**

K. **on the festering boil and burning and blister,**

---

*Sifra: The Judaic Commentary on Leviticus; A New Translation. The Leper, Leviticus 13:1–14:57* (Chico: Scholars Press for Brown Judaic Studies, 1985). Based on the translation of *Sifra Parashiyyot Negaim* and *Mesora* in *A History of the Mishnaic Law of Purities. VI. Negaim. Sifra* (with a section by Roger Brooks). See now my complete translation *Sifra* (Atlanta: Scholars Press for Brown Judaic Studies, 1988), I–III.

L. Their [those items in G] colors changed, whether to produce a lenient or a stringent ruling—

M. R. Eleazar b. Azarah declares clean.

N. R. Eleazar b. Hisma says, "To produce a lenient ruling—it is clean, and to produce a stringent ruling—let it be examined afresh."

O. R. Aqiba says, "Whether to produce a lenient or a stringent ruling, it is examined afresh [M. Neg. 7:11]."

P. Therefore it is said, *A man (Adam)—when there will be* (Lev. 13:1).

## N1:1

We begin with a citation of what I call the base verse, meaning the verse on which all further discourse rests, to which reference is constantly made. At B we see what has attracted the interest of the exegete. But that is only one point of interest, because, at G, we realize that the exegete has in mind a passage of the Mishnah, and what he has accomplished is to link that rule to the cited verse. The main point in both Scripture and the Mishnah is that when there *will be* the variations in skin tone, each must be treated in its own terms and examined afresh. We shall resume our brief comments on the abstracts at the end of a longer selection below.

A. *When there will be* (Lev. 13:2)—

B. [The use of the future tense, *when there will be a white spot,* indicates that the law applies only from the point of its pronouncement and onward, thus:] From the [time at which this law is] proclaimed [namely, Sinai] onward.

C. And is it not logical?

D. [Scripture] has declared uncleanness with reference to Zabim and has declared uncleanness with reference to plagues.

E. Just as in the case of Zabim, it declared clear [such appearances of uncleanness as occurred] before the pronouncement [of the Torah], so in reference to plagues, it declared clear [such appearances of uncleanness as occurred] on them before the pronouncement.

## N1:2

F. It [moreover] is an argument *a fortiori:* if in the case of Zabim, whose cleanness and uncleanness may be determined by anyone, it [Scripture] has declared free before the declaration, plagues, the uncleanness or cleanness of which may be declared only by a priest, it is not logical that it should declare them clear before the declaration?

G. No. If you have so stated concerning Zabim, whom it [Scripture] did not declare unclean when [the flux is] accidental, will you say so concerning plague, which is declared unclean [even when the uncleanness is] accidental?

H. Since it is declared unclean [even when the uncleanness is] accidental, will it declare them clear before the pronouncement [of the Scriptural law]?

I. Therefore Scripture says, *When it will be,* meaning, from the pronouncement [at Sinai] and onward.

### N1:3

A. *On the skin of his flesh* (Lev.13:2).

B. What does Scripture mean to say?

C. Because it is said, *And hair in the diseased spot has turned white* (Lev. 13:3), might one say I have reference only to a place which is suitable to grow white hair? But a place which is not suitable to grow white hair—how do we know [that it is susceptible]?

D. Scripture says, *On the skin of his flesh*—as an inclusionary clause.

[E. *A swelling or an eruption or a spot* (Lev. 13:2).]

F. *A swelling*—this is a swelling.

G. *A spot*—this a spot.

H. *An eruption (SPHT)*—this is secondary [in color] to the bright spot.

I. *And its shade is deep* [Lev. 13:3: *And the shade of the plague is deep*]— [the color of the SPHT is] secondary to that of the swelling.

J. What is the meaning of the word eruption? Prominent.

K. **Like the shades of the shadow, which are higher than the appearance of the sun.**

L. What is the meaning of the word deep?

M. **Deep as the shades of the sun, which are deeper than the shadow.**

N. What is the meaning of the word eruption? Secondary,

O. as it is said, *Put me (SPHYNY), I pray you, in one of the priest's places* (1 Sam. 2:36).

P. *And it will be* (Lev. 13:2)—teaches that **they [the colors] join together with one another to declare clear and to certify and to shut up.**

Q. *On the skin of his flesh* (Lev. 13:2)—on the skin of that flesh which can be seen [or: in accord with its appearance].

R. On this basis have they said: **A bright spot appears dim on a German and the dim one on the Ethiopian appears bright.**

### N1:4

S. **R. Ishmael says, "The house of Israel—lo, I am atonement for them—lo, they are like boxwood, not black and not white but intermediate."**

T. **R. Aqiba says, "The artists have pigments with which they color skin black, white, and intermediate. One brings the intermediate pigment and surrounds it [the bright spot] on the outer perimeter, and it will appear like the intermediate."**

U. R. Yosé says, "One Scripture says, *On the skin of the flesh* (Lev. 13:2), and another Scripture says, *On the skin of the flesh* (Lev. 13:2)."

V. We therefore find that
   **the specification of colors of plagues are meant to produce a lenient ruling, but not to produce a strict ruling. One therefore examines the German in accord with his skin tone to produce a lenient ruling.**

W. It comes out that [thereby] one carries out, *On the skin of* his *flesh.*

X. **And the Ethiopian is adjudged in accord with the intermediate pigment to produce a lenient ruling.**

Y. It comes out that [thereby] one carries out, *On the skin of the flesh.*

Z. **And sages say, "This [and this are adjudged in accord with] the intermediate [M. Neg. 2:1]."**

### N1:5

A. *And it will be on the skin of his flesh [for a plague]* (Lev. 13:2).

B. This teaches that he is pained by it.

C. And how do we know that also others are pained by it?

D. They see him, that he is pained by it.

E. Scripture says, *For a plague* (Lev. 13:2).

F. *A leprosy [sign]* (Lev. 13:2)—the size of a split bean.

G. And is it not logical?

H. It has declared unclean here [where there is white hair], and it has declared unclean in reference to quick flesh.

I. Just as quick flesh is the size of a split bean, so also here [we require] a sign the size of a split bean.

### N1:6

J. No. If you have said so concerning quick flesh, which must be the size of a lentil, will you say so concerning [a leprosy sign, marked as unclean by] white hair, for the space of white hair requires nothing [no specific area].

K. Scripture says, *Leprosy* (Lev. 13:2)—a sign the size of a split bean.

### N1:7

A. *And he will be brought to Aaron [the priest or to one of his sons the priests]* (Lev. 13:2).

B. I know only about Aaron himself.

C. How do we know to include another priest?

D. Scripture says, *The priest* (Lev. 13:2).

E. How do we know to include [as suitable examining priests] those [priests who are] injured?

F. Scripture says, *Among his sons* (Lev. 13:2).

G. Then perhaps should I also include profaned [disqualified priests, HLLYM]?

H. Scripture says, *The priests* (Lev. 13:2)—the disqualified priests are excluded.

I. And how do we know to include any Israelite [qualified to examine the plague]?

J. Scripture says, *Or to one.*

### N1:8

K. If we end up including every Israelite, why does Scripture say, *Or to one of his sons the priests?*

L. But it is to teach that the actual declaration of uncleanness or cleanness is only by a priest.

M. How so?

N. A sage who is an Israelite [and not necessarily a priest, but a sage and so informed about the law, as a priest may not be] examines the plagues **and says to the priest, even though he is an idiot, "Say, 'Unclean,' and he says, 'Unclean.' Say, 'Clean,' and he says, 'Clean' [M. Neg. 3:1]."**

O. Another matter:

P. Why does Scripture say, *Or to one of his sons the priests* (Lev. 13:2)?

Q. Since it is said, *In accord with their instructions will be every dispute and every plague* (Deut. 21:5), controversies are linked to plagues. Just as plagues must be decided by day, so controversies must be judged by day.

### N1:9

R. **Just as controversies may not be settled by relatives, so plagues may not be examined by relatives [M. Neg. 2:5].**

S. If [we should now attempt to continue]: Just as controversies must be with three [judges] so plagues must be examined by three [priests]—it is an argument *a fortiori.*

T. If his property [dispute] is settled by a decision of three judges, should his body not be examined by three?

U. Scripture says, *Or to one of his sons the priests* (Lev. 13:2).

V. This teaches that a single priest examines the plagues.

### N1:10

At **N1:2** we revert to the phrasing *when there will be.* The exegete interprets the verb's future tense to mean that the law applies only from the time that the Torah was given, and that uncleanness by reason of the skin ailment was not effective prior to the events on Mount Sinai. And then we see the wonderful inquiry: but will not mere logic tell me the same thing, on which account I do not require the stated exegesis of the words *will be?* Logic then invokes a parallel case to yield an argument *a fortiori*—from the lesser to the greater. Our task then is to violate the parallel and show that special traits distinguish the two cases that the proposed argument treats as analogous. We therefore prove that the analogy is incomplete or incorrect, **N1:3G.** We proceed from that point, **N1:4,** to a further phrase-by-phrase exegesis.

What we see is systematic glossing of the verse, and the glosses yield not clarification of the verse alone, but, in fact, rules that can apply to fresh cases, hence an exegesis meant to generate a syllogism. We invoke Mishnah-clauses in this process of clarification of the sense of Scripture. And the interweaving of Mishnah-clauses and scriptural verses goes forward, even where we do not ask whether we require Scripture's information at all. This underlines the point made earlier, that Mishnah's rules without Scripture's support are not reliable. N1:6 goes over the same ground yet another time, yielding at N1:7 the desired conclusion. What is important in the following abstract is simply the repetition of the exercises we have already seen. The reader therefore sees how uniform and cogent are the procedures at hand, which shows us that the mode of exegesis—that is, Midrash-interpretation—stands prior to the interpretation of the verses themselves—that is, Midrash-exegesis. And the mode of exegesis derives from the purposes of the document's authorship, that is, takes shape within the polemic the authors propose to undertake. First comes purpose of the exegesis, which the document as a whole defines for us; second, the exegetical method or process; and third and finally, the actual exegesis of the given verse.

### PARASHAT NEGAIM PARASHAH II

    A. *A white spot (Lev. 13:4: But if the spot is white in the skin of his body and appears no deeper than the skin . . .)*—

    B. I know only the white spot.

    C. How do we know that we should include the swelling?

    D. Scripture says below, *A white swelling* (Lev. 13:9: And if there is a white swelling in the skin . . .).

    E. And how do we know that we should include the other shades?

    F. Scripture says, *And if a bright spot.*

**NII:3**

G. Might one say that just as it is third in Scripture [(1) swelling, (2) eruption, (3) spot], so it should be third in the shades [of white] [that is, it need not be so white as the others]?

H. Scripture says, *White* (Lev. 13:4), *white* (Lev. 13:9).

I. It is white, and there is no brighter than it.

J. And how white must it be?

K. Like snow, as it is said, *And lo, Miriam was leprous like snow* (Num. 12:10).

### NII:2

L. Might one say that on account of every shade of snow they should be unclean, but [if they are as white as] all other shades [of white, except of the range of snow], they should be clean?

M. Scripture says, *It is a tetter* (Lev. 13:38).

N. [That which is as dull as] a tetter is unclean. From it [a tetter] and brighter, it is unclean.

### NII:3

O. On this basis have they said,

P. "The shades of plagues are two which are four.
"A bright spot is as bright as snow. Secondary to it is [white] as the plaster of the Temple.
"The rising is as white as the skin of an egg.
"Secondary to it is a shade of white like wool," the words of R. Meir.
And sages say, "The rising is [white] as wool, and secondary to it is [white] as the skin of an egg."

### NII:4

Q. "The variegation of the snow is like mixed wine.
"The variegation of the lime is like blood mixed in water," the words of R. Ishmael.

R. R. Aqiva says, "The reddishness which is in this and in that is like wine mixed in water.

S. "But that of snow is bright, and that of plaster is duller than it."

## NII:5

T. R. Hanina Prefect of the Priests says, "The shades of plagues are sixteen."

U. R. Dosa b. Harkinas says, "Thirty-six."

V. Aqavya b. Mehallel: "Seventy-two."

W. Said R. Yosé, "R. Joshua the son of R. Aqiva asked R. Aqiva, saying to him,

X. 'Why have they said, "The shades of plagues are two which are four"?'

Y. "He said to him, 'If not, what should they say?'

Z. "He said to him, 'Let them say, "From the white of the skin of an egg and brighter it is unclean, and they join together with one another." ' "

AA. Said R. Yosé, "R. Joshua the son of R. Aqiva asked R. Aqiva, saying to him, 'Why have they said, "The shades of plagues are two which are four"?'

BB. "He said to him, 'If not, what should they say?'

CC. "He said to him, 'Let them say, "From the shade of white like the skin of the egg and brighter is unclean." '

DD. "He said to him, 'To teach you that they join together with one another.'

EE. "He said to him, 'Let them say, "Anything which is as white as the skin of an egg or brighter is unclean, and they [the colors] join together with one another." '

FF. "He said to him, 'It teaches that if one is not an expert in them and in their names, he should not examine plagues' [M. Neg. 1:14, T. Neg. 1:1]."

## NII:6

A. *And its hair [has not turned white]* (Lev. 31:4)—

B. Not the hair of its quick flesh.

C. How so?

D. A bright spot the size of a split bean, and in it is quick flesh the size of a lentil—and white hair is in the midst of the quick flesh—

E. the quick flesh went away—it is unclean because of the white hair.

F. The white hair went away—it is unclean because of the quick flesh.

G. **R. Simeon declares clean, because the bright spot did not turn it [the hair white].**

H. He said to him, "And has it not already been said, *And hair in the plague has turned white* (Lev. 13:4)?

I. "This [quick flesh] is a plague in any event."

J. *And its hair has not turned white* (Lev. 13:4).

K. And not hair of part of it.

L. How so?

M. **A bright spot—**

N. **it [and] its quick flesh are the size of a split bean—**

O. **and white hair is in the midst of the bright spot—**

P. **the quick flesh went away—**

Q. **it is unclean because of the white hair.**

R. **The white hair went away—**

S. **it is unclean because of the quick flesh.**

T. **R. Simeon declares clean, because the bright spot the size of a split bean did not turn it [white].**

U. **And they agree [better: He (Simeon) agrees] that if there is in the place of white hair an area the size of a split bean, it is clean.**

V. *And its hair has not turned white, and he will shut up* (Lev. 13:4).

W. Lo, if there is in it black hair, it does not diminish it.

X. **The disciples asked R. Yosé, "A bright spot and in it is black hair: do we take account of the possibility that its place has diminished the bright spot to a size less than a split bean?"**

Y. **He said to them, "A bright spot, and [in it is] white hair—do we take account of the possibility that its place has diminished the bright spot to less than a split bean?"**

Z. **They said to him, "No. If you have said so concerning white hair, which is a sign of uncleanness [itself], will you say so concerning black hair, which is not a sign of uncleanness?"**

AA. **He said to them, "Lo, if there are in it ten white hairs, in any event are more than two of them tokens of uncleanness? Do we take account of the possibility that the excess has diminished the place of the bright spot to less than a split bean?"**

BB. They said to him, "No. If you have said so concerning white hair, which is a kind of uncleanness, will you say so concerning black hair, which in any event is not a variety of uncleanness?"

CC. He said to them, "Also black hair turns and becomes a kind of uncleanness [M. Neg. 4:6, T. Neg. 2:3].

DD. "But it says, *And its hair has not turned white, and he shuts up*—lo, if there is in it black hair, it does not diminish [the area of the spot]."

EE. *And the priest shall shut up the diseased spot seven days* (Lev. 13:5)—first [this is the first of two quarantines].

NII:9

Enough has been said to highlight the main points of this somewhat arcane discussion about the sense and meaning of Leviticus 13:1–5. What is important to us is the illustration of the basic proposition that the exegesis of the discrete verses time and again produces evidence in behalf of a fundamental syllogism, one that bears repetition and application to other cases altogether. In Sifré to Numbers and further abstracts in Parts Three and Four, we shall find more immediately engaging the subject matter of other passages. But none will show us so graphically how a single polemic will come to expression in multiple exegeses of diverse verses of Scripture or display more forcefully how in both form and content, plan and program, exegeses do yield a proposition. Seeing the same rhetorical program in the companion document, Sifré to Numbers, will now tell us how yet another authorship occupied itself with the same logical issues even while addressing a different topical program altogether.

## III. SIFRÉ TO NUMBERS

Sifré to Numbers 84 systematically spells out the potential meanings of Numbers 10:29–36, pursuing a rather diverse program. The same basic traits as before recur: explanation of the sense and meaning of individual verses, read in sequence, pointing toward a number of propositions (which we shall consider at the end) through a mass of detailed examples. The scriptural passage at hand, Numbers 10:29–36, is more immediately accessible than Leviticus 13:1ff.

### SIFRÉ TO NUMBERS 84 FOR NUMBERS 10:29–36

### LXXXIV:I.

1. A. *And whenever the ark set out, Moses said, "Arise, O Lord, and let your enemies be scattered, and let them that hate you flee before you." And when it rested, he said, "Return O Lord to the ten thousand thousands of Israel"* (Num. 10:29–36):

   B. [In the written version] there are dots above and below the word to indicate that this was not its correct place.

   C. Rabbi says, "It is because the pericope at hand constitutes a scroll unto itself."

   D. On the basis of this view they have said,

   E. **"In the case of a scroll which was blotted about, but in which eighty-five letters remained legible, as the number in the passage, *And whenever the ark set out,* imparts uncleanness to the hands [as does any holy scroll of the Torah] [M. Yad. 3:5]."**

   F. R. Simeon says, "In the written version there are dots above and below the word to indicate that this was not its correct place. And what ought to have been written instead of this passage? *And the people complained in the hearing of the Lord* (Num. 11:1ff.).

   G. "The matter may be compared to the case of people who said to the king, 'We shall see whether you will come with us to the ruler of Acre.' By the time they got to Acre, he had gone to Tyre. When they got to Tyre, he had gone to Sidon. When they got to Sidon, he had gone to Biri. When they got to Biri, he had gone to Antioch. When they got to Antioch, the people began to complain against the king, for they had wandered on the way, and the king had to complain against them, that on their account he too had wandered on the way.

   H. "So the Presence of God went on a single day a distance of thirty-six *mils* so that the Israelites should enter the land. The Israelites began to complain before the Omnipresent that they had wandered on the way. But the Omnipresent has to complain against them that on their account the Presence of God had gone on a single day thirty-six *mils* so that Israel should enter the land. [Each had held up the other. How to keep the two together, so that the one will not become separated from the other? That question is answered in the base verse: announce, *Arise, O Lord.*]"

The pericope before us in the written Torah is written out so as to stand distinct from its larger setting in the scroll of the Torah. Rabbi says that that is because it constitutes a distinct scroll, and E follows. Simeon's explanation is quite separate. He contributes the linkage between the present passage and what is to follow.

### LXXXIV:II.

1. A. *[And whenever the ark set out,] Moses said, "Arise, O Lord, [and let your enemies be scattered, and let them that hate you flee before you." And when it rested, he said, "Return O Lord to the ten thousand thousands of Israel"]* (Num. 10:29–36):

   B. While this verse says, *Whenever the ark set out, Moses said, "Arise, O Lord,"* another verse of Scripture says, *At the command of the Lord they encamped, and at the command of the Lord they set out* (Num. 9:23).

   C. How are both verses of Scripture to stand side by side? [Who gave the order to journey onward, God or Moses?]

   D. The matter may be compared to the case of a mortal king who said to his servant, "See to it that you so arrange things for me that I may go and hand over an inheritance to my son."

   E. Another matter: to what may the matter be compared? To the case of a mortal king who was going on the way and his ally went along with him. As he was setting out on the journey, he said, "I shall not set out until my ally comes." And when he encamps, he says, "I shall not make camp until my ally comes."

   F. In this way we may sustain both the statement [1] that it was on the orders *of Moses* that they made camp as well as the statement [2] that it was at the command of the *Lord* they made camp, thus on the command of Moses they journeyed, on the command of the Lord they journeyed.

The issue is how the two verses can be harmonized, since in the one case, the verse at hand, Moses is the one who gives the orders, while in the other, God tells them when to come and go. The solution is to compare the matter to a king who gives orders to his servant to arrange things as he wishes. That is in line with Simeon's account, above. The king will go his way, but only so as to set things up for his son later on. The *She-khinah* or Presence of God went its way, but only to provide an inheritance for the people, following. The second explanation, E–F, takes a different route: God gives the orders, but Moses so arranges matters as God wishes them.

## LXXXIV:III.

1.  A.  *[And whenever the ark set out, Moses said], "Arise, O Lord, and let your enemies be scattered, [and let them that hate you flee before you." And when it rested, he said, "Return O Lord to the ten thousand thousands of Israel"]* (Num. 10:29–36):

    B.  The enemies to be scattered are those who are gathered together.

    C.  *And let them that hate you flee before you:* these are those who pursue [Israel].

    D.  *From before you*—[so Israel says,] "[From before you] do they flee, but we are nothing before them. But when your presence is with us, we are a considerable force before them, and when your presence is not with us, we are as nothing before them."

    E.  And so Scripture says, *If your presence [face] does not go with us, do not bring us up from here* (Ex. 33:15).

    F.  And how does one know? It says, *And as they fled before Israel, while they were going down the ascent of Beth-horon, the Lord threw down great stones from heaven upon them as far as Azekah, and they died* (Josh. 10:11).

    G.  And it says, *O my God, make them like whirling dust, like chaff before the wind. As fire consumes the forest, as the flame sets the mountains ablaze, so do you pursue them with your tempest and terrify them with your hurricane* (Ps. 83:13–14).

The main point comes at C: God's presence makes all the difference. E and F then form secondary examples of evidence of what God's presence accomplishes. The syllogism is implicit but inescapable. We now move to the important corollary: God's presence in Israel means that those who hate Israel hate

God. That syllogism is both announced and then extensively proven by reference to the facts of Scripture, assembled in a sustained list of items all characterized by a single trait in common.

## LXXXIV:IV.

**1.**  A. *And let them that hate you flee before you:*

B. And do those who hate [come before] him who spoke and brought the world into being?

C. The purpose of the verse at hand is to say that whoever hates Israel is as if he hates him who spoke and by his word brought the world into being.

D. Along these same lines: *In the greatness of your majesty you overthrow your adversaries* (Ex. 15:7).

E. And are there really adversaries before him who spoke and by his word brought the world into being? But Scripture thus indicates that whoever rose up against Israel is as if he rose up against the Omnipresent.

F. Along these same lines: *Do not forget the clamor of your foes, the uproar of your adversaries, which goes up continually* (Ps. 74:23).

G. *For lo, your enemies, O Lord* (Ps. 92:10).

H. *For those who are far from you shall perish, you put an end to those who are false to you* (Ps. 73:27).

I. *For lo, your enemies are in tumult, those who hate you have raised their heads* (Ps. 83:2). On what account? *They lay crafty plans against your people, they consult together against your protected ones* (Ps. 83:3).

J. *Do I not hate those who hate you, O Lord? And do I not loathe them that rise up against you? I hate them with perfect hatred, I count them my enemies* (Ps. 139:21–22).

K. And so too Scripture says, *For whoever lays hands on you is as if he lays hands on the apple of his eye* (Zech. 2:12).

L. R. Judah says, "What is written is not 'the apple of an eye' but 'the apple of *his* eye.' It is as if Scripture speaks of him above, but Scripture has used a euphemism."

M. Along these same lines [are other anthropomorphic euphemisms]: *Why have you made me your mark, why have I become a burden to you?* ( Job 78:20), but Scripture has used a euphemism.

N. *Lo, they put the branch to their nose* (Ez. 8:17), but Scripture has used a euphemism.

O. Along these same lines: *Are you not from everlasting, O Lord my God, my Holy One? We shall not die* (Hab. 1:12), but Scripture has used a euphemism.

P. Along these same lines: *They exchanged the glory of God for the image of an ox that eats grass* (Ps. 106:20), but Scripture has used a euphemism.

Q. Along these same lines: *If you will deal thus with me, kill me at once, if I find favor in your sight, that I may not see my wretchedness* (Num. 11:15), but Scripture has used a euphemism.

R. Along these same lines: *But my people has exchanged its glory* (Jer. 2:11), but Scripture has used a euphemism.

S. Along these same lines: *Let her not be as one dead, of whom the flesh is half consumed when he comes out of his mother's womb* (Num. 12:13), but Scripture has used a euphemism.

T. So here too you say, "the apple of his eye."

U. R. Judah says, "What is written is not 'the apple of an eye' but 'the apple of *his* eye.' It is as if Scripture speaks of him above, but Scripture has used a euphemism."

V. And whoever gives help to Israel is as if he gives help to him who spoke and by his word brought the world into being, as it is said, *"Curse Meroz," says the angel of the Lord, "curse bitterly its inhabitants, because they came not to the help of the Lord, to the help of the Lord against the mighty"* (Judges 5:23).

W. R. Simeon b. Eleazar says, "You have no more prized part of the body than the eye and Israel has been compared to it. A further comparison: if a man is hit on his head, only his eyes feel it. Accordingly, you have no more prized part of the body than the eye, and Israel has been compared to it."

X. So Scripture says, *What, my son, What, son of my womb? what, son of my vows?* (Prov. 31:2).

Y. And it says, *When I was a son with my father, tender, the only one in the sight of my mother, he taught me and said to me, "Let your heart hold fast my words"* (Prov. 4:3–4).

Z. R. Yose b. Eleazar says, "It is like a man who puts his finger into his eye and scratches it. As to Pharaoh, who laid hands on you, what did I do to him? *The chariots of Pharaoh and his host sank into the sea* (Ex. 15:4).

AA. "As to Sisera, who laid hands on you, what did I do to him? *The stars in their courses fought against Sisera* (Judges 5:20).

BB. "As to Sennacherib, who laid hands on you, what did I do to him? *And an angel of the Lord came forth and smote the camp of Assyria* (2 Kgs. 19:35).

CC. "As to Nebuchadnezzar, who laid hands on you, what did I do to him? *And you shall be made to eat grass like an ox* (Dan. 4:32).

DD. "As to Haman, who laid hands on you, what did I do to him? *And they hung him on a tree* (Est. 8:7)."

EE. So you find, furthermore, that so long as Israel is subjugated, it is as if the Presence of God is subjugated with them, as it is said, *And they saw the God of Israel, and there was under his feet as it were a pavement of sapphire stone, like the very heaven for clearness* (Ex. 24:10).

FF. And so Scripture says, *In all their suffering is suffering for him* (Is. 63:9).

GG. I know only that that is the case for the suffering of the community. How do I know that it also is the case for the suffering of the individual?

HH. Scripture says, *When he calls me, I will answer him; I will be with him in trouble, I will rescue him and honor him* (Ps. 91:15).

II. And so Scripture says, *And Joseph's master took him and put him into the prison . . . and he was there in prison. But the Lord was with Joseph and showed him steadfast love and gave him favor in the sight of the keeper of the prison* (Gen. 39:20–21).

JJ. And so Scripture says, *On account of your people, whom you redeemed for yourself from Egypt, a people and its God [that is, God too was redeemed from Egypt]* (2 Sam. 7:23).

KK. R. Eliezer says, "An idol crossed over the sea with Israel. And what is it? It is the icon of Micah."

LL. R. Aqiba says, "If an available verse of Scripture had not said it, it would not have been possible to say it: Israel said before the Omnipresent, 'You have redeemed yourself.' "

MM. And so you find that everywhere [Israel] has been exiled, the Presence of God was with them, as it is said, *I revealed myself to the house of your father when they were in Egypt subject to the house of Pharaoh* (1 Sam. 2:27).

NN. When they were exiled to Babylonia, the Presence of God was with them: *On your account I was sent to Babylonia* (Is. 43:14).

OO. When they were exiled to Elam, the Presence of God was with them: *I set my throne in Elam* ( Jer. 49:38).

PP. When they were exiled to Edom, the Presence of God was with them: *Who is this who comes up from Edom, in crimsoned garments from Bozrah?* (Is. 63:1).

QQ. When they come back, the Presence of God will return with them, as it is said, *And the Lord your God will return your fortune* (Deut. 30:3). What is written is not *will return,* but *will come.*

RR. And Scripture further states, *With me from Lebanon, O bride, with me you shall come from Lebanon* (Song 4:8).

## LXXXIV:IV.

2. A. Rabbi says, "Here you say, '*Arise* O Lord,' and then, '*Return* O Lord.' How are the two verses of Scripture to be reconciled?

   B. "Scripture indicates that when the Israelites were journeying, the pillar of cloud stood bowed over, and did not move until Moses instructed it, '*Rise* O Lord,' and when they were encamped, the pillar of cloud stood bowed over, and it did not spread out until he said to it, "*Return* O Lord.' So you may reconcile the statement, '*Rise* O Lord' and also '*Return* O Lord.'"

No. 1 forms a vast construction of verses made to prove a series of syllogisms, none of which has a close bearing on the citing verse, beyond B. What is proved is that: (1) none can sustain hatred of God, followed by a list of proofs; then (2) whoever helps Israel is as if he helps God; (3) whoever persecutes Israel is as if he persecutes God; (4) God is with the community in all its trials; and (5) God is with the individual in all his trials. None of this focuses upon our verse in particular. The point of interest is much broader, a theory of the history of Israel as a nation and of the Israelite as an individual person, and of God's role in the destiny of both. No. 2 then returns us to the base verse and reconciles the two parts of the verse.

This stunning passage proves a powerful syllogism, which is that so long as Israel is subjugated, it is as if the Presence of God is subjugated with them, and that God is reliable to save Israel just as God shares the fate of Israel. The syllogism is expressed, but the important side is not the expression but the systematic testing of the proposition against the facts supplied by Scrip-

ture. To that matter the initial or base verse is really not critical, and the treatment of that verse serves only to allow for the
introduction and massive exposition and demonstration of the
stated syllogism. As we noticed, the role of Scripture now is
not to generate the proposition, let alone to guide discussion,
as in the case of Sifra. Rather, Scripture serves as a source of
indisputable facts, against which we are able to test our proposed theses, just as nature and logic serve philosophers. The
rabbinical sages think about matters of history and society, the
laws of social conduct and God's rule, and therefore Scripture
takes the place of nature. But the rigorous logic of philosophy,
testing propositions against appropriate and relevant facts,
governs as much here as it does in the natural philosophy of the
day in which the sages did their work.

## LXXXIV:V.

1.  A. *And when it rested, he said, "Return O Lord to the ten thousand thousands
       of Israel":*
    B. Scripture indicates that when the Israelites were journeying in their
       thousands, and encamping in their tens of thousands, as it were Moses
       said before the Omnipresent, "I shall not let the Presence of God rest
       until you will make Israel thousands and tens of thousands."
    C. For from the answer that he gave, you know what he had said to
       them:
    D. *"May the Lord, the God of your fathers, add to you numbers like yours, a
       thousand times over"* (Deut. 1:11).
    E. They said to him, "Moses our master, lo, we have been promised
       many blessings, for thus he has promised us that we should be like the
       stars of the heaven and the sand of the sea and the plants of the earth,
       and now you are setting a limit on the blessing that applies to us."
    F. He said to them, "I am a mere mortal, so there is a limit to the
       blessing that I on my part can bestow, but he will bless you just as
       he said to you, like the sand of the sea and the plants of the land and
       the fish of the sea and the stars of the heaven in multitude."

## LXXXIV:V.

2.  A. *And when it rested, he said, "Return O Lord to the ten thousand thousands
       of Israel:"*

B. Scripture indicates that the Presence of God rests above only for thousands and tens of thousands, as it is said, *With mighty chariotry, twice ten thousand, thousands upon thousands, the Lord came from Sinai into the holy place* (Ps. 68:17).

C. And just as the Presence of God rests above only for thousands and tens of thousands, so the Presence of God rests below only for thousands and tens of thousands.

D. Therefore Scripture says, *And when it rested, he said, "Return O Lord to the ten thousand thousands of Israel."*

The base verse now is expanded at No. 1 into the basis for a colloquy on Deuteronomy 1:11, joining the one to the other by reference to the numbers to which the verse refers. At No. 2 yet another verse that alludes to the same numbers is adduced in evidence.

## IV. THE ISSUE

Let us now move from the abstracts of our two documents to the issues addressed by the Midrash-exegeses collected in the Midrash-documents at hand. What is at stake in the Midrash-exegeses collected in the Midrash-compilations before us? Let me state the point made in the detailed exegeses and make explicit the recurring and implicit message of the forms of *external* exegesis as well as of the results achieved in the reading of passages of Leviticus and Numbers:

*Scripture stands paramount; logic, reason, analytical processes of classification and differentiation are secondary. Reason not built on scriptural foundations yields uncertain results. The Mishnah itself demands scriptural bases.*

Clearly, in the *extrinsic* exegeses that polemic is made explicit. But it is not so self-evidently present in those far more numerous Midrash-exegeses that simply cite verses and say what their several components mean. We therefore have to ask about the polemic present in the *intrinsic* exegetical exercises. This clearly does not allow for ready characterization.

As we saw, at least some of the intrinsic exegetical exercises focus on the use of logic—specifically, the logic of classification, comparison, and contrast of species of a genus—in the explanation of the meaning of verses of the book of Numbers. The internal dialectical mode, moving from point to point as logic dictates, underlines the main point already stated: logic produces possibilities, Scripture chooses among them. Again, the question *why is this passage stated?* commonly produces an answer generated by further verses of Scripture: this matter is stated here to clarify what otherwise would be confusion left in the wake of other verses. So Scripture produces problems of confusion and duplication, and Scripture—not logic, not differentiation, not classification—also resolves those problems. To state matters simply: Scripture is complete, harmonious, perfect. Logic not only does not generate truth beyond the limits of Scripture but also plays no important role in the harmonization of difficulties yielded by what appear to be duplications or disharmonies. These forms of internal exegesis then make the same point that the extrinsic ones do.

In so describing the fundamental points repeatedly illustrated by the rhetorical forms used in the inquiry into the verses of Scripture at hand, of course, we cover all but the single most profuse category of exegesis. These we have treated as simple and undifferentiated: (1) verse of Scripture or a clause, followed by (2) a brief statement of the meaning at hand. Here, among the vast evidences of both Midrash-compilations, I see no unifying polemic in favor of, or against, a given proposition. The most common form also proves the least pointed in its polemic in favor of a given syllogism: X bears this meaning, Y bears that meaning, or, as we have seen, citation of verse X, followed by "what this means is". . . . Whether simple or elaborate, the result is the same. What can be at issue when no polemic expressed in the formal traits of syntax and logic finds its way to the surface? What do I do when I merely clarify a phrase? Or, to frame the question more logically: what premises must validate my *intervention,* that is, my willingness to undertake to explain the meaning of a verse of Scripture? These seem to me propositions that must serve to justify the labor of intrinsic exegesis as we have seen its results here:

1. My independent judgment bears weight and produces meaning. I—that is, my mind—therefore may join in the process.

2. God's revelation to Moses at Sinai requires my intervention. I have the role, and the right, to say what that revelation means.

3. What validates my entry into the process of revelation is the correspondence between the logic of my mind and the logic of the document.

Why do I think so? Because of the implicit premise operative throughout—that my mind matches God's. Only if I think in accord with the logic of the revealed Torah can my thought processes join issue in clarifying what is at hand—the unfolding of God's will in the Torah. To state matters more accessibly: if the Torah does not make statements in accord with a syntax and a grammar of thought that I know and share, I cannot so understand the Torah as to explain its meaning. But if I can join in the discourse of the Torah, it is because I speak the same language of thought—syntax and grammar—at the deepest levels of my intellect. It follows that God's intellect and the intellect of the human being match: *in our image, after our likeness.*

4. Then to state matters affirmatively and finally: Since a shared logic of syntax and grammar joins my mind to the mind of God as revealed in the Torah, I can say what a sentence of the Torah means. So I too can amplify, clarify, expand, revise, rework, that is to say, create a commentary.

It follows that the intrinsic exegetical forms stand for a single proposition:

*While Scripture stands paramount and logic, reason, analytical processes of classification and differentiation secondary, nonetheless, the human mind joins God's mind when humanity receives and sets forth the Torah.*

It follows that the premise of Midrash in the first of the three trends of rabbinic Bible interpretation forms a large judgment on the nature of the human intellect. The sage, the model for humanity, enters into discourse with Scripture and explains its sense and meaning—because the sage, that is, the human being, can do so. The nature of the mind explains why.

Can we then state in a few words and in simple language what the formal rules of the document tell us about the purpose of the authorships of both Sifra and Sifré to Numbers? Beyond all concrete propositions, the document as a whole through its fixed and recurrent formal preferences or literary structures makes two complementary points.

1. *Reason unaided by Scripture produces uncertain propositions.*
2. *Reason operating within the limits of Scripture produces truth.*

These are the propositions yielded by Midrash-exegesis. To whom do these moderate and balanced propositions matter? Sages in particular, I think. The polemic addresses arguments internal to their circles. How do we know, and how may we be certain? If we contrast the polemic of our document about the balance between revelation and reason, Torah and logic, with the polemic of another canonical document about some other topic altogether, the contrast will tell. Then and only then shall we see the choices people faced. In that way we shall appreciate the particular choice the authorship at hand has made. With the perspective provided by an exercise of comparison, we shall see how truly remarkable a document we have in Sifré to Numbers. By itself the book supplies facts. Seen in context, the book makes points. So we require a context of comparison. And this draws us forward to Genesis Rabbah, Leviticus Rabbah, and Pesiqta deRab Kahana, each document serving through a proposition to conduct exegeses of selected verses of Scripture, all of them different in both plan and program from Sifra and Sifré to Numbers.

## V. WAY OF LIFE, BIBLICAL INTERPRETATION, AND THEOLOGICAL ORDER: THE PRIMACY OF SCRIPTURAL AUTHORITY IN THE EXEGESIS OF ISRAEL'S SANCTIFICATION

It is no accident that the verse-by-verse exegesis takes up the detailed interpretation of rules important to the priesthood in the books of Leviticus and Numbers. As we shall now see, the intersection of two verses, one drawn from a base text, another drawn from some other book of the Bible entirely, will characterize the treatment of the book of Genesis in Genesis Rabbah. For the larger message of the priestly compositions (whole or in part) of the biblical books of Leviticus and Numbers, as well as of their exegetes later on, concerned sanctification of the concrete and everyday life of holy Israel, and it is through the keeping of the rules *in detail* that that life attains the holiness described by God to Moses at Sinai. An interest in sanctification draws us to the here and now of little things, the minor matters of everyday life which all together form the arena of holiness, with the result that the detailed laws demand clarification and application, in the program of spelling out in detail the meaning and method of Israel's sanctification.

Another book of Scripture, the book of Genesis, by contrast, concerns history and questions of beginnings and endings, origins and long-term direction, hence the rules governing the social life of Israel now and the salvation of Israel at the end of time. That book with its teleological doctrine of salvation will require attention from exegetes who wish to understand the meaning of Israel's salvation at the coming end of history through exploring the historical rules of Israel's origin and destiny, as these are spelled out in the facts of the book of Genesis. And what will be important in the reading of Genesis, therefore—as the nature of teleology demands—will be not so much the details of this tale or that but rather the larger structures of time and the rules governing events—their direction, their purpose, their goal. And these structures will emerge not from one story but from many. They will be selected from diverse passages shown to make a single point, not from one case but from a multiplicity of cases, all of them testing and proving one proposition. Hence we shall expect the exegetes of Genesis to lead us not into detailed reading of the components of this verse or that (though they will make their contribution of small-scale Midrash-exegesis) but rather the large-scale interposition of cases, each represented by a verse of Scripture that refers to a fact of history, an event on its own. Bringing together diverse cases, that is, verses of Scripture constituting cases, deriving from various books of the Bible, that is, various times and places, the Midrash-exegetes will find it possible to set forth those fixed laws of history and society that, in the aggregate, add up to the textbook of salvation.

Accordingly, we recognize that the exegetes represented in Sifra and Sifré to Numbers have made choices. We see these choices still more clearly when we compare what one authorship has decided to accomplish with the purpose and plan of another authorship. Overall, the authorships of Sifra and Sifré to Numbers focus upon Israel's way of life, conducting a systematic labor of biblical interpretation in the interests of theological order. Specifically, they prove the primacy of scriptural authority in the exegesis of the details that, all together, add up to God's Torah for Israel's sanctification. Interest in detail, choice of forms that highlight explanation of detail, and large-scale proposition—all form one cogent Midrash-method, yielding out of diverse Midrash-exegeses remarkably coherent Midrash-compilations. The fact that what these exegetes have done in their working with Midrash represents a set of choices becomes still clearer when we conduct an exercise of comparison to what exegetes working with Midrash have done when reading another book of Scripture, with a different set of questions in mind. Then we shall see most clearly how a set of choices has confronted exegetes, and how each group of exegetes has made selections from those choices in such a way as to carry out a clear and purposive program.

The comparison requires brief description of another document of the same general venue, that is, a canonical document produced by sages after the formation of the Mishnah, in ca. A.D. 200, that is, a document emerging around ca. 400 C.E., in the time of the Talmud of the Land of Israel and perhaps of Sifra and Sifré to Numbers but some time before the closure of the Talmud of Babylonia, in ca. A.D. 600. For that purpose, I choose Genesis Rabbah, of which we shall see a fair amount in the next chapter. If we guess that Sifra and Sifré to Numbers reached closure sometime before 400, and we guess that Genesis Rabbah reached redaction at about that same time, we then are comparing two pieces of writing of pretty much the same period (give or take a hundred years).

The authorship of Genesis Rabbah focuses its discourse on the proposition that the book of Genesis speaks to the life and historical condition of Israel, the Jewish people. The entire narrative of Genesis is so formed as to point toward the sacred history of Israel, the Jewish people: its slavery and redemption, its coming Temple in Jerusalem, its exile and salvation at the end of time. The powerful message of Genesis in the pages of Genesis Rabbah proclaims that the world's creation commenced a single, straight line of events, leading in the end to the salvation of Israel and through Israel of all humanity. Therefore a given story will bear a deeper message about what it means to be Israel, on the one side, and what in the end of days will happen to Israel, on the other.

The single most important proposition of Genesis Rabbah is that in the story of the beginnings of creation, humanity, and Israel, we find the message of the meaning and end of the life of the Jewish people. The deeds of the founders supply signals for the children about what is going to come in the future. So the biography of Abraham, Isaac, and Jacob also constitutes the history of Israel later on. If the sages had announced a single syllogism and argued it systematically, that is the proposition on which they would have insisted. The sages understood that stories about the progenitors, presented in the book of Genesis, define the human condition and proper conduct for their children, Israel in time to come. Accordingly, they systematically asked Scripture to tell them how they were supposed to conduct themselves at the critical turnings of life.

We now ask ourselves a simple question: is the message of Sifré to Numbers the same as that of Genesis Rabbah? The answer is obvious. No, these are different books. They make different points in answering different questions. In plan and in program they yield more contrasts than comparisons. Why does that fact matter in my argument? The reason is that since these *are* different books, which *do* use different forms to deliver different messages, it must follow that there is nothing routine or given or to be predicted about the point that the authorship of Sifra or Sifré to Numbers wishes to make. Why not? Because it is not a point that is simply "there to be made." It is a striking and original point. We know it because when the sages who produced Genesis Rabbah read Genesis, they made a different point from the one at hand in the Midrash-compilations of Midrash-exegeses. So contrasting the one composition with the other shows us that each composition bears its own distinctive traits—traits of mind, traits of plan, traits of program. The medium matches the message and has been chosen for that reason.

The conclusion is simple. Once we characterize the persistent polemic of Sifra and of Sifré to Numbers and then compare that polemic to the characteristic point of argument of Genesis Rabbah (and, as it happens, Leviticus Rabbah as well), we see that Sifré to Numbers has chosen forms to advance its own distinctive, substantive argument. Its exegetical program points—explicitly in extrinsic exegesis, implicitly in intrinsic exegesis—to a single point, and that point is made on every page.

In plan and in program Sifra and Sifré to Numbers form a community. We shall now observe that Genesis Rabbah bears formal and substantive affinity to Leviticus Rabbah; the plan and program of both documents present an essential congruity and, moreover, fit well with Pesiqta deRab Kahana. The forms and polemic of Sifra and Sifré to Numbers cohere, with the forms designed so as to implicitly state and thus reinforce the substantive argument of both books. Further study suggests the same for the forms of Genesis Rabbah and Leviticus Rabbah and Pesiqta deRab Kahana. We may classify Sifra (serving Leviticus) and Sifré to Numbers as inner-directed, facing within, toward issues of the interior life of the community vis-à-vis revelation and the sanctification of the life of the nation, and, intellectually, as centered on issues urgent to sages themselves. For, as I said, to whom are the debates about the relationship between Torah and logic, reason and revelation, going to make a difference, if not to the intellectuals of the textual community at hand? Within the same classification scheme, Genesis Rabbah and Leviticus Rabbah appear outer-directed, addressing issues of history and salvation, taking up critical concerns of the public life of the nation vis-à-vis history and the world beyond. Sifra and Sifré to Numbers address sanctification, while Genesis Rabbah and Leviticus Rabbah and Pesiqta deRab Kahana address salvation.

The five documents respectively—the two we now have examined, the three that lie before—do not merely assemble discrete sayings, forming a hodgepodge of things people happen to have said about verses of Scripture chosen for reasons we do not know in a polemic we cannot specify. In the case of each document we can answer the question, Why this, not that? The documents are not compilations but compositions. Seen as a group, and compared with one another, they are not essentially the same, lacking all viewpoint, serving a single undifferentiated task of collecting and arranging whatever was at hand. Quite to the contrary, these documents of Midrash-compilations of the oral Torah's exegesis of the written Torah emerge as rich in differences from one another and sharply defined, each through its distinctive viewpoints and particular polemics, on the one side, and formal and aesthetic qualities, on the other.

# 3. MIDRASH AS EXEGESIS: (2) INTERPRETATION AS PROPOSITION YIELDING EXEGESIS

# 3. Genesis Rabbah

Genesis Rabbah presents the first complete and systematic Judaic commentary to the book of Genesis. Generally thought to have been closed ("redacted") at ca. 400 C.E., Genesis Rabbah provides a complete and authoritative account of how Judaism proposes to read and make sense of the first book of the Hebrew Scriptures as an account of the beginnings—and therefore, also of the endings—of the life of humanity in general and Israel in particular. The book of Genesis is changed from a genealogy and family history of Abraham, Isaac, Jacob, then Joseph, transformed into a book of the laws of history and rules of the salvation of Israel; the deeds of the founders become omens and signs for the final generations.

## I. THE DOCUMENT

Genesis Rabbah is a composite document. Some of the material in the compilation can be shown to have been put together before that material was used for the purposes of the late fourth-century compilers. Many times a comment entirely apposite to a verse of Genesis has been joined to a set of comments in no way pertinent to the verse of Genesis at hand. Proof for a given syllogism, furthermore, derives from a verse of Genesis as well as from verses of other books of the Bible. Such a syllogistic argument, therefore, has not been written for exegetical purposes particular to the verse at hand. The particular verse subject to attention serves that other, propositional plan. It is not the focus of discourse; it has not generated the comment but merely provided a proof for a syllogism. That is what I mean when I speak of a proposition's yielding an exegesis. The fundamental proposition displayed throughout Genesis Rabbah, which yields the specific exegeses of many of the verses of the book of Genesis and even whole stories, is that the beginnings point toward the endings, and the meaning of Israel's past points toward the message that lies in Israel's future. The things that happened to the fathers and mothers of the family, Israel, provide a sign for the things that will happen to the children later.

The mode of thought, we should expect, is the one of natural philosophy. It involves the classification of data, the testing of propositions against the facts of data, yielding the discovery of underlying rules out of a multiplicity of details; sages proposed and tested, against the facts provided by Scripture, the theses of Israel's salvation that demanded attention just then. But natural philosophy does not fully describe the sages' method. The issues were not so much philosophical as religious, in the sense that while philosophy addressed questions of nature and rules of enduring existence, religion asked about issues of history and God's intervention in time. Using distinction between nature, supernature, and sanctification on the one side, typified by the Mishnah and the Tosefta and the legal enterprise in general, and society, history, and salvation on the other, typified by Genesis Rabbah, Leviticus Rabbah, Pesiqta deRab Kahana, and the theological inquiry into teleology, we may distinguish our documents. Specifically, the document before us is a work of profound theological inquiry into God's rules for history and society in the here and now and for salvation at the end of historical time. That fundamental idea of searching in the account of the beginnings for the ending and meaning of Israel's society and history—hence the rules that govern and permit knowledge of what is to come—constitutes the generative proposition that yielded the specific exegesis of the book of Genesis in Genesis Rabbah.

Genesis Rabbah came to closure, all scholars generally concur, sometime after the end of the fourth century. The document in its final form therefore emerges from that momentous century in which the Roman Empire passed from pagan to

Christian rule, and in which, in the aftermath of Julian's abortive reversion to paganism, Christianity adopted the politics of repressing paganism that rapidly engulfed Judaism as well. The issue confronting Israel in the Land of Israel therefore proved immediate—the meaning of the new and ominous turn of history, the implications of Christ's worldly triumph for the otherworldly and supernatural people, Israel, whom God chooses and loves. The message of the exegete-compositors addressed a circumstance of historical crisis and generated remarkable renewal, a rebirth of intellect in the encounter with Scripture, intellect now in quest of the rules, not of sanctification—these had already been found—but of salvation. So the book of Genesis, which portrays how all things had begun, would testify to the message and the method of the end, the coming salvation of patient, hopeful, enduring Israel.

I therefore argue that, between categories of philosophy, including science and society, and religion, including history and teleology, Genesis Rabbah presents a deeply *religious* view of Israel's historical and salvific life, in much the same way that the Mishnah provides a profoundly *philosophical* view of Israel's everyday and sanctified existence. Just as the main themes of the Mishnah evoke the consideration of issues of being and becoming, the potential and the actual, mixtures and blends and other problems of physics, all in the interest of philosophical analysis, so Genesis Rabbah presents its cogent and coherent agendum as well. That program of inquiry concerns the way in which, in the book of Genesis, God set forth to Moses the entire scope and meaning of Israel's history among the nations and salvation at the end of days. The mode of thought by which the framers of Genesis Rabbah work out their propositions dictates the character of their exegesis, as to rhetoric, logical principle of cogent and intelligible discourse, and even as to topic. Once more we investigate the unities of message and medium.

The exegesis itself takes two forms, as, by now, we should expect. First, we find the exegesis of clauses of verses, read in sequence, just as we noted in Sifra and Sifré to Numbers. Second, sages use a not quite fresh, but vigorous and now fully exploited, exegetical technique. A sustained composition begins with a verse other than the one under analysis. That other verse intersects with the verse under discussion and is thus called the intersecting verse, while the verse under discussion is called the base verse. The power of this form—the juxtaposition of two verses, one derived from the document at hand, the other from some other document altogether—which will dominate from Genesis Rabbah (ca. 400–450) onward, is simple. On the surface, the intersecting verse expands the frame of reference of the base verse, introducing data otherwise not present. But just beneath the surface lies the implicit premise: *both the intersecting verse and the base verse make the same point; in their meeting, each rises out of its narrow framework as a detail or an instance of a rule and testifies to the larger picture, the encompassing rule itself.* The intersecting verse–base verse construction therefore yields a proposition that transcends both verses and finds proof in the cases of each. This powerful way of composing something new forms the centerpiece of Genesis Rabbah and the two documents that follow.

The reason that this rhetorical program works so well derives from the topical program of Genesis Rabbah—to demonstrate that reliable rules govern Israel's history, and to discover and validate those fixed rules within the details of stories of the origins of the family of Abraham, Isaac, and Jacob, which Israel now constitutes. Searching for the governing laws of history and society requires not specific cases but general rules, and an inductive process demands that sages generate rules out of cases. The meeting of rhetoric, logic, and topic takes place here. Putting together the cases represented by two verses, one deep within the narrative of Genesis, the other far distant from that narrative, the exegetes found it possible both to make an argument and to point toward an implicit generalization yielded by the two or more cases at hand. The rhetoric involves the recurrent arrangement of verses—the logic, the inquiry into the general rule that holds together two cases and makes of them a single statement of an overriding law—and the topic—the direction of the history of Israel, specifically, its ultimate salvation at the end of time.

In our sample we see how a very particular story turns into a very general statement about Israel's fate among the nations, and how each detail of the story is made to contribute to the validation of a law of Israel's history. Genesis Rabbah rhetorically marks a transition from primarily phrase-by-phrase exegeses of verses, characteristic of the two documents that mark the first trend in rabbinic Bible interpretation, to mainly propositional arguments, generating exegeses of verses only as a secondary interest, which marks the second trend. The passage before us is not as cogent as later documents, such as Leviticus Rabbah and Pesiqta deRab Kahana, which hew to a single topic and make a single point about that topic. But it is far more than the phrase-by-phrase commentary on diverse subjects, found in Sifra and Sifré to Numbers.

## II. A SAMPLE

### GENESIS RABBAH *PARASHAH* LXX TO GENESIS 28:20–29:30

#### LXX:I.

1.  A. *Then Jacob made a vow, saying, "If God will be with me and will keep me in this way that I go and will give me bread to eat and clothing to wear, so that I come again to my father's house in peace, then the Lord shall be my God. And this stone, which I have set up for a pillar, shall be God's house; and of all that you give me, I will give the tenth to you"* (Gen. 28:20–22):

    B. *I will perform for you my vows, which my lips have uttered and my mouth has spoken when I was in distress* (Ps. 66:13–14).

    C. Said R. Isaac the Babylonian, "One who takes a vow carries out a religious duty [if he does so in time of stress]."

    D. What is the meaning of the statement "Then Jacob made a vow, *saying*"? "Saying" to the future generations, so that they too will take vows in a time of stress.

What attracts the exegete's attention in Genesis 28:20 is the simple fact that Jacob has taken a vow, and the intersecting verse, Psalm 66:13–14, then underlines that fact. Isaac evaluates vow-taking, subjected to criticism, by saying that it can represent a meritorious action. D repeats the basic syllogism of Genesis Rabbah: what the founders do, the children carry on, and what happens to the founders tells what will happen to the children, and, finally, the merit accumulated by the founders serves the children later on as their inheritance and source of protection. The amplification of the opening encounter of base verse and intersecting verse follows. This order—base verse, then intersecting verse—is reversed in later compilations, which begin in the distant reaches of Scripture and only slowly and unpredictably recover the point articulated in what becomes the base verse.

**2.**  A. Jacob was the first to take a vow, therefore whoever takes a vow should make it depend only upon him.

B. Said R. Abbahu, "It is written, *How he swore to the Lord and vowed to the mighty one of Jacob* (Ps. 132:2).

C. "What is written is not 'how he swore to the Lord and vowed to the mighty one of Abraham' or 'of Isaac,' but 'of *Jacob*.'

D. "He made the vow depend upon the first person ever to take a vow."

The theme of the passage, taking vows, produces two important points. The first point, found in No. 1, is that while vowing in general does not meet sages' approval, in times of stress it does, and Jacob is the example of that fact. In No. 2, Jacob is the one who started the practice of vowing, so Jacob is the one to whom vows are made to refer, as in the cited passage. These two intersecting verses do not receive detailed exegesis on their own; they contribute themes and propositions. So the passage is not like those in which a long sequence of comments either brings the intersecting verse back to the base verse or reads the intersecting verse as an expression of the views of the principal of the base verse. Later, Jacob's failure to keep his vow in a prompt way elicits comment.

**LXX:II.**

1. A. R. Yudan in the name of R. Idi: "It is written, *Then the people rejoiced, for they offered willingly. Wherefore David blessed the Lord before all the congregation, and David said, 'Blessed be you, O Lord, the God of Israel our father'* (1 Chr. 29:9–10).

   B. "It was because they were engaged in carrying out religious duties that were acts of free will and that matters were successful that they rejoiced.

   C. "What is the meaning of the statement, *Wherefore David blessed the Lord before all the congregation, and David said, 'Blessed be you, O Lord, the God of Israel our father'*? Specifically, we note that what is written is not 'the God of Abraham, Isaac, and Israel,' but only 'God *of* Israel'?

   D. He made the vow depend upon the first person ever to take a vow."

   E. Said R. Yudan, "From the document at hand [the Torah, not merely the Writings] we do not lack further proof of that same fact. For example, *And Israel vowed* (Num. 21:2), meaning, our father, Israel.

   F. *"Then Jacob made a vow."*

The same point now recurs, with a different set of proof-texts. The rhetorically noteworthy point is at F: we revert to the base verse, and this will form a bridge to the systematic exposition of that base verse, which now begins.

**LXX:III.**

1. A. *Then Jacob made a vow:*

   B. Four made a vow, two vowed and lost out, and two vowed and benefited.

   C. Israel took a vow and Hannah took a vow, and they benefited.

   D. Jephthah took a vow and lost out, Jacob took a vow and lost out.*

The fragmentary comment serves the purpose of removing the impression that the text of Scripture goes over the same ground twice and contradicts itself. This same problem will be solved in a different way in what follows. Since, as we know, the pentateuchal books, including Genesis, are composed of a

---

*M. Freedman, *Genesis Rabbah* (London: Soncino, 1948), p. 637 n. 2: His vow was superfluous, since he had already received God's promise and therefore he lost thereby.

number of prior strands, some of which go over the same ground two or more times, the text itself, read by sages as single, linear, and unitary, presents its own problems for sages' attention.

## LXX:IV.

1. A. R. Aibu and R. Jonathan:
   B. One of them said, "The passage states matters out of the proper order."
   C. The other said, "The passage is entirely in the proper order."
   D. The one who has said, "The passage states matters out of the proper order" points to the following: *And lo, I am with you* (Gen. 28:15) contrasts to the statement "Then Jacob made a vow, saying, '*If God will be with me.*' "
   E. The other who has said, "The passage is entirely in the proper order" has then to explain the statement "If God will be with me" in light of the statement already at hand.
   F. His point is this: "If he will be with me" means "if all of the conditions that he has stipulated with me will be carried out" [then I will keep my vow].

2. A. R. Abbahu and rabbis:
   B. R. Abbahu said, " 'If God will be with me and will keep me in *this way*' refers to protection from gossip, in line with this usage: *And they turn their tongue in the way of slander,* * *their bow of falsehood* ( Jer. 9:2).
   C. "*Will give me bread to eat* refers to protection from fornication, in line with this usage: *Neither has he kept back any thing from me, except the bread which he ate* (Gen. 39:9), a euphemism for sexual relations with his wife.
   D. "*So that I come again to my father's house in peace* refers to bloodshed.
   E. "*Then the Lord shall be my God* so that I shall be protected from idolatry."
   F. Rabbis interpreted the statement *this way* to speak of all of these.
   G. [The rabbis' statement now follows:] "Specifically: *If God will be with me and will keep me in this way that I go* [by referring only to *way*] contains an allusion to idolatry, fornication, murder, and slander.
   H. "*Way* refers to idolatry: *They who swear by the sin of Samaria and say,*

---

*Freedman, p. 637 n. 4.

'*As your god, O Dan, lives, and as the way of Beer sheba lives*' (Amos 8:14).

I. "*Way* refers to adultery: *So is the way of an adulterous woman* (Prov. 30:20).

J. "*Way* refers to murder: *My son, do not walk in the way of them, restrain your foot from their path, for their feet run to evil and they make haste to shed blood* (Prov. 1:15–16).

K. "*Way* refers to slander: *And he heard the words of Laban's sons, saying, 'Jacob has taken away'* (Gen. 31:1)."

No. 1 goes over the problem of the preceding and makes it explicit. No. 2 then subjects the verse to a close exegesis, with the standard repertoire of mortal sins—murder, fornication, slander—now read into the verse. Jacob asks God's protection to keep himself from sinning. That interpretation rehabilitates Jacob, since the picture in Scripture portrays a rather self-centered person, and now Jacob exhibits virtue.

## LXX:V.

1. A. *Will give me bread to eat and clothing to wear:*

   B. Aqilas the proselyte came to R. Eliezer and said to him, "Is all the gain that is coming to the proselyte going to be contained in this verse: *And loves the proselyte, giving him food and clothing* (Deut. 10:18)?"

   C. He said to him, "And is something for which the old man [ Jacob] beseeched going to be such a small thing in your view, namely, *Will give me bread to eat and clothing to wear?* [God] comes and hands it over to [a proselyte] on a reed [and the proselyte does not have to beg for it]."

   D. He came to R. Joshua, who commenced by saying words to appease him: "*Bread* refers to Torah, as it is said *Come, eat of my bread* (Prov. 9:5). *Clothing* refers to the cloak of a disciple of sages.

   E. "When a person has the merit of studying the Torah, he has the merit of carrying out a religious duty. [So the proselyte receives a great deal when he gets bread and clothing, namely, entry into the estate of disciples].

   F. "And not only so, but his daughters may be chosen for marriage into the priesthood, so that their sons' sons will offer burnt offerings on the altar. [So the proselyte may also look forward to entry into the priests' caste. That statement will now be spelled out.]

> G. "*Bread* refers to the show-bread.
>
> H. "*Clothing* refers to the garments of the priesthood.
>
> I. "So lo, we deal with the sanctuary.
>
> J. "How do we know that the same sort of blessing applies in the provinces? *Bread* speaks of the dough-offering [that is separated in the provinces], while *clothing* refers to the first fleece [handed over to the priest]."

The interpretation of *bread* and *clothing* yields its own message, intersecting only at one point with the passage at hand. So at issue in this composition is not the exegesis of the base verse but the meaning of *bread* and *clothing* as applied to the proselyte. We now see how the components of the base verse are reread in terms of the base values of sages themselves: Torah and cult. Sages regard study of Torah as equivalent to a sacrifice, and the sage as equivalent to the priest. This typological reading of Israel's existence then will guide sages' interpretation of such specific passages as the one before us.

## LXX:VI.

1.   A.   *So that I come again to my father's house in peace, then the Lord shall be my God* (Gen. 28:20–22):

    B.   R. Joshua of Sikhnin in the name of R. Levi: "The Holy One, blessed be he, took the language used by the patriarchs and turned it into a key to the redemption of their descendants.

Now comes the main event in our passage: the reading, in the light of Israel's future history, that is, the story of Israel's salvation, of the deeds of the matriarchs and patriarchs and of God's love for them.

    C.   "Said the Holy One, blessed be he, to Jacob, 'You have said, *"Then the Lord shall be my God."* By your life, all of the acts of goodness, blessing, and consolation which I am going to carry out for your descendants I shall bestow only by using the same language:

    D.   "*Then in that day, living waters shall go out from Jerusalem* (Zech. 14:8). *Then in that day a man shall rear a young cow and two sheep* (Is. 7:21). *Then, in that day, the Lord will set his hand again the second time to recover the remnant of his people* (Is. 11:11). *Then, in that day, the mountains shall drop down sweet wine* (Joel 4:18). *Then, in that day, a great horn shall be blown and they shall come who were lost in the land of Assyria* (Is. 27:13).' "

The union of Jacob's biography and Israel's history yields the passage at hand. The explicit details, rather conventional in character, are less interesting than the basic syllogism, which is implicit and ubiquitous.

## LXX:VII.

1.  A. *And this stone, which I have set up for a pillar, shall be God's house; and of all that you give me, I will give the tenth to you* (Gen. 28:22):

The exegete's attention is arrested by the etiology of the Temple. God's house, to sages, of course is the Temple of Jerusalem. Then at issue is tithing the herd and the crop in support of the priestly caste and the Temple cult. The attached story is included because of its thematic relevance, not because it makes a point in the ongoing exposition of salvation history which the book of Genesis relates in the imagination of sages.

  B. A gentile asked R. Meir, "How is the firstling of an ass redeemed?"

  C. He said to him, "With a lamb, as it is written, *And the firstling of an ass you shall redeem with a lamb* (Ex. 34:20)."

  D. He said to him, "If one has no lamb?"

  E. He said to him, "With a goat."

  F. He said to him, "How do you know it?"

  G. He said to him, "It is written, *Your lamb shall be without blemish. You shall take it from the sheep or from the goats* (Ex. 12:5)."

  H. He said to him, "That passage speaks of the lamb used for the passover offering."

  I. He said to him, "But a goat also falls into the category of a lamb."

  J. He said to him, "How do you know it?"

  K. He said to him, "It is written, *These are the beasts which you may eat, the ox, the lamb of sheep, and the lamb of goats* (Deut. 14:4)."

  L. He got up and kissed him on his head.

2.  A. R. Joshua of Sikhnin in the name of R. Levi: "A Samaritan asked R. Meir, saying to him, 'Do you not maintain that Jacob told the truth?'

  B. "He said to him, 'Indeed so.'

C. "He said to him, 'And did he not say this: *And of all that you give me I will give the tenth to you*?'

D. "He said to him, 'Yes. And he separated the tribe of Levi as one of the ten.'

E. "He said to him, 'Then why did he not separate a tenth of the other two tribes?'

F. "He said to him, 'And were they twelve tribes? Were they not fourteen, as it is said, *Ephraim and Manasseh even as Reuben and Simeon shall be mine* (Gen. 48:5)?'

G. "He said to him, 'All the more so. You add more water, so you add more flour.'

H. "He said to him, 'But were there not four matriarchs?'

I. "He said to him, 'Yes.'

J. "He said to him, 'Deduct the four firstborn of each of the patriarchs from the fourteen, for the firstborn is holy, and what is already consecrated cannot serve to exempt what is consecrated [and that leaves ten, hence Levi was enough].'

K. "He said to him, 'Happy is your nation on account of what is within it.' "

The inclusion of this composition depends upon the use of the base verse as a prooftext. Otherwise there is no point of contact.

## LXX:VIII.

1. A. *Then Jacob lifted up his feet* (Gen. 29:1):
   B. Said R. Aha, "*A tranquil heart is the life of the flesh* (Prov. 14:30).
   C. "Since he had been given this good news, his heart carried his feet.
   D. "So people say: 'The stomach carries the feet.' "

What captures attention is the happiness that is expressed in the description of Jacob's onward journey. The good news carried him forward. But I do not see at this point what this good news (*gospel*) represents. However, what follows more than fills the gap. It is the gospel of Israel: its salvation, worked out in the principal components of its holy way of life of sanctification. So the base and intersecting verses prepare the way for a powerful and sustained statement. In the following protracted, six-part interpretation of the simple verse about seeing a well in the field, we see the full power of Midrash as proposition yielding exegesis. Elements of both sanctification and salvation are joined in a remarkable message.

2. A. *As he looked, he saw a well in the field:*
   B. R. Hama bar Hanina interpreted the verse in six ways [that is, he divides the verse into six clauses and systematically reads each of the clauses in light of the others and in line with an overriding theme]:
   C. "*As he looked, he saw a well in the field:* this refers to the well [of water in the wilderness, Num. 21:17].
   D. "*And lo, three flocks of sheep lying beside it:* specifically, Moses, Aaron, and Miriam.
   E. "*For out of that well the flocks were watered:* from there each one drew water for his standard, tribe, and family."
   F. *And the stone upon the well's mouth was great:*
   G. Said R. Hanina, "It was only the size of a little sieve."
   H. [Reverting to Hama's statement:] "*And put the stone back in its place upon the mouth of the well:* for the coming journeys."

Thus the first interpretation applies the passage at hand to the life of Israel in the wilderness. The premise is the prevailing syllogism: Israel's future history is lived out, the first time around, in the lives of the patriarchs and matriachs.

3. A. "*As he looked, he saw a well in the field:* refers to Zion.
   B. "*And lo, three flocks of sheep lying beside it:* refers to the three festivals.
   C. "*For out of that well the flocks were watered:* from there they drank of the Holy Spirit.
   D. "*The stone on the well's mouth was large:* this refers to the rejoicing of the house of the water drawing."
   E. Said R. Hoshaiah, "Why is it called 'the house of the water drawing'? Because from there they drink of the Holy Spirit."
   F. [Resuming Hama b. Hanina's discourse:] "*And when all the flocks were gathered there:* coming from *the entrance of Hamath to the brook of Egypt* (1 Kgs. 8:66).
   G. "*The shepherds would roll the stone from the mouth of the well and water the sheep:* for from there they would drink of the Holy Spirit.
   H. "*And put the stone back in its place upon the mouth of the well:* leaving it in place until the coming festival."

Thus the second interpretation reads the verse in light of the Temple celebration of the Festival of Tabernacles.

4. A. "*As he looked, he saw a well in the field:* this refers to Zion.

   B. "*And lo, three flocks of sheep lying beside it:* this refers to the three courts, concerning which we have learned in the Mishnah: **There were three courts there, one at the gateway of the Temple mount, one at the gateway of the courtyard, and one in the chamber of the hewn stones [M. San. 11:2].**

   C. "*For out of that well the flocks were watered:* for from there they would hear the ruling.

   D. "*The stone on the well's mouth was large:* this refers to the high court that was in the chamber of the hewn stones.

   E. "*And when all the flocks were gathered there:* this refers to the courts in session in the Land of Israel.

   F. "*The shepherds would roll the stone from the mouth of the well and water the sheep:* for from there they would hear the ruling.

   G. "*And put the stone back in its place upon the mouth of the well:* for they would give and take until they had produced the ruling in all the required clarity."

The third interpretation reads the verse in light of the Israelite institution of justice and administration. The intrusion of the cited passage of the Mishnah alerts us to the striking difference between this document and Sifra and Sifré to Numbers. The Mishnah-passage serves as mere illustration. It does not generate the question to be answered, nor does it come under detailed amplification itself. It is in no way a focus of interest.

5. A. "*As he looked, he saw a well in the field:* this refers to Zion.

   B. "*And lo, three flocks of sheep lying beside it:* this refers to the first three kingdoms [Babylonia, Media, Greece].

   C. "*For out of that well the flocks were watered:* for they enriched the treasures that were laid up in the chambers of the Temple.

   D. "*The stone on the well's mouth was large:* this refers to the merit attained by the patriarchs.

   E. "*And when all the flocks were gathered there:* this refers to the wicked kingdom, which collects troops through levies over all the nations of the world.

F. "*The shepherds would roll the stone from the mouth of the well and water the sheep:* for they enriched the treasures that were laid up in the chambers of the Temple.

G. "*And put the stone back in its place upon the mouth of the well:* in the age to come the merit attained by the patriarchs will stand [in defense of Israel]."

So the fourth interpretation interweaves the themes of the Temple cult and the domination of the four monarchies.

6.  A. "*As he looked, he saw a well in the field:* this refers to the Sanhedrin.

B. "*And lo, three flocks of sheep lying beside it:* this alludes to the three rows of disciples of sages that would go into session in their presence.

C. "*For out of that well the flocks were watered:* for from there they would listen to the ruling of the law.

D. "*The stone on the well's mouth was large:* this refers to the most distinguished member of the court, who determines the law decision.

E. "*And when all the flocks were gathered there:* this refers to disciples of the sages in the Land of Israel.

F. "*The shepherds would roll the stone from the mouth of the well and water the sheep:* for from there they would listen to the ruling of the law.

G. "*And put the stone back in its place upon the mouth of the well:* for they would give and take until they had produced the ruling in all the required clarity."

The fifth interpretation again reads the verse in light of the Israelite institution of legal education and justice.

7.  A. "*As he looked, he saw a well in the field:* this refers to the synagogue.

B. "*And lo, three flocks of sheep lying beside it:* this refers to the three who are called to the reading of the Torah on weekdays.

C. "*For out of that well the flocks were watered:* for from there they hear the reading of the Torah.

D. "*The stone on the well's mouth was large:* this refers to the impulse to do evil.

E. "*And when all the flocks were gathered there:* this refers to the congregation.

F. "*The shepherds would roll the stone from the mouth of the well and water the sheep:* for from there they hear the reading of the Torah.

G. "*And put the stone back in its place upon the mouth of the well:* for once they go forth [from the hearing of the reading of the Torah] the impulse to do evil reverts to its place."

The sixth and last interpretation turns to the twin themes of the reading of the Torah in the synagogue and the evil impulse, temporarily driven off through the hearing of the Torah. The six themes read in response to the verse cover (1) Israel in the wilderness, (2) the Temple cult on festivals with special reference to Tabernacles, (3) the judiciary and government, (4) the history of Israel under the four kingdoms, (5) the life of sages, and (6) the ordinary folk and the synagogue. The whole is an astonishing repertoire of fundamental themes of the life of the nation, Israel: at its origins in the wilderness, in its cult, in its institutions based on the cult, in the history of the nations, and, finally, in the twin social estates of sages and ordinary folk, matched by the institutions of the master-disciple circle and the synagogue. The vision of Jacob at the well thus encompassed the whole of the social reality of Jacob's people, Israel. The labor of interpreting this same passage in the profound, typological context already established now goes forward.

## LXX:IX.

1. A. R. Yohanan interpreted the statement in terms of Sinai:
   B. "*As he looked, he saw a well in the field:* this refers to Sinai.
   C. "*And lo, three flocks of sheep lying beside it:* these stand for the priests, Levites, and Israelites.
   D. "*For out of that well the flocks were watered:* for from there they heard the Ten Commandments.
   E. "*The stone on the well's mouth was large:* this refers to the Presence of God."
   F. *And when all the flocks were gathered there:*
   G. R. Simeon b. Judah of Kefar Akum in the name of R. Simeon: "All of the flocks of Israel had to be present, for if any one of them had been lacking, they would not have been worthy of receiving the Torah."
   H. [Returning to Yohanan's exposition:] "*The shepherds would roll the*

*stone from the mouth of the well and water the sheep:* for from there they
heard the Ten Commandments.

I. *"And put the stone back in its place upon the mouth of the well: You your-*
*selves have seen that I have talked with you from heaven (Ex. 20:19)."*

Yohanan's exposition adds what was left out, namely, reference to the revelation of the Torah at Sinai. We now go over
the same proposition again, with utterly fresh materials. That
shows that the proposed syllogism states the deep structure of
reality, that its syntax permits words to make diverse yet intelligible statements. Once we have taken up the challenge of the
foregoing, a still greater task requires us to make the same basic
point in utterly different cases, and that allows us definitively
to demonstrate that syllogism as it is tested against diverse cases
presented by Scripture's facts.

## LXX:X.

1. A. Jacob said to them, *"My brothers, where do you come from?"* They said,
   *"We are from Haran"* (Gen. 29:40):

   B. R. Yosé bar Haninah interpreted the verse at hand with reference to
   the Exile.

   C. "Jacob said to them, 'My brothers, where do you come from?' They said,
   'We are from Haran': that is, 'We are flying from the wrath of the
   Holy One, blessed be he.' [Here there is a play on the words for
   *Haran* and *wrath,* which share the same consonants.]

   D. "He said to them, *"Do you know Laban the son of Nahor?'* The sense is
   this, 'Do you know him who is destined to bleach your sins as
   white as snow?' [Here there is a play on the words for *Laban* and
   *bleach,* which share the same consonants.]

   E. "They said, 'We know him.' He said to them, 'Is it well with him?' They
   said, 'It is well.' On account of what sort of merit?

   F. [Yosé continues his interpretation:] "[The brothers go on,] *and see,*
   *Rachel his daughter is coming with the sheep (Gen. 29:6–7).*

   G. "That is in line with this verse: *Thus says the Lord, 'A voice is heard in*
   *Ramah, lamentation and bitter weeping, Rachel weeping for her children.*
   *She refuses to be comforted.' Thus says the Lord, 'Refrain your voice from*
   *weeping . . . and there is hope for your future,' says the Lord, and your*
   *children shall return to their own border (Jer. 31:15–16)."*

Now the history of the redemption of Israel is located in the colloquy between Jacob and Laban's sons. The themes pour forth in profusion.

**LXX:XI.**

1. A. [*He said to them, "Is it well with him?" They said, "It is well; and see, Rachel his daughter is coming with the sheep" (Lev. 29:6–7)]: He said to them, "Is it well with him? Is there peace between him and you?"*

   B. *They said, "It is well." And if it is gossip that you want, See, Rachel his daughter is coming with the sheep.*

   C. That is in line with this saying: *Women like gossip.*

2. A. *He said, "Behold, it is still [high day, it is not time for the animals to be gathered together; water the sheep and go, pasture them." But they said, "We cannot until all the flocks are gathered together, and the stone is rolled from the mouth of the well; then we water the sheep]" (Gen. 29:7–8):*

   B. He said to them, "If you are hired hands, *it is still high day.* [You have no right to water the flock so early in the day.]

   C. "If you are shepherding your own flock: it is not time for the animals to be gathered together. [It is not in your interest to do so.]"

3. A. *They said, "We cannot . . ." While he was still speaking with them, Rachel came (Gen. 29:9):*

   B. Said Rabban Simeon b. Gamaliel, "Come and note the difference between one neighborhood and the next.

   C. "Elsewhere [in Midian, when the daughters of Jethro came to water their flocks,] there were seven women, and the shepherds wanted to give them a hard time, as it is said, *And the shepherds came and drove them away* (Ex. 2:17).

   D. "Here, by contrast, there was only one woman, and yet not one of them laid a hand on her, because *The angel of the Lord encamps around about those who fear him and delivers them* (Ps. 34:8).

   E. "This refers to those who live in a neighborhood of those who fear him."

Nos. 1 and 2 articulate the conversation between Jacob and the shepherds. No. 3 draws a more general conclusion, using the base verse to demonstrate the contrast necessary for the syllogism. It is safer to live in a Jewish neighborhood.

**LXX:XII.**

1. A. *Now when Jacob saw Rachel, the daughter of Laban his mother's brother,*

*and the sheep of Laban, his mother's brother, Jacob went up and rolled the stone [from the well's mouth and watered the flock of Laban his mother's brother. Then Jacob kissed Rachel and wept aloud. And Jacob told Rachel that he was Rebecca's son, and she ran and told her father]* (Gen. 29:10–12):

B. Said R. Yohanan, "He did it without effort, like someone who takes a stopper out of a flask."

2.  A. *Then Jacob kissed Rachel:*

What follows is yet another mode of inquiry, namely, the laying out of a proposition by means of a list. The list collects the relevant data, and the proposition sorts out among the data the classifications that render the facts intelligible. In this pursuit of natural philosophy or science accomplished through making lists and classifying data on lists, sages turn to Scripture rather than to nature, but the mode of inquiry is the same. In this composition the base verse plays no important role. It is tacked on, simply a fact, which joins the prepared list to the larger context of the document at hand.

B. Every form of kissing is obscene except for three purposes, the kiss upon accepting high office, the kiss upon seeing someone at an interval after an absence, and the kiss of departure.

C. The kiss upon accepting high office: *Then Samuel took the vial of oil and poured it upon his head and kissed him* (1 Sam. 10:1).

D. The kiss upon seeing someone at an interval [after an absence]: *And he went and met him in the mountain of God and kissed him* (Ex. 4:27).

E. The kiss of departure: *And Orpah kissed her mother-in-law* (Ruth 1:4).

F. Said R. Tanhuma, "Also the kiss exchanged among kin: *Then Jacob kissed Rachel.*"

3.  A. *And he wept aloud:*

B. Why did Jacob weep?

C. [ Jacob thus] said, "Concerning Eliezer when he went to bring Rebecca, it is written in his regard: *And the servant took ten camels* (Gen. 24:10). But I do not have even a ring or a bracelet." [That is why he wept.]

4.  A. Another matter:

B. Why did Jacob weep?

C. Because he foresaw that she would not be buried with him.

D. That is in line with this statement that Rachel made to Leah: "*Therefore he shall lie with you tonight* (Gen. 30:15).

E. "With you he will sleep, and not with me."

5. A. Another matter:

B. Why did Jacob weep?

C. Because he saw that men were whispering with one another, saying, "Has this one now come to create an innovation in sexual licentiousness among us? [That is something we cannot permit.]"

D. For from the moment that the world had been smitten on account of the generation of the flood, the nations of the world had gone and fenced themselves away from fornication.

E. That is in line with what people say: "People of the east are meticulous about sexual purity."

No. 1 supplies a minor gloss. No. 2 uses the base verse as part of a syllogistic statement. No. 3 answers an obvious question. Nos. 4 and 5 answer the same question.

## LXX:XIII.

1. A. *And Jacob told Rachel that he was her father's brother and that he was Rebecca's son* (Gen. 29:12):

B. If it was a matter of deceit, then: *he was her father's brother.*

C. If it was a matter of righteous action, then: *he was Rebecca's son.* [He had traits of his mother's family.]

2. A. *He was Rebecca's son and she ran and told her father* (Gen. 29:12):

B. Said R. Yohanan, "A woman feels at home only in the house of her mother."

C. This objection was raised: *And she told her father's house* (Gen. 29:12).

D. He said to them, "It was because her mother was dead, so to whom would she report the matter if not to her father?"

3. A. *When Laban heard [the tidings of Jacob, his sister's son, he ran to meet him and embraced him and kissed him and brought him to his house. Jacob told Laban all these things, and Laban said to him, "Surely you are my bone and my flesh." And he stayed with him a month]* (Gen. 29:13–14):

B. He thought to himself, "Eliezer was the refuse of the household, and in his regard it is written, *And the servant took ten camels* (Gen. 24:10). This one, who is the favorite of the household, how much the more so!"

C. When he realized that he did not even notice a wallet [carrying money and gifts for the relatives], "he embraced him," thinking, "Perhaps he is carrying his money in his girdle."

D. When he did not find his money there, *he kissed him,* thinking, "Perhaps he brought pearls and has them in his mouth."

E. He said to him, "What are you thinking? That I came carrying money? I have come carrying nothing but *words* [that is precisely the thing with which they had sent his mother out]: *Jacob told Laban all these words.*"

Nos. 1 and 3 amplify the text at hand, supplying the motives of the participants or explaining their statements. No. 2 refers to the passage at hand in connection with its own proposition. The striking point of No. 3 is the correspondence between what Rebecca took away from her household and what Jacob brought back, a rather acute reading of details to form a single unified narrative.

## LXX:XIV.

1. A. *[When Laban heard the tidings of Jacob, his sister's son, he ran to meet him and embraced him and kissed him and brought him to his house. Jacob told Laban all these things,] and Laban said to him, "Surely you are my bone and my flesh." And he stayed with him a month* (Gen. 29:13–14):

B. He said to him, "I was thinking of making you king over me. But since you have nothing with you, *Surely you are my bone and my flesh.* Like a bone I shall crush you."

2. A. *And he stayed with him a month* (Gen. 29:13–14):

Another aspect of the use of Scripture as a rule book follows. Rules of society encompass proper conduct. So here, too, we learn proper conduct from what the patriarchs and matriarchs did.

B. Said R. Assi, "The Torah teaches you proper conduct.

C. To what extent does someone have to take up his relative's affairs? A month."

3. A. *Laban said to Jacob, "Because you are my kinsman, should you therefore serve me for nothing? [Tell me what shall your wages be?]"* (Gen. 29:15):

B. Was such an arrangement possible [either that Jacob would have worked for nothing, or that Laban could ever have been so scrupulous]? [Not very likely!]

C. But if he was working for ten *folarions,* Laban paid him only five, and if his load was worth six, he gave him three.

D. He said to him, "Do you think I came looking for money? I came only in order to take and marry your two daughters."

No. 1 reframes Laban's statement into a condemnation. No. 2 derives a lesson from the narrative. No. 3 gives Jacob a reply to Laban and also explains that Laban's conduct even at the outset was deceitful.

### LXX:XV.

1. A. *Now Laban had two daughters, the name of the older was Leah, and the name of the younger was Rachel* (Gen. 29:16):

   B. They were like two beams running from one end of the world to the other.

Once more we turn the family fable at hand into a paradigm of Israel's entire history, its genealogy, its destiny. The two matriarchs now stand at the head of long lines of Israel's history: its heroes, their deeds. The typology yields a paradigm.

   C. This one produced captains and that one produced captains, this one produced kings and that one produced kings, this one produced lion tamers and that one produced lion tamers, this one produced conquerors of nations and that one produced conquerors of nations, this one produced those who divided countries and that one produced dividers of countries.

   D. The offering brought by the son of this one overrode the prohibitions of the Sabbath, and the offering brought by the son of that one overrode the prohibitions of the Sabbath.

   E. The war fought by this one overrode the prohibitions of the Sabbath, and the war fought by that one overrode the prohibitions of the Sabbath.

   F. To this one were given two nights, and to that one were given two nights.

   G. The night of Pharaoh and the night of Sennacherib were for Leah, and the night of Gideon and the night of Mordecai were for Rachel, as it is said, *On that night the king could not sleep* (Est. 6:1).

2. A. *The name of the older [greater] was Leah:*

   B. She was greater in the gifts that came to her, receiving the priesthood forever and the throne forever.

C. *And the name of the younger [lesser] was Rachel* (Gen. 29:16):

D. She was lesser in the gifts she received, Joseph for a while, Saul for a while.

No. 1 links the whole history of Israel to the two daughters of Laban and their offspring. No. 2 effects the same exercise.

## LXX:XVI.

1. A. *The eyes of Leah were weak* (Gen. 29:17):

B. The Amoraic speaker of R. Yohanan explained the matter before him: "And Leah's eyes were [naturally] weak."

C. He said to him, "So let your mother's eyes be weak.

D. "What is the meaning of *weak*? They had been weakened on account of weeping, for people had assumed, 'This is the stipulation: the older daughter will be for the older son, [that is, Esau,] and the younger daughter for the younger son, [that is, Jacob].'

E. "So she wept, saying, 'May it be God's will that I not fall into the domain of the wicked Esau.' "

F. Said R. Huna, "Great is prayer, for it nullified the decree, and not only that, but she came before her sister."

The effect of the exegetical remark is to link the present story to the one about Esau, giving Leah a positive role in the matter.

## LXX:XVII.

1. A. *But Rachel was beautiful and lovely. Jacob loved Rachel, and he said, "I will serve you seven years for your younger daughter, Rachel"* (Gen. 29:17–18):

B. He said to him, "Since I know that people in your vicinity are a bunch of cheats, I am going to make my proposition perfectly clear to you."

C. *And he said, "I will serve you seven years for your younger daughter, Rachel."*

D. [Now clarifying Jacob's statement:] "*For Rachel,* not for Leah.

E. "*For your daughter,* and you cannot bring someone from the market-place whose name is Rachel.

F. "*The younger one,* so you may not change their names for one another."

G. But even if you put a wicked person in a carpenter's vise [an instrument of torture], you won't accomplish a thing.

2. A. *Laban said, "It is better that I give her to you than that I should give her to any other man; stay with me." So Jacob served seven years for Rachel, but they seemed to him but a few days because of the love he had for her* (Gen. 29:18):

B. Said R. Hinena bar Pazzi, "The word *a few* is written both in the present case and in the later one. Just as the reference to *a few* written later on, *And stay with him a few days* (Gen. 27:44), means seven years, so *a few* stated here means seven years."

No. 1 amplifies Jacob's statement to Laban and shows he took every precaution, to no avail. No. 2 then clarifies the meaning of a phrase.

## LXX:XVIII.

1. A. *Then Jacob said to Laban, "Give me my wife, that I may go in to her, for my time is completed"* (Gen. 29:21):

B. Said R. Aibu, "Even if a man is totally dissolute, he would not use this kind of blunt language.

C. "But this is what he said, 'Thus has the Holy One, blessed be he, decreed for me, that I am to produce twelve tribes. Now I am eighty-four years old, and if I do not produce them now, when am I going to produce them?'

D. "Thus the Scripture has to say, *Then Jacob said to Laban, 'Give me my wife, that I may go in to her, for my time is completed'* (Gen. 29:21)."

The exegete clarifies the rather coarse language imputed to Jacob. It is made into a statement of eagerness to carry out God's will. Thus far we have seen examples of Midrash as exegesis yielding proposition and Midrash as proposition yielding exegesis. What follows is our first instance of Midrash as narrative. The message comes at the end: there is an exact measure of justice, which operates for Jacob (hence, his children, Israel). Jacob is paid back for his deceiving Isaac by the deceit of Leah.

## LXX:XIX.

1. A. *So Laban gathered together all the men of the place and made a feast* (Gen. 29:22):

B. He brought together all of the men of the place. He said to them, "You know that we were in need of water. But once this righteous man came, the water has been blessed. [So let's keep him around here.]"

C. They said to him, "What is good for you is what you should do."

D. He said to them, "Do you want me to deceive him and give him Leah, and, since he loves Rachel more, he will stay and work here with you for another seven years?"

E. They said to him, "What is good for you is what you should do."

F. He said to them, "Give me your pledge that none of you will inform him."

G. They gave him their pledge. Then he went and with the pledges the neighbors had given got them wine, oil, and meat.

H. What follows is that he was called Laban the deceiver, since he deceived even the people who lived in his own town.

I. All that day the people were praising him. When the evening came, he said to them, "Why are you doing this?"

J. They said to him, "On your account benefits have been coming to us," and they sang praises before him, saying, *"Hey, Leah, Hey, Leah."*

K. In the evening they came to bring her in and they put out the lamps. He said to them, "Why so?"

L. They said to him, "Do you want us to be indecent the way you are? [Here we do not have sexual relations in the light.]"

M. All that night he would use the name of Rachel and she answered him. In the morning: *And in the morning, behold, it was Leah* (Gen. 29:24–25)!

N. He said, "How could you have deceived me, you daughter of a deceiver?"

O. She said to him, "And is there a book without faithful readers? [I know your story and so I followed your example.] Did not your father call you Esau, and you answered him accordingly? So you called me by a name other than my own, and I answered you accordingly."

2. A. *And Jacob said to Laban, "What is this that you have done to me? Did I not serve with you for Rachel? Why then have you deceived me?" And Laban said, "It is not so done in our country, to give the younger before the firstborn . . . Complete the week of this one and we will give you the other also in return for serving me another seven years"* (Gen. 29:25–27):

B. Said R. Jacob b. Aha, "On the basis of this statement we learn the rule that people may not confuse one occasion for rejoicing with some other."

No. 1 presents a sustained amplification of details of the story, ending with a stunning and apt observation about the appropriate conduct of Leah with Jacob. No. 2, by contrast, just draws a moral. The reference to the deeds of the patriarchs and matriarchs does not always yield complimentary judgments. Quite to the contrary, Jacob's conduct with Isaac accounts for Leah's conduct with Jacob. We look in vain for traces of sentimentality in the intellect of the exegetes at hand, who were engaged in a solemn search for the rules of life, not in a systematic apologetic for a merely sacred text.

### LXX:XX.

1. A. *[So Jacob did so and completed her work; then Laban gave him his daughter Rachel to wife]* . . . *So Jacob went in to Rachel also, and he loved Rachel more than Leah, and served Laban for another seven years* (Gen. 29:28–30):

   B. Said R. Judah b. Simon, "Under ordinary circumstances a worker works with a householder assiduously for two or three hours, but then he gets lazy at his work. But here just as the labor committed for the first years was complete, so the labor given in the latter seven years was hard and complete.

   C. "Just as the first years were worked out in good faith, so the last years were worked out in good faith."

2. A. Said R. Yohanan, "It is written, *And Jacob fled into the field of Aram, and Israel served for a wife, and for a wife he kept sheep* (Hos. 12:13).

   B. "He said to them, 'Your example is like Jacob. Just as Jacob was subjugated before he had married a wife and was also subjugated after he had married a wife, so you, before your redeemer was born, have been subjugated, and after your redeemer has been born you are still subjugated.' "

No. 1 makes a minor observation. No. 2 then joins the present story to the history of Israel. The subjugation after the birth of the redeemer is supposed to refer to the fact that the redeemer was born on the day the Temple was destroyed.*

---

* Freedman, *Genesis Rabbah*, p. 651 n. 1.

## III. THE ISSUE

Once more we ask what is at stake in our document. The issue concerns salvation, meaning, the sense of Israel's history now, the meaning and end of Israel's history then, at the end of time. The entire narrative of Genesis is so formed as to point toward the sacred history of Israel, the Jewish people: its slavery and redemption, its coming Temple in Jerusalem, its exile and salvation at the end of time. The powerful message of Genesis in the pages of Genesis Rabbah proclaims that the world's creation commenced a single, straight line of events, leading in the end to the salvation of Israel and through Israel all humanity. Therefore a given story will bear a deeper message about what it means to be Israel, on the one side, and what in the end of days will happen to Israel, on the other. The deeds of the founders supply signals for the children about what is going to come in the future. So the biography of Abraham, Isaac, and Jacob also constitutes the history of Israel later on. If the sages could announce a single syllogism and argue it systematically, that is the proposition on which they would insist.

The sages understood that stories about the progenitors, presented in the book of Genesis, define the human condition and proper conduct for their children, Israel in time to come. Accordingly, they systematically asked Scripture to tell them how they were supposed to conduct themselves at the critical turnings of life. In a few words let me restate what I conceive to be the program of the framers of Genesis Rabbah about the message and meaning of the book of Genesis:

We now know what will be in the future. How do we know it? Just as Jacob had told his sons what would happen in time to come, just as Moses told the tribes their future, so we may understand the laws of history if we study the Torah. And in the Torah, we turn to beginnings—the rules as they were laid out at the very start of human history. These we find in the book of Genesis, the story of the origins of the world and of Israel.

The Torah tells us not only what happened but why. The Torah permits us to discover the laws of history. Once we know those laws, we may also peer into the future and come to an assessment of what is going to happen to us—and, especially, of how we shall be saved from our present existence. Because everything exists under the aspect of a timeless will, God's will, and all things express one thing, God's program and plan, in the Torah we uncover the workings of God's will. Our task as Israel is to accept, endure, submit, and celebrate.

Now let me briefly restate what we have discovered concerning the premise and the implicit syllogism of the framers of the document. First, the premise:

We now know what will be then, just as Jacob had told his sons, just as Moses had told the tribes, because everything exists under the aspect of a timeless will, God's will, and all things express one thing, God's program and plan.

The record of Scripture tells us the facts of society and history, against which we test our proposed syllogistic construction, which aims at the following austere social policy:

Our task as Israel is to accept, endure, submit, and celebrate.

So in the Mishnah, we take up the philosophy of what we now call Judaism, while, in the polemical and pointed statements of the exegete-compositors of Genesis Rabbah, we confront the theology—which can only be teleological, that is, the theology of history—of that same Judaism.

When we follow Genesis Rabbah, we gain entry into the workings of Midrash, in this instance, the way in which the Judaism of the dual Torah would understand the stories of the creation of the world. These concern Adam's sin, Noah, and, especially, the founding family of Israel, in its first three generations, Abraham, Isaac, and Jacob, as well as Joseph. The sages show in detail the profound depths of the story of the creation of the world and Israel's founding family. Bringing their generative proposition about the character of the Scripture to the stories at hand, they systematically find in the details of the tales the history of the people Israel portrayed in the lives and deeds of the founders, the fathers and the mothers of this book of the Torah. It is no accident that the exegetes of the book of Genesis invoke large-scale constructions of history to make fundamental judgments about society—Israel's society. Nor is it merely happenstance that the exegetes bring into juxtaposition distinct facts—passages—of scriptural history or appeal to a typological reading of the humble details of the scriptural tale, for example, the simple statement that the shepherds had brought their flocks to the well. A large proposition has governed the details of exegesis, and the individual verses commonly, though not always, address their facts in the proof of an encompassing hypothesis, a theorem concerning Israel's fate and faith. Midrash works well in this other mode, the mode of interpreting Scripture by introducing a general proposition to be tested against the individual experiments of successive verses. When we come to Leviticus Rabbah, we find the interest in verse succeeding verse has waned; the proposition comes to the fore as the definitive and dominant organizing motif throughout. With Genesis Rabbah, the Sifra's and Sifré's mode of exegeting verses and their components—one by one in sequence—comes to its conclusion and a new approach commences. The mixed character of Genesis Rabbah, joining propositional to exegetical rhetoric in order to make points of both general intelligibility and also very specific and concrete amplification of detail, marks a transitional moment in the workings of Midrash. Now Midrash will take a very new way indeed—and that will make all the difference.

# 4. Leviticus Rabbah

The focus of Leviticus Rabbah and its laws of history is upon the society of Israel, its national fate and moral condition. Indeed, nearly all of the *parashiyyot* of Leviticus Rabbah deal with the national, social condition of Israel, and this in three contexts: (1) Israel's setting in the history of the nations, (2) the sanctified character of the inner life of Israel itself, (3) the future, salvific history of Israel. So the biblical book that deals with the holy Temple now is shown to address the holy people. Leviticus really discusses not the consecration of the cult but the sanctification of the nation—its conformity to God's will laid forth in the Torah, and God's rules. Leviticus Rabbah executes the paradox of shifting categories, applying to the nation—not a locative category—and its history the category that in the book subject to commentary pertained to the holy place—a locative category—and its eternal condition. So when we review the document as a whole and ask what is that something else that the base text is supposed to address, we find that in a stunning shift or transformation of the metaphor, *the sanctification of the cult in one place for all time stands for the salvation of the nation in every place at some one time.* So the nation now is like the cult then, the ordinary Israelite now like the priest then. The holy way of life lived now, through acts to which merit accrues, corresponds to the holy rites then. The process of metamorphosis is full, rich, complete. When everything stands for something else, the something else repeatedly turns out to be the nation. This is what our document spells out in exquisite detail, yet never missing the main point.

## I. THE DOCUMENT

The framers of Leviticus Rabbah abandoned the verse-by-verse mode of organizing discourse and struck out on their own to compose a means of expressing their propositions in a more systematic and cogent way. Specifically, they set forth, in the thirty-seven chapters (*parashiyyot*) into which their document is divided, thirty-seven propositions. Each of these chapters proves cogent, and all of them spell out their respective statements in an intellectually economical, if rich, manner. The message of Leviticus Rabbah is that the laws of history may be known, and that these laws, so far as Israel is concerned, focus upon the holy life of the community. If Israel then obeys the laws of society aimed at Israel's sanctification, then the foreordained history, resting on the merit of the ancestors, will unfold as Israel hopes. So there is no secret to the meaning of the events of the day, and Israel, for its part, can affect its destiny and effect salvation. The authorship of Leviticus Rabbah has thus joined the two great motifs of the Judaism of the dual Torah, sanctification and salvation, by reading a biblical book, Leviticus, that is devoted to the former in light of the requirements of the latter. In this way sages made their fundamental point, which is that salvation at the end of history depends upon sanctification in the here and now.

The distinctive mode of thought in Leviticus Rabbah (and, self-evidently, in other documents of the same sort, that is, appealing to a variation of the intersecting verse–base verse rhetorical pattern) appeals to metaphoric thinking. Reading one thing in terms of something else, one verse in terms of another as in the case of Genesis Rabbah, the builders of the document systematically adopted for themselves the reality of the Scripture, its history and doctrines. They transformed that history from a sequence of one-time events, leading from one place to some other, into an ever-present mythic world. No longer was there one Moses, one David, one set of happenings of a distinctive and never-to-be-repeated character. Now whatever happens, of which the thinkers propose to take account, must enter and be absorbed into that established and ubiquitous pattern and structure founded in Scripture. It is not that biblical history repeats itself. Rather, biblical history no longer constitutes history at all, that is, history as a story of things that happened once, long ago, and pointed to a single moment in the future. Biblical history becomes an account of things that happen every day—hence, an ever-present mythic world. In this way the basic trait of history in the salvific framework, its one-timeness and linearity, is reworked into the generative quality of sanctification, its routine and everyday, ongoing reality. When history enters a paradigm, it forms an exercise within philosophy, the search for the rules and regularities of the world. That is the profound achievement of the document before us.

And that is why, in Leviticus Rabbah, Scripture—the book of Leviticus—as a whole does not dictate the order of discourse, let alone its character. In this document the authorship at hand chose from Leviticus an isolated verse here, an odd phrase there. These then presented the pretext for propositional discourse commonly quite out of phase with the cited passage. Discussion shifts from the meanings conveyed by the quoted verses to the implications they contain; sages speak about something, anything, other than what the verses seem to be saying. So the *as-if* frame of mind brought to Scripture precipitates renewal of Scripture, requiring one to see everything with fresh eyes. And the result of the new vision in the fifth century was a reimagining of the social world envisioned by Leviticus Rabbah, that is, the everyday world of Israel in its Land in that same difficult time at which Genesis Rabbah was taking shape, the first century of the Christian West. For what the sages now proposed was a reconstruction of existence along the lines of the ancient design of Scripture as they read it. What that meant was that, from a sequence of one-time and linear events, everything that happened was turned into a repetition of known and already experienced paradigms, hence, once more, a mythic being. The source and core of the myth, of course, derive from Scripture—Scripture reread, renewed, reconstructed along with the society that revered Scripture.

So the mode of thought that dictated the issues and the logic of the document, telling the thinkers to see one thing in terms of something else, addressed Scripture in particular but verses of Scripture collectively. And thinking as they did, the framers of the document saw Scripture in a new way, just as they saw their own circumstance afresh, rejecting their world in favor of Scripture's, reliving Scripture's world in their own terms. That, incidentally, is why they did not write history, an account of what was happening and what it meant. It was not that they did not recognize or appreciate important changes and trends reshaping their nation's life. They could not deny that reality. In their apocalyptic reading of the dietary and leprosy laws, they made explicit their close encounter with the history of the world as they knew it. But they had another mode of responding to history. It was to treat history as if it were already known and readily understood. Whatever happened had already happened. Scripture dictated the contents of history, laying forth the structures of time, the rules that prevailed and were made known in events. Self-evidently, these same thinkers projected into Scripture's day the realities of their own, turning Moses and David into rabbis, for example. But that is how people think in that mythic, enchanted world in which, at first, reality blends with dream, and hope projects onto future and past alike how people want things to be.

From the logic of the document, which tells us how the authorship chose to make intelligible statements and argue persuasive propositions, we turn to its rhetorical plan. While Leviticus Rabbah focuses the discourse of each of its thirty-seven *parashiyyot* on a verse of the book of Leviticus, these verses in no way are sequential, that is, Leviticus 1:1, then Leviticus 1:2, in the way in which the structure of Genesis Rabbah dictates exegesis of the verses of the book of Genesis, read in sequence. The document's *parashiyyot* of chapters work out theses on a sequence of themes, for example, the evils of gossip or of drink, the unique character of Moses, and the like. But the respective themes cover a variety of propositions, and a *parashah* ordinarily displays and demonstrates more than a single cogent syllogism.

Concerning the classification of the units of discourse of which the *parashah* or chapter of Leviticus Rabbah is composed, we want to know the structure of the *parashah* as a whole. We ask where its largest subunits of thought begin and end and how they relate to one another. How shall we recognize a complete unit of thought? It will be marked off by the satisfactory resolution of a tension or problem introduced at the outset. A complete unit of thought may be made up of a number of subdivisions, many of them entirely spelled out on their own. But the composition of a complete unit of thought always will strike us as cogent, the work of a single conception of how a whole thought should be constructed and expressed. While that unitary conception draws upon already available materials, the main point is made by the composition as a whole, and not by any of its (ready-made) parts.

In the first classification we take up the single most striking recurrent literary structure of Leviticus Rabbah. It is the base verse–intersecting verse construction, already familiar from Genesis Rabbah, and to be repeated in Pesiqta deRab Kahana. In such a construction, a base verse, drawn from the book of Leviticus, is juxtaposed with an intersecting verse, drawn from any book other than a pentateuchal one. Then this intersecting verse is subjected to systematic exegesis. On the surface the exegesis is out of all relationship with the base verse. But in a stunning climax, all of the exegeses of the intersecting verse are shown to relate to the main point the exegete wishes to make about the base verse. What that means is that the composition as a whole is so conceived as to impose meaning and order on all of the parts, original or ready-made parts, of which the author of the whole has made use.

A variation of that form is the intersecting verse–base verse construction. Secondary in size and in exegetical complexity to the one just now surveyed, here the intersecting verse is worked out, then comes the base verse, given a simple exemplification. Just as in the first type, the exegete may assemble passages on that exemplificatory entry.

A third classification of rhetorical pattern, familiar from Sifra and Sifré to Numbers as well as from Genesis Rabbah, derives from the clause-by-clause exegesis of the base verse, with slight interest in intersecting verses or in illustrative materials deriving from other books of the Scripture. The base verse in this classification defines the entire frame of discourse, either because of its word choices or because of its main point. Where verses of other passages are quoted, they serve not as the focus of discourse but only as prooftexts or illustrative texts. They therefore function in a different way from the verses adduced in discourse in the first two classifications, for, in those former cases, the intersecting verses form the center of interest. The categories of units of discourse also explain the order of arrangement of types of units of discourse. First comes the base verse–intersecting verse construction; then comes intersecting verse–base verse construction; finally we have clause-by-clause exegetical constructions.

## II. A SAMPLE

Leviticus Rabbah *Parashah* XXVII to Leviticus 22:27

### XXVII:I.

1.   A.  *When a bull or sheep [or goat is born, it shall remain seven days with its mother; and from the eighth day on it shall be acceptable as an offering by fire to the Lord]* (Lev. 22:27).
     B.  *Your righteousness is like the mountains of God, [your judgments are like the great deep; man and beast you save, O Lord]* (Ps. 36:6).

The base verse announces that God does not wish the Israelites to offer the newborn sheep or calf but to leave it with the dam. Now the intersecting verse wishes us to recognize that this is an example of God's righteousness, in particular God's concern for the beast as much as for humanity. But before we reach that proposition, on which the chapter as a whole will dwell, we explore other meanings of the intersecting verse.

C. R. Ishmael and R. Aqiba:

D. R. Ishmael says, "With the righteous, who carry out the Torah, which was given *from the mountains of God,* the Holy One, blessed be he, does righteousness *like the mountains of God.*

E. "But with the wicked, who do not carry out the Torah, which was given *from the mountains of God,* the Holy One, blessed be he, seeks a strict accounting, *unto the great deep.*

F. "That is in line with the following verse of Scripture: *Your judgments are like the great deep* (Ps. 36:6)."

G. R. Aqiba says, "All the same are these and those: the Holy One, blessed be he, seeks a strict accounting with [all of] them in accord with strict justice.

H. "He seeks a strict accounting with the righteous, collecting from them the few bad deeds that they did in this world, in order to pay them an abundant reward in the world to come.

I. "And he affords prosperity to the wicked and gives them a full reward for the minor religious duties that they successfully accomplished in this world, in order to exact a full penalty from them in the world to come."

The first proposition has nothing to do with the base verse concerning God's mercy for animals. Rather, it underlines God's ultimate justice by recognizing that the wicked enjoy this world but not the next, and the righteous may suffer now but gain a just reward later on.

2. A. R. Meir says, *"The righteous are comparable to their abode [like the mountains of God] and the wicked are comparable to their dwelling [like the great deep].*

B. "The righteous are comparable to their abode: *I will feed them in a good pasture, and upon the high mountains of Israel will be their fold* (Ez. 34:14).

C. "The wicked are comparable to their abode: *In the day when he went down to the netherworld, [I caused the deep to mourn and cover itself for him]* (Ez. 31:15)."

D. R. Judah b. Rabbi said, "*I caused to mourn* (H'BLTY) is written, 'I brought down (HWBLTY).'

E. "You should notice that they do not make a cover for a bowl of silver, gold, copper, iron, tin, or lead [Num. 31:22] but only [for one] of clay, for it is a material of the same sort [as the bowl].

F. "So said the Holy One, blessed be he, 'Gehenna is dark, and the wicked are dark, and the deep is dark. Let the dark come and cover the dark in the dark,'

G. "as it is said, *For [the wicked] comes in vanity and departs in darkness and his name is covered with darkness* (Qoh. 6:4)."

3. A. R. Jonathan in the name of R. Josiah would rearrange the elements of this verse: *Your righteousness over your judgments [prevails] like the mountains of God over the great deep.*

B. "Just as these mountains conquer the great deep, so that it may not rise up and flood the entire world, so the deeds of the righteous overcome punishment, keeping it from spreading over the world.

C. "Just as these mountains have no end, so the reward of the righteous in the world to come will know no end.

D. *Your judgments are like the great deep* [Ps. 36:6]:

E. "Just as there is no searching out the great deep, so there is no searching out the punishment that is coming upon the wicked in the age to come."

4. A. Another interpretation: *Your righteousness is like the mountains of God:* Just as these mountains are sown and bring forth fruit, so the deeds of the righteous bring forth fruit.

B. That is in line with the following verse of Scripture: *Tell the righteous that it shall be well with them, for they shall eat the fruit of their deeds* (Is. 3:10).

C. *Your judgments are like the great deep:* Just as the great deep is not sown and does not bring forth fruit, so the deeds of the wicked do not bear fruit.

D. That is in line with the following verse of Scripture: *Woe to the wicked. It shall be ill with him, for what his hands have done shall be done to him* (Is. 3:11).

5. A. Another interpretation: *Your righteousness is like the mountains of God:* Just as the mountains are [readily] visible, so the deeds of the righteous are [readily] visible.

B. That is in line with the following verse of Scripture: *May they fear you in the sun* (Ps. 72:5).

C. *Your judgments are like the great deep:* Just as the deep is hidden [from view], so the deeds of the wicked are hidden [from view].

D. That is in line with the following verse of Scripture: *Whose deeds are in the dark* (Is. 29:15).

6.   A. Another interpretation: *Your righteousness is like the mountains of God:*

    B. Said R. Judah b. R. Simon, "The act of righteousness which you did with Noah in the ark is *like the mountains of God.*

    C. "That is in line with the following verse of Scripture: *And the ark rested . . . on the mountains of Ararat* (Gen. 8:4).

    D. *Your judgments are like the great deep:* The judgments which you meted out to his generation you exacted from them even to the great deep.

    E. "That is in line with the following verse of Scripture: *And on that day the springs of the great deep broke open* (Gen. 7:11).

    F. "And not only so, but, when you remembered him, it was not him alone that you remembered, but him and everyone that was with him in the ark.

    G. "That is in line with the following verse of Scripture: *And God remembered Noah and all the living creatures* (Gen. 8:1)."

7.   A. Another interpretation: *Your righteousness is like the mountains of God:*

    B. R. Joshua b. Hananiah went to Rome. There he saw marble pillars covered with tapestries, so that in the hot weather they should not crack from expansion and in the cold weather they should not crack from contraction.

    C. When he went out, he met a poor man with a mat of reeds underneath him and a mat of reeds on top of him.

    D. Concerning the marble pillars he recited the following verse of Scripture: *Your righteousness is like the mountains of God.*

    E. He said, "Where you give, you give lavishly."

    F. Concerning the poor man he recited this verse: *Your judgments are like the great deep.*

    G. "Where you smite, you pay close attention to every little detail."

8.   A. A tale: Alexander of Macedonia went to the king of Kasia, beyond the mountains of darkness. He came to a certain town, called Cartagena, and it was populated entirely by women.

    B. They came out before him and said to him, "If you make war on us and conquer us, word will go out about you in the world that you destroyed a town of women. But if we do battle with you and conquer you, word will go forth about you in the world that you made war on women and they beat you. And you'll never be able to hold up your head again among kings."

C. At that moment he turned his face away and left. After he went away, he wrote on the door of the gate of the city, saying, "I, Alexander the Macedonian, a king, was a fool until I came to the town called Cartagena, and I learned wisdom from women."

D. He came to another town, and it was called Africa. They came out and greeted him with golden apples, golden pomegranates, and golden bread.

E. He said, "Is this what you eat in your country?"

F. They said to him, "And is it not this way in your country, that you have come here?"

G. He said to them, "It is not your wealth that I have come to see, but it is your justice that I have come to see."

H. While they were standing there, two men came before the king for justice.

I. This one kept himself far from thievery, and so did that. One of them said, "I bought a carob tree from this man. I dug it open and found a jewel in it. I said to him, 'Take your jewel. I bought a carob. A jewel I didn't buy.' "

J. The other said, "When I sold the carob to that man, I sold him the carob tree and everything that is in it."

K. The king called one of them and said to him, "Do you have a male child?"

L. He said to him, "Yes."

M. The king called the other and said to him, "Do you have a daughter?"

N. He said to him, "Yes."

O. Then the king said to them, "Let this one marry that one, and let the two of them enjoy the jewel."

P. Alexander of Macedonia began to express surprise.

Q. He said to him, "Why are you surprised? Did I not give a good judgment?"

R. He said to him, "Yes, you did."

S. He said to him, "If this case had come to court in your country, how would you have judged it?"

T. He said to him, "We should have cut off the head of this party and cut off the head of that party, and the jewel would have passed into the possession of the crown."

U. He said to him, "Does rain fall on you?"

V. He said to him, "Yes."

W. "And does the sun rise for you?"

X. He said to him, "Yes."

Y. He said to him, "Are there small cattle in your country?"

Z. He said to him, "Yes."

AA. "Woe to you! It is on account of the merit of the small cattle that you are saved."

BB. That is in line with the following verse of Scripture: *Man and beast you save, O Lord* (Ps. 36:7).

CC. *Man on account of the merit of the beast do you save, O Lord.*

DD. *Man because of beast you save, O Lord.*

9. A. So did the Israelites say before the Holy One, blessed be he: "Lord of the world, we are mere men. Save us like a beast, for we are drawn after you."

B. That is in line with the following verse of Scripture: *Draw me, we will run after you* (Song 1:4).

C. "And whither are we drawn after you? To the Garden of Eden."

D. For it is written, *They feast on the abundance of your house, and you give them drink from the river of your delights* (Ps. 36:9).

E. Said R. Eleazar b. R. Menahem, " 'Your delight' is not written here, but rather, *'Your delights.'* On the basis of that fact we may conclude that every righteous person has an Eden unto himself."

10. A. Said R. Isaac, "Judgment is stated with regard to man, and judgment is stated with regard to beast.

B. "The judgment stated with regard to man: *And on the eighth day, he shall be circumcised* (Lev. 12:3).

C. "And the judgment stated with regard to beast: *When a bull or sheep or goat is born, it shall remain seven days [with its mother]; and from the eighth day on, it shall be acceptable as an offering by fire to the Lord* (Lev. 22:26)."

If I had to specify the proposition before us, it is that God rules man and beast alike, and there are just rules pertaining to each. The intersecting verse is worked out in reference to the righteous, compared to the mountains of God, while the wicked—those subject to judgment—are compared to the great deep. This general approach links Nos. 1 to 7. Once people read the verse in this way, the range of conclusions they propose is fairly standard. There are a few secondary developments, but in the main a single pattern is followed, for example, at Nos. 3 to 6. The only connection I can see between the Alexander fables and the intersecting verse is the reference to the "mountains of darkness." No. 9 is added because of the conclusion of No. 8. No. 10, however, is entirely germane to the base verse. But it is tacked on, since the connection to the preceding is tenuous. It too relies on Psalm 36:7, but it has no relationship to the earlier reading of the verse. The proposition that God's rule is just and reliable now is proved by a different proposition.

## XXVII:II.

1.  A. *Who has given me anything beforehand, that I should repay him? [Whatever is under the whole heaven is mine]* ( Job 41:11 [Heb. 41:3]).

    B. R. Tanhuma interpreted the verse to speak of a bachelor who was living in a town and who gave wages for scribes and Mishnah teachers: "Said the Holy One, blessed be he, 'It is my responsibility to pay him back for his goodness and to give him a male child.'

    C. "That is in line with the following verse of Scripture: *[He who is kind to the poor lends to the Lord], and he will repay him for his deed* (Prov. 19:17)."

2.  A. Said R. Jeremiah b. Eleazar, "An echo is going to proclaim on the tops of the mountains, saying, 'Whoever has worked with God'— whoever has worked with God shall come and collect his reward."

    B. "That is in line with the following verse of Scripture: *In time it will be said to Jacob and to Israel, What has God worked* [Num. 23:23].

    C. "Now let him come and collect his reward."

    D. "*And the Holy Spirit says, Who has given me anything beforehand? I shall repay him* ( Job. 41:11).

    E. "Who praised me before I gave him a soul, who was circumcised in my name before I gave him a male child, who made a parapet for me before I gave him a roof, who made a *mezuzah* for me before I gave him a house, who made a *sukkah* for me before I gave him a place [for it], who made a *lulab* for me before I gave him money, who made show fringes for me before I gave him a cloak, who separated *peah* for me before I gave him a field, who separated heave offering for me and tithe before I gave him a harvest, who separated dough offering for me before I gave him dough, who separated an offering for me before I gave him a beast!

    F. "*When a bull or a sheep or a goat [is born]* (Lev. 22:26)."

One who does his religious duties before he is obligated to do so is praised, in line with the cited verse of Job. That is the point of No. 1, and it is made still more explicit at No. 2. But one can do religious duties only if through God's grace one gets the opportunity: "Whatever is under the whole heaven is mine," so 2.E. The intersecting verse recovers the base verse because the latter speaks of when a bull or sheep is born—that is, by God's grace. Only then can one make an offering. We see a broad variety of cases pointing to the implicit syllogism, which is that God rules through righteousness, which extends to beasts as much as to humanity. But God's rule is not only just. It is also merciful, as we shall now see.

**XXVII:III.**

1.  A. R. Jacob b. R. Zabedi in the name of R. Abbahu opened [discourse by citing the following verse:] *"And it shall never again be the reliance of the house of Israel, recalling their iniquity, [when they turn to them for aid. Then they will know that I am the Lord God]* (Ez. 29:16).

    B. "It is written, *Above him stood the seraphim: [each had six wings, with two he covered his face, and with two he covered his feet, and with two he flew]* (Is. 6:2).

    C. *"With two he flew*—singing praises.

    D. *"With two he covered his face*—so as not to gaze upon the Presence of God.

    E. *"And with two he covered his feet*—so as not to let them be seen by the face of the Presence of God.

    F. "For it is written, *And the soles of their feet were like the sole of a calf's foot* (Ez. 1:6).

    G. "And it is written, *They made for themselves a molten calf* (Ex. 32:8).

    H. "So [in covering their feet, they avoided calling to mind the molten calf,] in accord with the verse, *And it shall never again be the reliance of the house of Israel, recalling their iniquity* (Ez. 29:16)."

The peculiar point is that God's righteousness extends to the mercy of not mentioning sins of the past, such as that of the golden calf. We shall now explore this point, which is invited by the topic of our base verse, the sheep or goat.

2.   A.  There we have learned in the Mishnah (M.R.H. 3:2): **All [horns] are suitable except for that of a cow.**

     B.  Why except for that of the cow? Because it is the horn of a calf.

     C.  And it is written, *They made for themselves a molten calf* (Ex. 32:8).

     D.  So [in not using the horn of a cow, they avoid calling to mind the molten calf, in accord with the verse], *And it shall never again be the reliance of the house of Israel, recalling their iniquity* (Ez. 29:16).

3.   A.  It has been taught: On what account does a wife accused of infidelity not drink from a cup used by another woman [the water that brings a curse]? So that people should not say, "Out of this cup another woman drank the water and died."

     B.  This is in line with the verse of Scripture: *And it shall never again be the reliance of the house of Israel, recalling their iniquity* (Ez. 29:16).

Yet another aspect of the same matter emerges at Leviticus 20:16, that particular sensitivity requiring the beast used in an act of bestiality to be put to death, another side of God's righteousness.

4.   A.  There we have learned: *And you shall kill the woman and the beast [that lay with her]* (Lev. 20:16). If a human being has sinned, what sin did the beast commit?

     B.  But since through that beast a disaster has come upon a human being, the Torah has said that it should be stoned.

     C.  Another consideration: That a beast should not walk through the market and people should say, "That is the beast on account of which So-and-so was stoned to death."

     D.  This is in line with the verse of Scripture: *And it shall never again be the reliance of the house of Israel, recalling their iniquity* (Ez. 29:16).

5.   A.  And so too here: *When a bull or a sheep or a goat is born* (Lev. 22:27).

     B.  Now is it born as a bull and not as a calf? But because it is said, *They made for themselves a molten calf,* therefore the Scripture refers to it as a bull and not as a calf: *A bull, a sheep, a goat.*

Here is a classic example of the systematic exposition of an intersecting verse leading, at the climax, to a new insight into the meaning of the base verse. The same point is made again and again, so that, when we reach the base verse, we readily grasp the pertinence of the intersecting verse. That diverse materials have been assembled is self-evident. What is striking is how they have been put together to make a single, entirely cogent point, five times over and fully spelled out. The next major point, within the same protracted syllogistic argument, is stated in XXVII:IV–V. It is that the just God consistently demands the blood of the victim from the hand of the persecutor. This point is made in two stages. First, there is nothing new: what has been is what will be. Second, what has been is the stated rule: God will favor the persecuted and avenge their blood. The unfolding of the argument is slow and majestic, appealing as it does to case after case.

### XXVII:IV.

1.  A. *That which is already has been, [that which is to be already has been. God seeks that which is pursued]* (Qoh. 3:15).

    B. R. Judah and R. Nehemiah:

    C. R. Judah says, "If someone should say to you that had the first Adam not sinned and eaten from that tree, he would have lived and endured even to this very day, tell him, *It already has been.* Elijah lives and endures forever.

    D. "*That which is to be already has been:* If someone should tell to you, it is possible that the Holy One, blessed be he, in the future is going to resurrect the dead, say to him, *It already has been.* He has already resurrected the dead through Elijah, Elisha, and Ezekiel in the valley of Dura."

    E. R. Nehemiah says, "If someone should say to you that it is possible that in the beginning the world was entirely made up of water in water, say to him, *It already has been,* for the ocean is full of diverse water.

    F. "*That which is to be already has been:* If someone should say to you, 'The Holy One, blessed be he, is going to dry [the sea] up,' say to him, '*It already has been.*' *And the children of Israel walked on dry land through the sea* (Ex. 15:19)."

2.  A. R. Aha in the name of R. Simeon b. Halapta: "Whatever the Holy One, blessed be he, is destined to do in the age to come already has he shown to [humanity] in this world.

    B. "That he is going to resurrect the dead: he has already resurrected the dead through Elijah, Elisha, and Ezekiel.

C. "That he is going to bring [people] through water on to dry land: *When you pass through water, I am with you* (Is. 43:2). He has already brought Israel through [water] with Moses: *And the children of Israel walked on dry land through the sea* (Ex. 15:19).

D. "*And through rivers they shall not overwhelm you* (Is. 43:2). This he has already accomplished through Joshua: *On dry land the Israelites crossed the Jordan* ( Josh. 4:22).

E. "*When you walk through fire you shall not be burned* (Is. 43:2). This he has already accomplished through Hananiah, Mishael, and Azariah.

F. "*And the flame shall not consume you* (Is. 43:2). This he has already accomplished: *[The fire had not had any power over the bodies of those men . . .] No smell of fire had come upon them* (Dan. 3:27).

G. "That God will sweeten bitter water, he has already accomplished through Moses: *The Lord showed him a tree, and he threw it into the water, and the water became sweet* (Ex. 15:25).

H. "That God will sweeten what is bitter through something bitter, he has already accomplished through Elisha: *Then he went to the spring of water and threw salt into it and said, 'Thus says the Lord, "I have made this water wholesome"* ' (2 Kgs. 2:21).

I. "That God blesses what is little [and makes it much], he already has accomplished through Elijah and Elisha: *For thus says the Lord, the God of Israel, 'The jar of meal shall not be spent, and the cruse of oil shall not fail, [until the day that the Lord sends rain upon the earth]'* (1 Kgs. 17:14).

J. "That God visits barren women, he has already accomplished through Sarah, Rebecca, Rachel, and Hannah.

K. "*The wolf and the lamb will pasture together* (Is. 65:25), he has already accomplished through Hezekiah: *The wolf shall dwell with the lamb* (Is. 11:6).

L. "*And kings will be your tutor* (Is. 49:23) he has already accomplished through Daniel: *Then the king Nebuchadnezzer fell upon his face and worshipped Daniel* [Dan. 2:46]."

The intersecting verse is thoroughly explained through scriptural examples, all of which make the point that whatever people believe will happen already has happened. The rather extensive illustration of that proposition occupies the entire passage. The base verse is reached only in the next passage.

**XXVII:V.**

1.  A.  *God seeks what has been driven away* (Qoh. 3:15).

    B.  R. Huna in the name of R. Joseph said, "It is always the case that *God seeks what has been driven away [favoring the victim]*.

    C.  "You find when a righteous man pursues a righteous man, *God seeks what has been driven away [favoring the victim]*.

    D.  "When a wicked man pursues a wicked man, *God seeks what has been driven away [favoring the victim]*.

    E.  "All the more so when a wicked man pursues a righteous man, *God seeks what has been driven away [favoring the victim]*.

    F.  "[The same principle applies] even when you come around to a case in which a righteous man pursues a wicked man, *God seeks what has been driven away [favoring the victim]*."

2.  A.  R. Yose b. R. Yudan in the name of R. Yose b. R. Nehorai says, "It is always the case that the Holy One, blessed be he, demands an accounting for the blood of those who have been pursued from the hand of the pursuer.

What follows is a most lucid instance in which a proposed proposition—God demands an accounting from the persecutor for the blood of the persecuted—is tested against a sequence of cases, which are composed into a long list, proving the basic proposition. The cases are drawn, as we expect, from biblical history, a set of facts that properly understood leads us deep into the regularities and rules of society and history.

    B.  "Abel was pursued by Cain, and God sought [an accounting for] the pursued: *And the Lord looked [favorably] upon Abel and his meal offering* (Gen. 4:4).

    C.  "Noah was pursued by his generation, and God sought [an accounting for] the pursued: *You and all your household shall come into the ark* (Gen. 7:1). And it says, *For this is like the days of Noah to me, as I swore [that the waters of Noah should no more go over the earth]* (Is. 54:9).

    D.  "Abraham was pursued by Nimrod, *and God seeks what has been driven away: You are the Lord, the God who chose Abram and brought him out of Ur* (Neh. 9:7).

    E.  "Isaac was pursued by Ishmael, *and God seeks what has been driven away: For through Isaac will seed be called for you* (Gen. 21:12).

F. "Jacob was pursued by Esau, *and God seeks what has been driven away: For the Lord has chosen Jacob, Israel for his prized possession* (Ps. 135:4).

G. "Moses was pursued by Pharaoh, *and God seeks what has been driven away: Had not Moses his chosen stood in the breach before him* (Ps. 106:23).

H. "David was pursued by Saul, *and God seeks what has been driven away: And he chose David, his servant* (Ps. 78:70).

I. "Israel was pursued by the nations, *and God seeks what has been driven away: And you has the Lord chosen to be a people to him* (Deut. 14:2).

Now we reach our particular topic, the base verse and the fact that it contributes to the syllogism under study.

J. "And the rule applies also to the matter of offerings. A bull is pursued by a lion, a sheep is pursued by a wolf, a goat is pursued by a leopard.

K. "Therefore the Holy One, blessed be he, has said, '*Do not make offerings before me from those animals that pursue, but from those that are pursued: When a bull, a sheep, or a goat is born*' (Lev. 22:27)."

Now the intersecting verse leads right back to the base verse and makes its point in a powerful way. God favors the persecuted over the persecutor, the pursued over the pursuer. This point is made in an abstract way at No. 1, and then through a review of the sacred history of Israel at No. 2. The intent of the whole is established at the outset, so we have a unitary composition. Still, 2.A–C speak of an accounting for blood, and 2.D–K resort to slightly different rhetoric. Since God is just, merciful, and reliable, Israel, for its part, can have no complaint with God. That is the next stage in the unfolding argument—and a key to what is at stake in the whole.

## XXVII:VI.

1. A. *O my people, what have I done to you, in what have I wearied you? Testify against me* (Mic. 6:3).

   B. Said R. Aha, "*Testify against me* and receive a reward, but *Do not bear false witness* (Ex. 20:13) and face a settlement of accounts in the age to come."

The prologue sets the stage for what is to follow, which is the settling of accounts. God now makes the point that whatever God does is righteous and is in accord with rule. No one has a legitimate complaint with God— just as we were told in the opening of this rather rich and complex, but essentially cogent exercise.

**2.** A. Said R. Samuel b. R. Nahman, "On three occasions the Holy One, blessed be he, came to engage in argument with Israel, and the nations of the world rejoiced, saying, 'Can these ever [dare] engage in an argument with their creator? Now he will wipe them out of the world.'

B. "One was when he said to them, *'Come, and let us reason together,' says the Lord* (Is. 1:18). When the Holy One, blessed be he, saw that the nations of the world were rejoicing, he turned the matter to [Israel's] advantage: *'If your sins are as scarlet, they shall be white as snow'* (Is. 1:18).

C. "Then the nations of the world were astonished, and said, 'This is repentance, and this is rebuke? He has planned only to amuse himself with his children.'

D. "[A second time was] when he said to them, *'Hear, you mountains, the controversy of the Lord'* (Mic. 6:2), the nations of the world rejoiced, saying, 'How can these ever [dare] engage in an argument with their creator? Now he will wipe them out of the world.'

E. "When the Holy One, blessed be he, saw that the nations of the world were rejoicing, he turned the matter to [Israel's] advantage: *'O my people, what have I done to you? In what have I wearied you? Testify against me'* (Mic. 6:3). *Remember what Balak king of Moab devised* (Mic. 6:5).

F. "Then the nations of the world were astonished, saying, 'This is repentance, and this is rebuke, one following the other? He has planned only to amuse himself with his children.'

G. "[A third time was] when he said to them, *'The Lord has an indictment against Judah, and will punish Jacob according to his ways'* (Hos. 12:2), the nations of the world rejoiced, saying, 'How can these ever [dare] engage in an argument with their creator? Now he will wipe them out of the world.'

H. "When the Holy One, blessed be he, saw that the nations of the world were rejoicing, he turned the matter to [Israel's] advantage. That is in line with the following verse of Scripture: *In the womb he [Jacob = Israel] took his brother [Esau = other nations] by the heel [and in his manhood he strove with God. He strove with the angel and prevailed, he wept and sought his favor]* (Hos. 12:3–4)."

3. A. Said R. Yudan b. R. Simeon, "The matter may be compared to a widow who was complaining to a judge about her son. When she saw that the judge was in session and handing out sentences of punishment by fire, pitch, and lashes, she said, 'If I report the bad conduct of my son to that judge, he will kill him now.' She waited until he was finished. When he had finished, he said to her, 'Madam, this son of yours, how has he behaved badly toward you?'

   B. "She said to him, 'My lord, when he was in my womb, he kicked me.'

   C. "He said to her, 'Now has he done anything wrong to you?'

   D. "She said to him, 'No.'

   E. "He said to her, 'Go your way, there is nothing wrong in the matter [that you report].'

   F. "So, when the Holy One, blessed be he, saw that the nations of the world were rejoicing, he turned the matter to [Israel's] advantage:

   G. "*In the womb he took his brother by the heel* (Mic. 12:3).

   H. "Then the nations of the world were astonished, saying, 'This is repentance and this is rebuke, one following the other? He has planned only to amuse himself with his children.' "

4. A. *And how have I wearied you?* (Mic. 6:3).

   B. Said R. Berekhiah, "The matter may be compared to the case of a king, who sent three messengers to a certain city, and the inhabitants of the city stood up before them and paid them service in awe, trembling, fear, and trepidation.

   C. "So the Holy One, blessed be he, said to Israel, 'I sent you three messengers, Moses, Aaron, and Miriam.

   D. "Now did they eat any of your food? Did they drink any of your drink? Did they impose upon you in any way? Is it not through their *merit* that you are maintained?

   E. 'The manna was through the merit of Moses, the well through the merit of Miriam, and the clouds of glory through the merit of Aaron.'

5. A. Said R. Isaac, "The matter may be compared to the case of a king

who sent his proclamation to a city. What did the inhabitants of the city do? They stood up and bared their heads and read the proclamation in awe, trembling, fear, and trepidation.

B. "So the Holy One, blessed be he, said to Israel, 'As to the proclamation of the *Shema* and the proclamation of mine [the Torah] [that I sent you], I did not impose on you by telling you to read [the *Shema*] either standing on your feet or having bared your heads, but only [at your convenience:] *When you sit in your house and when you walk by the way'* (Deut. 6:7)."

6. A. Said R. Judah b. R. Simon, "Said the Holy One, blessed be he, 'I handed ten beasts to you, three in your domain, and seven not in your domain.

B. 'The three in your domain: *the ox, sheep, and the goat* (Deut. 14:4).

C. 'The seven not in your domain: *the hart, gazelle, roebuck, wild goat, pygarg, antelope, and mountain sheep* (Deut 14:5).

D. 'I did not trouble you, and I did not tell you to go up into the mountains and to tire yourselves in the fields to bring me an offering of those beasts that are not within your domain.

E. "I asked only for those that are in your domain, the ones that grow at your crib: *Ox, sheep, or goat'* (Lev. 22:27)."

The systematic exposition of the intersecting verse, Micah 6:3, establishes a basic point, that God really does not trouble Israel, which leads us to the intersecting verse as climactic evidence of that point. God does not demand that the Israelites go to a great deal of trouble to find for the sacrifices animals not readily at hand. But before we reach that simple point, we work through a somewhat more complicated message. Whenever God begins a process of inquiry against Israel, the reaction of the nations of the world is such as to warn God off and to make him turn the process into an affirmation of God's love for Israel. This point comes in a number of versions, all of them following a single pattern of rhetoric and argument. There is a secondary motif, that, as Micah says, God does not impose inconvenience on Israel. And that draws us back to our base verse and makes the basic point of the *parashah* as a whole.

## XXVII:VII.

1. A. R. Levi opened [discourse by citing the following verse of Scripture:] *"Behold you are nothing, and your work is nought; [an abomination is he who chooses you]* (Is. 41:24).
   B. *"Nothing*—from nil, from a foul secretion.
   C. *"Nought* (M'P)—from the hundred (M'H) outcries (P'YWT) that a woman cries out when she is sitting on the birth stool, ninety-nine are for death, and one for life."

2. A. It has been taught: she bears three names, "the revived," "the pledged," and "the broken."
   B. "The revived," because she died and was brought back to life.
   C. "The pledged," because she had been pledged to death, in line with the following verse of Scripture: *"If you take your neighbor's garment as a pledge."*
   D. "The broken," because she was broken unto death.

3. A. *An abomination is he who chooses you* (Is. 41:24).
   B. Even though the infant emerges from his mother's belly filthy and soiled, covered with secretions and blood, everybody caresses and kisses him.

4. A. Another interpretation: *Behold, you are nothing* (Is. 41:24):
   B. Said R. Berekhiah, "The word *behold* (HN) is Greek, *hina,* meaning one.
   C. "Said the Holy One, blessed be he, 'I have only one nation among the nations of the world.' "
   D. *Nothing:* This refers to those about which it is written, *The nations are nothing before him* (Is. 40:17).
   E. *And your work is nought* (Is. 41:24):
   F. Said R. Levi, "All the good and comforting works that the Holy One, blessed be he, is going to do for Israel are only on account of a single exclamation (P'YYH) which you made before me at Sinai, when you said, *'Everything that the Lord has said we shall do and we shall hear'* (Ex. 24:7)."
   G. *An abomination is he who chooses you* (Is. 41:24):
   H. That abomination concerning which it is written, *They made for themselves a molten calf* (Ex. 22:8), is the same abomination [that] they shall bring to me as an offering:
   I. *Bull or sheep or goat* (Lev. 22:27).

The basic syllogism—the just and appropriate character of God's requirements—is expressed just now: what Israel brought as a god they will not bring as an offering to God. The intersecting verse, Isaiah 41:24, bears two distinct interpretations. In the first, Nos. 1 to 3, the verse is made to refer to the condition of the newborn child. In the second, No. 4, it refers to Israel, its redemption and God's forgiveness of Israel's sin with the golden calf. The stress then is on the sacrificial system as a mode of overcoming and expiating the idolatry of the people in the wilderness. The issue of the golden calf, already familiar, evidently strikes the exegetes as important in explaining the verse at hand. We shall see further instances of the same concern.

Now we come to the point of it all: the history of Israel as the illustration of reliable rules of society. The rule at issue is God's protection for Israel—this as a matter of justice. The entire composition now reaches its conclusion at just the point of deepest concern: the future history of Israel, that is, salvation.

### XXVII:VIII.

1.  A. *By their wickedness they make the king glad, [and the princes by their adultery]* (Hos. 7:3).

    B. Now why was the bull recognized as the first of all of the offerings *[bull, sheep, goat]* (Lev. 22:27)?

    C. Said R. Levi, "The matter may be compared to the case of a high-born lady who got a bad name on account of [alleged adultery with] one of the lords of the state.

    D. "The king looked into the matter and found nothing. What did the king do? He made a banquet and sat the [accused] man at the head of the guests.

    E. "Why so? To show that the king had looked into the matter and found nothing.

    F. "So the nations of the world taunt Israel and say to them, 'You made the golden calf!'

    G. "The Holy One, blessed be he, looked into the matter and found nothing. Accordingly, the bull was made the first among all the offerings: *Bull, sheep, goat* (Lev. 22:27)."

2.  A. R. Huna, R. Idi in the name of R. Samuel b. R. Nahman: "The [true] Israelites were saved from that act.

B. "For if the Israelites had themselves made the calf, they ought to have said, 'These are *our* gods, O Israel.' It was the proselytes who came up with Israel from Egypt [who made the calf]: *And also a mixed multitude came up with them* (Ex. 12:38).

C. "They are the ones who made the calf. They taunted them, saying to them, *'These are* your *gods, O Israel'* (Ex. 32:8)."

3.   A. Said R. Judah b. R. Simon, "It is written, *An ox knows its owner, and an ass its master's crib, but Israel does not know* (Is. 1:3).

B. "Did they really not know? Rather, they trampled under heel [God's commandments]. [They did not pay adequate attention and sinned by inadvertence.]"

C. Along these same lines: *For my people is foolish. Me they have not known* (Jer. 4:22). Did they not know? Rather, they trampled under heel.

D. Along these same lines: *And she did not know that it was I who gave her the grain, wine, and oil* (Hos. 2:8). Did she not know? Rather, she trampled under heel.

No. 1 carries forward the familiar line of thought that the sin of the calf had long since been found to be null. The intersecting text provokes 1.C. No. 2 then explains why: the true Israelites did not commit the sin at all. No. 3 carries forward the view that the prophets exaggerated Israel's guilt, but in fact Israel was not deliberately sinning at all. It is not that they were worse than the beasts but rather that they paid no attention and so sinned through inadvertence.

## XXVII:IX.

1.   A. *A bull, a sheep, or a goat* (Lev. 22:27):

B. *A bull* on account of the merit of Abraham, as it is said: *And Abraham ran to the herd and took a calf* (Gen. 18:7).

C. *A sheep* on account of the merit of Isaac, as it is written, *And he looked, and behold, a ram caught by its horns* (Gen. 22:13).

D. *A goat* on account of the merit of Jacob, as it is written in his regard, *Now go to the flock and get me two good kid goats* (Gen. 27:9).

2.   A. What is the meaning of *good*?

B. R. Berekhiah in the name of R. Helbo: "Good for you, good for your children.

    C. "Good for you, for on their account you will receive indications of blessing.

    D. "Good for your children, for on their account you will have atonement on the Day of Atonement: *For on this day atonement will be made for you* (Lev. 16:30), [including the atonement of the sacrifice of the goat] (Lev. 16:9)."

The exegesis of the verse is clear as specified. The several beasts now are related to the patriarchs, a fairly standard approach to the amplification of Scripture. The secondary development of Genesis 27:9 presents no problems. We see how a mode of thought powerful in Genesis Rabbah affects the interpretation of Leviticus Rabbah as well.

## XXVII:X.

1.    A. *[When a bull or sheep or goat is born,] it shall remain seven days with its mother; [from the eighth day on it shall be acceptable as an offering by fire to the Lord]* (Lev. 22:27).

    B. Why for seven days?

    C. So that the beast may be inspected, for if the dam should have gored it, or if some disqualifying blemish should turn up on it, lo, it will be invalid and not be suitable for an offering.

    D. For we have learned (M. Nid. 5:1): **That which goes forth from the side [delivered by Caesarean section]—they do not sit out the days of uncleanness and the days of cleanness [Lev. 12:1ff.] on its account, and they are not liable on its account for an offering.**

    E. **R. Simeon says, "Lo, this is like one that is born [naturally] [so that the rules of Lev. 12:1ff. do apply]."**

We note that, while a Mishnah-passage is cited, there is no polemic associated with the exegetical disquisition. It is merely an illustration.

2.    A. Another interpretation: *It shall remain seven days with its mother* (Lev. 22:27).

    B. Why for seven days?

    C. R. Joshua of Sikhnin in the name of R. Levi said, "The matter may be compared to the case of a king who came into a town and made decrees, saying, 'None of the residents who are here will see me before they first see my lady.'

D. "Said the Holy One, blessed be he, 'You will not make an offering before me until a Sabbath shall have passed over [the animal that is to be offered], for seven days cannot pass without a Sabbath, and [for the same reason] the rite of circumcision [takes place on the eighth day] so that it cannot take place without the advent of a Sabbath.

E. "*And from the eighth day on it shall be acceptable [as an offering by fire to the Lord]* (Lev. 22:27)."

3. A. Said R. Isaac, "A rule is written with regard to a man, and the same rule is written with regard to a beast:

B. "The rule with regard to a man: *And on the eighth day the flesh of his foreskin will be circumcised* (Lev. 12:3).

C. "The same rule with regard to a beast: *And from the eighth day on, it shall be acceptable* (Lev. 22:27)."

The comparability of the just rule for man and beast is repeated here. The connection of 1.D–E to 1.A–C is not at all clear. The interpretation given by 1.A–C presents no surprises. No. 2 introduces the matter of the Sabbath, which any reference to eight days should provoke.

Up to now, the reader may have wondered why I stressed the point that Leviticus Rabbah presents the rules of history and sets forth the regulations of Israel's salvation. We shall now see how the sizable disquisition up to now has been pointing toward just that message of Israel's salvation through the living of the holy life.

## XXVII:XI.

1. A. *And whether the mother is a cow or a ewe, [you shall not kill both her and her young in one day]* (Lev. 22:28).

B. R. Berekhiah in the name of R. Levi: "It is written, *A righteous man has regard for the life of his beast, but the mercy of the wicked is cruel* (Prov. 12:10).

C. "*A righteous man has regard* refers to the Holy One, blessed be he, in whose Torah it is written, *You will not take the dam with the young* (Deut. 22:6).

D. "*But the mercy of the wicked is cruel* refers to Sennacherib, the wicked one, concerning whom it is written, *The mother was dashed into pieces with her children* (Hos. 10:14)."

2.    A. Another interpretation: *A righteous man has regard for the life of his beast* refers to the Holy One, blessed be he, in whose Torah it is written, *And whether the mother is a cow or a ewe, you shall not kill both her and her young in one day* (Lev. 22:28).

   B. *But the mercy of the wicked is cruel* refers to the wicked Haman, concerning whom it is written, *To destroy, to slay, to obliterate all Jews* (Est. 3:13).

3.    A. Said R. Levi, "Woe for the wicked, who make conspiracies against Israel, each one saying, 'My plan is better than your plan.'

   B. "Esau said, 'Cain was a fool, since he killed his brother while his father was yet alive. He did not know that his father would continue to be fruitful and multiply. That is not how I am going to do things.' Rather: *The days of mourning for my father are approaching; [only upon his death] will I kill my brother Jacob* (Gen. 27:41).

   C. "Pharaoh said, 'Esau was a fool. For he said, *The days of mourning for my father are approaching.* But he did not know that his brother would continue to be fruitful and multiply in the lifetime of his father. That is not how I am going to do things. But while they are still little, under their mother's belly, I will strangle them.' That is in line with the following verse of Scripture: *Every son that is born you shall cast into the river* (Ex. 1:22).

   D. "Haman said, 'Pharaoh was a fool, for he said, *Every son that is born* . . . He did not realize that the daughters would marry husbands and be fruitful and multiply with them. That is not how I am going to do things. Rather: *To destroy, to slay, to obliterate all Jews* (Est. 3:13).' "

   E. Said R. Levi, "So, too, Gog, in time to come, is going to say the same, 'The ancients were fools, for they made conspiracies against Israel and did not know that they have a patron in Heaven. That is not how I am going to do things. First I shall seek a confrontation with their patron, and afterward I shall seek a confrontation with them.' That is in line with the following verse of Scripture: *The kings of the earth set themselves, and the rulers take counsel together, against the Lord and against his anointed* (Ps. 2:2).

   F. "Said to him the Holy One, blessed be he, 'Wicked man! Do you seek a confrontation with me? By your life, I shall make war with you.' That is in line with the following verse of Scripture: *The Lord will go forth as a mighty man* (Is. 42:13).

   G. "*And the Lord will go forth and fight against those nations* (Zech. 14:3).

H. "And what is written there? *The Lord will be king over all the earth* (Zech. 14:9)."

The exegeses of Leviticus 22:27ff., XXVII:VIII–XI, reach a climax and conclusion with an eschatological motif. The first two units treat Proverbs 12:10 in an entirely appropriate way, tying it closely to the substance of the base verse. But it is not a construction built on the basis of the intersecting verse. Nos. 1 and 2 make essentially the same point, one with Sennacherib, the other with Haman. Levi's systematic picture of Cain, Esau, and Haman then is tacked on because of the prior allusion to Sennacherib and Haman. Nothing in No. 3 alludes to the base verse. And yet the theme still resonates: the cruelties of the wicked, now the ever-increasing but ever-more-futile folly of the wicked who conspire against Israel. The cruelty of each is what joins No. 3 to Nos. 1–2. Nonetheless, it is difficult to deny that No. 3 was framed for its own purpose, prior to its serving to amplify the reference to Haman at No. 2.

## XXVII:XII.

1. A. *And when you sacrifice a thanksgiving sacrifice to the Lord* (Lev. 22:29).

   B. R. Phineas and R. Levi and R. Yohanan in the name of R. Menahem of Gallia: "In time to come all offerings will come to an end, but the thanksgiving offering will not come to an end.

   C. "All forms of prayer will come to an end, but the thanksgiving prayer will never come to an end.

   D. "That is in line with that which is written, *The voice of joy and the voice of gladness, the voice of the bridegroom and the voice of the bride, the voice of them that say, 'Give thanks to the God of Hosts'* (Jer. 33:11). This refers to the thanksgiving prayer.

   E. "*Who brings a thanksgiving offering to the house of the Lord* (Jer. 33:11). This refers to the thanksgiving offering.

   F. "And so did David say, '*Your vows are incumbent upon me, O God! I shall render thanksgivings to you*' (Ps. 56:13).

   G. "*I shall render thanksgiving to you* is not written here, but rather, *I shall render thanksgivings [plural] to you* (Ps. 56:13). The reference [of the plural usage] then is to both the thanksgiving prayer and the thanksgiving offering."

The passage serves the next verse in sequence, Leviticus 22:29. But it treats the theme, rather than the particular statement at hand, and serves equally well at **IX:VII,** above.

## III. THE ISSUE

Let us turn now from these stylized, therefore somewhat confusing, exercises to a concrete account of what has happened through the concrete detail we have surveyed, in particular, when the thinkers at hand undertook to reimagine reality—both their own and Scripture's. How did they think about one thing in terms of another, and what did they choose to recognize in this rather complex process of juggling unpalatable present and unattainable myth? We turn to the specifics by reverting to the tried and true method of listing all the data and classifying them. Exactly what did the framers of Leviticus Rabbah learn when they opened the book of Leviticus? When they read the rules of sanctification of the priesthood, they heard the message of the salvation of all Israel. Leviticus became the story of how Israel, purified from social sin and sanctified, would be saved. A brief account of the whole document makes that point clear.

Let us turn, then, to the classifications of rules that sages located in the social laws of Leviticus. The first, and paramount, category takes shape within the themes associated with the national life of Israel. The principal lines of structure flow along the fringes: Israel's relationships with the nations are, so to speak, horizontal, and with God, vertical. But from the viewpoint of the framers of the document, the relationships form a single, seamless web, for Israel's vertical relationship dictates the horizontals as well; when God wishes to punish Israel, the nations come to do the work. The relationships that define Israel, moreover, prove dynamic, not static, in that they respond to the movement of the Torah through Israel's history. When the Torah governs, the vertical relationship is stable and felicitous and the horizontal one is secure; when not, God obeys the rules and the nations obey God. As in the case of Genesis Rabbah, the recurrent messages of Leviticus Rabbah may be stated in a few words.

God loves Israel and therefore gave it the Torah, which defines its life and governs its welfare. Israel is alone in its category (*sui generis*), so what is a virtue to Israel is a vice to the nation, life-giving to Israel, poison to the gentiles. True, Israel sins, but God forgives that sin, having punished the nation on account of it. Such a process has yet to come to an end, but it will culminate in Israel's complete regeneration.

Meanwhile, Israel's assurance of God's love lies in the many expressions of special concern for even the humblest and most ordinary aspects of the national life: the food the nation eats, the sexual practices by which it procreates. These life-sustaining, life-transmitting activities draw God's special interest, as a mark of his general love for Israel. Israel then is supposed to achieve its life in conformity with the marks of God's love.

These indications moreover signify also the character of Israel's difficulty, namely, subordination to the nations in general, but to the fourth kingdom, Rome, in particular. Both food laws and skin diseases stand for the nations. Yet another category of sin is also collective and generates collective punishment, and that is social sin. The moral character of Israel's life, the treatment of people by one another, the practice of gossip and small-scale thuggery—these too draw down divine penalty.

The nation's fate therefore corresponds to its moral condition. The moral condition, however, emerges not only from the current generation. Israel's richest hope lies in the merit of the ancestors, thus in the scriptural record of the merits attained by the founders of the nation, those who originally brought it into being and gave it life.

The world to come is so portrayed as to restate these same propositions. Merit overcomes sin, and doing religious duties or supererogatory acts of kindness will win merit for the nation that does them. Israel will be saved at the end of time, and the age or world to follow will be exactly the opposite of this one. Much that we find in the account of Israel's national life, worked out through the definition of the liminal relationships, recurs in slightly altered form in the picture of the world to come. The world to come will right all presently unbalanced relationships. What is good will go forward, what is bad will come to an end. The simple message is that the things people revere—the cult and its majestic course through the year—will go on; Jerusalem and the Temple will come back in all their glory. Israel will be saved through the merit of the ancestors, atonement, study of Torah, practice of religious duties. The prevalence of the eschatological dimension at the formal structures, with its messianic and other expressions, here finds its counterpart in the repetition of the same few symbols in the expression of doctrine. The theme of the moral life of Israel produces propositions concerning not only the individual but, more important, the social virtues that the community as a whole must exhibit.

This brings us to the laws of society. The message to the individual constitutes a revision, for this context, of the address to the nation: humility as against arrogance, obedience as against sin, constant concern not to follow one's natural inclination to do evil or to overcome the natural limitations of the human condition. Israel must accept its fate, obey, and rely on God's special love and the merits accrued through the ages. The individual must conform, in ordinary affairs, to this same paradigm of patience and submission. Great men and women, that is, individual heroes within the established paradigm, conform to that pattern, exemplifying the national virtues. Among these, of course, Moses stands out; he has no equal. The special position of the humble Moses is complemented by the patriarchs and by David, all of whom knew how to please God and left as an inheritance to Israel the merit they had thereby attained.

Another theme is so commonplace that we should have to list the majority of paragraphs of discourse in order to provide a complete list. It is the list, such as that found in the climactic moment of Leviticus Rabbah, of events in Israel's history, meaning, in this context, Israel's history solely in scriptural times, down through the return to Zion. The one-time events—the generation of the flood, Sodom and Gomorrah, the patriarchs and the sojourn in Egypt, the exodus, the revelation of the Torah at Sinai, the golden calf, the Davidic monarchy and the building of the Temple, Sennacherib, Hezekiah, and the destruction of northern Israel, Nebuchadnezzar and the destruction of the Temple in 586, the life of Israel in Babylonian captivity, Daniel and his associates, Mordecai and Haman—all occur over and over again. They serve as paradigms of sin and atonement, steadfastness and divine intervention, and other equivalent lessons. We find, in fact, a fairly standard repertoire of scriptural heroes or villains, on the one side, and conventional lists of Israel's enemies and their actions and downfall, on the other. The boastful, for instance, include the generation of the flood, Sodom and Gomorrah, Pharaoh, Sisera, Sennacherib, Nebuchadnezzar, the wicked empire (Rome), contrasted to Israel, "despised and humble in this world." The four kingdoms recur again and again, always ending, of course, with Rome, with the repeated message that after Rome will come Israel. But Israel has to make this happen through its faith and submission to God's will. Lists of enemies ring the changes on Cain, the Sodomites, Pharaoh, Sennacherib, Nebuchadnezzar, Haman.

Accordingly, the mode of thought brought to bear upon the theme of history remains exactly the same as before: list making, with data that exhibits similar taxonomic traits drawn together into lists based on common monothetic traits or definitions. These lists, then, through the power of repetition make a single enormous point. They prove a social law of history. The catalogues of exemplary heroes and historical events serve a further purpose. They provide a model of how contemporary events are to be absorbed into the biblical paradigm. Since biblical events exemplify recurrent happenings, sin and redemption, forgiveness and atonement lose their one-time character. At the same time and in the same way, current events find a place within the ancient, but eternally present, paradigmatic scheme. So no new historical events, other than exemplary episodes in lives of heroes, demand narration because, through what is said about the past, events taking place in the times of the framers of the Leviticus Rabbah also come under consideration. This mode of dealing with biblical history and contemporary events produces two reciprocal effects. The first is the mythicization of biblical stories, their removal from the framework of ongoing, unique patterns of history and sequences of events and their transformation into accounts of things that happen all the time. The second is that contemporary events too lose all their specificity and enter the paradigmatic framework of established mythic existence. So (1) the Scripture's myth happens every day, and (2) every day produces reenactment of the Scripture's myth.

Salvation and sanctification join together in Leviticus Rabbah. The laws of the book of Leviticus, focused as they are on the sanctification of the nation through its cult, in Leviticus Rabbah indicate the rules of salvation as well. The message of Leviticus Rabbah attaches itself to the book of Leviticus, as if that book had come from prophecy and addressed the issue of the meaning of history and Israel's salvation. But the book of Leviticus came from the priesthood and spoke of sanctification. The paradoxical syllogism—the as-if reading, the opposite of how things seem—of the composers of Leviticus Rabbah therefore reaches simple formulation. In the very setting of sanctification we find the promise of salvation. In the topics of the cult and the priesthood we uncover the national and social issues of the moral life and redemptive hope of Israel. The repeated comparison and contrast of priesthood and prophecy, sanctification and salvation, produce a complement, which comes to most perfect union in the text at hand.

Seen in sequence, the three documents, Genesis Rabbah, Leviticus Rabbah, and Pesiqta deRab Kahana, to which we now turn, show us three developing stages in the history of syllogistic discourse within the Midrash-compilations. The first makes a variety of points, not cogent with one another in sequence but entirely cogent seen as a whole, and allows those points to unfold in whatever direction the sequence of verses dictates. The second makes a variety of points, but the order of verses plays no role in the spelling out of those propositions; the unit of discourse is the complete *parashah,* thematically composed, rather than the individual component of a *parashah* centered on a given verse of Scripture. The third then resorts to the framework of a complete chapter, in Pesiqta deRab Kahana called a *pisqa* (=*parashah*) to make a single point, that is, to display and demonstrate a single syllogism. The structure once more shifts. Once the authorship of Leviticus Rabbah determined that they did not require a sequence of verses but only a key verse, the logical next step was to abandon altogether the structure supplied (even if only in pretense) by a biblical book. Pesiqta deRab Kahana's authorship organized its syllogistic discourse not around the verses of a book of Scripture but around the sacred calendar of the holy days of the synagogue, with special reference to synagogue lections on occasions of consequence.

# 5. Pesiqta deRab Kahana

The profoundly cogent statement made through the composition of Pesiqta deRab Kahana, a document of twenty-eight chapters or *pisqaot,* each presenting its own cogent syllogism, is this: God loves Israel, that love is unconditional, and Israel's response to God must be obedience to the religious duties that God has assigned, which will produce merit. God is reasonable, and when Israel has been punished, it is in accord with God's rules. God forgives penitent Israel and is abundant in mercy. God will save Israel personally at a time and circumstance of his own choosing. Israel may know what the future redemption will be like, because of the redemption from Egypt. Organized not around the verses of a book of Scripture but around the sacred calendar of the synagogue and its lections on holy days, the composition links to the theme of Israel's one-time salvation each of the synagogual lections in the ongoing rhythm of holy time. The authorship of Pesiqta deRab Kahana has appealed to the ongoing life of the synagogue, with its rhythms of time and its continual celebrations of the passing seasons, to introduce the propositions of the disruptive and one-time event of Israel's salvation. It has therefore imposed upon the rules of sanctification in synagogue service, which form the counterpart of the Temple's cult and its position in the eternity of unending time, the propositions of salvation, leading from somewhere to somewhere, once and for all time. That blending of the two great themes of the Judaism of the dual Torah constitutes a triumph in the unfolding of the workings of Midrash as the rabbinic circles interpreted the Hebrew Bible. Joining the historical themes of Israel's sorrowful past to the existential topics of the everyday life of the Jew in the world of sin and atonement and imposing on the whole the ineluctable certainty of coming salvation, the authorship of Pesiqta deRab Kahana through its Midrash-exegesis of specific verses has imposed the primacy of scriptural paradigms upon the exegesis of Israel's salvation.

## I. THE DOCUMENT

Pesiqta deRab Kahana therefore has been assembled so as to exhibit a viewpoint, a purpose of its particular authorship—and one quite distinctive, in its own context (if not in a single one of its propositions!) to its framers or collectors and arrangers. Such a characteristic literary purpose is so powerfully particular to one authorship that nearly everything at hand can be shown to have been chosen, and, furthermore, much has been arranged and even (re)shaped for the ultimate purpose of the authorship at hand. These, then, are collectors and arrangers who demand the title of authors. In form and in polemic, in plan and in program, the materials assembled in Pesiqta deRab Kahana cohere to such a degree that on the basis of traits of cogency we can differentiate materials in Pesiqta deRab Kahana that are original to Leviticus Rabbah from those distinctive to Pesiqta deRab Kahana. Not only so, but the program, the framing of a position on the role of logic and reason in the mind of sages, and the plan, the defining of recurrent rhetorical forms and patterns, join into a single statement. And since they do cohere, we may conclude that the framers of the document indeed have followed a single plan and a program.

In Pesiqta deRab Kahana, therefore, we take up not a composite but a composition accomplished as a collage, a work of integrity, a message addressed to a particular place, time, and circumstance by a distinct and singular authorship. The message of the framers derives from Sinai: Israel is in the hands of a loving and forgiving God, who will save Israel in his own good time. But the chosen medium of organization and proportion, sense and meaning, appealing to the orderly and reliable passage of the seasons, testifies to the pertinence of the framers' message. And that choice is original, not received but invented. The single definitive trait of Pesiqta deRab Kahana derives from the structure of the document, which generates the fundamental principle of organization and topical selection, and the distinctive and differentiating traits of rhetoric. It is, as I said, the remarkably original decision to organize the completed document, all of discourse, around the synagogue lections—whether of the Pentateuch or the prophets—for various holy days. The structure of the document derives not from Scripture at all, but from the unfolding of the liturgical calendar of the synagogue and, in particular, its lections on special occasions.

The authorship of Pesiqta deRab Kahana builds its cogent discourses (*pisqaot*) by illustrating an unstated, but everywhere implicit, syllogism—twenty-eight syllogisms in all, corresponding to the twenty-eight *pisqaot.* In this respect the present authorship would not have surprised that of Leviticus Rabbah. But the syllogism refers to and rests on the proof found not in a verse of Scripture. Rather, the theme and also the proposition derive from a special occasion in the holy calendar, specifically the synagogual lections for holy days. Thus the proposition rests not on the foundation of syllogisms stated in the language and terms of the authorship alone but rather on the basis of syllogisms that refer to or borrow from another, prior writing. That writing we may call *the text* selected by the authorship of Pesiqta deRab Kahana for the foundation for a commentary. But I make that statement only with the proviso that the word *text* may refer to a variety of structures, not solely to Scripture. Each *pisqa* repeatedly refers to data clearly outside the frame of discourse of the authorship and treated as authoritative within that same frame.

To turn briefly to detail, Pesiqta deRab Kahana follows the synagogual lections from early spring through fall, in the Western calendar, from late February or early March through late September or early October, approximately half of the solar year, twenty-seven weeks, and somewhat more than half of the lunar year. On the surface, the basic building block is the theme of a given lectionary Sabbath—that is, a Sabbath distinguished by a particular lection—and not the theme dictated by a given passage of Scripture, let alone the exposition of the language or proposition of such a scriptural verse. The topical program of the document may be defined very simply: expositions of themes dictated by special Sabbaths or festivals and their lections.

## II. A SAMPLE

### PESIQTA deRAB KAHANA *PISQA* 19

The base verse of this *pisqa* is as follows: *I, even I, am he who comforts you. [Who are you that you are afraid of a man who dies, of the son of man who is made like grass, and have forgotten the Lord, your Maker, who stretched out the heavens and laid the foundations of the earth, and fear continually all the day because of the fury of the oppressor, when he sets himself to destroy? And where is the fury of the oppressor? He who is bowed down shall speedily be released; he shall die and go down to the Pit, neither shall his bread fail. For I am the Lord your God, who stirs up the sea so that its waves roar—the Lord of hosts is his name. I have put my words in your mouth and have covered you in the shadow of my hand that I may plant the heavens and lay the foundations of the earth, and say to Zion, you are my people]* (Is. 51:12–16). The passage is the lection for the fourth Sabbath after the ninth of Ab, one of the seven Sabbaths of consolation after the day of mourning for the destruction of the Temple. Braude and Kapstein state the syllogism as follows: "Israel's obedience to three basic commands makes her worthy of being God's own people."* After we have surveyed the same pisqa, we shall state a different syllogism, one that encompasses the whole all together and all at once.

---

*William G. Braude and Israel J. Kapstein, *Pesiqta de-Rab Kahana* (Philadelphia: Jewish Publication Society of America, 1975), ad loc. But we shall now see a different syllogism entirely. While at many points I differ with Braude and Kapstein, I think their basic approach—attempting to locate a basic proposition in each chapter—is quite correct.

**XIX:I.**

1. A. *[You know what reproaches I bear, all my anguish is seen by you.] Reproach has broken my heart, my shame and my dishonor are past hope; I looked for consolation and received none, for comfort and did not find any* (Ps. 69:19–21):

   B. "The reproach that has broken us" are the Ammonites and Moabites.

   C. You find that when sin had made it possible for the gentiles to enter Jerusalem, the Ammonites and Moabites came in with them.

   D. They came into the house of the holy of holies and took the cherubim and put them onto a bier and paraded them around the streets of Jerusalem, saying, "Did not the Israelites say, 'We do not worship idols'? See what they were doing."

   E. That is in line with this verse of Scripture: *Moab and Seir say, "Behold the house of Judah is like all the other nations"* (Ez. 25:8).

   F. What did they say? "Woe, woe, all of them are as one."

   G. From that time the Holy One, blessed be he, said *"I have heard the shame of Moab and the blaspheming of the children of Ammon, who have shamed my people, the children of Israel, and aggrandized their border . . . therefore as I live," says the Lord of hosts, the God of Israel, "surely Moab shall be as Sodom and the children of Amon as Gomorrah"* (Zeph. 2:9).

We note that the intersecting verse has not yet met the base verse, and, it follows, we do not know the proposition that is subject to exposition. But we can already come to a sound guess. It must derive from the fact that God has punished Israel, and that Israel complains that it has looked for consolation and received none. Then the base verse will respond with great force: *I, even I, am he who comforts you.*

2. A. *Shame:*

   B. the sense of the word is, Upon me has come a powerful blow, which has drained my strength.

3. A. *I looked for consolation and received none, for comfort and did not find any* (Ps. 69:19–21):

   B. Said the Holy One, blessed be he, *"I, even I, am he who comforts you. [Who are you that you are afraid of a man who dies, of the son of man who is made like grass, and have forgotten the Lord, your Maker, who stretched out the heavens and laid the foundations of the earth, and fear continually*

*all the day because of the fury of the oppressor, when he sets himself to de-*
*stroy? And where is the fury of the oppressor? He who is bowed down shall*
*speedily be released; he shall die and go down to the Pit, neither shall his*
*bread fail. For I am the Lord your God, who stirs up the sea so that its*
*waves roar—the Lord of hosts is his name]"* (Is. 51:12–15).

The intersecting verse is well chosen, since it presents a dramatic contrast between the complaint, that there is no comfort,
and God's statement that he is the one who brings comfort.
The prior exposition of the intersecting verse in terms of the
Moabites bears its own relevance, since it sets the stage for the
catastrophe from which Israelite claims to derive no comfort.
So the whole is cogent and the message is exceedingly sharp.

## XIX:II.

1. A. *Hear me when I groan, with no one to comfort me. [All my enemies, when*
      *they heard of my calamity, rejoiced at what you had done, but hasten the*
      *day you have promised when they shall become like me]* (Lam. 2:21):

Further intersecting verses will harp on the theme of having
no one to give comfort.

   B. R. Joshua of Sikhnin in the name of R. Levi interpreted the verse of
      Scripture to represent Aaron, the high priest:
   C. "You find that when Aaron, the high priest, died, the Canaanites
      came and made war against Israel, in line with the following verse
      of Scripture: *When the Canaanite, the king of Arad, who dwelled in the*
      *south, heard tell that Israel came by the way of Atarim* (Num. 21:1).
   D. "What is the meaning of *by the way of Atarim?*
   E. "It is that Aaron had died, the great pathfinder of theirs, who ex-
      plored the path for them.
   F. *"With no one to comfort me:*
   G. "Moses was in mourning, Eleazar was in mourning. *All my enemies,*
      *when they heard of my calamity, rejoiced at what you had done.*
   H. "They said, 'It is time to go and come against them, it is time to go
      and destroy their enemies [that is, them].' "
2. A. Rabbis interpreted the cited verse to speak of the nations of the
      world:

B. "You find that when the sins of Israel made it possible for the gentiles to enter Jerusalem, they made the decree that in every place to which they would flee, they should close [the gates before them].

C. "They tried to flee to the south, but they did not let them: *Thus says the Lord, 'For three transgressions of Gaza, yes for four, I will not reverse it [because they permitted an entire captivity to be carried away captive by delivering them up to Edom]'* (Amos 1:6).

D. "They wanted to flee to the east, but they did not let them: *Thus says the Lord, 'For three transgressions of Damascus, yes for four, I will not reverse it'* (Amos 1:3).

E. "They wanted to flee to the north, but they did not let them: *Thus says the Lord, 'For three transgressions of Tyre, yes for four, I will not reverse it'* (Amos 1:21).

F. "They wanted to flee to the west, but they did not let them: *The burden upon Arabia* (Is. 21:13).

G. "Said to them the Holy One, blessed be he, 'Lo, you outraged them.'

H. "They said before him, 'Lord of the ages, are you not the one who did it? *[All my enemies, when they heard of my calamity, rejoiced at what you had done].*' "

3. A. They drew a parable. To what may the matter be compared?

B. To the case of a king who married a noble lady, and gave her instructions, saying to her: "Do not talk with your neighbors, and do not lend anything to them, and do not borrow anything from them."

C. One time she made him mad, so he drove her out and dismissed her from his palace, and she made the rounds of the households of her neighbors, but there was not a single one who would accept her.

D. The king said to her, "Lo, you outraged them."

E. She said to him, "My lord, king, are you not the one who did it? Did you not give me instructions, say to me, 'Do not talk with your neighbors, and do not lend anything to them, and do not borrow anything from them.' If I had borrowed something from them or had lent something to them, which one of them would have seen me pass through her household and not accept me in her home?"

F. That illustrates the verse: *All my enemies, when they heard of my calamity, rejoiced at what you had done.*

G. Said Israel before the Holy One, blessed be he, "Lord of the ages, are you not the one who did this: Did you not write for us in the

Torah: *You shall not make marriages with them: your daughter you shall not give to his son, nor his daughter shall you take for your son* (Deut. 7:3).

H. "If we had taken children in marriage from them, or given children in marriage to them, which one of them would have seen a son or daughter standing in trouble and would not have received him?"

I. That illustrates the verse: *All my enemies, when they heard of my calamity, rejoiced at what you had done.*

God is the one who has made Israel an object of derision. Therefore: God owes comfort—a daring allegation indeed, but one we can find in other documents of the age, for example, "hatred of Israel descended from Sinai," a play on the word for hatred, *sinah,* and *Sinai.*

4. A. *But hasten the day you have promised when they shall become like me* (Lam. 2:21):

B. Like me in sorrow, not like me in prosperity.

5. A. *With no one to comfort me:*

B. Said the Holy One, blessed be he, *"I, even I, am he who comforts you. [Who are you that you are afraid of a man who dies, of the son of man who is made like grass, and have forgotten the Lord, your Maker, who stretched out the heavens and laid the foundations of the earth, and fear continually all the day because of the fury of the oppressor, when he sets himself to destroy? And where is the fury of the oppressor? He who is bowed down shall speedily be released; he shall die and go down to the Pit, neither shall his bread fail. For I am the Lord your God, who stirs up the sea so that its waves roar—the Lord of hosts is his name]"* (Is. 51:12–15).

The cited verse is applied to three cases, with the third one leading us directly to the base verse. First we speak of Aaron, or, rather, of Israel at the time that Aaron died. This application seems to me not very rich, since all we have is a reference to one clause of the intersecting verse, the rejoicing of enemies at what God had done. No. 2, by contrast, confronts each of the clauses, making the point that it is God who caused the entire catastrophe, specifically, Israel's loyalty to God's commandments. The parable in No. 3 restates in general terms what No. 2 has told us in very particular ones. Then the parable is applied to make the point that No. 2 has made. Nos. 4 and 5 then bring the whole to the point at which we started, the base verse, in which God comforts Israel, who now has accepted the accusation that God also has brought the trouble on Israel's head.

### XIX:III.

1. A. *As a father has compassion on his children so has the Lord compassion on all who fear him. [For he knows how we were made, who knows full well that we are dust]* (Ps. 103:13–14):

   B. Like which father?

   C. R. Hiyya taught on Tannaite authority: "Like the most merciful among the patriarchs."

   D. And who is the most merciful among the patriarchs?

   E. R. Azariah in the name of R. Aha, "This is our father Abraham.

   F. "You find that before the Holy One, blessed be he, brought the flood on the Sodomites, our father Abraham said before the Holy One, blessed be he, 'Lord of the ages, you have bound yourself by an oath not to bring a flood upon the world. What verse of Scripture indicates it? *These days recall for me the days of Noah, as I swore that the waters of Noah's flood should never again pour over the earth, [so now I swear to you never again to be angry with you or reproach you]* (Is. 54:9). True enough, you are not going to bring a flood of water, but you are going to bring a flood of fire. Are you now going to act deceitfully against the clear intent of that oath? [If so, you will not carry out the oath!]

   G. "*Far be it from you to do this thing, to kill the righteous like the wicked* (Gen. 18:25)."

   H. Said R. Levi, "*Will not the judge of all the earth do justly?* (Gen. 18:25). If you want to have a world, there can be no justice, and if justice is what you want, there can be no world. You are holding the rope at both ends, you want your world and you want justice. If you don't give in a bit, the world can never stand."

2. A. R. Joshua b. Nehemiah interpreted the verse to speak of our father, Jacob:

   B. "*And he himself went on before them and he bowed down* (Gen. 33:3):

   C. "What is the meaning of the statement *and he?*

   D. "He was still in distress. He said, 'It is better that he lay hands on me and not on my children.'

E.   "What did he do? He armed them, and then dressed them in white garments on the outside and prepared himself for three matters: to say a prayer, to give a gift, and to fight a battle.

F.   "To say a prayer: *Save me, I pray you, from the hand of my brother* (Gen. 32:2).

G.   "To give a gift: *And the gift passed before him* (Gen. 32:22).

H.   "And to fight a battle: *And he said, 'If Esau comes to the one camp and smites it'* (Gen. 32:9).

I.   "From this point onward, we shall have a battle with him."

3.   A.   Said R. Samuel, "It is the way of the father to have compassion: *As a father has compassion on children* (Ps. 103:13).

B.   "It is the way of the mother to have compassion: *Like a man whose mother comforts him* (Is. 66:13).

C.   "Said the Holy One, blessed be he, 'I shall do the part of the father, I shall do the part of the mother.'

D.   " 'I shall do the part of the father: *As a father has compassion on children* (Ps. 103:13).

E.   " 'I shall do the part of the mother: *Like a man whose mother comforts him* (Is. 66:13).'

F.   "Said the Holy One, blessed be he, '*I, even I, am he who comforts you. [Who are you that you are afraid of a man who dies, of the son of man who is made like grass, and have forgotten the Lord, your Maker, who stretched out the heavens and laid the foundations of the earth, and fear continually all the day because of the fury of the oppressor, when he sets himself to destroy? And where is the fury of the oppressor? He who is bowed down shall speedily be released; he shall die and go down to the Pit, neither shall his bread fail. For I am the Lord your God, who stirs up the sea so that its waves roar—the Lord of hosts is his name]'* (Is. 51:12–15)."

The intersecting verse proves entirely congruent to the task of illuminating the base verse, and the message of God's personal role in comforting Israel is stated with great emotional power by introducing the parallel of the mercy of the patriarchs, on the one side, Nos. 1 and 2, and then of the natural father and mother, on the other, No. 3. God does the work of both father and mother, leading us to the base verse, which underlines the idea that it is God personally who brings comfort. By this time we realize that the single implicit syllogism—God comforts Israel—will recur over and over again. The effect of the intersecting verse on the base verse is to ask the question Who comforts Israel? so that the base verse may then answer it: God alone and personally.

## XIX:IV.

1.  A. R. Abba Kahana in the name of R. Yohanan: "The matter may be compared to the case of a king who betrothed a noble lady and wrote for her in the marriage settlement a sizable pledge: 'So and so many marriage canopies I shall prepare for you, such and so ornaments I shall provide for you, so and so many treasurers I shall give you.'

   B. "He then left her and went overseas, and she waited there for many years. Her friends were making fun of her, saying, 'How long are you going to sit? Get yourself a husband while you are still young, while you are still vigorous.'

   C. "And she would go into her house and take the document of her marriage settlement and read it and find comfort. After some time the king came home from overseas. He said to her, 'My daughter, I am surprised at how you have had faith in me all these years.'

   D. "She said to him, 'My lord, king, were it not for the substantial marriage settlement that you wrote out for me, my friends would have made you lose me.'

   E. "So too, since in this world, the nations of the world ridicule Israel, saying to them, 'How long are you going to be put to death for the sake of your God and give your lives for him and be put to death for him? How much pain does he bring on you, how much humiliation he brings on you. Come to us and we shall appoint you commanders and governers and generals.'

   F. "Then the Israelites enter their meeting places and study halls and take the scroll of the Torah and read in it: *And I shall walk in your midst, and I shall make you prosper, and I shall make you numerous, and I shall carry out my covenant with you* (Lev. 26:9).

   G. "When the end will come, the Holy One, blessed be he, will say to Israel, 'I am surprised at how you have had faith in me all these years.'

   H. "And Israel will say before the Holy One, blessed be he, 'Lord of the ages, were it not for the scroll of the Torah which you wrote out for us, the nations of the world would have succeeded in destroying us for you.

I. "That is in line with this verse of Scripture: *I recall to mind, therefore I have hope* (Lam. 3:21).

J. "And so too David says, '*Unless your Torah had been my delight, I should then have perished in my affliction*' (Ps. 119:92)."

I cannot imagine a more powerful statement, but why it serves our *pisqa* I cannot say, since it is at best thematically relevant. But it ignores the work at hand. The parable states in general terms what the exegesis proceeds to spell our in particular ones. My best sense is that the composition has been worked out in its own terms and then selected for use here because of its obvious thematic pertinence.

## XIX:V.

1. A. Another interpretation of the verse *I, even I, am he who comforts you. [Who are you that you are afraid of a man who dies, of the son of man who is made like grass, and have forgotten the Lord, your Maker, who stretched out the heavens and laid the foundations of the earth, and fear continually all the day because of the fury of the oppressor, when he sets himself to destroy? And where is the fury of the oppressor? He who is bowed down shall speedily be released; he shall die and go down to the Pit, neither shall his bread fail. For I am the Lord your God, who stirs up the sea so that its waves roar—the Lord of hosts is his name]* (Is. 51:12–15).

   B. R. Abun in the name of R. Simeon b. Laqish: "The matter may be compared to the case of a king who grew angry with his noble wife and drove her out and put her away from his palace. After some time he wanted to bring her back. She said, 'Let him double the sum promised in my marriage settlement and then he can bring me back.'

   C. "So too [in the case of Israel] thus said the Holy One, blessed be he, to Israel, 'My children, at Sinai I said to you one time, "*I am the Lord your God*" (Ex. 20:2), but in Jerusalem in the coming age I shall say it to you two times: "*I, even I, am he who comforts you.*" ' "

We now move to the statement of the syllogism through the exposition of the salient traits of the components of the base verse. In this case it is the repeated reference, *I, even I,* and that draws attention when we compare it to the formulation of Exodus 20:2.

2. A. R. Menahamah in the name of R. Abin, "[God said,] 'Of that very consolation that you laid before me at Mount Sinai, when you said, *"All that the Lord has spoken we shall do and we shall hear"* (Ex. 24:7), [you are assured of comfort]. *Why are you afraid* (Is. 51:12).

   B. " 'Are you not the one who said to me at the sea, *"Who is like you* (Ex. 15:11)?" *Then are you afraid of a man who dies, of the son of man who is made like grass?'* "

3. A. R. Berekhiah in the name of R. Helbo, R. Samuel bar Nahman in the name of R. Jonathan: "The Israelites were worthy of being annihilated in the time of Haman. But they relied on the judgment of the elder and said, 'If our father, Jacob, whom the Holy One, blessed be he, promised, saying to him, *"Lo, I shall be with you and guard you wherever you go"* (Gen. 28:15), nonetheless feared, how much the more so should we fear!'

   B. "That is why the prophet rebukes them, saying to them, '*Have you forgotten the Lord, your Maker, who stretched out the heavens and laid the foundations of the earth?*

   C. " '*Have you forgotten what I said to you, "If heaven is measured and the foundations of the earth search out beneath, then will I cast off all the seed of Israel for all that they have done, says the Lord?"* ( Jer. 31:37).

   D. " '*Have you seen heaven measured or the foundations of the earth searched out?*

   E. " '*From the stretching out of the heavens and the laying of the foundations of the earth you should have learned. But rather, You fear continually all the day because of the fury of the oppressor, when he sets himself to destroy? [And where is the fury of the oppressor? He who is bowed down shall speedily be released; he shall die and go down to the Pit, neither shall his bread fail. For I am the Lord your God, who stirs up the sea so that its waves roar—the Lord of hosts is his name]* (Is. 51:12–13).' "

4. A. Said R. Isaac, "[The reason that *you fear continually all the day because of the fury of the oppressor*] is that troubles follow in close succession."

5. A. *And where is the fury of the oppressor?*

   B. That is Haman and his party.

   C. *When he sets himself to destroy:* in the first month, that is the month of Nisan (Est. 3:7).

6. A. *He who is bowed down shall speedily be released; he shall not die and go down to the Pit:*

   B. Said R. Abbahu, "There are six things that are a good sign for one who is sick: sneezing, sweating, sleeping, a nocturnal emission, dreaming, and regular bowel movements:

C. "Sneezing: *His sneezings flash forth light* ( Job 41:10);

D. "Sweating: *In the sweat of your face you shall eat bread* (Gen. 3:19);

E. "A nocturnal emission: *Seeing seed, he shall prolong his days* (Is. 53:10);

F. "Sleeping: *I should have slept, then I would have been at ease* ( Job 3:13);

G. "Dreaming: *You caused me to dream and made me live* (Is. 38:16);

H. "And regular bowel movements: *He who is bowed down shall speedily be released; he shall not die and go down to the Pit.*"

I. Said R. Haggai, "And that is on condition that he should not lack for bread [but eats regularly]."

We proceed to the phrase-by-phrase exegis of the base verse. No. 1, as I said, once more lights on the doubling, *I, even I*. This is given a strong application. Nos. 2 and 3 yield some textual problems, though I believe I have stated the gist of the matter accurately. No. 3 clearly wishes to read one clause in the light of another. No. 4 seems another fragment. No. 5 also does not appear to be fully spelled out. No. 6 presents a syllogism independent of our setting, to which the base verse contributes a prooftext. The remainder of the *pisqa* will now dwell on further clauses of the base verse.

## XIX:VI.

1. A. *For I am the Lord your God, who stirs up the sea so that its waves roar—the Lord of hosts is his name]* (Is. 51:12):

   B. And why did the sea flee?

   C. R. Judah and R. Nehemiah:

   D. R. Judah said, "It was the staff of Moses that the sea saw and from which it fled."

   E. R. Nehemiah said, "It was the Ineffable Name that was incised on it: *the Lord of hosts is his name,* that the sea saw and on account of which it fled."

2. A. *I have put my words in your mouth and have covered you in the shadow of my hand that I may plant the heavens and lay the foundations of the earth* (Is. 51:16):

   B. There we have learned in a passage of the Mishnah: **Simeon the righteous was one of the last of the remnants of the Great**

Assembly. [He would say, "On three things the world endures: Torah, deeds of lovingkindness, and the Temple service"] (Fathers 1:2).

3. A. R. Huna in the name of R. Aha: "Those who passed through the sea explained the matter: *You in your kindness have led the people which you have redeemed* (Ex. 15:13).

B. "This refers to acts of lovingkindness.

C. "*You have guided them in your strength* (Ex. 15:14):

D. "This refers to the Torah.

E. "*When the Lord gave strength to his people, he blessed them with peace* (Ps. 29:11).

F. "Yet the world still trembles. When will the world be set on a secure foundation?

G. "When *they come to your holy habitation* (Ex. 15:14) [that is to say, the Temple, the third item in Simeon's list]."

4. A. There we have learned: **Rabban Simeon ben Gamaliel says, "the world is established on three things. . . . And all of them derive from a single verse of Scripture: *These are the things you shall do: speak every man the truth to his neighbor, do justice, and make peace in your gates* (Zech. 8:16)."**

5. A. R. Joshua of Sikhnin in the name of R. Levi: "*I have put my words in your mouth and have covered you in the shadow of my hand that I may plant the heavens and lay the foundations of the earth:*

B. "*I have put my words in your mouth:* this refers to words of Torah.

C. "*And have covered you in the shadow of my hand:* this refers to acts of lovingkindness.

D. "This serves to teach you that whoever is occupied with study of the Torah and with acts of lovingkindness gains the merit of taking refuge in the shadow of the Holy One, blessed be he."

E. That is in line with this verse of Scripture: *How precious is your lovingkindness which you commanded; because of it men take refuge in the shadow of your wings* (Ps. 36:8).

F. "*That I may plant the heavens and lay the foundations of the earth:* this refers to the offerings."

G. *And say to Zion, you are my people:*

H. Said R. Hanina bar Papa, "We have made the rounds of the whole of Scripture and have never found another passage in which Israel is called Zion.

I. "But where is there such a passage? *And say to Zion, you are my people.*"

The exegesis of the concluding clause of the base verse is somewhat disjointed, since No. 1 does not serve our passage but merely draws upon it as a prooftext for its own purpose. No. 2 has in mind to link our concluding phrase to the matter of Torah, deeds of lovingkindness, and the sacrificial cult, and this exposition does succeed, though it too is not without its imperfections. For instance, No. 3 interrupts the exposition, and No. 4 is irrelevant. But at No. 5 we have a most successful exercise, and a suitable conclusion to the whole.

## III. THE ISSUE

Each *pisqa,* like the one before us, contains an implicit proposition, and that proposition may be stated in a simple way. It emerges from the intersection of an external verse with the base verse, an intersection that recurs throughout the *pisqa,* and then is restated by the systematic dissection of the components of the base verse, each of which is shown to say the same thing as all the others. As these form a coherent statement, let me now specify the implicit propositions of each of the *pisqaot* of Pesiqta deRab Kahana. In three simple statements I specify the recurrent and cogent syllogism of the document. In order to reach these three statements, I combine the implicit syllogisms each of the twenty-eight *pisqaot* into a single composite.*

## 1. God loves Israel, that love is unconditional, and Israel's response to God must be obedience to the religious duties that God has assigned, which will produce merit.

Israel's obedience to God is what will save Israel. That means doing the religious duties as required by the Torah, which is the mark of God's love for—and regeneration of—Israel. The tabernacle symbolizes the union of Israel and God.

---

*In my *Pesiqta deRab Kahana: An American Translation* (Atlanta: Scholars Press for Brown Judaic Studies, 1987), vol. 3, I present an inductive introduction to the document, in which the conclusions now presented are worked out in detail.

When Israel does what God asks above, Israel will prosper down below. If Israel remembers Amalek down below, God will remember Amalek up above and will wipe him out. A mark of Israel's loyalty to God is remembering Amalek. God does not require the animals that are sacrificed, since humans could never sate God's appetite, if that were the issue, but the savor pleases God [as a mark of Israel's loyalty and obedience]. The first sheaf returns to God his fair share of the gifts that God bestows on Israel, and those who give it to God benefit, while those who hold it back suffer. Observing religious duties, typified by the rites of The Festival, brings a great reward of the merit that ultimately leads to redemption. God's ways are just, righteous, and merciful, as shown by God's concern that the offspring remain with the mother for seven days. God's love for Israel is so intense that he wants to hold them back for an extra day after The Festival (that is, Tabernacles, *Sukkot*) in order to spend more time with them, because, unlike the nations of the world, Israel knows how to please God. This is a mark of God's love for Israel.

## 2. God is reasonable, and when Israel has been punished, it is in accord with God's rules. God forgives penitent Israel and is abundant in mercy.

The good and the wicked die in exactly the same circumstance or condition. Laughter is vain because it is mixed with grief. A wise person will not expect too much joy. But when people suffer, there ordinarily is a good reason for it. That is only one sign that God is reasonable. God never did anything lawless and wrong to Israel or made unreasonable demands, and, therefore, Israel had no reason to lose confidence in God or to abandon him. God punished Israel, to be sure. But this was done with reason. Nothing happened to Israel of which God did not give fair warning in advance; Israel's failure to heed the prophets brought about its fall. And God will forgive a faithful Israel. Even though the Israelites sinned by making the golden calf, God forgave them and raised them up. On the

New Year, God executes justice, but the justice is tempered with mercy. The rites of the New Year bring about divine judgment and also forgiveness because of the merit of the fathers and mothers. Israel must repent and return to the Lord, who is merciful and will forgive them for their sins. The penitential season of the New Year and Day of Atonement is the right time for confession and penitence, and God is sure to accept penitence. By exercising his power of mercy, the already-merciful God grows still stronger in mercy.

## 3. God will save Israel personally at a time and circumstance of his own choosing. Israel may know what the future redemption will be like, because of the redemption from Egypt.

The paradox of the red cow—that what imparts uncleanness, namely touching the ashes of the red cow, produces cleanness—is part of God's ineffable wisdom, which humanity cannot fathom. Only God can know the precise moment of Israel's redemption. But God will certainly fulfill the predictions of the prophets about Israel's coming redemption. The Exodus from Egypt is the paradigm of the coming redemption. Israel has lost Eden but can return home, and, with God's help, will do so. God's unique power is shown through Israel's unique suffering. In God's own time, he will redeem Israel. The lunar calendar, particular to Israel, marks Israel as favored by God, for the new moon signals the coming of Israel's redemption, and the particular new moon that will mark the actual event is that of Nisan. When God chooses to redeem Israel, Israel's enemies will have no power to stop him, because God will force Israel's enemies to serve Israel, because of Israel's purity and loyalty to God. Israel's enemies are punished, and what they propose to do to Israel, God does to them. Both directly and through the prophets, God is the source of true comfort, which he will bring to Israel. Israel thinks that God has forsaken the people. But it is Israel who forsook God; God's love has never failed and will never fail. Even though he has been angry, his mercy still is near, and God has the power and will to save Israel. God has designated the godly ones for himself and has already promised to redeem them. He will assuredly do so. God personally is the one who will comfort Israel. While Israel says there is no comfort, in fact, God will comfort Israel. Zion/Israel is like a barren woman, but Zion will bring forth children, and Israel will be comforted. Both God and Israel will bring light to Zion, which will give light to the world. The rebuilding of Zion will be a source of joy for the entire world, not for Israel alone. God will rejoice in Israel, Israel in God, like bride and groom.

These three fundamental syllogisms, all of them implicit, rest upon the proofs of historical facts contained in Scripture. In this regard the mode of argument is that made familiar by Genesis Rabbah and Leviticus Rabbah: natural philosophy applied to society and appealing to firm facts presented in the scriptural record of Israel's society in history. But the organization of argument—the rhetoric at its deepest structure—around the sacred calendar, with its rhythmic response to the movement of the moon in relationship to the sun and the seasons, joins history to nature. The whole, therefore, presents a powerful union of the themes of Israel in both nature and history, sanctification and salvation. Through the synagogual lections the rhythm of time moves toward a caesura in time; the record of God's intervention into God's own system and structure is repeated, celebrated, and turned into a petition and a promise of things to come.

## IV. WORLD VIEW, BIBLICAL INTERPRETATION AND THEOLOGICAL IMAGINATION: THE PRIMACY OF SCRIPTURAL PARADIGMS IN THE EXEGESIS OF ISRAEL'S SALVATION

What we have learned about the three Midrash-compilations in which propositions generate exegeses of specific verses emerges when we compare one to the next. The rabbinic Bible interpretation in which a proposition yields exegesis, we see, refers over and over again to a single proposition, one that was hardly urgent to the authorships behind Sifra and Sifré to Numbers. All three Midrash-compilations in which proposition generates exegesis take up the theme of salvation.

Our comparison of the three Midrash-documents that portray Midrash as proposition yielding exegesis shows interesting points of difference. Pesiqta's treatment of the subject is rhetorically the most original of the three, just as that of Genesis Rabbah is the most conservative. The liturgical calendar dictates lections and themes that also govern the organization of Pesiqta deRab Kahana in particular. The *pisqaot* that link up with holy days, moreover, tell us why the document does the things it does: *why this,* not only *why not that.* Other authorships, prior to the one at hand, moreover, did precisely what that of Pesiqta deRab Kahana did *not* do, and none built a cogent unit of sustained and protracted discourse on the basis chosen by Pesiqta's, that is, the character and theme of a holy day. The framers of Sifra and Sifré to Numbers (not to mention Sifré to Deuteronomy) follow the verses of Scripture and attach to them whatever messages they wish to deliver. The authorship of Genesis Rabbah follows suit, though less narrowly guided by verses and more clearly interested in their broader themes. The framers of Leviticus Rabbah attach rather broad, discursive, and syllogistic statements to verses of the book of Leviticus, but these verses do not follow in close sequence, one, then the next, as in Sifra and its friends.

The documentary distinctiveness of Leviticus Rabbah strikes more forcefully when we compare that composition to its closest neighbors, fore and aft, Genesis Rabbah and Pesiqta deRab Kahana. The framers of Leviticus Rabbah treat topics, not particular verses. They make generalizations that are freestanding. They express cogent propositions through extended compositions, not episodic ideas. Earlier, in Genesis Rabbah, we saw that things people wished to say were attached to predefined statements based on an existing text, constructed in accord with an organizing logic independent of the systematic expression of a single, well-framed idea. That is to say, the sequence of verses of Genesis and their contents played a massive role in the larger-scale organization of Genesis Rabbah and expression of its propositions. Now the authors of Leviticus Rabbah collect and arrange their materials so that an abstract proposition emerges. That proposition is not expressed solely or mainly through episodic restatements, assigned, as I said, to an order established by a base text (whether Genesis or Leviticus or a Mishnah-tractate). Rather, the proposition emerges through a logic of its own. What is new is the move from an essentially exegetical mode of logical discourse to a fundamentally philosophical one. It is the shift from discourse framed around an established (hence old) text to syllogistic argument organized around a proposed (hence new) theorem or proposition. What changes, therefore, is the way in which cogent thought takes place, as people move from discourse contingent on some prior principle of organization to discourse independent of a ready-made program inherited from an earlier paradigm. But, as we have seen, the authorship of Pesiqta deRab Kahana moves far beyond the position staked out in Leviticus Rabbah, in freeing itself entirely of the restraints of a particular biblical book and selecting instead the rhythms of the sacred calendar as its text and point of organization.

Were we now to define the world of rabbinic Bible interpretation and the working of Midrash, we should insist on one of the following two propositions. First, Midrash as rabbis execute it focuses upon Scripture's particular verses, rather than on large-scale themes or tales. Or, second, Midrash is propositional and argumentative, stating syllogisms and working them out in appeals to evidence provided by Scripture. So Midrash provides us with an essentially philosophical, therefore necessarily philological, reading of Scripture. It examines the meanings of words and phrases to yield propositions. Or it brings to the test of Scripture propositions that can be analyzed in terms of Scripture's words and phrases. Midrash as a large-scale reworking neither of scriptural verses nor of propositions read in relationship to Scripture has yet to make its appearance.

And yet, once the authorship of Pesiqta deRab Kahana had freed itself from the dominance of Scripture's basic structures—books of the Hebrew Bible, read section by section (as in Sifra, Sifré to Numbers) or at least by verses, as in Leviticus Rabbah—the way lay open for a different approach entirely, one in which the message would derive from the medium of narrative, and narrative of a particular order, crafted to the needs of Midrash-exegesis on a large scale. That approach to Midrash through the medium of storytelling would direct attention not to concrete statements of Scripture, whether in sequences of verses or merely individual verses or even words or phrases, but to entire compositions of Scripture—themes, stories. Another mode of Midrash-exegesis, one of which we have seen very little as yet, would then generate Midrash as narrative: the (re)telling of Scripture's stories in such a way as to recast those stories and to make new and engaging points through the recasting. In this third major trend in which Midrash works, in addition to the trends of exegesis generating proposition and proposition yielding exegesis, Midrash effects its reading of Scripture through storytelling. Sifra and Sifré to Numbers, we recall, matched medium to message, making their points in an eloquent and powerful way both by how and also by what was said. Genesis Rabbah, Leviticus Rabbah, and Pesiqta deRab Kahana left us no doubt as to the overriding themes and recurrent tensions that precipitated Bible interpretation among their authorships. Once again, we were able to relate the medium to the message of Midrash, Midrash-hermeneutics to Midrash-exegesis to Midrash-compilation. Whether or not the new medium, that of narrative, carries with it a new message, and whether we may discern a fresh issue, in addition to those posed so urgently by the first two trends of Midrash-compilation, now remains to be seen.

# 4. MIDRASH AND NARRATIVE: INTERPRETATION AS STORY

# 6. The Fathers According to Rabbi Nathan

The authorship of The Fathers According to Rabbi Nathan, which flourished at an indeterminate time but which fits into the framework of the larger authorship of the Talmud of Babylonia, hence probably in the fifth or sixth century, composed a large amplification of Mishnah-tractate Avot, The Fathers. It was through narrative, in particular, that the framers made their important points in response to tractate Avot. Indeed, they resorted to several types of narrative to deal with the received document, and these types differ as the subject changes, from a scriptural topic to a tale about a sage to an event in the holy nation's history. To understand their mode of Midrash in respect to Scripture in particular, which was the Midrash-trend marked by interpretation through storytelling, we have to grasp their broader aesthetic-theological program in respect to narrative.

## I. THE DOCUMENT

Our specific task is to see how, for one sort of exegetical purpose, the authors told one sort of tale, and for another, a different kind altogether. When we appreciate the striking difference between the mode of telling stories about scriptural figures, on the one side, and the manner of narrating stories about sages, on the other, we shall see how sharply and clearly the authorship at hand has matched its aesthetic plan to its larger theological program of interpretation. Once more we may hope to match the medium to the message. For each topic—sage, scriptural hero—in the narrators' and compositors' minds required its own particular type of narrative. Let me classify narratives over all, as these occur in the document before us, and then deal with the two that, in showing the workings of Midrash, I shall compare.

A narrative conveys a message through telling a sequential tale of things that happened rather than through framing a message in general and abstract language. A narrative contains some action, even if only implicit. Let me make this point negatively, then positively. "Someone came and said" does not constitute a narrative; "He said to him . . . He said to him . . ." does not form the substrate of implicit action, for what is said is ordinarily a position in logical analysis and practical reason. But "someone came and did, and the rabbi, seeing the action, ruled" does constitute a narrative. But that type of narrative differs from one in which a sequence of sustained actions, each described in adequate detail, with beginning, middle, and end, constitutes the account and bears the main message. So too, "walking along one day, he saw a skull in the water and said" forms a narrative, even though the narrative serves only to provide a setting for the saying. So the trait of all sustained narrative discourse, absent in all nonnarrative discourse, is that a point is made through describing action, not merely through reporting a position or principle that is established through what is said. I emphasize that the description of action may be implicit in what is said, for example, "Why did you do such and so?" "Because I wanted. . . . " But implicit action is different from the statement of a principle, for instance, "Why do you maintain so and so?" "Because the verse says . . . ," or, "Because the established principle is. . . . " That mode of discourse reports on a conversation, to be sure, but it does not portray an event, tell a tale, evoke a pictorial tableau of completed action, or indicate something that someone has done.

Within the genus *narrative* a message may be portrayed in several ways. In The Fathers I find four such divisions: (1) the parable, (2) the setting for, or formal precipitant of, a saying, (3) the (ordinarily legal, but sometimes moral) precedent, and (4) the story. These constitute the four species of narrative.

The fourth, the story, is further divided into two subspecies: the one dealing with a biblical figure, hence a Midrash-story, the other relating to a hero in the sages' world, hence a sage-story; thus the two types are scriptural and sagacious. I shall show that in narrative technique these are sufficiently different from one another to justify separate classification. Before proceeding, let me spell out the traits of each of the five types of narrative—the four divisions and the two subdivisions of the story.

## 1. THE PARABLE

A parable\* is like a story, in that the narrative centers on things people do, rather than on what they say, and the message is carried by the medium of described action, commonly with a point of tension introduced at the outset and resolved at the end. A parable is different from a story in that its author presents a totally abstract tale, not mentioning specific authorities nor placing the action in concrete time and setting nor invoking an authoritative text (for example, a prooftext of Scripture). Like a story, a parable does not prove a point of law or supply a precedent. But while a story centers on a sage's exemplary actions as the point of tension and resolution, a parable ordinarily focuses on wisdom or morality, which the parable's narrator proposes to illustrate. A parable teaches its lesson explicitly; a story about a sage is rarely explicit in specifying its lesson, and the implicit lesson is always the exemplary character of the sage and what he does—whatever it is, whatever its verbal formulation as a lesson. So there is a very considerable difference between the parable and the story.

---

\*The literature on the parable has not helped me in my inquiry, because the parable is treated as a constant among the diverse documents at hand. I do not know of a study that differentiates the form and use of the parable in one document from the form and use of the parable in some other. The literary form (if that is what it is) is treated as uniform throughout. But the failure to undertake any sort of sustained analysis and differentiation leaves open to question all the conclusions and propositions about *the* parable that have been laid forth. I do not know to begin with that there is such a thing as *the* parable.

One example of a parable, so labeled in our document, is at Fathers According to Rabbi Nathan **I:XIII.2:**

**I:XIII.**

**2.** A. R. Simeon b. Yohai says, "I shall draw a parable for you. To what may the First Man be compared? He was like a man who had a wife at home. What did that man do? He went and brought a jug and put in it a certain number of dates and nuts. He caught a scorpion and put it at the mouth of the jug and sealed it tightly. He left it in the corner of his house.

B. "He said to her, 'My daughter, whatever I have in the house is entrusted to you, except for this jar, which under no circumstances should you touch.' What did the woman do? When her husband went off to market, she went and opened the jug and put her hand in it, and the scorpion bit her, and she went and fell into bed. When her husband came home from the market, he said to her, 'What's going on?'

C. "She said to him, 'I put my hand into the jug, and a scorpion bit me, and now I'm dying.'

D. "He said to her, 'Didn't I tell you to begin with, "Whatever I have in the house is entrusted to you, except for this jar, which under no circumstances should you touch"?' He got mad at her and divorced her.

E. "So it was with the First Man.

F. "When the Holy One, blessed be he, said to him, *Of all the trees of the garden you certainly may eat, but from the tree of knowledge of good and evil you may not eat, for on the day on which you eat of it, you will surely die* (Gen. 2:17),

G. "On that day he was driven out, thereby illustrating the verse, *Man does not lodge overnight in honor* (Ps. 49:24)."

Simeon's point is that by giving Man the commandment, God aroused human interest in that tree and led humans to do what they did. So God bears a measure of guilt for the fall of humanity. This is a narrative meant to make a point, and the parable carries that point, as clearly as an explicit proposition would have conveyed it.

The trait of the parable that draws our attention is its impersonality: the details of the narrative point toward the lesson to be drawn, and not to the specifics of the name of the man and the day of the week and the place of the event. These have no bearing, obviously, because the parable is parabolic, intended to state in a particular narrative a general point. The parable in its narrative traits is the opposite of a historical story, such as we find told about sages. The one is general, universal, pertinent to humanity wherever and whenever the narrated event takes place. The other is specific, particular, relevant to a concrete circumstance and situation and person.

## 2. THE NARRATIVE SETTING FOR A SAYING

What I call formal setting, or *precipitant,* for a saying merely portrays a situation to which a saying pertains, for example, "He saw a skull and said." That hardly adds up to a substantial story, since nothing happens to draw out the significance of the event, *he saw,* but it does demand classification as a narrative, because something has happened, not merely been said. Such a formal setting for a saying may prove substantial, but it will not constitute a narrative in the way that a story does, because not the action but the saying forms the focus of interest, and the potentialities of tension and resolution constituted by the precipitating action ("One day he saw a skull and said. . . . ") are never explored. Here is an example of a story that provides merely a narrative setting for a saying, no different from "He saw a skull and said. . . . " The setting for a saying is like a parable in its generality and exemplary character, but it is unlike a parable in that the burden of the narrative is carried not by what is done, as in the parable, but only by what is said. What follows materially differs in no way from that brief lemma.

I provide only as much of the actual citation of Eleazar's speech to indicate that the setting, the "narrative," has no bearing upon the substance of the "saying," that is, the speech.

**XVIII:I.**

**4.** A. He called R. Eleazar b. Azariah a peddler's basket. . . .

**XVIII:II.**

1. A. When R. Joshua got old, his disciples came to visit him. He said to them, "My sons, what was the new point that you had today in school?"

   B. They said to him, "We are your disciples, and your water [alone] do we drink."

   C. He said to them, "God forbid! It is impossible that there is a generation of sages that is orphaned [and without suitable guidance]. Whose week was it to teach?"

   D. They said to him, "It was the week of R. Eleazar b. Azariah."

   E. He said to them, "And what was the topic of the narrative today?"

   F. They said to him, "It was the passage that begins, *Assemble the people, the men and the women and the children* (Deut. 31:12)."

   G. He said to them, "And what did he expound in that connection?"

   H. They said to him, "This is how he interpreted it." 'The men come to learn, the women to listen, but why do the children come? It is to provide the occasion for the gaining of a reward for those who bring them."

   I. He said to them, "You had a good pearl in your hands, and you wanted to make me lose it! If you had come only to let me hear this one thing, it would have been enough for me."

**XVIII:II.**

2. A. They said to him, "There was another exposition today, concerning the following verse: *The words of the wise are as goads and as nails well fastened are those that sit together in groups; they are given from one shepherd* (Qoh. 12:11)."

   B. " 'Just as a goad guides the cow in its furrow, so the words of the Torah guide a person to the ways of life.' "

The treatments of the cited verses of Scripture would not have surprised the authorships of the Midrash-compilations we have reviewed. We have a cited verse, then a secondary amplification of its meaning. The medium is a very old one. But the narrative setting is just that; it has no bearing on the message imputed to the cited verse. What follows works out the speech and never refers back to the narrative setting. That is why I maintain that the elaborate narrative setting has no impact upon the point of what is portrayed and from the viewpoint of the message is simply a formality.

## 3. A PRECEDENT OR ILLUSTRATION OF A LAW

A precedent narrates a case, often enough in the form of a tale of something that was done, not merely said. The setting is always discourse on the law, but what marks the precedent as different from a story is not its setting but its narrative quality. Specifically, the precedent portrays a tableau of completed action, in which the tension is established not by the action but by the ruling, and in which the resolution of the tension is accomplished solely by the same component, the decision of the sage. There is rarely a beginning, middle, and end, such as there is in a parable and a story. The precedent or illustration is concrete and specific, in the way a story is, but not to a distinctive, named person and time and place, in the way a story is. The precedent, unlike a story, is paradigmatic and makes a general point, rather than historical and particular to a distinctive situation. A precedent or illustration of the law is like a parable in that it presents no concrete details that allow us to identify a particular place or actor.

The species *precedent* includes a subspecies called the *illustrative tale,* invoked not to prove a point but only to make one concrete. The narrative of the illustration is laconic and narrowly descriptive of known, this-worldly circumstances. What marks the parable, its enchanted setting, for example, a king in an indeterminate place or time, never makes an impact on the illustration.

The precedent is readily recognized, since in the Mishnah and related documents, it is commonly marked by the word *ma'aseh,* which, in the context of legal discourse, routinely points toward a story bearing legal weight as a precedent. The illustration is not always so designated but is readily identified. I have translated the word *ma'aseh* as *precedent* in the following story, which bears upon sages' teaching to build a fence around the law by observing stricter rules than the law on its own demands. I present the whole narrative, because its traits of exposition contribute to our inquiry into the story. Specifically, we ask how a story in its narrative qualities differs from the precedent.

**II:I.**

2.   A.   There is the precedent of a man who studied much Scripture, repeated much Mishnah, extensively served as a disciple of sages, but died when his years were only half done, and his wife took his *tefillin* and made the circuit of synagogues and schoolhouses, crying and weeping, saying to them, "My lords, it is written in the Torah, *For it is your life and the length of your days* (Deut. 30:20).

      B.   "On what account did my husband, who studied much Scripture, repeated much Mishnah, extensively served as a disciple of sages, die when his years were only half done?"

      C.   No one knew what to answer her. But one time Elijah, of blessed memory, was appointed to deal with her, saying to her, "My daughter, on what account are you crying and weeping?"

      D.   She said to him, "My lord, my husband studied much Scripture, repeated much Mishnah, extensively served as a disciple of sages, but died when his years were only half done."

      E.   He said to her, "When you were in your period, on the first three days of your period, what was your practice?"

      F.   She said to him, "My lord, God forbid, he never touched me, even with his little finger. But this is what he said to me, 'Do not touch a thing, perhaps you may come into doubt about something.' "

      G.   "As to the last days of your period, what was your practice?"

      H.   She said to him, "My lord, I ate with him, drank with him, and in my clothing slept with him in the same bed, and, while his flesh touched mine, he never had the intention of any inappropriate action [such as sexual relations before the period had fully ended]."

      I.   He said to her, "Blessed be the Omnipresent, who killed him. For so is it written in the Torah: *To a woman during the unclean time of her menstrual period you shall not draw near* (Lev. 18:17)."

This is a highly formal and well articulated narrative, introducing the question with great clarity and repeating the circumstance at A, B, and D, setting up a crisis or point of narrative tension at C ("no one knew . . . "), then invoking the supernatural, also at C, to resolve the tension. So there are really two narratives, A–B, and C and following, which prepare the way for the detailed articulation of the point the storyteller wishes to make, which is at H–I, with the conclusion that things have worked out just as they should.

A more usual kind of precedent ties a story to a legal ruling, as in the following item. Here the narrative includes the name of the authority, as it must, but the personality and role of the named authority make no impact, since the narrative points toward J, the ruling, which occurs also at M. B.Q. 8:7, cited verbatim and here given in boldface type:

### III:III.

1. A. There was a man who violated the instructions of R. Aqiba by pulling off a woman's hair covering in the market place.

   B. She brought complaint before R. Aqiba and he imposed on the man a fine of four hundred *zuz*.

   C. The man said to him, "My lord, give me time [to pay up this substantial sum]."

   D. He gave him time.

   E. When the man left court, his friend said to him, "I'll tell you how you won't have to pay her even something worth a penny."

   F. He said to him, "Tell me."

   G. He said to him, "Go and get yourself some oil worth an *issar* and break the flask at the woman's door."

   H. [He did so.] What did that woman do? She came out of her house and let her hair down in the marketplace and mopped up the oil with her hands and wiped it on her hair.

   I. Now the man had set up witnesses and came back to R. Aqiba's court and said to him, "Should I pay off four hundred *zuz* to this contemptible woman? Now because of a mere *issar*'s worth of oil, this woman could not forego the dignity owing to herself, but rather came out of her house and let her hair down in the marketplace and mopped up the oil with her hands and wiped it on her hair."

   J. He said to him, "You have no legitimate claim at all. For [since the rule is that] **if a person inflicts injury on herself, even though one is not permitted to do so, is exempt from penalty, others who do injury to that person are liable,** [it must follow that] she who does injury to herself is exempt from penalty, while you, who have done injury to her [are liable]. Go and pay her the four hundred *zuz*."

The words in boldface type occur in the Mishnah. The narrative points toward the ruling at J, and the details of the tale are so formed as to provide a concrete illustration for the abstract ruling. The narrator sets up the point of tension by the device of having the defendant ask for and receive time, with E–H providing the incident and the action. Then I works out the consequence and makes the point, with everything finding resolution at J. The difference between this narrative-precedent and the foregoing is less than meets the eye, since the former one also is composed so as to point toward the climactic ruling.

Another kind of narrative, within the same species as the precedent, serves the related purpose of illustrating the law. The important difference from the foregoing is only that the narrative that illustrates the law does not serve as a precedent in a concrete case, while the one involving Aqiba does. But we noticed that Aqiba's precedent simply illustrates the abstract law in a concrete way, and so does the story that follows. So I perceive no intrinsic difference in the formation of the narrative, only in its function, and that is on account of the redactors' selection and use and not the tale's intrinsic characteristics.

### 4. THE STORY (SCRIPTURAL OR SAGE)

A story is like an illustration in that it presents a narrative: such and such is what happened. It also resembles the story in its interest in the concrete and specific way of framing a point. But it is different in one fundamental and definitive way. Its importance requires emphasis: *while meaning to provide a good example of how one should behave, the teller of a story always deals with a concrete person and a particular incident.*

The person is concrete in that he is always specified by name. (In this document, while we find women in precedents and other sorts of narratives, there is not a single story about a woman.) The story concerns a particular incident in that the viewpoint of the narrator makes clear the one-timeness and specificity of the event that is reported. The story always happens in historical time, and the point it wishes to make is subordinate to the description of action, the development of a point of tension, at which the story commences, and its resolution, at which the story concludes: beginning, middle, and end.

A nearly universal, definitive trait of the story is that the story itself ignores the main point the redactor of the document in which the story appears has introduced the story to amplify. In negative terms, the storyteller is never bound by the requirements of a larger redactional purpose and intent. While we cannot say that the story is told "for its own sake," since I cannot define the traits of a story told "for its own sake," we must conclude that the generative and definitive power of the story derives from internal precipitants and not extrinsic interests. The storyteller wishes to compose the narrative along lines required by the generative tension of the story at hand, not those imposed by the redactional purpose supplied by the (planned) setting of the story. The power of the story—its definitive function—is intrinsic to the narrative and self-evident within the narrative. Any further point that the story proves or illustrates lies outside of the imaginative framework.

We turn now to the differences between stories about scriptural topics and stories about sages. We review the exempla of the one, then the other, and, finally, establish the fact that they are, as exercises of narrative, distinct subspecies of the story. Along the way we shall further see how the narrative serves in a powerful way to accomplish Midrash-exegesis of Scripture, so constituting the third of the three major trends of rabbinic Bible interpretation. We shall time and again note how the first two trends find a place as well.

## II. NARRATIVE AND MIDRASH: (1) CREATION

Two questions define our reading of stories on scriptural figures. First, we wish to find out whether the subject matter—scriptural themes rather than sages' lives and deeds—imposes narrative literary conventions that differ from those that guide writers of stories about sages. Second, we ask what, if any, points emerge from stories about scriptural themes and how these propositions (if any) relate to those of stories about sages. The Fathers According to Rabbi Nathan contains stories on two fundamental themes: (1) creation, encompassing the First Man and Woman, and (2) Moses and Israel.

All stories about the First Man and Woman, as well as creation, occur in a single vast anthology, in The Fathers According to Rabbi Nathan Chapter One. At the outset we see the reason for inserting the anthology, that is, the specification of "the fence that the first man made around his words," to which the amplification of Avot 1:1 alludes. Then a good example of the matter is given, **I:VIII.1.C–D,** which is given its own amplification at **I:VIII.5.** And afterward, the entire composition follows. Let us first review the whole, with some comments on the components. I shall then account for the arrangement of the parts and finally turn to the issue of narrative and story.

**I:VIII.**

1. A. What is the fence that the First Man made around his words?

   B. Lo, Scripture says, *And the Lord God laid a commandment on Man, saying, "Of all the trees of the garden you may certainly eat, but from the tree of knowledge of good and evil you may not eat, for on the day of your eating of it you will surely die* (Gen. 2:17)."

   C. Man did not want to state the matter to Woman as the Holy One, blessed be he, had stated it to him, but rather he said to her, "*Of the fruit of the tree which is in the midst of the garden God has said, You may not eat and* you may not touch it *lest you die* (Gen. 3:3)." [He made a fence around his words by extending the matter from eating to merely touching.]

   D. At that moment the wicked snake thought to himself, saying, "Since I cannot make Man stumble, I shall go and make Woman stumble." He went and entered discourse with her and had a long conversation with her, saying to her, "If it was as to not touching the tree that you say the Holy One, blessed be he, has laid a commandment on us, lo, I am going to touch it, but I shall not die. You too may touch it and you will not die."

E. What did the wicked snake do at that moment? He went and touched the tree with his hands and feet and shook it until its fruit fell to the ground.

F. But some say he did not touch it at all. But when the tree saw [the snake], it said, "Wicked! Wicked! Don't touch me!" For it is said, *Let not the foot of pride overtake me and let not the hand of the wicked shake me* (Ps. 36:12).

We see why the story falls into the large classification of Midrash, in that the important points are tied to the citation of specific verses of Scripture. We also see how the story before us differs from the two kinds of Midrash-exegesis, the workings of which we have already surveyed. In neither of the former kinds—exegetical, propositional—does narrative play a role. But here it is at the heart of matters.

### I:VIII.

2. A. Another interpretation of the verse, *Let not the foot of pride overtake me and let not the hand of the wicked shake me* (Ps. 36:12).

B. This refers to the wicked Titus, may his bones be pulverized, for, with wand [penis] in hand he hit the altar saying, "Wolf, wolf! You are a king and I am a king, come and make war against me! How many oxen were slaughtered on you, how many fowl were killed on you, how much wine was poured out on you, how much incense was burned up on you! You are the one who consumes the entire world," as it is said, *O Ariel, Ariel, the city where David encamped, add year to year, let the feasts come around* (Is. 29:1).

### I:VIII.

3. A. [Continuing **I:VIII.1.D:**] And the snake further said to her, "If it was as to not eating of the tree that you say the Holy One, blessed be he, has laid a commandment on us, lo, I am going to eat of it, but I shall not die. You too may eat of it and you will not die."

B. Now what did Woman think to herself? "All the things that my lord [Man] has taught me from the very beginning are lies." (For Woman would call the first Man only "my lord.")

C. So she went and took of the fruit and ate it and gave it to Man and he ate, as it is said, *And the Woman saw that the tree was good for eating and an appealing sight* (Gen. 3:6).

**I:VIII.**

4.   A. At that moment Eve was assigned ten curses [below: three decrees, cf. **I:XIV.3**], as it is said, *To the Woman he said, "I will greatly multiply your pain and your travail; in pain you shall bring forth children; and your desire will be to your husband; and he shall rule over you* (Gen. 3:16)."

    B. *I will greatly multiply your pain* refers to the two kinds of blood that a woman discharges, one the pain of menstrual blood, the other that of hymeneal blood.

    C. *And your travail* refers to the pain of pregnancy.

    D. *In pain you shall bring forth children* bears the obvious meaning [and refers to the pain of giving birth].

    E. *And your desire will be to your husband* refers to the fact that a woman lusts after her husband when he goes off on a journey.

    F. *And he shall rule over you* refers to the fact that a man asks explicitly for what he wants, while a woman just aches in her heart for it, cloaked as in mourning, imprisoned, cut off from all men [other than her husband].

The mixture of Midrash-as-story with Midrash-as-exegesis alerts us to the fact that the several modes of Midrash coexist quite comfortably. The actual narrative portion of the whole, we see, is substantially shorter than the larger part of the composite.

**I:VIII.**

5.   A. [Reverting to the opening proposition:] Now what is it that led to the woman's touching the tree? It was the fence that the First Man erected around his words.

    B. On this basis they have said: "If someone puts too much of a fence around what he says, he will not be able to stand by his words."

    C. On this basis they have said: "A person should not embellish [a report, when repeating] what he hears."

    D. R. Yosé says, "Better a fence ten handbreadths high that stands than one a hundred handbreadths high that falls down."

*Fence,* here, means an embellishment or an addition to what one says, aimed at adding to effect. A fence reinforces something one should not do rather than something one should do. So when at **I:VI.1.B** we were told that the First Man made a fence around his words, we expected that that is something we should emulate. But as we see, the point is just the opposite. The First Man embellished the instructions that God had given to him, with the result that is spelled out. It seems to me this composition is singularly inappropriate to the present context. At least part of it, a systematic collection conglomerated around Psalm 36:12, surely took shape before insertion here. Then there is an independent exegesis of Genesis 3:16. I:VIII.5 pretends to carry us all the way back to our opening proposition. But, of course, as we already realize, that is an error, since the opening proposition was that one should set up a hedge around one's statements, but the closing one—quite appropriate to the large and complex composition before us—is that one should not do so, a separate and essentially contradictory position. We now go on to a further exposition of the topic that has made possible this treatment of the proposition, that is, the fall of Man and Woman.

### I:IX.

1.   A.  At that time, the wicked snake reflected, "I shall go and kill Man and marry his wife and be king over the whole world and walk upright and eat all the gourmet foods of the world."

       B.  Said to him the Holy One, blessed be he, "You have said, 'I shall kill Man and marry Woman.' Therefore: *I shall put hatred between you and Woman* (Gen. 3:15).

       C.  "You have said, 'I shall be king over the whole world.' Therefore: *You are most cursed of all cattle* (Gen. 3:14).

       D.  "You have said, 'I shall walk upright.' Therefore: *On your belly you shall walk* (Gen. 3:15).

       E.  "You have said, 'I shall eat all the gourmet foods of the world.' Therefore: *You will eat dirt all the time you live.*"

The systematic exegesis of Genesis 3:14–15, reasoning backward from God's curse to the original motivation of the snake, simply serves as a thematic supplement to the foregoing. In no way does it advance the argument concerning setting up (or not setting up too high) a fence around one's words. This same thematic miscellany continues.

**I:X.**

1. A. R. Simeon b. Menassia says, "What a loss of a great servant, for if the snake had not been cursed, every Israelite would have had two snakes in his house, one to send westward, the other eastward, to bring back good sardony, jewels, pearls, every sort of desirable thing in the world, and no one could do them any harm.

   B. "Not only so, but they would have served as beasts of burden in place of camels, asses, mules, bringing manure out to the fields and orchards."

The principle of aggregation is simple: more on the same theme as the foregoing.

**I:XI.**

1. A. R. Judah b. Bathera says, "The First Man was reclining in the Garden of Eden, with the ministering angels serving as his retinue, roasting meat for him, cooling wine for him.

   B. "The snake came and saw all this glory and was filled with envy."

**I:XII.**

1. A. What was the order of the creation of the First Man? [The entire sequence of events of the creation and fall of Man and Woman took place on a single day, illustrating a series of verses of Psalms that are liturgically used on the several days of the week.]

   B. In the first hour [of the sixth day, on which Man was made] the dirt for making him was gathered, in the second, his form was shaped, in the third, he was turned into a mass of dough, in the fourth, his limbs were made, in the fifth, his various apertures were opened up, in the sixth, breath was put into him, in the seventh, he stood on his feet, in the eighth, Eve was made as his match, in the ninth, he was put into the Garden of Eden, in the tenth, he was given the commandment, in the eleventh, he turned rotten, in the twelfth, he was driven out and went his way.

   C. This carries out the verse: *But Man does not lodge overnight in honor* (Ps. 49:13).

   D. On the first day of the week [with reference to the acts of creation done on that day], what Psalm is to be recited? *The earth is the Lord's and the fullness thereof, the world and they who dwell in it* (Ps. 24:1). For [God] is the one who owns it and transfers ownership of it, and he is the one who will judge the world.

E. On the second day? *Great is the Lord and greatly to be praised in the city of our God* (Ps. 48:2). He divided everything he had made [between sea and dry land] and was made king over his world.

F. On the third day? *God is standing in the congregation of the mighty, in the midst of the mighty he will judge* (Ps. 82:1). He created the sea and the dry land and folded up the land to its place, leaving a place for his congregation.

G. On the fourth day? *God of vengeance, O Lord, God of vengeance, appear* (Ps. 94:1). He created the sun, moon, stars, and planets, which give light to the world, but he is going to exact vengeance [from those who serve them].

H. On the fifth? *Sing aloud to God our strength, shout to the God of Jacob* (Ps. 81:2). He created the fowl, fish, mammals of the sea, who sing aloud in the world [praises of God].

I. On the sixth? *The Lord reigns, clothed in majesty, the Lord is clothed, girded in strength, yes, the world is established and cannot be moved* (Ps. 93:1). On that day he completed all his work and arose and took his seat on the heights of the world.

J. On the seventh? *A Psalm, a song for the Sabbath day* (Ps. 92:1). It is a day that is wholly a Sabbath, on which there is no eating, drinking, or conducting of business, but the righteous are seated in retinue with their crowns on their heads and derive sustenance from the splendor of God's presence, as it is said, *And they beheld God and ate and drank* (Ex. 24:11), like the ministering angels.

K. And [reverting back to B] why [was man created last]?

L. So that [immediately upon creation on the sixth day] he might forthwith take up his Sabbath meal.

The order of creation is worked out at A and B. The sizable insertion, D–J, then goes over the order of creation as it is celebrated in psalms recited in the cult. Only K and L take up where B has left off. That D–J has been composed in its own terms we need not doubt, and the entire complex has been tacked on for essentially the same reason as the foregoing: an enormous thematic supplement to what was originally irrelevant to the exposition of the matter at hand.

**I:XIII.**

1. A. R. Simeon b. Eleazar says, "I shall draw a parable for you. To what may the First Man be compared? He was like a man who married a

proselyte, who sat and gave her instructions, saying to her, 'My daughter, do not eat a piece of bread when your hands are cultically unclean, and do not eat produce that has not been tithed, and do not profane the Sabbath, and do not go around making vows, and do not walk about with any other man. Now if you should violate any of these orders, lo, you will be subject to the death penalty.'

B. "What did the man himself do? He went and in her presence ate a piece of bread when his hands were cultically unclean, ate produce that had not been tithed, violated the Sabbath, went around taking vows, and with his own hands placed before her [an example of what he had himself prohibited].

C. "What did that proselyte say to herself? 'All of these orders that my husband gave me to begin with were lies.' So she went and violated all of them."

## I:XIII.

2.　A. R. Simeon b. Yohai says, "I shall draw a parable for you. To what may the First Man be compared? He was like a man who had a wife at home. What did that man do? He went and brought a jug and put in it a certain number of dates and nuts. He caught a scorpion and put it at the mouth of the jug and sealed it tightly. He left it in the corner of the house.

B. "He said to her, 'My daughter, whatever I have in the house is entrusted to you, except for this jar, which under no circumstances should you touch.' What did the woman do? When her husband went off to market, she went and opened the jug and put her hand in it, and the scorpion bit her, and she went and fell into bed. When her husband came home from the market, he said to her, 'What's going on?'

C. "She said to him, 'I put my hand into the jug, and a scorpion bit me, and now I'm dying.'

D. "He said to her, 'Didn't I tell you to begin with, "Whatever I have in the house is entrusted to you, except for this jar, which under no circumstances should you touch"?' He got mad at her and divorced her.

E. "So it was with the First Man.

F. "When the Holy One, blessed be he, said to him, '*Of all the trees of the garden you certainly may eat, but from the tree of knowledge of good and evil you may not eat, for on the day on which you eat of it, you will surely die* (Gen. 2:17),'

G. "on that day he was driven out, thereby illustrating the verse, *Man does not lodge overnight in honor* (Ps. 49:24)."

I am puzzled by the point of Simeon's statement at **I:XIII.1.** I do not see how the parable is relevant to Adam as the story has been expounded here. For it was Eve who violated Adam's instructions, and the one error Adam made was stated above, "Man did not want to state the matter to Woman as the Holy One, blessed be he, had stated it to him, but rather he said to her, *Of the fruit of the tree which is in the midst of the garden God has said, You may not eat and* you may not touch it *lest you die.*" That has no bearing on Adam's violating his *own* instructions, which is the point of the story before us. Clearly, the point of pertinence comes at C, which intersects explicitly with the following: "Now what did Woman think to herself? All the things that my lord [Man] has taught me from the very beginning are lies." But that is on account of the exaggeration of Man's statement of God's instruction, that is to say, Man had built too high a fence around God's words. But that point has no bearing here. The upshot is that the parable intersects with, but does not illustrate, the materials before us. That forms a still stronger argument for the proposition that the person who has collected these materials as a thematic appendix has had very little role in making the materials up, and also had no strong theory of what he wished to say through the compilation of the document, beyond the mere development of a scrapbook on certain themes.

The pertinence of the second parable, **I:XIII.2,** is clear. Simeon's point is somewhat odd, however, since what he wishes to say is that by giving Man the commandment, God aroused his interest in that tree and led man to do what he did. So God bears a measure of guilt for the fall of humanity. F–G clearly is tacked on and out of place, since it does not revert to the parable at all and makes its own point, Psalm 49:24.

**I:XIV.**

1.   A.   On the very same day Man was formed, on the very same day Man

was made, on the very same day his form was shaped, on the very
same day he was turned into a mass of dough, on the very same day
his limbs were made and his various apertures were opened up, on
the very same day breath was put into him, on the very same day he
stood on his feet, on the very same day Eve was matched for him,
on the very same day he was put into the Garden of Eden, on the
very same day he was given the commandment, on the very same
day he went bad, on the very same day he was driven out and went
his way,

B. thereby illustrating the verse, *Man does not lodge overnight in honor*
(Ps. 49:24).

## I:XIV.

2. A. On the very same day two got into bed and four got out.
   B. R. Judah b. Beterah says, "On the very same day two got into bed
   and seven got out."

## I:XIV.

3. A. On that very same day three decrees were issued against Man,
   B. as it is said, *And to Man he said, Because you have obeyed your wife, cursed
   is the ground on your account; in labor you shall eat its produce . . . thorns
   also and thistles it will produce for you, and you shall eat the herb of the
   field* (Gen. 3:17–18).
   C. When the First Man heard what the Holy One, blessed be he, said
   to him, namely, "*You shall eat the herb of the field,*" his limbs trembled, and he said before him, "Lord of the world, shall I and my
   cattle eat in a single crib?"
   D. Said to him the Holy One, blessed be he, "Since your limbs have
   trembled, *in the sweat of your face you shall eat bread* (Gen. 3:19)."
   E. And just as three decrees were issued against the First Man, so three
   decrees were issued against Woman.
   F. For it is said, *To the woman he said, I will greatly multiply your pain and
   your travail; in pain you shall bring forth children; and your desire will be
   to your husband; and he shall rule over you* (Gen. 3:16).
   G. *I will greatly [multiply] your pain* refers to the fact that, when a woman produces menstrual blood at the beginning of her period, it is
   painful for her.
   H. *I will [greatly] multiply your pain* refers to the fact that when a woman has sexual relations for the first time, it is painful for her.

I. *In pain you shall conceive* refers to the fact that, when a woman first gets pregnant, for the first three months her face is distorted and pale.

No. 1 goes over familiar materials. It is tacked on because it goes over the same prooftext as is given earlier. No. 2 carries forward the formulaic pattern of No. 1, and so does No. 3.

## I:XV.

1. A. When evening fell, the First Man saw the world growing dark as the sun set. He thought to himself, "Woe is me! Because I turned rotten, the Holy One, blessed be he, on my account brings darkness to the entire world." But he did not know that that is how things are.

   B. At dawn when he saw the world grow light with sunrise, he rejoiced. He went and built altars and brought an ox whose horns extended beyond its hooves and offered it up as a whole offering [retaining no parts for his own food],

   C. as it is said, *And it shall please the Lord better than an ox whose horns extend beyond its hooves* (Ps. 69:32).

## I:XV.

2. A. As to the ox that the First Man offered, the bull that Noah offered, and the ram that Abraham, our father, offered in place of his son on the altar, all of them were *beasts in which the horns extended beyond the hooves.*

   B. For it is said, *And Abraham looked up, and he saw, lo, another ram, caught by its horns in the bush* (Gen. 22:13).

The anthology on the First Man runs its course. We have at No. 1 a set piece, which, so far as I can see, does not continue any prior discussion. It is simply inserted whole. No. 2 is attached to No. 1 because of its pertinence to the theme of the particularly desirable animal for sacrifice.

## I:XVI.

1. A. At that moment three groups of ministering angels descended, with lutes, lyres, and diverse other musical instruments in their hands, and with [the First Man] they recited a song.

B. For it is said, *A Psalm, a song, for the sabbath day. It is good to give thanks to the Lord . . . to declare your lovingkindness in the morning and your faithfulness at night* (Ps. 92:1–3).

C. *To declare your lovingkindness in the morning* refers to the world to come, as it is said, *They are new every morning, great is your faithfulness* (Lam. 3:23).

D. *And your faithfulness at night* refers to this world, which is compared to night, as it is said, *The burden of Dumah. One calls to me out of Seir, watchman, what of the night? Watchman, what of the night?* (Is. 21:11).

The long narrative about the First Man on the day of the fall from grace proceeds on its own lines. The rhetorical-formulaic that links one piece to the next, "on that very same day," or, "at that time," provides the outline of a reasonably cogent narrative program.

**I:XVII.**

1.  A. At that time said the Holy One, blessed be he, "If I do not judge the snake, I shall turn out to destroy the entire world."

    B. And he thought to himself, "This one that I crowned and made king over the entire world has gone wrong and eaten of the fruit of the tree."

    C. He forthwith turned on him and cursed him,

    D. as it is said, *And the Lord God said to the snake* (Gen. 3:14).

    E. R. Yose says, "If the curse concerning the snake had not been stated in Scripture [following Goldin, p. 15:] after theirs [the curse of Man and Woman], [the snake] would have destroyed the entire world."

The narrative proceeds apace. The reason for including it—the reference to the First Man and the fence that he (wrongly) erected around his words—has long since fallen from sight.

**I:XVIII.**

1.  A. When the Holy One, blessed be he, created the First Man, he formed a face on him both in front and in back,

    B. for it is said, *You have fashioned me in back and in front and laid your hand upon me* (Ps. 139:5).

    C. Then the ministering angels came down to destroy him, so the Holy One, blessed be he, took him and placed him under his wings, as it is said, *and laid your hand upon me.*

**I:XVIII.**

2. A. Another interpretation of the clause, *And laid your hand upon me:*

   B. Once [the First Man] went rotten, the Holy One, blessed be he, took away one of [the two faces he had originally given to Man].

**I:XVIII.**

3. A. On this basis [we derive the fact that] the First Man and the Temple, when they were created, were created with both of God's hands.

   B. How do we know that [when Man was created,] he was created with both hands?

   C. As it is said, *Your hands have made me and formed me* (Ps. 119:73).

   D. How do we know that the Temple was created with two hands?

   E. As it is said, *The sanctuary, O Lord, which your hands have established* (Ex. 15:17); *And he brought them to his holy border, the mountain, which his right hand had gotten* (Ps. 78:543); *The Lord shall reign for ever and ever* (Ex. 15:18).

The long narrative on the creation of the First Man reaches its conclusion with a final miscellany. Pertinent verses are adduced to provide a further fact, Nos. 1–2. No. 3 follows as an appropriate appendix.

I see four definitive traits of the scriptural story, as exemplified here. The first, and the paramount, trait is the profligate use of verses of Scripture. Scripture verses predominate and govern, and—more important than mere quantity—the amplification of the sense of those verses proves a dominant interest. Indeed, more often than not, in a scriptural story, the point of the story is to clarify the scriptural verse or its broader narrative. When we come to stories about sages, by contrast, we shall locate few prooftexts and slight concern for the exposition of the meaning of verses of Scripture. The sage story never takes as its point of tension and departure the clarification of the meaning of a verse of Scripture, and, it follows, citation of verses of Scripture will be economical and tangential to the sequence of action and thrust of narrative.

A second trait of the scriptural story is the invariably dominant role of the narrator (unseen, unidentified). The story is told not through dialogue alone or principally, but through the narrator's constant intervention. It is he who tells us what the snake was thinking (**I:VIII.1**) as well as what he did. The interest in describing action is not paramount; rather, interest lies in ascertaining motivation and the consequence of improper deed resulting from inappropriate motivation.

A third (already-familiar) trait, characteristic of the story in relationship to Scripture, is the redactor's insistence upon including along with a story other important exegeses of a verse of Scripture cited in the story. That accounts for the intrusion of **I:VIII.2,** interrupting the flow from **I:VIII.1.D** to **I:VIII.3.** The redactor's point of interest becomes clear: the verse, with focus on *its* exposition—whether through concrete narrative or through abstract paraphrase and amplification. Stories about sages do not ordinarily bear the freight of (to us, intruded) exegeses of verses cited in those stories. They run their course, beginning to end, without so sizable an interruption as is represented by **I:VIII.2** and its counterparts throughout. An instance is at **I:VIII.4,** continuing **I:VIII.3.** "At that moment" provides the narrator with the form of a story, but the substance is a set-piece exegesis of Genesis 3:16. In terms of the original classification, **I:VIII.4** constitutes nothing more than the setting for a saying, or a "precipitant." **I:IX.1f.** follows suit; once more, "at that time" makes up whatever narrative we are going to be given. **I:X.1** does not change the picture. **I:VIII.5,** of course, does not present us with anything like a story. It is important, however, and serves the principal interest of the ultimate redactor of the entire composite.

A fourth trait of the scriptural story is the striking absence of movement, of a tale with beginning, middle, end, of tension and resolution, not to mention sustained interest in the characterization of the figures at hand. Scriptural story figures ordinarily serve as cardboard characters, composing a tableau, which, frozen and at rest, in the aggregate makes its point. Stories about sages, by contrast, make their point not through a fixed and stationary tableau but through the unfolding of action, whether "he said to him . . . , he said to him . . . ," or the tale of what actually is done.

When we come to **I:XII.1** through inductive observation of the unfolding narrative, we therefore begin to realize that what we have before us hardly constitutes a story at all. The ultimate interest of the redactor predominates not only in the selection and arrangement of what is before us, but also in the substance of the narrative. In fact, the narrative tells no story at all but—as we observed tentatively a moment ago–presents a setting for an exposition that is not a narrative at all. **I:XII.1** pretends to "narrate" the order of creation, but in fact it proposes to demonstrate the proposition that the liturgical psalms, recited on each day of the week in the Temple, form the counterpart to "events"—which are not events at all but rather stages in the unfolding of creation and the fall of Man. **I:XIII.1–2** follows suit. The parables do not constitute stories, for reasons already specified. **I:XIV.1** presents the illusion of a narrative by beginning, "On the very same day," which functions as "at that hour." In fact, we have no narrative at all, up to **I:XIV.3.** Then we do have a brief narrative, **I:XIV.3.C–D,** but the narrative contains no action, recounted or implied. Rather, it simply allows us to juxtapose two verses, which tell a lesson. What has been said applies to the remainder of the anthology, which contains narratives but little action, making points not so much through what happens or even through what is said as through the invocation of verses of Scripture. As a generalization, therefore, we may say that the story on a theme drawn from Scripture is not a story at all. We may then distinguish both in subject matter and in narrative technique the story based on Scripture and the story based on the sage, that is, the story within the setting of the written Torah, as read by sages, and the story within the oral Torah, as read by the same authorities.

Having made the distinction, we need not dwell on the point of these stories. A brief catalogue suffices to show the disparate and random topics. These excerpts underline the striking difference between a Midrash-compilation interested in narrative and Midrash-compilation focused upon propositions:

| I:VIII. | One should not make too high a fence around one's words, in such a way as to distort the meaning. |
|---|---|
| I:IX. | If one wishes something one should not desire, he gets the opposite of what he wants. |
| I:X. | Had the curse of the snake not taken place, Israel would have had a good servant. |
| I:XI. | The snake envied man. |
| I:XII. | *Man does not lodge overnight in honor.* |
| I:XIII. | *Man does not lodge overnight in honor.* But the further point of the parable is that a commandment may serve to rouse one's interest in sinning. |
| I:XIV. | *Man does not lodge overnight in honor.* |
| I:XV. | The course of the natural world brought Man reassurance, and he makes a sacrifice to express his gratification. |
| I:XVI. | This world contrasted to world to come. |
| I:XVII. | The snake was cursed. |
| I:XVIII. | Creation of Man and Temple were both done with God's hands. |

The opening point ties the entire anthology to the larger setting in which it has been located. It is difficult to see how propositions in particular (as distinct from the larger general theme) join one item to the next, fore or aft. Nor can I explain the order of the propositions. I see a group formed by **I:X-I-XIV,** but otherwise it seems to me nothing more than a set of miscellanies, not spun out around a common proposition or sequence of points, but all joined, more or less randomly, solely because of an unfolding theme.

In conclusion, let us answer the questions with which we began.

First, does the subject matter—scriptural themes—generate its own narrative literary conventions that differ from those that guide writers of stories about sages? On the surface, the answer clearly is yes. The materials in parts IVff. will confirm that impression.

Second, do we find propositions emerging from stories on scriptural themes? Clearly we do, but these do not on the surface relate to large historical questions, such as we shall locate in the stories about sages. This brings us to the archetypal sage, Moses, "our lord," and stories told about a scriptural figure who also falls into the classification of the sage.

## III. NARRATIVE AND MIDRASH: (2) MOSES AND ISRAEL

Moses, the mediating figure, and others of his classification, such as Abraham, now come to the fore. Do stories about Moses in particular exhibit traits characterizing stories about scriptural figures or traits indicating (as we shall presently see) stories about sages? The answer to that question will tell us whether the point of origin of the theme of a story—the written Torah or Scripture, the oral Torah or the life of the sage of the Mishnah—imposes points of narrative differentiation upon the narrative and doctrinal program of the story itself. Moses is called "our Rabbi," and he serves as the paragon of the sage. At the same time, of course, he is a scriptural hero, so he forms the bridge between the model of virtuous hero deriving from Scripture, the written Torah, on the one side, and the counterpart deriving from the world of sages, that is, the realm of the oral Torah, on the other. The figure of Moses allows us to find out whether merely because a sage derives from Scripture, that is, the written Torah, stories about him will differ from stories about sages of the oral Torah. The answer is, they do. And that fact proves the validity of the distinction between the scriptural story and the sage story.

One decisive point of differentiation is now proved. Stories about the first man make profligate use of verses of Scripture. Verses predominate and govern, and amplifying the sense of those verses is a primary interest of redactors. That is why narratives about scriptural topics are called Midrash: they always contain an element of exegesis of particular passages of Scripture. In stories about sages, by contrast, we shall locate few prooftexts and slight concern for the exposition of the meaning of scriptural verses. The focus is on the sage and the event at hand, and exegesis of a verse of Scripture, where it occurs, takes a subordinate position. Further differences will soon appear.

The first example deals with a hero of the written Torah, Abraham, and one of the oral Torah, Hanina b. Dosa. The same point is made with reference to both figures.

### VIII:VI.

1.    A. Just as the righteous men in ancient times were pious, so their cattle were pious.

      B. They say that the cattle of Abraham, our father, never went into a house that contained an idol,

      C. as it is said, *For I have cleared the house and made room for the camels* (Gen. 24:31), meaning, *I have cleared the house of teraphim.*

      D. And on what account does Scripture say, *And made room for the camels?*

      E. This teaches that they would not enter Laban the Aramaean's house until they had cleared away all the idols from before them.

### VIII:VI.

2.    A. There was the case of the ass of R. Hanina b. Dosa, which bandits stole and tied up in the courtyard. They set before it straw, barley, and water, but it would not eat or drink.

      B. They said, "Why should we leave it here to die and make a stink for us in the courtyard?" They went and opened the gate and sent it out, and it went along, braying, until it came to the house of R. Hanina b. Dosa.

      C. When it got near the house, [Hanina's] son heard its braying.

      D. He said to him, "Father, it appears to me that the braying is like the braying of our beast."

      E. He said to him, "My son, open the gate for it, for it must be nearly dying of starvation."

      F. He went and opened the gate for it, and put before it straw, barley, and water, and it ate and drank.

G.  Therefore they say: Just as the righteous men in ancient times were pious, so their cattle were pious.

The contrast between the two stories could not be drawn more sharply. In the story about the biblical hero, prooftext follows prooftext. In fact, nothing like a narrative appears. "They say" that such and such did or did not do so and so: hardly a story at all. Then comes a lesson, E. By contrast, making the same point using Hanina's ass does involve a fully expounded narrative. The hero is the animal, not the authority. The story works out its message without the need for G, since the point is made within the limits and discipline of the story itself, with its point of tension—the stolen beast that finds its way home, that is released because of its own pious behavior— and the resolution thereof. The juxtaposed stories indicate that where the written Torah supplies the materials for a narrative, the consequent tale hardly qualifies as a story at all.

We come now to stories about the rabbi *par excellence,* Moses "our lord" or Rabbi.

## XII:I.

5.  A.  And there are those who say that for this reason it is said, *Every member of the house of Israel wept for Aaron for thirty days:*
    B.  Whoever can see Eleazar and Phineas, sons of high priests, standing and weeping, and not join in the weeping?

## XII:II.

1.  A.  At that moment Moses asked for a death like the death of Aaron,
    B.  for he saw the bier of Aaron lying in state in great honor, with bands of ministering angels lamenting for him.
    C.  But did he ask for such a death in the presence of some other person? Was it not in the privacy of his own heart? But the Holy One, blessed be he, heard what he had whispered to himself.
    D.  And how do we know that Moses asked for a death like the death of Aaron and [the Holy One, blessed be he,] heard what he had whispered to himself?
    E.  As it is said, *Die in the mountain to which you go up, and be gathered to your people as Aaron your brother died in Mount Hor* (Deut. 32:50).

F. Thus you have learned that Moses asked for a death like the death of Aaron.

**XII:II.**

2.  A. At that time [the Holy One, blessed be he,] said to the angel of death, "Go, bring me the soul of Moses."

    B. The angel of death went and stood before him, saying to him, "Moses, give me your soul."

    C. Moses grew angry with him and said to him, "Where I am sitting you have no right even to stand, yet you have said, 'Give me your soul'!" He threw him out with outrage.

    D. Then the Holy One, blessed be he, said to Moses, "Moses, you have had enough of this world, for lo, the world to come is readied for you, for a place is prepared for you from the first six days of creation."

    E. For it is said, *And the Lord said, "Behold a place by me, and you shall stand upon the rock* (Ex. 33:21)."

    F. The Holy One, blessed be he, took the soul of Moses and stored it away under the throne of glory.

    G. And when he took it, he took it only with a kiss, as it is said, *By the mouth of the Lord* (Deut. 34:5).

**XII:II.**

3.  A. It is not the soul of Moses alone that is stored away under the throne of glory, but the souls of the righteous are stored away under the throne of glory,

    B. as it is said, *Yet the soul of my Lord shall be bound in the bundle of life with the Lord your God* (1 Sam. 25:29).

    C. Is it possible to imagine that that is the case also with the souls of the wicked?

    D. Scripture says, *And the souls of your enemies, those he shall sling out as from the hollow of a sling* (1 Sam. 25:29).

    E. For even though one is tossed from place to place, it does not know on what to come to rest.

    F. So too the souls of the wicked go roving and fluttering about the world and do not know where to come to rest.

**XII:II.**

4.  A. The Holy One, blessed be he, further said to the angel of death, "Go, bring me the soul of Moses."

B. The angel of death went in search of him in his place but did not find him. He went to the Great Sea and said to it, "Has Moses come here?"

C. The sea replied, "From the day on which the Israelites passed through me, I have not seen him."

D. He went to the mountains and hills and said to them, "Has Moses come here?"

E. They replied, "From the day on which Israel received the Torah on Mount Sinai, we have not seen him."

F. He went to Sheol and Destruction and said to them, "Has Moses come here?"

G. They said to him, "His name we have heard, but him we have never seen."

H. He went to the ministering angels and said to them, "Has Moses come here?"

I. They said to him, "*God understands his way and knows his place* [Goldin: cf. Job 28:23]. God has hidden him away for the life of the world to come, and no one knows where."

J. So it is said, *But wisdom, where shall it be found? and where is the place of understanding? Man does not know its price, nor is it found in the land of the living. The deep says, "It is not in me," and the sea says, "It is not with me."... Destruction and death say, "We have heard a rumor thereof with our ears* ( Job 28:13–15, 22)."

**XII:II.**

5. A. Joshua too was seated and grieving for Moses,

   B. until the Holy One, blessed be he, said to him, "Joshua, why are you grieving for Moses? *Moses, my servant, is dead* ( Joshua 1:2)."

The narrative begins at **XII:II** with the now-familiar "at that moment," which introduces a narrative effect for the statement of a proposition on a scriptural theme or passage. **XII:II** then does not tell a story at all. It simply makes the point that Moses asked to die the way Aaron had. That proposition is proved by reference to the indicated prooftexts. But **XII:II.2** (complemented by No. 3) does seem to me a fine example of a story. The narrative has a beginning, middle, and end: the angel of death is told to go and get Moses' soul, but Moses refuses to hand it over, until God tells Moses that he has to do so. We cannot point to the story as an example of dramatic art, but it is more than a mere setting for a wise saying, on the one side, or proof or illustration of a proposition, on the other. **XII:II.4** forms a far more powerful story on precisely the same theme. Now we have a sequence of stunning conversations, within a narrative framework that makes its impact upon what is said. This second story makes the same point as did the first—Moses' soul is hidden God knows where—but it makes it in a massive, dramatic framework, invoking heaven and earth, the sea, the mountains, and so on. And yet, if we ask once again, Does the story exhibit marks of dramatic intent? the answer is negative. Still more consequential, the story unfolds through what is said, rather than both through what is said and through what is done. No described action carries a part of the burden of the story. In fact, in the several stories, we note, nothing much happens: no one gets killed, no building gets burned. These stories contain only the thinnest narrative core of action, explicit or implicit.

**XVII:II.**

1. A. **And get yourself ready to learn Torah, for it does not come as an inheritance to you:** how so?

**XVII:II**

2. A. When Moses, our master, saw that his sons had no knowledge of the Torah that would qualify them to succeed him in the leadership, he cloaked himself and stood in prayer.

  B. He said before him, "Lord of the world, tell me who will go in [and] who will come out at the head of all this people?"

  C. For it is said, *And Moses spoke to the Lord, saying, "Let the Lord, the God of the spirits of all flesh, set a man over the congregation, who may go out before them and who may come in before them"* (Num. 27:15ff.).

  D. Said the Holy One, blessed be he, to Moses, *"Moses, take Joshua"* (Num. 27:15).

  E. Said the Holy One, blessed be he, to Moses, "Go and act as his voice so that he may give an exposition in your presence at the head of all the great men of Israel [and that will signify that he is heir]."

  F. At that moment Moses said to Joshua, "Joshua, as to this people that I am handing over to you, I am giving you not goats but kids, not sheep but lambs, for as yet they are not much experienced in the practice of religious duties, and they have not yet reached the growth of goats and sheep."

G. So it is said, *If you do not know, O you fairest among women, go your way forth by the footsteps of the flock and feed your kids beside the shepherds' tents* (Song 1:8).

The base clause is illustrated by the case of Moses' sons, but only in a general way. For the focus of the story is Moses' leaving the people in Joshua's hands and warning Joshua that the people is still in an immature state. This story has nothing to do with the exposition of the notion that the Torah is no one's inheritance, although the story does intersect with that notion. What follows is tacked on because it invokes the prooftext, Song 1:8. The same narrative traits characterize the materials at hand as mark the earlier stories about Moses. That is to say, very little actually happens, and the narrative framework serves only to define the arena for dialogue. The story such as it is makes its point through that dialogue. Moses realizes that his sons will not inherit, and God tells him to choose Joshua. Moses does that and gives him some advice, and the tale ends.

In conclusion, let us answer the questions with which we began.

First, does the subject matter—scriptural themes—generate its own narrative literary conventions that differ from those guiding writers of stories about sages? On the surface, the answer clearly is yes.

Do we find propositions emerging from stories on scriptural themes? Clearly these propositions are particular and limited; they do not on the surface relate to large historical questions. Stories about the archetypal sage, Moses, "our lord" turn out not very different from stories on other scriptural topics. The striking contrast in the narrative qualities of the story about Hanina's and Abraham's beasts tells the whole tale. These propositions will take on greater power when we turn to sage stories.

## IV. NARRATIVE, BUT NOT MIDRASH: THE SAGE

While we shall observe numerous differences in narrative conventions governing Scripture stories as against sage stories, three prove definitive:

1. The story about a sage has a beginning, middle, and end, and the story about a sage also rests not only (or mainly) on verbal exchanges ("he said to him . . . , he said to him. . . . "), but on described (occasionally, merely implied) action.

2. The story about a sage unfolds from a point of tension and conflict to a clear resolution and remission of the conflict.

3. The story about a sage rarely invokes a verse of Scripture and never proves a proposition concerning the meaning of a verse of Scripture.

The traits of stories about scriptural figures and themes in retrospect prove opposite:

1. In the story about a scriptural hero there is no beginning, middle, and end, and little action. The burden of the narrative is carried by "he said to him . . . , he said to him. . . ." Described action is rare and plays slight role in the unfolding of the narrative. Often the narrative consists of little more than a setting for a saying, and the point of the narrative is conveyed not through what is told but through the cited saying.

2. The story about a scriptural hero is worked out as a tableau, with description of the components of the stationary tableau placed at the center. There is little movement, no point of tension that is resolved.

3. The story about a scriptural hero always invokes verses from Scripture and makes the imputation of meaning to those verses the center of interest.

Presented with stories taken from The Fathers According to Rabbi Nathan that lack all markings to indicate their subject matter, we could readily identify those focused upon scriptural heroes as distinct from those centered upon sages. When the narrators wished to talk about sages, they invoked one set of narrative conventions, deemed appropriate to that topic, and when they made up stories on scriptural heroes and topics, they appealed to quite different narrative conventions.

We turn to one type of sage story—the one that narrates the sage's role in history—to illustrate these points. The sage here plays a public, not solely a private, role. Within the genealogical theory of Israel as one extended family, the sage as supernatural father forms the critical element in the history of the family, Israel. That history, of course, is defined by the encounter with Rome in particular. If the sage stands for Israel, then Rome will be represented by its *persona,* and that can only be the emperor. All stories in The Fathers According to Rabbi Nathan that do not deal with the lives and deeds of sages concern the large historical question facing Israel—its history in this world and destiny in the world to come. The same issue predominates in the propositions of Genesis Rabbah, Leviticus Rabbah, and Pesiqta deRab Kahana. History finds its definition in a single event, the encounter with Rome, which involves two aspects: (1) the destruction of the Temple and the sages' role in dealing with that matter; (2) the (associated, consequent) repression of Torah sages and their study. Israel's history in this world works itself out in the encounter with Rome, Israel's counterpart and opposite, and that history in the world coming soon will see a reversal of roles. The centrality of study of the Torah in securing Israel's future forms the leitmotif of the stories at hand.

We therefore take up the important story about the destruction of the Temple. That protracted story is set in an exegesis of the saying in The Fathers that the world stands on deeds of lovingkindness. These, then, are found by the exegete at Hosea 6:6, and the intrusion of that verse carries in its wake a narrative—not a story but a narrative setting for a saying—about Yohanan ben Zakkai and his disciple, Joshua, in the ruins of the Temple. Only at the end of the matter do we find the major historical story of the destruction.

**IV:V.**

1.   A.   **On deeds of lovingkindness:** how so?

      B.   Lo, Scripture says, *For I desire mercy and not sacrifice, [and the knowledge of God rather than burnt offerings]* (Hos. 6:6).

      C.   To begin with, the world was created only on account of lovingkindness.

      D.   For so it is said, *For I have said, the world is built with lovingkindness, in the very heavens you establish your faithfulness* (Ps. 89:3).

**IV:V.**

2.   A.   One time [after the destruction of the Temple] Rabban Yohanan b. Zakkai was going forth from Jerusalem, with R. Joshua following after him. He saw the house of the sanctuary lying in ruins.

      B.   R. Joshua said, "Woe is us for this place which lies in ruins, the place in which the sins of Israel used to come to atonement."

      C.   He said to him, "My son, do not be distressed. We have another mode of atonement, which is like [atonement through sacrifice], and what is that? It is deeds of lovingkindness.

      D.   "For so it is said, *For I desire mercy and not sacrifice, [and the knowledge of God rather than burnt offerings]* (Hos. 6:6)."

**IV:V.**

3.   A.   So we find in the case of Daniel, that most desirable man, that he carried out deeds of lovingkindness.

      B.   And what are the deeds of lovingkindness that Daniel did?

      C.   If you say that he offered whole offerings and sacrifices, do people offer sacrifices in Babylonia?

      D.   And has it not in fact been said, *Take heed that you not offer your whole offerings in any place which you see but in the place which the Lord will select in the territory of one of the tribes. There you will offer up your whole offerings* (Deut. 12:13–14).

      E.   When, then, were the deeds of lovingkindness that Daniel did?

      F.   He would adorn the bride and make her happy, join a cortege for the deceased, give a penny to a pauper, pray three times every day,

      G.   and his prayer was received with favor,

      H.   for it is said, *And when Daniel knew that the writing was signed, he went into his house—his windows were open in his upper chamber toward Jerusalem—and he kneeled upon his knees three times a day and prayed and gave thanks before his God as he did aforetime* (Dan. 6:11).

This entire construction serves as a prologue to what follows, an account of the destruction of the Temple, which forms the background to **IV:VI.1.** We have not a story but a narrative that forms a setting for a saying, so **IV:V.2.** From "One time . . . ," we are given the occasion on which the colloquy of B–C took place. Still, a narrative side emerges in the implicit movement from B to C. But classifying the passage as a story seems to me not justified.

## IV:VI.

1.  A. Now when Vespasian came to destroy Jerusalem, he said to [the inhabitants of the city,] "Idiots! Why do you want to destroy this city and burn the house of the sanctuary? For what do I want of you, except that you send me a bow or an arrow [as marks of submission to my rule], and I shall go on my way?"

    B. They said to him, "Just as we sallied out against the first two who came before you and killed them, so shall we sally out and kill you."

    C. When Rabban Yohanan b. Zakkai heard, he proclaimed to the men of Jerusalem, saying to them, "My sons, why do you want to destroy this city and burn the house of the sanctuary? For what does he want of you, except that you send him a bow or an arrow, and he will go on his way?"

    D. They said to him, "Just as we sallied out against the first two who came before him and killed them, so shall we sally out and kill him."

    E. Vespasian had stationed men near the walls of the city, and whatever they heard, they would write on an arrow and shoot out over the wall. [They reported] that Rabban Yohanan b. Zakkai was a loyalist of Caesar's.

    F. After Rabban Yohanan b. Zakkai had spoken to them one day, a second, and a third, and the people did not accept his counsel, he sent and called his disciples, R. Eliezer and R. Joshua, saying to them, "My sons, go and get me out of here. Make me an ark and I shall go to sleep in it."

    G. R. Eliezer took the head and R. Joshua the feet, and toward sunset they carried him until they came to the gates of Jerusalem.

    H. The gate keepers said to them, "Who is this?"

I. They said to him, "It is a corpse. Do you not know that a corpse is not kept overnight in Jerusalem?"

J. They said to them, "If it is a corpse, take him out," so they took him out and brought him out at sunset, until they came to Vespasian.

K. They opened the ark and he stood before him.

L. He said to him, "Are you Rabban Yohanan b. Zakkai? Indicate what I should give you."

M. He said to him, "I ask from you only Yavneh, to which I shall go, and where I shall teach my disciples, establish prayer [Goldin: a prayer house], and carry out all of the religious duties."

N. He said to him, "Go and do whatever you want."

O. He said to him, "Would you mind if I said something to you?"

P. He said to him, "Go ahead."

Q. He said to him, "Lo, you are going to be made sovereign."

R. He said to him, "How do you know?"

S. He said to him, "It is a tradition of ours that the house of the sanctuary will be given over not into the power of a commoner but of a king, for it is said, *And he shall cut down the thickets of the forest with iron, and Lebanon* [which refers to the Temple] *shall fall by a mighty one*" (Is. 10:34).

T. People say that not a day, two, or three passed before a delegation came to him from his city indicating that the [former] Caesar had died and they had voted for him to ascend the throne.

U. They brought him a [Goldin:] catapult and drew it up against the wall of Jerusalem.

V. They brought him cedar beams and put them into the catapult, and he struck them against the wall until a breach had been made in it. They brought the head of a pig and put it into the catapult and tossed it toward the limbs that were on the Temple altar.

W. At that moment Jerusalem was captured.

X. Rabban Yohanan b. Zakkai was in session and with trembling was looking outward, in the way that Eli had sat and waited: *Lo, Eli sat upon his seat by the wayside watching, for his heart trembled for the ark of God* (1 Sam. 4:13).

Y. When Rabban Yohanan b. Zakkai heard that Jerusalem had been destroyed and the house of the sanctuary burned in flames, he tore his garments, and his disciples tore their garments, and they wept and cried and mourned.

**IV:VI.**

2.  A.  Scripture says, *Open your doors, O Lebanon, that the fire may devour your cedars* (Zech. 11:1).

    B.  That verse refers to the high priests who were in the sanctuary [on the day it was burned].

    C.  They took their keys in their hands and threw them upward, saying before the Holy One, blessed be he, "Lord of the world, here are your keys which you entrusted to us, for we have not been faithful custodians to carry out the work of the king and to receive support from the table of the king."

**IV:VI.**

3.  A.  Abraham, Isaac, and Jacob, and the twelve tribes were weeping, crying, and mourning.

**IV:VI.**

4.  A.  Scripture says, *Wail, O cypress tree, for the cedar is fallen, because the glorious ones are spoiled. Wail, O you oaks of Bashan, for the strong forest is come down* (Zech. 11:2).

    B.  *Wail, O cypress tree, for the cedar is fallen* refers to the house of the sanctuary.

    C.  *Because the glorious ones are spoiled* refers to Abraham, Isaac, and Jacob, and the twelve tribes [who were weeping, crying, and mourning].

    D.  *Wail, O you oaks of Bashan* refers to Moses, Aaron, and Miriam.

    E.  *For the strong forest is come down* refers to the house of the sanctuary.

    F.  *Hark the wailing of the shepherds, for their glory is spoiled* (Zech. 11:3) refers to David and Solomon his son.

    G.  *Hark the roaring of young lions, for the thickets of the Jordan are spoiled* (Zech. 11:3) speaks of Elijah and Elisha.

While the larger composite in which the story occurs bears its burden of Midrash-exegesis, the story forms a cogent and complete statement on its own. It unfolds in a smooth way from beginning to end. It serves, overall, as an account of the power of the Torah to lead Israel through historical crises. Specifically, the storyteller at three points—(1) the comparison of Vespasian and the Jewish troops and Yohanan and the Jewish troops, (2) Vespasian and Yohanan in their direct encounter, then at the end, (3) the destruction itself—places the sage into the scale against the emperor, Israel against Rome. Then the Torah makes the difference, for, in the end, Israel will outweigh Rome. The story's themes all form part of the larger theme of Torah-learning. The centerpiece is Yohanan's knowledge that the Temple is going to be destroyed. This he acquired in two ways. First of all, his observation of the conduct of the Israelite army led him to that conclusion. But, second and more important, his knowledge of the Torah told him the deeper meaning of the event, which was in two parts. In the first part of the event, Rome got a new emperor. On the other hand, Israel got its program for the period beyond the destruction. The opening unit of the story, A–T, seems to me seamless. I can point to no element that could have been omitted without seriously damaging the integrity of the story. I see no intrusions of any kind. If that is a correct judgment, then the climax must come only at S, confirmed by T and what follows. That is to say, it is the power of the sage to know the future because of his knowledge of the Torah. Establishing a place for the teaching of disciples and the performance of other holy duties forms a substrate of the same central theme. And yet, deeper still, lies the theme of the counterpart and opposite: Israel and Rome, sage and emperor. That motif occurs originally at A–C, where Vespasian and Yohanan say precisely the same thing, with one difference. Vespasian calls the Jewish army "idiots," and Yohanan calls the troops, "my sons." Otherwise the statements are the same. And the replies, B and D, are also the same. So the first episode sets up the emperor and the sage as opposites and counterparts.

The second episode shows the people unwilling to listen to the sage—the emperor has no role here—leading the sage to conclude that it is time to "make an ark and go to sleep in it." If I had to choose a point of reference, it would be not the sleep of death—then Yohanan would have wanted a bier—but the ark of Noah. Yohanan then forms the counterpart, in the storyteller's choice of the word at hand, to Noah, who will save the world beyond the coming deluge. I then see F–G as a chapter in a complete story. E, on the one side, and H–J, on the other, link that cogent chapter to the larger context. E prepares us to understand why Vespasian recognizes Yohanan, an important detail added precisely where it had to come, and H–J forms the necessary bridge to what is coming.

The next component of the unitary story again places Vespasian in the balance against Yohanan. Now Yohanan tells Vespasian what is going to happen. Each party rises to power as a direct outcome of the destruction of the Temple: sage versus emperor, one in the scale against the other. The colloquy with Vespasian, L–S, forms the only part of the story to rely upon a narrative consisting of "he said to him . . . he said to him. . . ." The point, of course, is clear, as already stated. Then comes the necessary denouement, in two parts. First, the Temple actually was destroyed, and we are told how in T–W; second, Yohanan responded in mourning, X–Y. Here too we have that same counterpart and opposite: Rome, then Israel, with Israel represented by the sage, Rome by the emperor. What follows, of course, is not narrative, let alone story. **IV:VI.2** provides an exegisis A–B, followed by a colloquy. **IV:VI.3** is a singleton, and **IV:VI.4** joins the destruction of the Temple to the history of Israel and its heroes, all of whom wept as did Yohanan. But I do not see in the inclusion of **IV:VI.4** an attempt to compare Yohanan to the named heroes. This is virtually certain, since the story itself at **IV:VI.1.X** invokes the figure of Eli, who is noteworthy for his omission in **IV:VI.4.**

A simple point emerges in the sage story before us: through knowledge of the Torah the sage leads Israel toward the age to come, when Israel will supplant Rome. The leadership of zealots on the battlefield led to the destruction of the Temple, the senseless destruction of the food supply of Jerusalem, the calamity that had overtaken Israel. The leadership of the sages, armed with foresight and backed by God, will show the right way. The story invokes these narrative conventions: the story about a sage has a beginning, middle, and end; the story about a

sage also rests not only on verbal exchanges ("he said to him
..., he said to him..."), but on (described or implicit) action;
the story about a sage unfolds from a point of tension and conflict to a clear resolution and remission of the conflict; the story about a sage never proves a proposition concerning the
meaning of a verse of Scripture. Does the subject matter—
sages—generate its own narrative literary conventions that
differ from those that guide writers of stories about scriptural
figures? Indeed so. But these conventions apply to all types of
stories about sages. Do we find cogent propositions emerging
from stories on sages? Yes, we do, and these propositions intersect, whether the story concerns the origin of the sage, his particular sagacity, or his role in the history of Israel. And the plan
and program of stories about sages do differ from those that
govern the narratives concerning scriptural heroes.

The story about a sage never proves a proposition concerning the meaning of a verse of Scripture. The subject matter—
the sage, hero of the oral Torah, as distinct from the hero of the
written Torah—does generate its own narrative literary conventions, differing from those that guide writers of stories
about scriptural figures, and a few remarkably cogent propositions do emerge from stories on sages.

## V. THE MEDIUM AND THE MESSAGE

We search in vain for points of differentiation among the
three trends of rabbinic Bible interpretation, that is, among the
messages of Midrash-as-narrative, the messages of Midrash-as-
exegesis-yielding-proposition and the messages of Midrash-
as-proposition-yielding-exegesis. Midrash-as-story makes
points that in no way would have astonished the authorships
and compositors of other Midrash-compilations.

By contrast, the medium of the sage story provides the authorship of The Fathers According to Rabbi Nathan an opportunity to make a number of points quite distinctive to that
group. We can show that fact by comparing the message con-

veyed through sage stories with the messages of the base document, The Fathers (or tractate Avot), which The Fathers According to Rabbi Nathan amplifies and interprets—a "Midrash" in the simplest sense. When we compare the propositions of the present document with those of the composition on which it stands, we see that the medium of the sage story, with all its distinctive traits, bears a message of its own as well. And that fact underlines the point just now made, that whatever the mode of Midrash as exegesis of Scripture, the points remain constant and cogent.

To turn to the case at hand, the authorship of The Fathers According to Rabbi Nathan has presented a set of propositions that would have surprised the authorship of The Fathers. And, as we shall now briefly see, in the stories not told by the earlier authorship but narrated by the later one, we find evidences of a considerable shift in viewpoint and perspective. Points of emphasis in The Fathers According to Rabbi Nathan lacking development in The Fathers include: (1) an assertion that one should study the Torah and other things will take care of themselves—a claim of a more supernatural character than the one in The Fathers; (2) a portrayal of sages as supernatural figures rather than mainly as political leaders, eager to conciliate and reconcile the other; (3) an eschatological answer given to the teleological question—an answer altogether lacking in the earlier document.

This third point requires a brief explanation. The sayings collected in The Fathers focus on the individual and his or her personal salvation in the life of the world to come. The shift in The Fathers According to Rabbi Nathan is to the nation as a whole and national salvation in the coming age, distinguished from this historical epoch. It follows that, for the authorship before us, the definitive category is social, therefore national, raising the issue not of the private person but of holy Israel, not of the private life and destiny, but of the national history and future of Israel. The concern, then, is what will happen to the nation in time to come, meaning the coming age, not the coming life of the resurrection. The systemic teleology shifts its focus to the holy people, and, alongside, to the national history of the holy people—now and in the age to come. The Fathers According to Rabbi Nathan is consistent and one-sided when it addresses not so much the individual as the nation. The framers of The Fathers According to Rabbi Nathan redefine the teleology at hand and focus it upon historical and social categories, rather than upon issues emerging from the life and death of the individual. In so doing, they bring The Fathers According to Rabbi Nathan into close alignment with the propositions that emerge in Genesis Rabbah, Leviticus Rabbah, and Pesiqta deRab Kahana. But the authorship before us makes those points through sage stories rather than through Scripture stories, let alone through Midrash-exegeses or Midrash-propositions.

The Midrash-compilations that stress issues of salvation, like the sage stories we have reviewed just now, move far from the range of topics treated in The Fathers, just as the Midrash-exegeses and Midrash-propositions carry us far from the Mishnah, served by The Fathers. For sayings in that document do not allude to the destruction of the Temple and say nothing about Rome. A simple comparison between stories *not* told in The Fathers but told in The Fathers According to Rabbi Nathan, begins in that simple fact. Were we to rely upon The Fathers for knowledge of the world in which Israel lived—the circumstances in which the sayings before us were to be carried out—we would know nothing whatsoever. In The Fathers According to Rabbi Nathan the message of the sage story is twofold: the centrality of the sage and his Torah in the supernatural life of Israel, and the critical role of the sage in the movement of the age from this world, with Rome in command, to the coming age, the time of Israel and sages. But the sage story and the Scripture story do come together. In both cases the story concerns history. The medium fits the message: the sage story carries the burden of history. In bearing that heavy weight, the sage story finds its fit with the Scripture story, and the two kinds of narrative—both classified as story—join the vast propositional Midrash-compilations to repeat a single message, now on the authority of Scripture, now on the authority of the sage. That message proves particularly apt for the medium of the story, since when we speak of history and salvation, we find in narrative in general, and in the story of salvation in particular, a strikingly appropriate mode of discourse.

# 5. THE WORKINGS OF MIDRASH

# 7. The World of Rabbinic Bible Interpretation

We have described the workings of Midrash, as the ancient rabbis practiced the art of biblical interpretation, through the three major trends exhibited by whole Midrash-compilations. Yet Midrash-exegesis took yet another documentary form. That form is found in the two principal compositions devoted to Mishnah-exegesis, the Talmud of the Land of Israel (or Yerushalmi) and the Talmud of Babylonia (or Bavli), ca. 400 and 600 C.E., respectively. In two senses one might therefore classify the two Talmuds as Midrash-compilations as well. First, in them we find Midrash-exegesis, with the proviso that the base text is not Scripture but the Mishnah. Second, and more important, in them we also find Midrash-compositions, if not entire documents such as we have already reviewed. In the two Talmuds large-scale discourse takes shape around the sequence of Mishnah-paragraphs, read in the sequence of Mishnah-chapters as these unfold in Mishnah-tractates. This mode of organizing discourse is, of course, familiar from Sifra and Sifré to Numbers. In this way (as in others), the Midrash-exegesis of verses of Scripture parallels the Midrash-exegesis of passages of the Mishnah.

## I. SCRIPTURE AND THE ORGANIZATION OF THOUGHT

What is important to the unfolding of the three principal trends in Midrash-exegesis is that in the two Talmuds we find a reprise of all three modes of Midrash-exegesis and Midrash-compilation familiar from the sequence of documents we have surveyed, from Sifra and Sifré to Numbers, through Genesis

Rabbah, Leviticus Rabbah, Pesiqta deRab Kahana, and The Fathers According to Rabbi Nathan. It goes without saying that the methods of Midrash-interpretation, moreover, remain constant in the Talmuds. We shall now see that precisely as in Sifra and Sifré to Numbers the base verse governs the organization of thought, so in the two Talmuds, the exegesis of a given verse proceeds systematically and in an orderly way, clause by clause, so that thought follows the program of that verse. Just as in Genesis Rabbah, Leviticus Rabbah, and Pesiqta deRab Kahana, a powerful proposition generates exegesis of diverse verses of Scripture, all of them selected to test and validate the generative proposition, so in the two Talmuds, the authorships of sustained compositions that present propositions appeal to verses of Scripture for factual proof of those propositions. The sustained compositions presented by these two types of Midrash-document find counterparts, as we shall see, in the two Talmuds.

But the Talmud of Babylonia contains an unanticipated counterpart to the Midrash-document in yet a third aspect: the large and sustained thematic or propositional composition that in a Midrash-document we called a chapter, or a *pisqa* or a *parashah*, is found also within the Talmud of Babylonia. The several Midrash-compilations are composed of whole and fully spelled out statements, whether the exegesis of a sizable cluster of verses that add up to a *pisqa*, as in Sifré to Numbers, or the presentation of a large and internally cogent statement on a complete biblical unit of thought, as the *parashiyyot* in Genesis Rabbah, or the display of an equally large and still more coherent statement of a proposition proved through a systematic repertoire of verses of Scripture, as in the *pisqaot* of Pesiqta deRab Kahana. Moving yet a step further, we may say that what makes a Midrash-compilation whole is the conglomerate of its parts, and these parts comprise the *parashah* or the *pisqa*. Once we have recognized that unit in the construction of the Midrash-documents, we find in the Talmud of Babylonia a parallel mode of discourse. For the Talmud of Babylonia comprises not only large-scale discourse about sequential paragraphs of the Mishnah, but also large-scale interpretation of sequential verses of Scripture.

The Talmud of Babylonia is, in fact, a composite of both Mishnah-interpretation and Scripture-interpretation—both Midrash of the oral Torah and Midrash of the written Torah. In my probe of three tractates of the Talmud of the Land of Israel and the Talmud of Babylonia,* I found no material differences between the two Talmuds in the types of Midrash-exegeses presented by each. But I did find that while a negligible proportion of the large-scale compositions of the Talmud of the Land of Israel is devoted to the systematic exegesis of verses or topics of Scripture, a sizable part of the Talmud of Babylonia forms a counterpart to the Midrash-compilation at the level of the *pisqa* or *parashah*. In the sample of my probe, sixty percent of the sustained compositions address the exegesis of the Mishnah and its law, while forty percent provide equivalent, sustained exegesis of Scripture and its theology, including narrative.

When, therefore, we trace the three trends in Midrash as rabbinic Bible interpretation, we should realize that those trends come to literary expression in two ways. First, as we have seen, each trend dominates in a particular kind of Midrash-compilation. Second, as we shall now see, all three trends come to full and complete statement in the Talmud of Babylonia. In its vast enterprise of joining the two Torahs, written and oral, into a single statement, the authorship of the Talmud of Babylonia brought to a triumphant conclusion the work of Sinai, announced at The Fathers 1:1: *Moses received Torah at Sinai and handed it on.* . . . Midrash—the work of interpretation of Scripture as exegesis yielding propositions, interpretation of Scripture in the mode of propositions yielding exegesis, as well as interpretation of Scripture in the mode of the retelling of the scriptural story—reached its ultimate and

*Judaism: Classical Statement; The Evidence of the Bavli* (Chicago: University of Chicago Press, 1986).

conclusive statement not in a Midrash-document but in an important, if subordinated, component of the Talmud of Babylonia. The Talmud of Babylonia, read through the ongoing process of exegesis applied equally to it as to Scripture and the Mishnah, has defined Judaism from that time to the present.

## II. ORGANIZING PROPOSITIONS AROUND VERSES OF SCRIPTURE: THE YERUSHALMI

We begin with an example of how, in the Talmud of the Land of Israel, or Yerushalmi, discourse develops around the structure defined by exegesis of the topics of individual verses. We shall find ourselves entirely at home with the mode of discourse worked out in Sifra and Sifré to Numbers. In the following passage, Mishnah-passages appear in boldface type, and, when cited in the body of the Talmud, again cited in boldface type. The Yerushalmi is composed of four elements: a passage of the Mishnah, a passage of the Tosefta (cited also in boldface type), verses of Scripture occurring in both (cited in italics), and discourse particular to the Yerushalmi, given in plain type.

### TALMUD YERUSHALMI SANHEDRIN 10:4

A. **"The generation of the wilderness has no portion in the world to come and will not stand in judgment,**

B. **"for it is written, *In this wilderness they shall be consumed and there they shall die* (Num. 14:35)," the words of R. Aqiba.**

C. **R. Eliezar says, "Concerning them it says, *Gather my saints together to me, those that have made a covenant with me by sacrifice* (Ps. 50:5)."**

D. **"The party of Korah is not destined to rise up,**

E. **"for it is written, *And the earth closed upon them* (Num. 16:33) [—in this world].**

F. ***"And they perished from among the assembly* (Num. 16:33) [—in the world to come]," the words of R. Aqiba.**

G. **And R. Eliezar says, "Concerning them it says, *The Lord kills and resurrects, brings down to Sheol and brings up again* (1 Sam. 2:6)."**

The Mishnah-paragraph concerns a proposition, and the authorship draws upon Scripture for facts useful in testing the proposition as laid forth by each party. The verses of Scripture have not provided the framework of discourse, but the exegesis of those verses is critical to the unfolding of the passage.

I.  A. **"The generation of the wilderness has no portion in the world to come and will not live in the world to come,**

B. **"as it is said, *In this wilderness they shall be consumed and there they shall die* (Num. 14:35).**

C. **"*They shall be consumed*—in this world.**

D. **"*And there they will die*—in the world to come.**

E. **"And so it says, *Therefore I swore in my anger that they should not enter my rest* (Ps. 95:11)," the words of R. Aqiba.**

F. **R. Eliezer says, "Concerning them it is said, *Gather my saints together to me, those that have made a covenant with me by sacrifice* (Ps. 50:5)" [T. San. 13:10].**

G. R. Joshua says, "*I have sworn an oath and confirmed it* (Ps. 119:106).

H. Hananiah nephew of R. Joshua says, **"It is written, *Therefore I swore in my anger . . .* (Ps. 95:11)—**

I. *"In my anger did I swear, but I retract it"* [T. San. 13:11]

J. It was taught, **R. Simeon b. Menassia says, "Concerning them does Scripture state, *Gather to me my faithful ones, who made a covenant with me by sacrifice!* (Ps. 50:5).**

K. **"*My faithful ones*—who acted faithfully with me.**

L. **"*Who have made a covenant with me*—who are cut in my behalf.**

M. **"*With me by sacrifice*—who exalted me and are sacrificed in my name."**

N. It was taught: **R. Joshua b. Qorha says, "Concerning these generations, Scripture states, *And then the ransomed of the Lord shall return, [and come singing to Zion]*" (Is. 35:10) [T. San. 13:11].**

The Tosefta-passage amplifies the Mishnah-passage, supplying more opinions and adducing in evidence further pertinent verses of Scripture, but in no way shifting the issue under discussion.

    O.  Rabbi says, "Both these and those do have a portion in the world to come."

    P.  What is the scriptural basis for this viewpoint?

    Q.  *And in that day a great trumpet will be blown, and those who were lost in the land of Assyria [and those who were driven out to the land of Egypt will come and worship the Lord on the holy mountain at Jerusalem]* (Is. 27:13).

    R.  *In the land of Assyria*—these are the ten tribes.

    S.  *And those who were driven out to the land of Egypt*—this is the generation of the wilderness.

    T.  These and those *will come and worship the Lord on the holy mountain at Jerusalem.*

May we see Rabbi's position as a systematic exegesis of the base verse, rather than as a component of the larger propositional debate? Yes and no. As we have Rabbi's statement, it simply continues the foregoing. But seen on its own, with an appropriately specific subject for the initial proposition, what we have is a systematic treatment of Isaiah 27:13, each of its elements nicely spelled out in its own terms. Rabbi's statement as an interpretation of the base verse is cogent and complete on its own.

II.    A.  **The party of Korach has no portion in the world to come and will not live in the world to come.**

    B.  What is the scriptural basis for this view?

    C.  **[So they and all that belonged to them went down alive into Sheol] and the earth closed over them, and they perished from the midst of the assembly (Num. 16:33).**

    D.  **The earth closed over them—in this world.**

    E.  **And they perished from the midst of the assembly—in the world to come [M. San. 10:4D–F].**

    F.  It was taught: **R. Judah b. Batera says, "[The contrary view] is to be derived from the implication of the following verse:**

    G.  **"I have gone astray like a lost sheep; seek thy servant [and do not forget thy commandments] (Ps. 119:176).**

H. "Just as the lost object which is mentioned later on in the end is going to be searched for, so the lost object which is stated herein is destined to be searched for [T. San. 13:9]."

I. Who will pray for them?

J. R. Samuel bar Nahman said, "Moses will pray for them."

K. *Let Reuben live, and not die, [nor let his men be few]* (Deut. 33:6).

L. R. Joshua b. Levi said, "Hannah will pray for them."

M. This is the view of R. Joshua b. Levi, for R. Joshua b. Levi said, "Thus did the party of Korach sink ever downward, until Hannah went and prayed for them and said, *The Lord kills and brings to life; he brings down to Sheol and raises up* (1 Sam. 2:6)."

While the individual exegeses of Scripture are submerged in the larger propositional composition, still in a few instances we are able to see complete and cogent statements made up solely of a clause-by-clause reading of a base verse. The present exemplification of Midrash as exegesis yielding a proposition, while casual and unimportant, shows us that a vast labor of interpretation along these lines went forward not only in order to produce such sustained documents as Sifra and Sifré to Numbers, but also in its own terms, that is, on a verse-by-verse level. Where, when, and why this other-than-documentary work was carried on frames a question deserving attention in due course.

We come, second, to the counterpart, within the Yerushalmi, of the interpretation of Scripture as proposition yielding exegesis. In the case at hand, the proposition is that the merit of the patriarchs always sustained Israel through its history and always will sustain Israel in the future, to the age to come. That proposition is implicit, but the entire formation and direction of the passage aims at making the point clearly and decisively. In this composition, diverse verses of Scripture, drawn from everywhere, form an assembly of proofs for individual propositions as to the point at which the merit of the patriarchs was exhausted, and then the whole, seen only when complete, states the important but unexpressed syllogism. The syllogistic passage conforms to the interests in issues of salvation that predominate in the other propositional Midrash-compilations of Midrash-exegeses, particularly Leviticus Rabbah and Pesiqta deRab Kahana. But the syllogisms worked out through propositions generating exegeses do not fit within the limitation of that one theme.

### YERUSHALMI SANHEDRIN 10:1

**VI.** A. How long did the merit of the patriarchs endure [to protect Israel]?

B. R. Tanhuma said in the name of R. Hiyya the Great, Bar Nahman stated in the name of R. Berekiah, R. Helbo in the name of R. Ba bar Zabeda: "Down to Joahaz."

C. *But the Lord was gracious to them and had compassion on them, [because of his covenant with Abraham, Isaac, and Jacob, and would not destroy them; nor has he cast them from his presence until now* (2 Kings 13:23).

D. "Up to that time the merit of the patriarchs endured."

E. Samuel said, "Down to Hosea."

F. *Now I will uncover the lewdness in the sight of her lovers, and no man shall rescue her out of my hand* (Hos. 2:12).

G. "Now *man* can refer only to Abraham, as you say, *Now then restore the man's wife; for he is a prophet, [and he will pray for you, and you shall live. But if you do not restore her, know that you will surely die, you, and all that are yours]* (Gen. 20:7).

H. "And *man* can refer only to Isaac, as you say, '[Rebekah said to the servant,] *Who is the man yonder, walking in the field to meet us? [The servant said, It is my master. So she took her veil and covered herself]* (Gen. 24:65).

I. "And *man* can refer only to Jacob, as you say, *[When the boys grew up, Esau was a skillful hunter, a man of the field,] while Jacob was a quiet man, [dwelling in tents]* (Gen. 25:27)."

J. R. Joshua b. Levi said, "It was down to Elijah."

K. *And at the time of the offering of the oblation, Elijah the prophet came near and said, "O Lord, God of Abraham, Isaac, and Israel, let it be known this day that thou art God in Israel, and that I am thy servant, [and that I have done all these things at thy word]"* (1 Kings 18:36).

L. R. Yudan said, "It was down to Hezekiah."

M. *Of the increase of his government and of peace there will be no end, [upon the throne of David, and over his kingdom, to establish it, and to uphold it with justice and righteousness from this time forth and for evermore. The zeal of the Lord of hosts will do this]* (Is. 9:6).

Now comes the climactic statement of the fundamental proposition:

N. Said R. Aha, "The merit of the patriarchs endures forever [to protect Israel]."

O. *For the Lord your God is a merciful God; [he will not fail you or destroy you or forget the covenant with your fathers which he swore to them]* (Deut. 4:31).

Everything that follows is tacked on as a kind of thematic appendix, in some parts addressing the cited verse, in others amplifying facts that point toward the desired conclusion. The secondary expansion leads us to a message for the time of the authorship itself, which is that the way of reinforcing the merit of the patriarchs and matriarchs is to practice acts of lovingkindness (steadfast love).

P. This teaches that the covenant is made with the tribes.

Q. R. Yudan bar Hanan in the name of R. Berekiah: "Said the Holy One, blessed be he, to Israel, 'My children, if you see the merit of the patriarchs declining, and the merit of the matriarchs growing feeble, go and cleave unto the trait of steadfast love.' "

R. What is the scriptural basis for this statement?

S. *"For the mountains may depart and the hills be removed, [but my steadfast love shall not depart from you, and my covenant of peace shall not be removed," says the Lord, who has compassion on you* (Is. 54:10).

T. *For the mountains may depart*—this refers to the merit of the patriarchs.

U. *And the hills be removed*—this refers to the merit of the matriarchs.

V. Henceforth: *"But my steadfast love shall not depart from you, and my covenant of peace shall not be removed," says the Lord, who has compassion on you.*

What is interesting is that Q–V may stand entirely by itself, a complete and cogent statement on its own. Then the point that the authorship has made is worked out through the specific verse at hand, and, turning matters around, we have an example of interpretation as an exegesis yielding a proposition. But in its larger context, the prevailing proposition holds the whole together and transforms an independent statement into a subordinated component of a much larger and still more cogent composition.

We come next to the work of interpretation carried out through the retelling of biblical stories. In both cases the narrative emphasizes the points important to the storyteller, without regard to the narrative thrust of the original story.

### YERUSHALMI SANHEDRIN 10:1

**VII. A. An Epicurean [M. San. 10:1D(3)].**
   B. R. Yohanan and R. Eleazar—
   C. one said, "It is a priest who said, 'Now is *that* a scribe?!' "
   D. The other said, "It is a priest who said, 'Now are *those* rabbis?!' "

The Epicurean to which the Mishnah refers in its list of those who will not enter the world to come is an unbeliever. Sages then identify such a person with one who denies the standing of sages.

   E. R. Eleazar and R. Samuel bar Nahman—
   F. one said, "It [unbelief] is comparable to a pile of stones. Once one of them shifts, all of them tumble down."
   G. And the other said, "It is comparable to a storehouse full of straw. Even though you take out all of the straw that is in the storehouse, there still is straw that eventually will weaken the walls."

We turn now to the theme of the archetypal unbeliever, who was Korach. He rejected the authority of Moses, the model for the sage today. Moses, called "our Rabbi," then stands for the sage in his confrontation with the unbeliever, Korach. In retelling the story of Korach, sages thus make the biblical narrative into an exercise challenging the authority of sages. And the character of the challenge is defined with great precision: it has to do with the sensibility of sages' rulings on matters of law, that is to say, the very issue prominent in the everyday workings of the sages' life. Consequently, in retelling the biblical tale, the exegetes make a powerful case of their own concerning their authority as against the unbelievers' rejection of their authority. And the result? Those who accept sages' authority enter the world to come, while the earth opens up and swallows those who do not. This wonderful vision of politics as fantasy unfolds in the passage that follows.

H. Rab said, "Korach was very rich. [The location of] Pharaoh's treasures was revealed to him, between Migdol and the sea." [This item breaks off here.]

I. Rab said, "Korach was an Epicurean. What did he do? He went and made a prayer shawl that was entirely purple [although the law is that only the fringe was to be purple]."

J. "He went to Moses, saying to him, 'Moses, our rabbi: A prayer shawl that is entirely purple, what is the law as to its being liable to show fringes?' "

K. "He said to him, 'It is liable, for it is written,' *You shall make yourself tassels [on the four corners of your cloak with which you cover yourself]* (Deut. 22:12)."

L. [Korach continued,] "A house that is entirely filled with holy books, what is the law as to its being liable for a *mezuzah* [containing sacred Scripture, on the doorpost]?"

M. He said to him, "It is liable for a *mezuzah,* for it is written, *And you shall write them on the doorposts of your house [and upon your gates]* (Deut. 6:9)."

N. He said to him, "A bright spot the size of a bean, what is the law [as to whether it is a sign of uncleanness in line with Lev. 13:2ff., which we saw in our inquiry into Sifra, above]?"

O. He said to him, "It is a sign of uncleanness."

P. "And if it spread over the whole of the man's body?"

Q. He said to him, "It is a sign of cleanness." [Scripture itself states that paradoxical ruling.]

R. At that moment Korach said, "The Torah does not come from Heaven, Moses is no prophet, and Aaron is not a high priest." [The rulings of the Torah are nonsense.]

S. Then did Moses say, "Lord of all worlds, if from creation the earth was formed with a mouth, well and good, and if not, then make it now!"

T. *But if the Lord creates [something new, and the ground opens its mouth, and swallows them up, with all that belongs to them, and they go down alive to Sheol, then you shall know that these men have despised the Lord]* (Num. 16:30).

The narrative has recast the Korach story by supplying the necessary dialogue. But is is not a mere aesthetic improvement, since, as we see, the dialogue makes the point important to the storytellers. This example of Midrash as narrative is now complemented with a series of further remarks. The reason for the inclusion of the whole is at W.

U. Said R. Simeon b. Laqish, "Three denied their prophetic gift on account of the baseness [with which they were treated].

V. "And these are they: Moses, Elijah, and Micha."

W. Moses said, *If these men die the common death of all men, [or if they are visited by the fate of all men, then the Lord has not sent me]*" (Num. 16:29).

X. Elijah said, "*Answer me, O Lord, answer me, [that this people may know that thou, O Lord, art God, and that thou hast turned their hearts back]*" (1 Kgs. 18:37).

Y. Micah said, "*[And Micaiah said,] 'If you return in peace, the Lord has not spoken by me.' [And he said, 'Hear all you peoples!']* (1 Kings 22:28)."

Z. *So they and all that belonged to them went down alive into Sheol; [and the earth closed over them, and they perished from the midst of the assembly]* (Num. 16:33).

AA. R. Berekiah in the name of R. Helbo: "Even the mention of their names flew off the pages of the record books [of bonds and documents] containing them."

BB. Said R. Yose b. Haninah, "Even a needle belonging to them which has been lent to an Israelite by them was swallowed up with them,

CC. "as it is written, *So they and all that belonged to them went down alive into Sheol* (Num. 16:33)."

DD. And who prayed in their behalf?

EE. R. Samuel bar Nahman said, "Moses prayed in their behalf: *Let Reuben live and not die, [nor let his men be few]* (Deut. 33:6)."

FF. R. Joshua b. Levi said, "Hannah prayed in their behalf."

GG. That indeed is the view of R. Joshua b. Levi, for R. Joshua b. Levi said in the name of R. Yosé. "So did the band of Korach sink and fall, until Hannah went and prayed for them.

HH. "She said, *The Lord kills and brings to life; he brings down to Sheol and raises up* (1 Sam. 2:6)."

A second example of Midrash as narrative in the Yerushalmi allows us to see yet another polemic unfolding through exegesis of a biblical tale. This polemic concerns the downfall of Israel, and it addresses two issues. First, the story tells us the character of Israel's enemies by describing Balaam, a figure acknowledged as a prophet, but a prophet who used his divine gifts to do evil to Israel. Second, it warns Israel about not going over to the enemy, however inviting the enemy appears, and, especially, avoiding those traits of licentiousness that cause the downfall of Israel. Balaam, we recall, appears on the list of those who will not enter the world to come. Why not?

### YERUSHALMI SANHEDRIN 10:2

**VII.** A. Now what did the evil Balaam do [to warrant losing his portion in the world to come]?

B. It was because he gave advice to Balak son of Zippor on how to cause Israel's downfall by the sword.

C. He said to him, "The God of this nation hates fornication. So put up your daughters for fornication, and you will rule over them."

D. He said to him, "And will [the Moabites] listen to me [when I tell them to turn their daughters into whores]?"

E. He said to him, "Put up your own daughter first, and they will see and then accept what you say to them."

F. That is in line with the following verse of Scripture: *[And the name of the Midianite woman who was slain was Cozbi the daughter of Zur,] who was the head of the people of a father's house in Midian* (Num. 25:15).

G. What did they do? They built for themselves temples from Beth HaJeshimmon to Snowy Mountain, and they set in them women selling various kinds of sweets. They put the old lady outside, and the young girl inside.

H. Now the Israelites would then eat and drink, and one of them would go out to walk in the marketplace, and he would buy something from a stallkeeper. The old lady then would sell him the thing for whatever it was worth, and the young girl would say, "Come on in and take it for still less." So it was on the first day, the second day, and the third day. And then, she would say to him, "From now on, you belong here. Come on in and choose whatever you like."

I. When he came in [he found there] a flagon of wine, Ammonite wine, which is very strong. And it serves as an aphrodisiac to the body, and its scent was enticing. (Now up to this time the wine of gentiles had not been prohibited for Israelite use by reason of its being libation wine.)

J. Now the girl would say to him, "Do you want to drink a cup of wine?" and he would reply to her, "Yes." So she gave him a cup of wine, and he drank it.

K. When he drank it, the wine would burn in him like the venom of a snake. Then he would say to her, "Surrender yourself [sexually] to me." She would say to him, "Do you want me to 'surrender' myself to you?" And he would say "Yes." Then she took out an image of Peor from her bosom, and she said to him, "Bow down to this, and I'll surrender myself to you." And he would say to her, "Now am I going to bow down to an idol?" And she would say to him, "You don't really bow down to it, but you expose yourself to it."

L. This is in line with that which sages have said [in the Mishnah], **"He who exposes himself to Baal Peor—this is the appropriate manner of worshipping it; and he who tosses a stone at Merkolis—this is the appropriate manner of worshipping it."**

M. cw0[When he came in, he found] there a flagon full of wine, Ammonite wine, which is very strong. And it serves as an aphrodisiac to incite the body to passion, and its scent was enticing. (Now up to this time the wine of gentiles had not been prohibited for Israelite use by reason of its being libation wine.) Now the girl would say to him, "Do you want to drink a cup of wine?" and he would reply to her, "Yes." So she gave him a cup of wine, and he drank it. When he drank it, the wine would burn in him like the venom of a snake. Then he would say to her, "Surrender yourself to me."

N. And she would say to him, "Separate yourself from the Torah of Moses, and I shall 'surrender' myself to you."

O. That is in line with the following verse of Scripture: [*Like grapes in the wilderness, I found Israel. Like the first fruits on the fig tree, in its first season, I saw your fathers.*] *But they came to Baal Peor, and consecrated themselves to Baal, and became detestable like the thing they loved* (Hos. 9:10).

P. They became detested until they became detestable to their Father who is in Heaven.

Q. Said R. Eleazar, "Just as this nail—one cannot separate it from the door without a piece of wood, so it is not possible to separate from Peor without [the loss of] souls."

R. There was this story: Subetah from Ulam hired out his ass to a gentile woman, [to take her] to bow down to Peor. When they got to Peor's house, she said to him, "Wait for me here, while I go in and worship Peor." When she came out, he said to her, "Wait for me here, until I go in and do just what you did." What did he do? He went in and took a shit, and he wiped his ass on the nose of Peor. Everyone present praised him, and said to him, "No one ever did it the way this one did it!"

S. There was this story: Menahem of Gypta Ary was moving jugs. The chief of Peor came to him by night. What did he do? He took the spit and stood up against him, and [the chief] fled from him. He came to him the next night. Menahem said to him, "How are you going to curse me? You are afraid of me!" And he said to him, "I'm not going to curse you anymore."

T. There was this story: An officer came from overseas to bow down to Peor. He said to them, "Bring me an ox, a ram, a sheep, to worship Peor." They said to him, "You don't have to go to all that trouble. All you have to do is expose yourself to it." What did he do? He called up his troops, who beat them and broke their skulls with staves, and he said to them, "Woe for you and for this big 'mistake' of yours!"

U. It is written: *And the Lord was angry at Israel, and the Lord said to Moses, "Take all the chiefs of the people, and hang them in the sun before the Lord, [that the fierce anger of the Lord may turn away from Israel]"* (Num. 25:4).

V. He said to him, "Appoint their heads as judges over them, and let them put the sinners to death toward the sun."

W. This is in line with the following verse of Scripture: *And Moses said to the judges of Israel, "Every one of you slay his men who have yoked themselves to Baal Peor"* (Num. 25:5).

X. And how many are the judges of Israel? They are 78,600 [calculation as follows:]

Y. Heads of thousands are six hundred.

Z. Heads of hundreds are six thousand.

AA. Heads of troops of fifty are twelve thousand.

BB. Heads of troops of ten are sixty thousand.

CC. It thus turns out that the judges of Israel [heads of all units] are 78,600.

DD. He said to them, "Each one of you kill two." So 157,200 turned out to be put to death.

EE. *And behold, one of the people of Israel came and brought a Midianite woman to his family, in the sight of Moses [and in the sight of the whole congregation of the people of Israel, while they were weeping at the door of the tent of meeting]* (Num. 25:6).

FF. What is the meaning of *In the sight of Moses*?

GG. It was like someone who says, "Here—right in your eye!"

HH. He said [to Moses] "Is your Zipporah not Midianite, and are not her feet cloven? [Is she not clean for you, fit to be your wife?] This one [Zipporah] is clean but that one [my woman] is unclean?!"

II. Now Phineas was there. He said, "Is there no man here who will kill him even at the expense of his life?"

JJ. "Where are the lions?"

KK. *Judah is a lion's whelp; [from the prey, my son, you have gone up. He stooped down, he crouched as a lion, and as a lioness who dares to rouse him?]* (Gen. 49:9).

LL. *[And of Dan he said,] "Dan is a lion's whelp, [that leaps forth from Bashan]"* (Deut. 33:22).

MM. *Benjamin is a ravenous wolf, [in the morning devouring the prey, and at evening dividing the spoil]* (Gen. 49:27).

The theme of the tale now turns to another way in which Israel is defeated: dissension and sectarianism.

NN. When he [Phineas] saw that no Israelite did a thing, forthwith, Phineas stood up from his Sanhedrin seat and took a spear in his hand and put the iron head of it under his *fascia*. He leaned on the wood [of the spear, concealing its purpose] until he reached his door. When he came to his door, [the occupant] said to him, "Whence and whither, Phineas?"

OO. He said to them, "Do you not agree with me that the tribe of Levi is near the tribe of Simeon under all circumstances?"

PP. They said to him, "Leave him [me] alone. Maybe the separatists have permitted this matter [after all]!

QQ. When he got in, the Holy One, blessed be he, did six miracles.

RR. The first miracle: It is the usual way [after fucking] to separate from one another, but the angel of the Lord kept them stuck together.

SS. The second miracle: He aimed the spear directly into the belly of the woman, so that the man's penis would stick out of her belly.

TT. And this was on account of the nitpickers, so that they should not go around saying, "He too shouldered his way in and did what came naturally."

UU. The third miracle: The angel sealed their lips, so that they could not cry out.

VV. The fourth miracle: They did not slip off the spear but remained in place. [Phineas lifted them up on the spear.]

WW. The fifth miracle: The angel raised the lintel [so that he could carry the two of them on the spear], so that both of them could go out on his shoulders.

XX. The sixth miracle: When he went out and saw the plague afflicting the people, what did he do? He threw them down to the ground and stood and prayed.

YY. This is in line with the following verse of Scripture: *Then Phineas stood up and interposed, and the plague was stayed* (Ps. 106:30).

ZZ. Now when the Israelites came to take vengeance against Midian, they found Balaam ben Beor there.

AAA. Now what had he come to do?

BBB. He had come to collect his salary for the twenty-four thousand Israelites who had died in Shittim on his account.

CCC. Phineas said to him, "You did not do what you said, and you also did not do Balak's bidding.

DDD. "You did not do what you said, for he said to you, 'You shall not go with the messengers of Balak,' but you went along with them.

EEE. "And you did not do what Balak said, for he said to you, 'Go and curse Israel,' but you blessed them.

FFF. "So, for my part, I'm not going to withhold your salary!"

GGG. That is in line with that which is written in Scripture: *Balaam also, the son of Beor, the soothsayer, the people of Israel killed with the sword among the rest of their slain* (Josh. 13:22).

HHH. What is the meaning of among the rest of their slain?

III. That he was equal to all the other slain put together.

JJJ. Another interpretation: *Among the rest of their slain*—just as their slain no longer have substance, so he was of no substance.

KKK. Another interpretation: *Among the rest of their slain,* for he hovered [in the air] over their slain, and Phineas showed him the [priestly] frontlet, and he fell down [to earth].

The long narrative runs through verses of the story of Balaam but in no way limits itself to the exposition of meanings of words or phrases of those verses. The narrator has his own program, as much as the framer of the foregoing brought his proposition to the exegesis of individual verses. In working out the narrative in his own interests, the narrator has used verses of Scripture in a cogent statement of his own.

Now that we have seen how Midrash-exegesis in the Talmud of the Land of Israel takes shape in precisely the ways in which, in the several documents, we have followed its unfolding, let us move upward to the largest cogent structure of Midrash-exegesis, the complete statement of a given theme or proposition that frames a full and autonomous "chapter," such as is called the *parashah* or *pisqa*. As I said, in the Talmud of the Land of Israel, we have few such whole chapters corresponding to the treatment of an entire chapter of the Mishnah. The compositors of the Talmud of Babylonia and the authorships behind its major components build a significant proportion of the whole in precisely that way, as systematic and ongoing exercises in Midrash-exegesis worked out through Midrash-documents.

## III. ORGANIZING DISCOURSE AROUND VERSES OF SCRIPTURE: THE BAVLI

In many instances sustained discourse takes shape around a biblical topic, specifically given expression through the Midrash-exegesis of a sequence of verses. One example is strikingly relevant to the materials we have been surveying, that is, the amplification of the Mishnah's discourse on those who will or will not enter the world to come. Here is the treatment of Jeroboam in an enormous and sustained discourse, held together both through the single cogent theme and also through the unfolding of the verses of Scripture, read sequentially, on that theme. As before, Mishnah or Tosefta citations appear in bold-face type, and verses of Scripture are in italics.

## BAVLI SANHEDRIN 10:2

### CXLVI.

A. **Three kings and four ordinary folk [have no portion in the world to come. Three kings: Jeroboam, Ahab, and Manasseh]** [M. 11:2A–B]:

B. Our rabbis have taught on Tannaite authority:

C. *Jeroboam:* for he treated the people as his sexual object.

D. Another matter: *Jeroboam:* for he made strife in the people.

E. Another matter: *Jeroboam:* for he brought strife between the people of Israel and their father in heaven.

F. *Son of Nebat,* a son who saw [a vision] but did not see [its meaning].

### CXLVII.

A. On Tannaite [authority it was stated]:

B. Nebat is the same as Micah and Sheba son of Bichri.

C. Nebat: because he saw a vision but did not see [its meaning].

D. Micah: because he was [Freedman, *Sanhedrin*]: crushed in the building.*

E. But what was his real name? It was Sheba, son of Bichri.

### CXLVIII.

A. Our rabbis have taught on Tannaite authority:

B. There were three who saw [a vision] but did not see [its meaning], and these are they: Nabat, Ahitophel, and Pharaoh's astrologers.

C. Nabat saw fire coming forth from his penis. He thought that [it meant that] he would rule, but that was not the case. It was that Jeroboam would come forth from him [who would rule].

D. Ahitophel saw *saraat* [the skin ailment mentioned in Leviticus 13] spread over him and over his penis. He thought that it meant that he would be king, and that was not the case. It was Sheba, his daughter, from whom Solomon would come forth.

---

*Freedman, pp. 688–89 n. 11: According to legend, when the Israelites in Egypt did not complete their tale of bricks, their children were built into the walls instead. On Moses' complaining thereof to God, he answered him that he was thus weeding out the destined wicked. As proof, he was empowered to save Micah, who had already built it, but only to become an idolator on his reaching manhood. Rashi also gives an alternative rendering: he became impoverished through building—presumably his idolatrous shrine.

E. The astrologers of Pharaoh: In line with what R. Hama, son of R. Hanina, said, "What is the meaning of the verse of Scripture, *These are the waters of rebellion, because they strove* (Num. 20:13)?

F. "These are the waters which the astrologers of Pharaoh foresaw, and about which they erred.

G. "They saw that the savior of Israel would be smitten because of water. So [Pharaoh] decreed, *Every son that is born you shall cast into the river* (Ex. 1:22).

H. "But they did not know that it was on account of the water of rebellion that he would be smitten."

**CXLIX.**

A. And how do we know that [Jeroboam] will not come into the world to come?

B. As it is written, *and this thing became sin to the house of Jeroboam, even to cut if off and to destroy it from off the face of the earth* (1 Kgs. 13:34).

C. *To cut if off*—in this world.

D. *And to destroy it*—in the world to come.

This brief unit can, of course, stand on its own as an exegesis of 1 Kings 13:34. But in our context it forms part of a majestic, sustained essay on Jeroboam. The topical program is rather logical in its sequence. We have worked out the main topic. Now we turn to the history and biography: why he ruled, how he ruled, and what sins he committed. All these questions are answered in an orderly way, just as the Mishnah lays out its topics in a logical and orderly manner, and just as the Mishnah-exegetes in two Talmuds follow and amplify the statements of the Mishnah-paragraphs and chapters under discussion.

**CL.**

A. Said R. Yohanan, 'On what account did Jeroboam have the merit to rule?

B. "Because he reproved Solomon.

C. "And on what account was he punished?

D. "Because he reproved him publicly.

E. "So it is said, *And this was the cause that he lifted up his hand against the king: Solomon built Millo and repaired the breaches of the city of David his father* (1 Kgs. 11:27).

F. "He said to him, 'David your father made breaches in the wall so that the Israelites might come up for the pilgrim festivals, but you have filled them in so as to collect a tax for the daughter of Pharaoh.' "

G. And what is the meaning of the phrase, *That he lifted up his hand against the king* (1 Kgs. 11:27)?

H. Said R. Nahman, "Because he took off his phylacteries in his presence." [Sages regarded it as an act of merit to wear phylacteries at all times and discouraged Jews from removing their phylacteries in the presence of gentile authorities.]

**CLI.**

A. Said R. Nahman, "The arrogance that characterized Jeroboam is what drove him out of the world.

B. "For it is said, *Now Jeroboam said in his heart, 'Now shall the kingdom return to the house of David. If this people go up to sacrifice in the house of the Lord at Jerusalem, then shall the heart of this people turn to their Lord, even to Rehoboam, king of Judah, and they shall kill me and go again to Rehoboam, king of Judah'* (1 Kgs. 12:27–28).

C. "He said, 'We have a tradition that no one may sit down in the Temple courtyard except kings of the house of Judah alone. When the people see that Rehoboam is sitting down and I am standing, they will think that he is king, and I am merely a servant.

D. " 'But if I sit down, I shall be in the position of rebelling against the monarchy, and they will kill me and follow.'

E. "Forthwith: *Wherefore the king took counsel and made two calves of gold and said to them, 'It is too much for you to go up to Jerusalem. Behold your gods, O Israel, who brought you up out of the land of Egypt,' and he put one in Beth El and the other he put in Dan* (1 Kgs. 12:28)."

Now we know the motivation of Jeroboam, which is pride, the opposite of that humility, which sages urged as the correct attitude for Israel.

F. What is the meaning of the phrase, *The king took counsel*?

G. Said R. Judah, "That he sat a wicked person next to a righteous person. He said to them, 'Will you sign everything that I do?'

H. "They said to him, 'Yes.'

I. "He said to them, 'I want to be king.'

J. "They said to him, 'Yes.'

K. "He said to them, 'Will you do whatever I say?'

L. "They said to him, 'Yes.' "

M. " 'Even to worship an idol.'

N. "The righteous one said to him, 'God forbid.'

O. "The wicked one said to the righteous one, 'Do you think that a person such as Jeroboam would really worship an idol? Rather, what he wants to do is to test us to see whether or not we shall accept his word [102A].' "

P. "Even Ahijah the Shilonite made a mistake and signed, for Jehu was a very righteous man, as it is said, *And the Lord said to Jehu, 'Because you have done well in executing what is right in my eyes and have done to the house of Ahab according to all that was in my heart, your children of the fourth generation shall sit upon the throne of Israel'* (2 Kgs. 10:30).

Q. "But is is written, *But Jehu took no heed to walk in the law of the Lord God of Israel with all his heart, for he did not depart from the sins of Jeroboam, which he had made Israel to sin* (2 Kgs. 10:31)."

R. What caused it?

S. Said Abayye, "A covenant made orally, as it is said, *And Jehu gathered all the people together and said to them, 'Ahab served Baal a little, but Jehu shall serve him much'* (2 Kgs. 10:18)."*

T. Raba said, "He saw the signature of Ahijah the Shilonite, and he erred on that account."

## CLII.

A. It is written, *And the revolters are profound to make slaughter, though I have been a rebuke of all of them* (Hos. 5:2):

B. Said R. Yohanan, "Said the Holy One, blessed be he, 'They have gone deeper than I did. I said, "Whoever does not go up to Jerusalem for the festival transgresses an affirmative requirement," but they have said, "Whoever does go up to Jerusalem for the festival will be stabbed with a sword." ' "

## CLIII.

A. *And it came to pass at that time, when Jeroboam went out of Jerusalem, that the prophet Ahijah the Shilonite found him in the way, and he had clad himself with a new garment* (1 Kgs. 11:20):

---

*Freedman, p. 691 n. 5: These words, though spoken guilefully, had to be fulfilled.

B. It was taught on Tannaite authority in the name of R. Yose, "It was a time designated for punishment." [Freedman, p. 691 n. 9: "On that occasion Ahijah prophesied the division of the kingdom as a punishment for Solomon's backsliding."]

C. *In the time of their visitation they shall perish* ( Jer. 51:18):

D. It was taught on Tannaite authority in the name of R. Yose, "A time designated for punishment."

E. *In an acceptable time I have heard you* (Is. 49:8):

F. It was taught on Tannaite authority in the name of R. Yose, "A time designated for good."

G. *Nevertheless in the day when I visit, I will visit their sin upon them* (Ex. 32:34):

H. It was taught on Tannaite authority in the name of R. Yose, "A time designated for punishment."

I. *And it came to pass at that time, that Judah went down from his brethren* (Gen. 38:1):

J. It was taught on Tannaite authority in the name of R. Yose, "A time designated for punishment."

K. *And Rehoboam went to Shechem, for all Israel were come to Shechem to make him king* (1 Kgs. 12:1):

L. It was taught on Tannaite authority in the name of R. Yose, "A time designated for punishment. In Shechem men raped Dinah, in Shechem his brothers sold Joseph, in Shechem the kingdom of David was divided."

## CLIV.

A. *Now it came to pass at that time that Jeroboam went went out of Jerusalem* (1 Kgs. 11:29):

B. Said R. Hanina b. Pappa, "He went out of the realm of Jerusalem."

## CLV.

A. *And the prophet Ahijah the Shilonite found him in the way, and he clad himself with a new garment, and the two were alone in the field* (1 Kgs. 11:29):

B. What is this *new garment?*

C. Said R. Nahman, "It was as with a new garment: just as a new garment has no sort of blemish, so the Torah-learning of Jeroboam had no sort of flaw."

D. Another matter: *A new garment:*

E. It was that they said things so new that no ear had ever heard them.

F. *And the two were alone in the field* (Kgs. 11:29): What is the meaning of this statement?

G. Said R. Judah said Rab, "It is that all the disciples of sages were as grass of the field before them [and of no account]."

H. And there is he who says, "It is that the reasons for the rulings of the Torah were revealed to them in the open as in a field."

## CLVI.

A. *Therefore shall you give parting gifts to Moresheth-gath; the houses of Achzib shall be a lie to the kings of Israel* (Mic. 1:14):

B. Said R. Hanina b. Pappa, "An echo came forth and said to them, 'He who killed the Philistine and gave you possession of Gath—to his sons you will give parting gifts.' "

C. *Therefore the houses of Achzib shall be a lie to the kings of Israel* (Mich. 1:14). [Freedman, p. 693 n. 2: "Since you deal treacherously with the house of David, preferring the rule of the kings of Israel, therefore you shall be delivered into the hands of the heathen, whose religion is false."]

## CLVII.

A. Said R. Hinnena b. Pappa, "Whoever derives benefit from this world without reciting a blessing is as if he steals from the Holy One, blessed be he, and the community of Israel.

B. "For it is said, *Who robs from his father or his mother and says, 'It is no transgression,' is the companion of a destroyer* (Prov. 28:24).

C. "*His father* is only the Holy One, blessed be he, as it is said, *Is not [God] your father, who has bought you* (Deut. 32:6), and *his mother* can mean only the congregation of Israel, as it is said, *My son, hear the instruction of your father and do not forsake the Torah of your mother* (Prov. 1:8)."

D. "*What is the sense of He is the companion of a destroyer* (Prov. 28:24)?

E. "He is companion of Jeroboam, son of Nebat, who destroyed Israel for their father in heaven."

## CLVIII.

A. *And Jeroboam drove Israel from following the Lord and made them sin a great sin* (2 Kgs. 17:21):

B. Said R. Hanin, "It was like two sticks that rebound from one another."

## CLIX.

A. *[These are the words which Moses spoke to all Israel in the wilderness] and Di Zahab* (Deut. 1:1):

B. Said a member of the house of R. Yannai, "Moses said before the Holy One, blessed be he, 'Lord of the world, on account of the silver and gold which you showered on Israel until they said, "Enough," they were caused to make for themselves gods of gold.'

C. "It is comparable to the case of a lion, who does not tear and roar on account of what is in a basket containing straw, but because of what is in a basket of meat."

D. Said R. Oshaia, "Up to the time of Jeroboam, the Israelites would suck from a single calf [sinning on account of only one], but from that time on, it was from two or three calves."

E. Said R. Isaac, "Any sort of punishment that comes upon the world contains at least one twenty-fourth of part of the overweight of a litra of the first calf.

F. "For it is written, *Nevertheless in the day when I visit, I will visit their sin upon them* (Ex. 32:34)."

G. Said R. Hanina, "After twenty-four generations this verse of Scripture will be exacted: *He cried also in my ears with a loud voice, saying, 'Cause the visitations of the city to draw near, even every man with his destroying weapon in his hand* (Ez. 9:1)."*

We see in this sustained and rather complex composition how the whole is held together in one way only, through the exposition of a sequence of verses on a given topic and through the concomitant program of issues invited by that topic. In the Bavli, therefore, we are able to locate a counterpart to those large-scale building blocks of sustained discourse of which each of our documents, from Sifra through Pesiqta deRab Kahana, is made up. In the Bavli, as much as in the Midrash-compilations, Midrash emerges as a whole and major unit, a document on its own.

---

*Freedman, p. 694 n. 4: "The use of 'visitations' suggests that this was the fulfillment of the doom threatened in Ex. 32:34. There were twenty-four generations from that of the wilderness, when the calf was made, to that of Zedekiah, in whose reign the state was overthrown and Judah was deported to Babylonia."

The upshot is that Midrash comprises both many documents on its own and also forms important components of the first of the two Talmuds and a principal building block of the second. Midrash-exegesis, moreover, governs the reading of both components of the dual Torah, Scripture and Mishnah, and in due course the result of Midrash-exegesis yields further canonical documents, such as those we have reviewed: the Midrash-compilations, on the one side, and the two Talmuds on the other. That means that the mode of thought characterizing the Judaism of the dual Torah, which generates the means of engaging in intelligible discourse (logic), the manner of composing persuasive propositions (rhetoric), and the message of discourse, finds accurate representation in one word, *Midrash*. We may therefore say that the Judaism of the dual Torah unfolds through the processes of Midrash, and that the world of rabbinic Bible interpretation encompasses the whole of that Judaism.

And that leads us to the final questions. What are we, the present generation, to make of Midrash, and what do we learn from Midrash about Judaism as a religion perpetually engaged in an exercise in exegesis? When we find answers to these questions, we—Jews and Christians alike—who by reason of the character of our culture are engaged by Scripture, will understand the character and continuity of Western civilization, with its powerful and concrete response, age after age, to the Scriptures of ancient Israel. Of still greater consequence, we who believe that God reveals Torah at Sinai will gain a greater understanding of ourselves as God sees us and in the Torah—whether the canon of the Judaism of the dual Torah or the canon of the Christianity of the dual Testament—instructs us.

# 8. Midrash and Us: Four Contemporary Issues

Our survey of the workings of Midrash brings us back to our own time. For acutely contemporary concerns of theology and culture are at stake in understanding Midrash. The issues begin, in the nature of things, with Judaism but address all religious women and men in the West. For Judaism, along with Christianity and Islam—the three religions that appeal to the Holy Scriptures of ancient Israel—has defined the West, and therefore the world. How Judaism mediates between the Holy Scriptures of ancient Israel and the living age forms a paradigm for the continuity of culture in the West, through time and through change perpetually framed in response to that singular piece of privileged writing. Neglecting to apply what we learn in the ancient writings of the rabbis to our understanding of the condition of the West and of the world deprives us of the relevant and the valuable and leaves us only the academic and the interesting.

## I. THEOLOGY, CULTURE, AND MIDRASH

In particular, four issues deserve attention. These concern: (1) the definition of a "biblical religion," whether Christianity, Islam, or Judaism, but in this case, Judaism; (2) the interpretation of religious literature, in this instance, the writings of the ancient rabbis; (3) the character of a continuing culture, in the example at hand, that of Israel, the Jewish people, from remote to late antiquity; and (4) the nature and meaning of humanity in relationship to God, beginning with Israel, God's first love and suffering servant.

At stake are four hermeneutical propositions. First, Midrash says what Scripture says. Scripture therefore defines the permissible limits of Midrash, and, by implication, of all interpretation. Valid biblical interpretation says only what Scripture says: paraphrase and application. That position is contained within the view that in Midrash we see Judaism as a biblical religion. The hermeneutical implication is that in principle exegesis constitutes paraphrase enlivened by wit, erudition, free association.

Second, Midrash stands for totally undisciplined free association, something people make up as they go along in the encounter with a given verse, read wholly out of a defining and limiting context. This position, maintained in literary criticism, represents Midrash as interpretation unbound by tradition. The hermeneutical implication, appealing for precedent (if not authority) to Midrash is that we can make things up as we go along and call the result the (a, one) meaning of the text.

The third and fourth hermeneutical propositions treat two aspects of a position I hold that pertains to culture and theology alike: first, Midrash stands for the interplay of freedom and tradition, imagination and authority, the continuous and the contemporary in culture and theology. But in the end, the implications of Midrash for religious thinking about culture prove subordinate. For, second, I find the ultimate meaning of Midrash in its message about who we are in relationship to God: in the search for proportion and balance between—in theological terms—our reason and God's revelation, our power to understand and God's power to instruct. Midrash mediates, and that is its meaning. Midrash, properly understood, lays down a position on that recurrent, anguished question: precisely what does it mean for us mortals to be "in our image, after our likeness"?

## II. IS JUDAISM A "BIBLICAL RELIGION"?

A theological claim of apologetics in both Judaism and Christianity, therefore a bitterly debated issue, is which party truly carries forward the revelation of Sinai, the Torah of Israel in ancient times. Judaism claims that it states, here and now, the true intent and meaning of Scripture, and it appeals for proof of its claim to the Midrash-documents we have surveyed. The Bavli, for instance, has presented us with a *summa* composed of the two Torahs, oral and written. It is, therefore, the authoritative and encompassing statement of the Judaism of the dual Torah, oral and written. Thus we have to face a final question of description, namely, whether and how Midrash as a principal component of the oral Torah leads us to Scripture, the written Torah. Specifically, Midrash in the hands of the rabbinic exegetes links the principal legal and theological doctrines of the oral and written Torahs. This is the persistent effect of Midrash-exegesis, the continuing claim of the Midrash-compilations, the verification and validation of Midrash-processes. The upshot is that Midrash in its three modes constitutes a massive testimony of the union of the Torah in two media and Judaism, in all its distinctive character, constitutes the religion that, today, speaks authoritatively in behalf of the Hebrew Scriptures.

Let me spell out the apologetic in behalf of Judaism contained within the proposition at hand. That claim, implicit throughout but made explicit every time a sage cites a verse of the written Torah as proof for a proposition of the oral Torah, raises this question: Does Midrash prove that Judaism is the true statement of the Hebrew Scriptures? The answer always affirms that what a sage says paraphrases what Scripture means. Judaism, therefore—Judaism, not Christianity or Islam—says what the Holy Scriptures mean. For Judaism commonly is described as "the religion of the book," meaning the Hebrew Scriptures or the Old Testament. The great apologists for Judaism in the nineteenth and twentieth centuries have faced the Christian and gentile world, both hostile and friendly, with that claim. That view rests upon the notion that what Judaism says in theology and law simply restates the fundamental, revealed truths of Scripture. Accordingly, if people wish to come to Sinai, then the straight and true road passes through Judaism. The law and theology of Judaism derive from "the book," the Bible. And that is true, but not in the sense in which people make the statement. For "the Bible," meaning "the Old Testament and the New Testament," is a Protestant category, accepted neither by Roman Catholic Christianity, with its appeal to Scripture and also tradition preserved by the Holy Church, nor by Judaism, with its appeal to the Torah in two media, oral and written.

In my judgment, Judaism states the profound theological and legal doctrines of the written Torah just as accurately and definitively as the New Testament imparts its full and complete meaning upon the Old Testament—no less, no more. That is to say, the claim authentically and authoritatively to speak in behalf of the Hebrew Scriptures, common to both heirs of ancient Israel, and the means of making that claim stick through Midrash (whether rabbinic or Christian) appeals to history to validate the faith. The component of history appealed to is the original, hence historical, meaning of the verses of the Scripture of ancient Israel. If one can show, for example, through Midrash, that the original sense of a verse of Scripture pointed to precisely the conclusion reached by the Judaic or Christian exegete-theologian or exegete-legist, then Judaism or Christianity, in that detail, correctly states the original, historical, therefore valid sense of Scripture, the verse of Scripture at hand. And, it must follow, "Judaism is right," because, through Midrash, Judaism can show that Scripture originally took the positions that, later on, would be announced in the distinctive documents of the oral Torah, in particular in the climactic statement of the Bavli at the end, with its joining of the two Torahs into one Judaism.

That apologetic, with its conclusion that Judaism really does emerge from the written Torah or Hebrew Scriptures and is therefore the authentic and legitimate heir of ancient Israel's Bible, simply misses the point. The fact is that the Judaism of the dual Torah constitutes a whole and complete system, and that system is what has generated the issues addressed to Scripture. Both issues of inner meaning to sages, such as those involved in whether reason alone or only Scripture provides solid facts of law, and issues of intense interest to the nation, Israel, at large, such as those concerning salvation, derive from the Judaism of the dual Torah. The system comes prior to its canon, that is, the canonical doctrine of the two Torahs, and the system shapes the issues that are addressed to the canon and resolved through exegesis—Midrash-exegesis in the several modes and trends we have reviewed. To allege that "Judaism is a biblical religion" therefore proves monumentally irrelevant to the definitive claim of Judaism concerning the dual Torah, encompassing both biblical and extrabiblical writings from the Mishnah forward.

The exegesis of the dual Torah followed that recognition of the components of the canon. What we have in the Midrash-compilations, as part of the canon of the Judaism of the dual Torah, therefore, is the result of the mode of thought of philosophers and scientists. The framers proposed, not to lay down, but to discover rules governing Israel's life. For them Scripture provided a principal source of facts, against which the propositions of the system—the Judaism of the dual Torah—had to be verified. The inquiry was inductive, in the sense I have proposed. But the propositions demanding validation—the law and theology of the Judaism of the dual Torah—emerged originally from the Judaism of the dual Torah, and only when wholly framed within the system that made those propositions urgent did they come under the scrutiny of the facts of the written Torah. If the Judaism of the dual Torah *were* a "biblical religion," it by definition could not be what it was. For the Judaism of the dual Torah rejected as insufficient and incomplete the (merely) written record of the revealed Torah at Sinai and announced itself as more than the religion of the written Torah. *Judaism cannot be a biblical religion because Judaism is the one whole Torah of Moses, our Rabbi, revealed by God at Sinai in the two media of revelation, writing and memory.*

## III. WERE THE RABBIS JOKING?

If Midrash does not—and should not—demonstrate that Judaism is "the religion of the Old Testament," then what good is Midrash at all? One might wish to conclude that in Midrash-compilations we learn only how people long ago and far away read Scripture—nothing urgent for our own day, no message, not even a model of interpretation. Midrash then presents an instance of mere formalism: things people say about arrangements of words, messages perceived in mere words read out of all cultural context, therefore social setting. Contemporary literary critics invoke Midrash as an example of hermeneutics wholly out of historical context, maintaining that Midrash-exegesis begins and ends with the verse subject to analysis on the one side, and constitutes a kind of highly academic game, a *jeu d'esprit,* a joke, on the other. That is why we wonder whether, in the end, the extravagant imagination displayed in Midrash-exegesis and Midrash-narrative marks Midrash as a kind of erudite game, something in which, for all but the players, nothing much is at stake. In moving from what I believe is a wrong theological conclusion about Judaism as a biblical religion to a wrong literary-cultural conclusion about Midrash as a set of word games, we confront another broadly held misconstruction.

Many take the view that each Midrash-exegesis is to be read out of all context but the verse subject to interpretation and therefore is to be seen as little more than a show of academic ingenuity. In recent times, none has stated matters more explicitly and with greater certainty than James Kugel. Having spent a great deal of effort to explain how a given verse has precipitated a received exegesis, in his essay "Two introductions to Midrash,"* Kugel concludes that exegeses begin with the problems of verses. Having reached that position, furthermore, he appears not to have spent a great deal of time analyzing rhetoric, on the

---

*In *Midrash and Literature,* ed. Geoffrey Hartman and Sanford Buddick (New Haven: Yale University Press, 1986), pp. 81ff.

one side, or inquiring into the principles of logical cogency and intelligible discourse, on the other. This has further discouraged him from asking whether a document as a whole proposes to make a point or to register a syllogism or a set of syllogisms.

Let us survey some of the more important positions concerning Midrash taken by the Jewish literary critics represented by Kugel. Among these, three pertain directly to the issue of what we, for our own times and lives, may learn from Midrash.

Kugel maintains that Midrash is precipitated by the character of the verse subject to exegesis, stating, "Midrash's precise focus is most often what one might call surface irregularities in the text: a good deal of the time, it is concerned with . . . *problems*."* In detail, Kugel may well be right. That is to say, once an exegete has chosen the verse and knows what he wishes, in general, to prove, then a set of the properties of a given verse may attract attention. Why one type of property, rather than some other? Why one issue, not another? These are questions to which the discrete exegesis of a verse on its own does not respond. And, as we have seen, in the comparison of such Midrash-compilations as the two families we have examined, Sifra and Sifré to Numbers on the one side, Genesis Rabbah, Leviticus Rabbah, and Pesiqta deRab Kahana on the other, we can propose theses in response to those questions—the ones of why this, not that?—and we can test those theses against the traits of rhetoric, logic, and even topic. In all, I do not set forth a one-sided disagreement with the position represented by Kugel that the traits of a given verse register in the formation of an exegesis of that verse. I am certain that the received exegetical literature, the thousand-year tradition of reading the Midrash-exegeses precisely the way Kugel and others wish to read them, enjoys ample proof in result and detail. But it begs the question to conclude *post hoc, ergo propter hoc,* as Kugel and his friends do.

Along these same lines, Kugel takes the view that Midrash is an exegesis of biblical verses, not of books, saying, "Midrash

*Ibid., p. 92.

is an exegesis of biblical verses, not of books. The basic unit of the Bible for the midrashist is the verse: this is what he seeks to expound, and it might be said that there simply is no boundary encountered beyond that of the verse until one comes to the borders of the canon itself."* It is simply false to claim that there is no boundary between Midrash-exegesis of a single verse and the entirety of the canon of Judaism. The opposite is the fact. And yet, here too Kugel is not completely wrong. Some materials do travel freely from document to document, though apart from verses of Scripture, I know of nothing that appears in every document of the dual Torah in its repertoire of late antiquity, through the Talmud of Babylonia. Kugel is talking about facts, if not (in proportion to the whole) a great many, and if not (in weight of evidence) probative ones.

Kugel further entertains the notion that authorships compose their documents essentially through free association.* The components of Midrash-compositions are interchangeable, as Kugel states, "Our midrashic compilations are in this sense potentially deceiving, since they seem to treat the whole text bit by bit; but with the exception of certain patterns, these 'bits' are rather atomistic, and, as any student of rabbinic literature knows, interchangeable, modifiable, combinable—in short, not part of an overall exegesis at all."* Kugel is wrong. He does not demonstrate that the components of Midrash-exegesis are mere atoms, readily interchanged, modified, combined in diverse ways. In his defense, I point to what I said at

---

*Ibid., p. 93.

*The conception that authorships play an active role in the formation of what they include in their documents is not new to me or particular to my school. It is in fact a routine inquiry, one that has produced interesting results for diverse scholars. I call attention, for example, to Steven Fraade, "Sifré Deuteronomy 26 (ad Deut. 3:23): How Conscious the Composition," *Hebrew Union College Annual* 54 (1983): 245–302. Despite his certainty on these matters, I can find in Kugel's notes no reference to, or argument with, Fraade. My own debate with Fraade appears in my *Religious Studies of Judaism: Description, Analysis, and Interpretation,* Studies in Judaism no. 5 (Lanham: University Press of America, 1986), 1:93–128, in particular, pp. 104–8, "Fraade vs. Fraade." But Fraade in his HUCA paper is certainly on the right track.

*Ibid., p. 95.

the third proposition. Some (few) Midrash-exegeses do occur in a number of passages. Characterizing all of them as Kugel does, however, violates the facts of close to eighty or ninety percent of the Midrash-exegeses in the documents we have examined.

Kugel's final proposition is that the rabbis presented in Midrash a kind of joking. He makes the statement explicitly. Let me cite the entire context in which this judgment appears, italicizing the relevant words:

Forever after, one cannot think of the verse or hear it recited without also recalling the solution to its problematic irritant—indeed, remembering it in the study-house or synagogue, one would certainly pass it along to others present, and together appreciate its cleverness and erudition. And so midrashic explications of individual verses no doubt circulated on their own, independent of any larger exegetical context. Perhaps in this sense it would not be inappropriate to compare their manner of circulating to that of jokes in modern society; *indeed, they were a kind of joking, a learned and sophisticated play about the biblical text, and like jokes they were passed on,* modified, and improved as they went, until a great many of them eventually entered into the common inheritance of every Jew, passed on in learning with the text of the Bible itself.*

Kugel does not demonstrate that we deal with "a kind of joking." How this literary judgment, which I regard as unproved and probably groundless, accords with the theological position stated with power and force in the Midrash-compilations surveyed in Parts Two, Three, and Four I cannot say. What I find stunning in the Midrash-compilations as well as in their contents, the Midrash-exegeses, is the urgency and immediacy of matters, not the cleverness and erudition demonstrated therein. Israel, the people of God, turned with deep anxieties about salvation to Genesis, Leviticus, and the sacred calendar. I find nothing amusing, merely clever, or particularly erudite in what the sages found there. In my description, analysis, and interpretation of the Midrash-compilations, I find

*Ibid., p. 95.

messages of self-evident truth in response to questions of life and death.

## IV. HISTORY AND MIDRASH: THE AUTHORITY OF SCRIPTURE, THE FREEDOM OF INTERPRETATION, AND THE CONTINUITY OF CULTURE

If Judaism *were* "the religion of the Bible," then the Midrash, as Judaic theologians maintain, would say only what the Scriptures do—or, at least, truly intended. That is not true. If the ancient rabbi-exegetes could say anything they wanted, attaching to a verse of choice a message made up on the spot, then, as literary critics hold, Midrash would hardly differ from mere free association. Nothing could be further from the truth. Then if it is not utter replication of Scripture nor utter invention of new garments, manufactured out of whole cloth, what is this Bible as the ancient rabbis read the Hebrew Scriptures, this Midrash? The answer comes in theory, then in example. Midrash shows us how the Judaic sages mediated between God's word and their own world, finding bridges from the one to the other, invoking the one as a metaphor for the other, equally and reciprocally. They learned from Scripture what it meant for humanity to be "in our image, after our likeness," and they learned in the difficult world in which they lived how life in God's image of humanity, as Scripture set forth that image, was to be not only endured but lived in full holiness: the godly life on earth (in the language of Judaism), God incarnate (in the language of Christianity), life as the imitation of God (in language shared by both).

In concrete terms, in the Midrash we see not "the Old Testament" or "the Hebrew Bible" but the one whole Torah, oral and written, that is Judaism. In that Torah Scripture read in the prism of Midrash forms a commentary on everyday life—as much as everyday life brings with it fresh understanding of Scripture. That theological conviction frames a cultural policy, one that constantly refers to Scripture in the interpretation of everyday life, and to everyday life in the interpretation of Scripture. Such a policy invokes both the eternal and continuing truths of Scripture and also the ephemeral but urgent considerations of the here and the now. Midrash then forms the bridge, defines the metaphor. It reads the one in light of the other, imparting one meaning to both, drawing each toward the plane of the other. Midrash reads the everyday as the metaphor against which the eternal is to be read, and the eternal as the metaphor against which the everyday is to be reenacted. It is exemplified in the powerful reading of Genesis by Genesis Rabbah, of Leviticus by Leviticus Rabbah, in both cases bringing to Scripture the anguish and the terror of difficult times— and learning from Scripture God's plan and program for all times. That is what it means to read the everyday in the metaphor of the eternal. (In my final statement, I shall explain what it means to read the eternal in the metaphor of the everyday, that is, to investigate the mind of God through creation.)

In Midrash there is a constant interplay, an ongoing interchange, between everyday affairs and the word of God in the Torah—Scripture. What we see reminds us of what Scripture says, and what Scripture says informs our understanding of the things we see and do in everyday life. That is what, in my view, the critical verse of Scripture, "In all thy ways, know him," means. And the deep structure of human existence, framed by Scripture and formed out of God's will as spelled out in the Torah, forms the foundation of our everyday life. Here and now, in the life of the hour, we can and do know God. So everyday life forms a commentary on revealed Scripture—on the Torah—and Scripture, the Torah, provides a commentary on everyday life. Life flows in both directions.

Midrash thus rests upon two pillars: first, the authority of Scripture; second (for theological reasons I spell out in the final section), the freedom of interpretation. In joining these two, each in balance and proper proportion, Midrash realizes in the here and now the continuity of culture. Forming a profoundly conservative and constructive power in the cultural and also

the political life of Israel, the Jewish people, Midrash legiti-
mates innovation in the name of the received revelation, while
preserving the vitality and ongoing pertinence of revelation in
the present age. Eternity in time comes to realization in the
processes of Midrash, which, through literary means, define a
sacred society, a consecrated culture.

The founders of Judaism as we know it, who flourished in
the first seven centuries of the Common Era, brought Scripture
into their world, and their world into Scripture. They therefore show us how people shaped their understanding of the
world out of the resources of God's revelation of the beginnings of humanity, and, especially, of God's people, Israel. The
great sages, honored with the title of rabbi, transformed the
Torah into a plan and design for the world, the everyday as an
instance of the eternal. They read Scripture as God's picture of
creation and humanity. They read the life of the streets and
marketplaces, the home and the hearth, the nations and the
world, as an ongoing commentary on Scripture and the potentialities (not all of them good) of creation. So, as I said, Torah
flows in both directions.

Let us take Genesis Rabbah, for example. Reading Genesis as
sages did, against the background of their world, we encounter
the story of the beginnings of humanity in a new way. It is now
an account not of a distant past, but of a living and abiding
present. Reading Leviticus as acutely revelant to their world,
understanding Numbers as an urgent message for their particular human setting, sages came to Scripture as God's living
word for their day. Sages turned Scripture into a paradigm of
truth, which accounts for their use of the cases of Scripture as
modes of testing the validity of social laws, historical rules,
paradigms of natural philosophy extended to society and history. Genesis, the story of beginnings, lays forth the meaning and
end of humanity. In the book of Genesis, as the sages who in
the fourth century composed Genesis Rabbah saw things, God
set forth to Moses the entire scope and meaning of Israel's history among the nations and salvation at the end of days. They

read Genesis not as a set of individual verses, one by one, but as a single and coherent statement, whole and complete. What happened to the patriarchs and matriarchs signalled what would happen to their descendants: the model of the ancestors sends a message for the children. So the importance of Genesis, to the sages of Genesis Rabbah, derived not from its lessons about the past but its message for Israel's and humanity's present—and, especially, future. Their conviction was that what Abraham, Isaac, and Jacob did shaped the future history of Israel. If, therefore, we want to know the meaning of events now and tomorrow, we look back at yesterday to find out.

Why did the sages of the Jewish people, in the Land of Israel, come to Genesis and the other books of Scripture with the questions of their own day? Because, they maintained, the world reveals not chaos but order, and God's will works itself out not once but again and again. If they could find out how things got going, they might also find meaning in the present and see method in the direction they were heading. That is why they looked to a reliable account of the past and searched out the meaning of their own days. Bringing to the stories of Genesis the conviction that the book of Genesis tells not only the story of yesterday but also the tale of tomorrow, the sages transformed a picture of the past into a prophecy for a near tomorrow. That transformation constitutes Midrash, whether of the book of Genesis or—in the later trends in the rabbinic Bible interpretation—of the text of the sacred calendar of the synagogue itself.

The sages who in the third, fourth, and fifth centuries created Genesis Rabbah, Leviticus Rabbah, Sifré to Numbers, and the other great readings of Scripture offer a model—therefore, a cultural policy—of how through Midrash people mediated between the received and the givens of their own time. In the written Torah they hoped to find, and they did find, the story of the day at hand, which, they anticipated, would indeed form the counterpart and conclusion to the story of beginnings. From creation to conclusion, from the beginnings of salvation in the patriarchs and matriarchs to the ending of salvation and its fulfillment in their own day—this is what the sages sought to discover. Genesis Rabbah in its reading of one-time history as paradigm and rule for all time presents us with a model of freedom balanced with discipline. It shows us how the sages of ancient times read Scripture in light of their own concerns—but then listened carefully to the teachings of the Torah about contexts like their own and circumstances such as those they faced. They exercised a freedom of interpretation by insisting that God speaks through the Torah to Israel everywhere and continually. But when they brought to the written Torah the deepest anguish of the age, they allowed that component of the Torah to speak to them in the here and now.

So, as I said, the bridge carried traffic in both directions, from the sages' present back to Sinai, from Sinai forward to the present moment. That is what I mean when I represent Midrash as mediator. The principal mode of thinking in Midrash translates the metaphor into a policy of culture: it requires us to look deeply at something, for, in the depths, we find something else; each thing stands for another, and all things possess a potentiality of meaning never close to the surface, always in the depths of God's revealed will in the Torah. And that account of the continuity of culture under the aspect of Midrash leads us to the limits of this world and the threshold of the other.

## V. REASON AND REVELATION: OUR PLACE IN GOD'S PLAN

Midrash is to Scripture as science is to creation. In following Midrash into the inner structure of revelation, in the case of Scripture, and in following natural science into the inner structure of creation, in the case of natural philosophy, we enter into the mind of God—that one God who revealed the Torah and created the world and who thereby exposed for us the inner workings of God's mind.

What does this final theological proposition mean? To understand the theological premise of Midrash we revert to the issue addressed in the first of the three trends of rabbinic Bible interpretation, the practice of reading individual verses of Scripture to yield general propositions. As we reviewed the forms and propositions of Sifra and Sifré to Numbers, we found the implicit syllogism that the human mind can make sense of the Torah and even clarify its meaning, an assumption that formed the premise of all rabbinic Midrash-exegesis from that time onward. Just as Genesis and Leviticus Rabbah teach us lessons of Midrash for issues of culture, so Sifra and Sifré to Numbers alert us to the lessons of Midrash for issues of theology.

We recall several propositions implicit in the theological position of those Midrash-compilations: First, while Scripture stands paramount and logic, reason, and analytical processes of classification and differentiation are secondary, nonetheless, the sage's mind joins God's mind when the sage receives and sets forth the Torah.

Second, reason unaided by Scripture produces uncertain propositions. Reason operating within the limits of Scripture produces truth. This is because humanity is "in our image, after our likeness," and the aspect of humanity that is like God is not the external and material but the interior: the heart, the soul, the mind. The heart of God, the prophets say, feels the way the heart of humanity does: pain and joy, jealousy and loyalty. The soul of God forms the model for that of humanity.

It follows that through the Torah, humanity enters even into the mind of God, in particular that corner of God's mind revealed in the plan and program that God laid forth in the effects of creation. Humanity may receive Scripture and explain its meaning because humanity—the sage, in our context—reasons as God reasons, feels as God feels, thinks and responds as God does. So the theological premise of Midrash, like the theological premise of the Talmuds, celebrates humanity "in our image, after our likeness." *God's plan revealed in the Torah opens up God's mind to humanity, because humanity guided by the processes of Midrash can grasp the metaphor for God that Torah, seen in creation and revelation alike, reveals.*

In this way Midrash forms the counterpart to natural science. As science examines nature, so Midrash examines Scripture. Both science and Midrash teach us about the wonders of God, who revealed the Torah and created the world. Science constitutes the exegesis of nature. Midrash does its work through exegesis of verses of the Torah. It makes a statement, through exegesis, of propositions demonstrated by the Torah. Through the display in exegesis achieved through narrative, it sets forth the full and whole meaning of the metaphors of person and of action in the Torah. Through Midrash sages discover God's rules for reality in the here and now and at the end of time.

These convictions come to explicit expression in Genesis Rabbah, with which we bring this account of the major trends of rabbinic Bible interpretation to a close. The authorship of that document announces as its initial syllogism that God looked into the Torah as plan and model for the creation of the world. The Torah therefore leads us into God's plan and intention for the world, and when, through Midrash, we penetrate into the profound and hidden layers of that being and that reality, we reach into the mind of God.

This conviction forms the foundation for sages' reading of today in light of the Torah and of the Torah in light of today—*and for their understanding of the whole of time, now and eternity beyond through that mind common to humanity and God, the shared intellect that, in method and in message, in Midrash mediates between Heaven and earth.* Let us conclude by listening to how sages state this conviction.

GENESIS RABBAH I:I

1. A. *In the beginning God created* (Gen. 1:1):
   B. R. Oshaia commenced [discourse by citing the following verse:] *Then I was beside him like a little child, and I was daily his delight [rejoic-*

*ing before him always, rejoicing in his inhabited world, and delighting in the sons of men]* (Prov. 8:30–31).

We read the intersecting verse as though the Torah were speaking. Hence the Torah says of itself that the Torah was beside God *like a little child.* But the word for *child* bears other meanings, and it is one of these that brings us to our conclusion.

2. A. *In the beginning God created* (Gen. 1:1). [As to the verse, *Then I was beside him like a little child, and I was daily his delight [rejoicing before him always, rejoicing in his inhabited world, and delighting in the sons of men]*:

B. the word [for *child* also may be read to] mean "workman."

C. [In the cited verse] the Torah speaks, "I was the work-plan of the Holy One, blessed be he."

D. In the accepted practice of the world, when a mortal king builds a palace, he does not build it out of his own head, but he follows a work-plan.

E. And [the one who supplies] the work-plan does not build out of his own head, but he has designs and diagrams, so as to know how to situate the rooms and the doorways.

F. Thus the Holy One, blessed be he, consulted the Torah when he created the world.

G. So the Torah stated, *By means of "the beginning"* [*that is to say, the Torah*] *did God create . . .* (Gen. 1:1).

H. For the word for *beginning* refers only to the Torah, as Scripture says, *The Lord made me as the beginning of his way* (Prov. 8:22).

# Selected Hebrew Texts

## CHAPTER 1: MISHNAH BERACHOT 8*

אֵלּוּ דְבָרִים שֶׁבֵּין בֵּית שַׁמַּאי וּבֵית הִלֵּל בַּסְעוּדָה. בֵּית שַׁמַּאי
אוֹמְרִים: מְבָרֵךְ עַל הַיּוֹם, וְאַחַר כָּךְ מְבָרֵךְ עַל הַיַּיִן. וּבֵית הִלֵּל אוֹמְרִים:
מְבָרֵךְ עַל הַיַּיִן, וְאַחַר כָּךְ מְבָרֵךְ עַל הַיּוֹם. בֵּית שַׁמַּאי אוֹמְרִים: נוֹטְלִין
לַיָּדַיִם, וְאַחַר כָּךְ מוֹזְגִין אֶת הַכּוֹס. וּבֵית הִלֵּל אוֹמְרִים: מוֹזְגִין אֶת הַכּוֹס,
וְאַחַר כָּךְ נוֹטְלִין לַיָּדַיִם. בֵּית שַׁמַּאי אוֹמְרִים: מְקַנֵּחַ יָדָיו בַּמַּפָּה, וּמַנִּיחָהּ
עַל הַשֻּׁלְחָן. וּבֵית הִלֵּל אוֹמְרִים: עַל הַכֶּסֶת.

בֵּית שַׁמַּאי אוֹמְרִים: מְכַבְּדִין אֶת הַבַּיִת, וְאַחַר כָּךְ נוֹטְלִין לַיָּדַיִם.
וּבֵית הִלֵּל אוֹמְרִים: נוֹטְלִין לַיָּדַיִם, וְאַחַר כָּךְ מְכַבְּדִין אֶת הַבַּיִת.

בֵּית שַׁמַּאי אוֹמְרִים: נֵר, וּמָזוֹן, וּבְשָׂמִים, וְהַבְדָּלָה. וּבֵית הִלֵּל
אוֹמְרִים: נֵר, וּבְשָׂמִים, וּמָזוֹן, וְהַבְדָּלָה. בֵּית שַׁמַּאי אוֹמְרִים: 'שֶׁבָּרָא
מְאוֹר הָאֵשׁ'; וּבֵית הִלֵּל אוֹמְרִים: 'בּוֹרֵא מְאוֹרֵי הָאֵשׁ'.

אֵין מְבָרְכִין לֹא עַל הַנֵּר, וְלֹא עַל הַבְּשָׂמִים שֶׁלַּגּוֹיִם, וְלֹא עַל הַנֵּר,
וְלֹא עַל הַבְּשָׂמִים שֶׁלַּמֵּתִים, וְלֹא עַל הַנֵּר, וְלֹא עַל הַבְּשָׂמִים שֶׁלִּפְנֵי
עֲבוֹדָה זָרָה. וְאֵין מְבָרְכִין עַל הַנֵּר עַד שֶׁיֵּאוֹתוּ לְאוֹרוֹ.

מִי שֶׁאָכַל וְשָׁכַח וְלֹא בֵרַךְ—בֵּית שַׁמַּאי אוֹמְרִים: יַחֲזֹר לִמְקוֹמוֹ
וִיבָרֵךְ. וּבֵית הִלֵּל אוֹמְרִים: יְבָרֵךְ בַּמָּקוֹם שֶׁנִּזְכַּר. עַד אֵימָתַי הוּא מְבָרֵךְ?
עַד כְּדֵי שֶׁיִּתְעַכֵּל הַמָּזוֹן שֶׁבְּמֵעָיו.

בָּא לָהֶם יַיִן לְאַחַר הַמָּזוֹן, וְאֵין שָׁם אֶלָּא אוֹתוֹ הַכּוֹס—בֵּית שַׁמַּאי
אוֹמְרִים: מְבָרֵךְ עַל הַיַּיִן, וְאַחַר כָּךְ מְבָרֵךְ עַל הַמָּזוֹן. וּבֵית הִלֵּל אוֹמְרִים:
מְבָרֵךְ עַל הַמָּזוֹן, וְאַחַר כָּךְ מְבָרֵךְ עַל הַיַּיִן. עוֹנִין אָמֵן אַחַר יִשְׂרָאֵל
הַמְבָרֵךְ, וְאֵין עוֹנִין אָמֵן אַחַר הַכּוּתִי הַמְבָרֵךְ, עַד שֶׁיִּשְׁמַע אֶת כָּל הַבְּרָכָה.

---

*Author's Note: Selected Hebrew texts edited by Stephen A. Kaufman with
Michael Arsers.

## CHAPTER 2: SIFRA NEGAIM PARASHAH ONE

פרק א אֲוַיְדַבֵּר ה׳ אֶל־מֹשֶׁה וְאֶל־אַהֲרֹן לֵאמֹר. אָדָם כִּי־יִהְיֶה בְעוֹר־
בְּשָׂרוֹ. מַה תַּלְמוּד לוֹמַר לְפִי שֶׁנֶּאֱמַר כִּי־יִהְיֶה
בְעוֹר־בְּשָׂרוֹ בֶּהָרוֹת בֶּהָרוֹת טְהוֹרוֹת. אֵין צָרִיךְ לוֹמַר בֶּהָרוֹת שֶׁאֵין בָּהֶם
מַרְאוֹת נְגָעִים וְשֶׁלֹּא בָאוּ לִכְלָל אֶלָּא בֶהָרוֹת שֶׁבָּהֶם מַרְאוֹת נְגָעִים שֶׁהָיוּ
בְגוֹי וְנִתְגַּיֵּיר. בְּקָטָן וְנוֹלַד. בְּקֵמֶט וְנִגְלָה בְרֹאשׁ וּבַזָּקָן בִּשְׁחִין וּבְמִכְוָה
בְּקָרַחַת ᵇהַמּוֹרְדִין נִשְׁתַּנּוּ מַרְאֵיהֶם בֵּין לְהָקֵל בֵּין לְהַחֲמִיר. ר׳ אֶלְעָזָר בֶּן
עֲזַרְיָה מְטַהֵר. רַבִּי אֶלְעָזָר בֶּן חִסְמָא אוֹמֵר לְהָקֵל טָהוֹר וּלְהַחֲמִיר תֵּרָאֶה
כַתְּחִלָּה רַבִּי עֲקִיבָא אוֹמֵר בֵּין לְהָקֵל בֵּין לְהַחֲמִיר תֵּרָאֶה כַתְּחִלָּה לְכָךְ נֶאֱמַר
אָדָם כִּי־יִהְיֶה: (ב) כִּי יִהְיֶה מִן ᵍהַדִּיבֵּר וְהֵילָךְ. וַהֲלֹא דִין הוּא. טִימֵּא בַזָּבִים
וְטִימֵּא בַנְּגָעִים מַה־זָבִים פָּטַר בָּהֶם לִפְנֵי הַדִּיבֵּר אַף נְגָעִים פָּטַר בָּהֶם
לִפְנֵי הַדִּיבֵּר: (ג) קַל וָחוֹמֶר וּמָה אִם זָבִים שֶׁטּוּמְאָתָן וְטָהֳרָתָן בְּכָל אָדָם
פָּטַר בָּהֶם לִפְנֵי הַדִּיבֵּר. נְגָעִים שֶׁאֵין טוּמְאָתָם וְטָהֳרָתָן אֶלָּא בְכֹהֵן אֵינוּ
דִין שֶׁיִּפָּטוֹר בָּהֶם לִפְנֵי הַדִּיבֵּר. לֹא אִם אָמַרְתָּ בַּזָּבִים שֶׁלֹּא טִימֵּא בָהֶם
אֲנוּסִים. תֹּאמַר בַּנְּגָעִים שֶׁטִּימֵּא בָהֶם אֲנוּסִים. הוֹאִיל וְטִימֵּא בָהֶם
אֲנוּסִים יִפָּטוֹר בָּהֶם לִפְנֵי הַדִּיבֵּר תַּלְמוּד לוֹמַר כִּי־יִהְיֶה מִן הַדִּיבֵּר
וְאֵילָךְ: (ד) בְעוֹר־בְּשָׂרוֹ מַה תַּלְמוּד לוֹמַר לְפִי שֶׁנֶּאֱמַר וְשֵׂעָר בַּנֶּגַע
הָפַךְ לָבָן שֶׁיָּכוֹל אֵין לִי אֶלָּא מָקוֹם שֶׁהוּא רָאוּי לְגַדֵּל שֵׂעָר לָבָן. מָקוֹם
שֶׁאֵינוּ רָאוּי לְגַדֵּל שֵׂעָר לָבָן מִנַּיִן תַּלְמוּד לוֹמַר בְעוֹר־בְּשָׂרוֹ רִיבָּה.
ᵈשְׂאֵת זוֹ שְׂאֵת. בַּהֶרֶת זוֹ בַהֶרֶת. סַפַּחַת זוֹ שֵׁנִי לְבַהֶרֶת. וּמַרְאֵהוּ
עָמֹק. שֵׁנִי לִשְׂאֵת. מַה לָּשׁוֹן שְׂאֵת. מוּבְהֶקֶת. כְּמַרְאֶה הַצֵּל שֶׁהֵם
גְּבוֹהִים מִמַּרְאֵה הַחַמָּה. מַה לָּשׁוֹן עָמֹק. עֲמוּקָה כְּמַרְאֵה הַחַמָּה שֶׁהֵם
עֲמוּקִים מִן הַצֵּל. מַה לָּשׁוֹן סַפַּחַת טְפֵילָה. שֶׁנֶּאֱמַר סְפָחֵנִי נָא אֶל־אַחַת
הַכְּהֻנּוֹת. ʰוְהָיָה מְלַמֵּד שֶׁהֵם מִצְטָרְפִים זֶה עִם זֶה לִפְטוֹר וּלְהַחֲלִיט
וּלְהַסְגִּיר. בְעוֹר בָּשָׂר. בְעוֹר בָּשָׂר שֶׁל נִרְאָה. ʸמִיכָּן אָמְרוּ בַהֶרֶת
עַזָּה נִרְאֵית כְּגַרְמָנִי. כֵּהָה. וְהַכֵּהָה כְּכוּשִׁי עַזָּה: (ה) רַבִּי יִשְׁמָעֵאל

אוֹמֵר בֵּית יִשְׂרָאֵל הֲרֵינִי כְּפַרְתָּן הֲרֵי הֵן כְּאֶשְׁכְּרוֹעַ לֹא שְׁחוֹרִים וְלֹא
לְבָנִים אֶלָּא בֵּינוֹנִיִּים. רַבִּי עֲקִיבָא אוֹמֵר יֵשׁ לַצַּיָּירִים סַמְמָנִים שֶׁהֵם
צָרִים עוֹרוֹת שְׁחוֹרוֹת לְבָנוֹת וּבֵינוֹנִיּוֹת מֵבִיא סַם בֵּינוֹנִית וּמַקִּיפוֹ
מִבַּחוּץ וְתֵרָאֶה כְּבֵינוֹנִי. רַבִּי יוֹסֵי אוֹמֵר כָּתוּב אֶחָד אוֹמֵר בְּעוֹר בָּשָׂר
וְכָתוּב אֶחָד אוֹמֵר בְּעוֹר־הַבָּשָׂר. מָצִינוּ שֶׁמַּרְאוֹת נְגָעִים לְהָקֵל. אֲבָל לֹא
לְהַחְמִיר רוֹאֶה הַגֶּרְמָנִי בִּבְשָׂרוֹ לְהָקֵל נִמְצֵאת נִמְקַיֵּים בְּעוֹר בְּשָׂרוֹ.
וְהַכּוּשִׁי בְּבֵינוֹנִית לְהָקֵל נִמְצֵאת מְקַיֵּים בְּעוֹר־הַבָּשָׂר וַחֲכָמִים אוֹמְרִים
זֶה בְּבֵינוֹנִי: (ו) 'וְהָיָה בְעוֹר־בְּשָׂרוֹ שֶׁהוּא מְלַמֵּד שֶׁהוּא מִצְטַעֵר מִמֶּנּוּ. וּמִנַּיִן
שֶׁאַף אֲחֵרִים מִצְטַעֲרִים מִמֶּנּוּ רוֹאִים אוֹתוֹ שֶׁהוּא מִצְטַעֵר מִמֶּנּוּ תַּלְמוּד
לוֹמַר לְנָגַע. צָרַעַת כִּגְרִיס. הֲלֹא דִין הוּא טִימֵּא כָּאן וְטִימֵּא בְּמִחְיָה מַה
מִחְיָה כִּגְרִיס אַף כָּאן כִּגְרִיס: (ז) לְלֹא אִם אָמַרְתָּ בְּמִחְיָה שֶׁהִיא צְרִיכָה
כַּעֲדָשָׁה תֹּאמַר בְּשֵׂיעָר לָבָן בְּשֵׂיעָר מָקוֹם שֵׁיעָר לָבָן צָרִיךְ כְּלוּם תַּלְמוּד
לוֹמַר צָרַעַת כִּגְרִיס: (ח) חְוְהוּבָא אֶל־אַהֲרֹן. אֵין לִי אֶלָּא אַהֲרֹן עַצְמוֹ.
מִנַּיִן לְרַבּוֹת כֹּהֵן אַחֵר תַּלְמוּד לוֹמַר הַכֹּהֵן. מִנַּיִן לְרַבּוֹת בַּעֲלֵי מוּמִים
הַלְמוּד לוֹמַר מִבָּנָיו. אוֹ יָכוֹל שֶׁאֲנִי מְרַבֶּה חֲלָלִים. תַּלְמוּד לוֹמַר הַכֹּהֲנִים
יָצְאוּ חֲלָלִים. וּמִנַּיִן לְרַבּוֹת כָּל יִשְׂרָאֵל תַּלְמוּד לוֹמַר אוֹ אֶל־אַחַד: (ט) אִם
סוֹפִינוּ לְרַבּוֹת כָּל יִשְׂרָאֵל מַה תַּלְמוּד לוֹמַר אוֹ אֶל אַחַד מִבָּנָיו הַכֹּהֲנִים.
אֶלָּא לְלַמֵּד שֶׁאֵין טוּמְאָה וְטָהֳרָה אֶלָּא מִפִּי כֹהֵן. הָא כֵּיצַד חָכָם שֶׁבְּיִשְׂרָאֵל
רוֹאֶה אֶת הַנְּגָעִים וְאוֹמֵר לְכֹהֵן אַף עַל פִּי שׁוֹטֶה אֱמוֹר טָמֵא וְהוּא אוֹמֵר
טָמֵא. אֱמוֹר טָהוֹר וְהוּא אוֹמֵר טָהוֹר. דָּבָר אַחֵר מַה תַּלְמוּד לוֹמַר אוֹ
אֶל־אַחַד מִבָּנָיו הַכֹּהֲנִים לְפִי שֶׁנֶּאֱמַר עַל־פִּיהֶם יִהְיֶה כָּל־רִיב וְכָל־נָגַע
טְהִקִּישׁ רִיבִים לִנְגָעִים מַה נְגָעִים בַּיּוֹם אַף רִיבִים בַּיּוֹם: (י) מָה רִיבִים
שֶׁלֹּא בִקְרוֹבִים. אַף נְגָעִים שֶׁלֹּא בִקְרוֹבִים. אִי מָה רִיבִים בִּשְׁלֹשָׁה אַף
נְגָעִים בִּשְׁלֹשָׁה קַל וָחוֹמֶר אִם מָמוֹנוֹ בִּשְׁלֹשָׁה. אֵינוֹ דִין שֶׁלֹּא יְהָא גוּפוֹ
בִּשְׁלֹשָׁה. תַּלְמוּד לוֹמַר אוֹ אֶל אַחַד מִבָּנָיו הַכֹּהֲנִים מְלַמֵּד שֶׁכֹּהֵן אֶחָד
רוֹאֶה אֶת הַנְּגָעִים.

## CHAPTER 2: SIFRA NEGAIM PARASHAH TWO

**פרשה ב** בַּהֶרֶת לְבָנָה אֵין לִי אֶלָּא בַהֶרֶת לְבָנָה. מְנַיִן לְרַבּוֹת אֶת
הַשְׂאֵת תַּלְמוּד לוֹמַר לְמַטָּן שְׂאֵת לְבָנָה. וּמְנַיִן לְרַבּוֹת שְׁאָר
הַמַּרְאוֹת תַּלְמוּד לוֹמַר וְאִם־בַּהֶרֶת: (ב) יָכוֹל כְּשֵׁם שֶׁהוּא שְׁלִישִׁי לְכָתוּב
כָּךְ תְּהֵא שְׁלִישִׁי לְמַרְאוֹת תַּלְמוּד לוֹמַר לְבָנָה ˊלְבָנָה הִיא לְבָנָה (היא)
וְאֵין לְמַעֲלָה הֵימֶנָּה. וְכַמָּה תְהֵא לַבְנוּנִיתָה כַּשֶּׁלֶג שֶׁנֶּאֱמַר וְהִנֵּה מִרְיָם
מְצוֹרַעַת כַּשָּׁלֶג: (ג) יָכוֹל לְכָל מַרְאֵה הַשֶּׁלֶג יִהְיוּ טְמֵאִים וּשְׁאָר כָּל
הַמַּרְאוֹת יִהְיוּ טְהוֹרִים תַּלְמוּד לוֹמַר בּוֹהַק הוּא. בּוֹהַק טָהוֹר הוּא מִמֶּנּוּ
וּלְמַעֲלָה טָמֵא: (ד) מִיכָּן אָמְרוּ מַרְאוֹת נְגָעִים שְׁנַיִם שֶׁהֵם אַרְבָּעָה בַּהֶרֶת
עַזָּה כַּשֶּׁלֶג. שְׁנִיָּיה לָה כְּסִיד הַהֵיכָל. הַשְׂאֵת כְּקִרוּם בֵּיצָה שְׁנִיָּיה לָה
כְּצֶמֶר לָבָן דִּבְרֵי רַבִּי מֵאִיר. וַחֲכָמִים אוֹמְרִים הַשְׂאֵת כְּצֶמֶר וּשְׁנִיָּיה לָה
כְּקִרוּם בֵּיצָה: (ה) ˢהַפָּתוּךְ שֶׁבַּשֶּׁלֶג כַּיַּיִן הַמָּזוּג. הַפָּתוּךְ שֶׁבַּסִּיד כַּדָּם
הַמָּזוּג בְּחָלָב דִּבְרֵי רַבִּי יִשְׁמָעֵאל. רַבִּי עֲקִיבָא אוֹמֵר אֲדַמְדָּם שֶׁבָּזֶה
וְשֶׁבָּזֶה כַּיַּיִן הַמָּזוּג בְּמַיִם. אֶלָּא שֶׁל שֶׁלֶג עַזָּה וְשֶׁל סִיד כֵּהָה הֵימֶנָּה:
(ו) ˊרַבִּי חֲנַנְיָה סְגַן הַכֹּהֲנִים אוֹמֵר מַרְאוֹת נְגָעִים שִׁשָּׁה עָשָׂר. רַבִּי דוֹסָא
בֶּן הַרְכִּינַס אוֹמֵר שְׁלֹשִׁים וְשִׁשָּׁה. עֲקַבְיָא בֶּן מַהֲלַלְאֵל שִׁבְעִים וּשְׁנַיִם.
ˣאָמַר רַבִּי יוֹסֵי שָׁאַל רַבִּי יְהוֹשֻׁעַ בְּנוֹ שֶׁל רַבִּי עֲקִיבָא אֶת רַבִּי עֲקִיבָא
אָמַר לוֹ מִפְּנֵי מָה אָמְרוּ מַרְאוֹת נְגָעִים [שְׁתַּיִם] שֶׁהֵם אַרְבָּעָה אָמַר לוֹ אִם
לָאו מַה יֹּאמְרוּ אָמַר לוֹ יֹאמְרוּ מִקְּרוּם בֵּיצָה וּלְמַעֲלָה טָמֵא וּמִצְטָרְפִים
זֶה עִם זֶה. אָמַר רַבִּי יוֹסֵי שָׁאַל רַבִּי יְהוֹשֻׁעַ בְּנוֹ שֶׁל רַבִּי עֲקִיבָא אֶת
רַבִּי עֲקִיבָא אָמַר לוֹ מִפְּנֵי מָה אָמְרוּ מַרְאוֹת נְגָעִים [שְׁתַּיִם] שֶׁהֵם
אַרְבָּעָה אָמַר לוֹ אִם לָאו מַה יֹּאמְרוּ אָמַר לוֹ יֹאמְרוּ מִקְּרוּם בֵּיצָה וּלְמַעֲלָה
טָמֵא אָמַר לוֹ לוֹמַר לָךְ שֶׁמִּצְטָרְפִים זֶה עִם זֶה אָמַר לוֹ וְיֹאמַר כָּל שֶׁהוּא
מִקְּרוּם בֵּיצָה וּלְמַעֲלָה טָמֵא וּמִצְטָרְפִים זֶה עִם זֶה אָמַר לוֹ מְלַמֵּד שֶׁאִם
אֵינוֹ בָקִי בָהֶם וּבִשְׁמוֹתֵיהֶם לֹא יִרְאֶה אֶת הַנְּגָעִים: (ז) ˊוּשְׂעָרָה לֹא
שִׂעֵר מִחְיָתָה בֵּיצַד בַּהֶרֶת כִּגְרִיס וּבָה מִחְיָה כַּעֲדָשָׁה וְשִׂעֵר לָבָן

בְּתוֹךְ הַמִּחְיָה. הָלְכָה הַמִּחְיָה טְמֵאָה מִשּׁוּם שֵׂעָר לָבָן. הָלְכָה שֵׂעָר
לָבָן טָמֵא מִשּׁוּם הַמִּחְיָה. רַבִּי שִׁמְעוֹן מְטַהֵר מִפְּנֵי שֶׁלֹּא הֲפַכַתּוּ הַבַּהֶרֶת
אָמַר לוֹ וַהֲלֹא כְּבָר נֶאֱמַר וְשֵׂעָר בַּנֶּגַע הָפַךְ לָבָן נֶגַע זֶה בְּכָל מָקוֹם:
(ח) וּשְׂעָרָה לֹא הָפַךְ לָבָן וְלֹא שֵׂעָר מִקְצָתָהּ כֵּיצַד בַּהֶרֶת הִיא מִחְיָתָהּ
כִּגְרִיס וְשֵׂעָר לָבָן בְּתוֹךְ הַבַּהֶרֶת הָלְכָה הַמִּחְיָה טְמֵאָה מִשּׁוּם שֵׂעָר
לָבָן הָלַךְ שֵׂעָר לָבָן טָמֵא מִשּׁוּם הַמִּחְיָה. רַבִּי שִׁמְעוֹן מְטַהֵר מִפְּנֵי שֶׁלֹּא
הֲפַכַתּוּ הַבַּהֶרֶת כִּגְרִיס. וּמוֹדִים שֶׁאִם יֵשׁ בַּמָּקוֹם שֵׂעָר לָבָן כִּגְרִיס
שֶׁהוּא טָמֵא. (ט) ³וּשְׂעָרָה לֹא הָפַךְ לָבָן וְהִסְגִּיר הָא אִם יֵשׁ בָּהּ שֵׂעָר
שָׁחוֹר אֵינוֹ מְמַעֲטָהּ. שֶׁאֵלּוּ הַתַּלְמִידִים אֶת רַבִּי יוֹסֵי בַּהֶרֶת וּבָהּ שֵׂעָר
שָׁחוֹר חוֹשְׁשִׁים אָנוּ שֶׁמָּא מִיעֵט מִמְּקוֹמוֹ אֶת הַבַּהֶרֶת מִכְּגְרִיס אָמַר לָהֶם
בַּהֶרֶת וּבְשֵׂעָר לָבָן חַיָּישִׁינָן שֶׁמָּא מִיעֵט מְקוֹמָהּ אֶת דְּבַהֶרֶת כִּגְרִיס
אָמְרוּ לוֹ לֹא אִם אָמַרְתָּ בְּשֵׂעָר לָבָן שֶׁהוּא סִימַן טוּמְאָה תֹּאמַר בְּשֵׂעָר
שָׁחוֹר שֶׁאֵינוֹ סִימַן טוּמְאָה אָמַר לָהֶן הֲרֵי שֶׁיֵּשׁ בָּהּ עֶשֶׂר שְׂעָרוֹת לְבָנוֹת
כְּלוּם הֲרֵי הֵם סִימָנֵי טוּמְאָה אֶלָּא שְׁתַּיִם. חוֹשְׁשִׁים אָנוּ עַל הַמּוֹתָר שֶׁמָּא
מִיעֵט מִמְּקוֹמוֹ אֶת בַּהֶרֶת מִכְּגְרִיס. אָמְרוּ לוֹ לֹא אִם אָמַרְתָּ בְּשֵׂעָר לָבָן
שֶׁהוּא מִין טוּמְאָה תֹּאמַר בְּשֵׂעָר שָׁחוֹר שֶׁאֵינוֹ מִין טוּמְאָה. אָמַר לָהֶם
אַף שֵׂעָר שָׁחוֹר הוֹפֵךְ וְהוֹוֶה מִין טוּמְאָה וְאוֹמֵר וּשְׂעָרָה לֹא הָפַךְ לָבָן.
וְהִסְגִּיר הָא יֵשׁ בָּהּ שֵׂעָר שָׁחוֹר אֵינוֹ מְמַעֲטָהּ וְהִסְגִּיר הַכֹּהֵן אֶת הַנֶּגַע
שִׁבְעָה יָמִים תְּחִלָּה:

## CHAPTER 2: SIFRÉ TO NUMBERS 84

(פד) וַיְהִי בִּנְסֹעַ הָאָרֹן נָקוּד עָלָיו מִלְמַעְלָה וּמִלְמַטָּה מִפְּנֵי שֶׁלֹּא

הָיָה זֶה מְקוֹמוֹ רַבִּי אוֹמֵר מִפְּנֵי שֶׁהוּא סֵפֶר בְּעַצְמוֹ מִיכָּן אָמְרוּ סֵפֶר

שֶׁנִּמְחַק וְנִשְׁתַּיֵּיר בּוֹ שְׁמוֹנִים וְחָמֵשׁ אוֹתִיּוֹת כְּפָרָשַׁת וַיְהִי בִּנְסֹעַ הָאָרֹן

מְטַמֵּא אֶת הַיָּדַיִם ר' שִׁמְעוֹן אוֹמֵר נָקוּד עָלָיו מִלְמַעְלָה וּמִלְמַטָּה מִפְּנֵי

שֶׁלֹּא הָיָה זֶה מְקוֹמוֹ וּמֶה הָיָה רָאוּי לִיכָּתֵב תַּחְתָּיו וַיְהִי הָעָם כְּמִתְאוֹנְנִים

מָשָׁל לְמָה הַדָּבָר דּוֹמֶה לִבְנֵי אָדָם שֶׁאָמְרוּ לַמֶּלֶךְ הַנִּרְאֶה שֶׁתַּגִּיעַ עִמָּנוּ

אֵצֶל מוֹשָׁל עַכּוֹ הִגִּיעַ לְעַכּוֹ הָלַךְ לוֹ לְצוֹר הִגִּיעַ לְצוֹר הָלַךְ לוֹ לְצִידוֹן

הִגִּיעַ לְצִידוֹן [הָלַךְ לוֹ לִבְירִי הִגִּיעַ לִבְירִי] הָלַךְ לוֹ לְאַנְטוֹכְיָה הִגִּיעַ

לְאַנְטוֹכְיָה הִתְחִילוּ בְּנֵי אָדָם מִתְרָעֲמִים עַל הַמֶּלֶךְ שֶׁנִּתְלַבְּטוּ עַל דֶּרֶךְ זוֹ

וְהַמֶּלֶךְ צָרִיךְ לְהִתְרָעֵם עֲלֵיהֶם שֶׁבִּשְׁבִילָם נִתְלַבֵּט עַל דֶּרֶךְ זוֹ כָּךְ הָלְכָה

שְׁכִינָה בּוֹ בַיּוֹם שְׁלֹשִׁים וְשִׁשָּׁה מִיל כְּדֵי שֶׁיִּכָּנְסוּ יִשְׂרָאֵל לָאָרֶץ הִתְחִילוּ

יִשְׂרָאֵל מִתְרָעֲמִים לִפְנֵי הַמָּקוֹם שֶׁנִּתְלַבְּטוּ עַל דֶּרֶךְ זוֹ וְהַמָּקוֹם צָרִיךְ

לְהִתְרָעֵם עֲלֵיהֶם שֶׁבִּשְׁבִילָם הִילְכָה שְׁכִינָה בּוֹ בַיּוֹם שְׁלֹשִׁים וְשִׁשָּׁה

מִילִין כְּדֵי שֶׁיִּכָּנְסוּ יִשְׂרָאֵל לָאָרֶץ.

וַיֹּאמֶר מֹשֶׁה קוּמָה ה' וְכָתוּב אֶחָד אוֹמֵר עַל פִּי ה' יַחֲנוּ וְעַל־פִּי ה'

יִסָּעוּ (במדבר ט כג) כֵּיצַד יִתְקַיְּימוּ שְׁנֵי כְתוּבִים הַלָּלוּ מָשָׁל לְמֶלֶךְ בָּשָׂר

וָדָם שֶׁאָמַר לְעַבְדּוֹ הַנִּרְאֶה שֶׁתַּעֲמִידֵנִי בִּשְׁבִיל שֶׁאֲנִי הוֹלֵךְ לִיתֵּן יְרוּשָׁה

לִבְנִי דָבָר אַחֵר לְמָה הַדָּבָר דּוֹמֶה לְמֶלֶךְ בָּשָׂר וָדָם שֶׁהָיָה מְהַלֵּךְ בַּדֶּרֶךְ

וְנָהַג אוֹהֲבוֹ עִמּוֹ כְּשֶׁהוּא נוֹסֵעַ אוֹמֵר אֵינִי נוֹסֵעַ עַד שֶׁיָּבֹא אוֹהֲבִי וּכְשֶׁהוּא

חוֹנֶה אוֹמֵר אֵינִי חוֹנֶה עַד שֶׁיָּבֹא אוֹהֲבִי נִמְצֵאתָ מְקַיֵּים עַל פִּי מֹשֶׁה יַחֲנוּ

וְנִמְצֵאתָ מְקַיֵּים עַל פִּי ה' יַחֲנוּ וְעַל פִּי מֹשֶׁה יִסָּעוּ וְעַל פִּי ה' יִסָּעוּ.

קוּמָה ה' וְיָפוּצוּ אוֹיְבֶיךָ, אֵלּוּ הַמְכֻנָּסִים: וְיָנוּסוּ מְשַׂנְאֶיךָ, אֵלּוּ

הָרוֹדְפִים: מִפָּנֶיךָ, מִפָּנֶיךָ הֵם נָסִים וְאֵין אָנוּ כְלוּם לִפְנֵיהֶם אֶלָּא כְשֶׁפָּנֶיךָ

אִתָּנוּ אָנוּ כְלוּם לִפְנֵיהֶם וּכְשֶׁאֵין פָּנֶיךָ אִתָּנוּ אֵין אָנוּ כְלוּם לִפְנֵיהֶם וְכֵן

הוּא אוֹמֵר וַיֹּאמֶר אֵלָיו אִם־אֵין פָּנֶיךָ הוֹלְכִים אַל־תַּעֲלֵנוּ מִזֶּה (שמות לג טו)

וּבַמֶּה יוֹדֵעַ אֵיפוֹא וְאוֹמֵר וְאוֹמֵר וַיְהִי בְּנֻסָם מִפְּנֵי יִשְׂרָאֵל הֵם בְּמוֹרַד בֵּית־חוֹרוֹן
וַה' הִשְׁלִיךְ עֲלֵיהֶם אֲבָנִים גְּדוֹלוֹת (יהושע י יא) וְאוֹמֵר אֱלֹהַי שִׁיתֵמוֹ כַגַּלְגַּל
כְּקַשׁ לִפְנֵי־רוּחַ כְּאֵשׁ תִּבְעַר־יָעַר וּכְלֶהָבָה תְּלַהֵט הָרִים (תהלים פג יד־טו).

וְיָנוּסוּ מְשַׂנְאֶיךָ, וְכִי יֵשׁ שׂוֹנְאִים לִפְנֵי מִי שֶׁאָמַר וְהָיָה הָעוֹלָם אֶלָּא
מַגִּיד הַכָּתוּב שֶׁכָּל מִי שֶׁשּׂוֹנֵא אֶת יִשְׂרָאֵל כְּאִלּוּ שׂוֹנֵא אֶת מִי שֶׁאָמַר
וְהָיָה הָעוֹלָם כַּיּוֹצֵא בּוֹ אַתָּה אוֹמֵר וּבְרוֹב גְּאוֹנְךָ תַּהֲרֹס קָמֶיךָ (שמות טו ז)
וְכִי יֵשׁ קָמִים לִפְנֵי מִי שֶׁאָמַר וְהָיָה הָעוֹלָם אֶלָּא מַגִּיד הַכָּתוּב שֶׁכָּל מִי
שֶׁקָּם עַל יִשְׂרָאֵל כְּאִלּוּ קָם עַל הַמָּקוֹם וְכֵן הוּא אוֹמֵר אַל־תִּשְׁכַּח קוֹל
צֹרְרֶיךָ שְׁאוֹן קָמֶיךָ עוֹלֶה תָמִיד (תהלים עד כג) [כִּי הִנֵּה אוֹיְבֶיךָ ה' (שם צב י)
כִּי־הִנֵּה רְחֵקֶיךָ יֹאבֵדוּ (שם עג כז)] כִּי־הִנֵּה אוֹיְבֶיךָ יֶהֱמָיוּן וּמְשַׂנְאֶיךָ נָשְׂאוּ
רֹאשׁ (שם פג ג) מִפְּנֵי מָה עַל־עַמְּךָ יַעֲרִימוּ סוֹד (שם ד) הֲלֹא־מְשַׂנְאֶיךָ
ה' אֶשְׂנָא וּבִתְקוֹמְמֶיךָ אֶתְקוֹטָט תַּכְלִית שִׂנְאָה שְׂנֵאתִים לְאוֹיְבִים הָיוּ
לִי (שם קלט כא־כב) וְכֵן הוּא אוֹמֵר כִּי הַנּוֹגֵעַ בָּכֶם כְּנוֹגֵעַ בְּבָבַת עֵינוֹ
(זכריה ב יב) ר' יְהוּדָה אוֹמֵר בְּבָבַת עַיִן לֹא נֶאֱמַר אֶלָּא בָּבַת עֵינוֹ כִּבְיָכוֹל
כְּלַפֵּי מַעֲלָה הַכָּתוּב מְדַבֵּר אֶלָּא שְׁכִינָה הַכָּתוּב כַּיּוֹצֵא בּוֹ לָמָה שַׂמְתַּנִי
לְמִפְגָּע לָךְ וָאֶהְיֶה עָלַי לְמַשָּׂא (איוב ז כ) אֶלָּא שְׁכִינָה הַכָּתוּב כַּיּוֹצֵא בּוֹ
וְהִנָּם שׁוֹלְחִים אֶת־הַזְּמוֹרָה אֶל־אַפָּם (יחזקאל ח יז) אֶלָּא שְׁכִינָה הַכָּתוּב
כַּיּוֹצֵא בּוֹ הֲלֹא אַתָּה מִקֶּדֶם ה' אֱלֹהַי קְדֹשִׁי וְלֹא נָמוּת (חבקוק א יב) אֶלָּא
שְׁכִינָה הַכָּתוּב כַּיּוֹצֵא בּוֹ וַיָּמִירוּ אֶת־כְּבוֹדָם בְּתַבְנִית שׁוֹר אוֹכֵל עֵשֶׂב
(תהלים קו כ) אֶלָּא שְׁכִינָה הַכָּתוּב כַּיּוֹצֵא בּוֹ וְאִם־כָּכָה אַתְּ־עֹשֶׂה לִי הָרְגֵנִי
נָא הָרוֹג אִם־מָצָאתִי חֵן בְּעֵינֶיךָ וְאַל־אֶרְאֶה בְּרָעָתִי (במדבר יא טו) אֶלָּא
שְׁכִינָה הַכָּתוּב [כַּיּוֹצֵא בּוֹ וְעַמִּי הֵמִיר כְּבוֹדוֹ (ירמיה ב יא) אֶלָּא שְׁכִינָה
הַכָּתוּב] כַּיּוֹצֵא בּוֹ אַל־נָא תְהִי כַמֵּת אֲשֶׁר בְּצֵאתוֹ מֵרֶחֶם אִמּוֹ וַיֵּאָכֵל חֲצִי
בְשָׂרוֹ (במדבר יב יב) אֶלָּא שְׁכִינָה הַכָּתוּב [אַף כָּאן אַתָּה אוֹמֵר בָּבַת עֵינוֹ
ר' יְהוּדָה אוֹמֵר בָּבַת הָעַיִן לֹא נֶאֱמַר אֶלָּא בָּבַת עֵינוֹ כִּבְיָכוֹל כְּלַפֵּי מַעֲלָה
הַכָּתוּב מְדַבֵּר] וְכָל מִי שֶׁעוֹזֵר אֶת יִשְׂרָאֵל כְּאִלּוּ עוֹזֵר אֶת מִי שֶׁאָמַר

וְהָיָה הָעוֹלָם שֶׁנֶּאֱמַר מֵרוֹז אָמַר מַלְאַךְ ה' אוֹרוּ אָרוֹר יוֹשְׁבֶיהָ כִּי
לֹא־בָאוּ לְעֶזְרַת ה' לְעֶזְרַת ה' בַּגִּבּוֹרִים (שופטים ה כג) רַבִּי שִׁמְעוֹן בֶּן
אֶלְעָזָר אוֹמֵר אֵין לְךָ חָבִיב בְּכָל הַגּוּף כָּעַיִן וּמָשָׁל בָּהּ אֶת יִשְׂרָאֵל מָשָׁל
אָדָם לוֹקֶה עַל רֹאשׁוֹ אֵינוֹ אוֹמֵר אֶלָּא עֵינָיו הָא אֵין לְךָ חָבִיב בְּכָל הַגּוּף
כָּעַיִן וּמָשָׁל בָּהּ אֶת יִשְׂרָאֵל וְכֵן הוּא אוֹמֵר מַה־בְּרִי וּמַה־בַּר־בִּטְנִי וּמֶה
בַּר־נְדָרָי (משלי לא ב) וְאוֹמֵר כִּי־בֵן הָיִיתִי לְאָבִי רַךְ וְיָחִיד לִפְנֵי אִמִּי (שם ד ג)
ר' יוֹסֵי בֶּן אֶלְעָזָר אוֹמֵר כְּאָדָם שֶׁמּוֹשִׁיט אֶצְבָּעוֹ לְתוֹךְ עֵינוֹ וּמְחַטְטָה
פַּרְעֹה שֶׁנָּגַע בָּכֶם מֶה עָשִׂיתִי לוֹ מַרְכְּבֹת פַּרְעֹה וְחֵילוֹ יָרָה בַיָּם (שמות טו ד)
סִיסְרָא שֶׁנָּגַע בָּכֶם מֶה עָשִׂיתִי לוֹ מִן־שָׁמַיִם נִלְחָמוּ הַכּוֹכָבִים מִמְּסִלּוֹתָם
נִלְחֲמוּ עִם־סִיסְרָא (שופטים ה כ) סַנְחֵרִיב שֶׁנָּגַע בָּכֶם מֶה עָשִׂיתִי לוֹ וַיֵּצֵא
מַלְאַךְ ה' וַיַּךְ בְּמַחֲנֵה אַשּׁוּר (מלכים ב' יט לה) נְבוּכַדְנֶצַּר שֶׁנָּגַע בָּכֶם מֶה
עָשִׂיתִי לוֹ וְעִשְׂבָּא כְתוֹרִין יֵאכֻל (דניאל ד ל) הָמָן שֶׁנָּגַע בָּכֶם מֶה עָשִׂיתִי
לוֹ וְאוֹתוֹ תָּלוּ עַל־הָעֵץ (אסתר ח ז) וְכֵן אַתָּה מוֹצֵא כָל זְמָן שֶׁיִּשְׂרָאֵל
מְשׁוּעְבָּדִים כִּבְיָכוֹל שְׁכִינָה מִשְׁתַּעְבֶּדֶת עִמָּהֶם שֶׁנֶּאֱמַר וַיִּרְאוּ אֶת אֱלֹהֵי
יִשְׂרָאֵל וְתַחַת רַגְלָיו כְּמַעֲשֵׂה לִבְנַת הַסַּפִּיר (שמות כד י) וְכֵן הוּא אוֹמֵר
בְּכָל־צָרָתָם לוֹ צָר (ישעיה סג ט) אֵין לִי אֶלָּא צָרַת צִבּוּר צָרַת יָחִיד מִנַּיִן
תַּלְמוּד לוֹמַר יִקְרָאֵנִי וְאֶעֱנֵהוּ עִמּוֹ אָנֹכִי בְצָרָה (תהלים צא טו) וְכֵן הוּא
אוֹמֵר וַיִּקַּח אֲדֹנֵי יוֹסֵף אוֹתוֹ וְגו' וַיְהִי ה' אֶת־יוֹסֵף (בראשית לט כ־כא) וְכֵן
הוּא אוֹמֵר מִפְּנֵי עַמְּךָ אֲשֶׁר פָּדִיתָ לְּךָ מִמִּצְרַיִם גּוֹי וֵאלֹהָיו (שמואל ב' ז כג).
ר' אֱלִיעֶזֶר אוֹמֵר עֲבוֹדָה זָרָה עָבְרָה בַיָּם עִם יִשְׂרָאֵל וְאֵיזֶה זֶה זֶה פִּסְלוֹ
שֶׁל מִיכָה ר' עֲקִיבָא אוֹמֵר אִלְמָלֵא מִקְרָא שֶׁכָּתוּב אִי אֶפְשָׁר לְאוֹמְרוֹ אָמְרוּ
יִשְׂרָאֵל לִפְנֵי הַמָּקוֹם פָּדִיתָ אֶת עַצְמְךָ וְכֵן אַתְּ מוֹצֵא שֶׁכָּל מָקוֹם שֶׁגָּלוּ
שְׁכִינָה עִמָּהֶם שֶׁנֶּאֱמַר הֲנִגְלֹה נִגְלֵיתִי אֶל־בֵּית אָבִיךָ בִּהְיוֹתָם בְּמִצְרַיִם
בְּבֵית פַּרְעֹה (שמואל א' ב כז) גָּלוּ לְבָבֶל שְׁכִינָה עִמָּהֶם שֶׁנֶּאֱמַר לְמַעַנְכֶם
שֻׁלַּחְתִּי בָבֶלָה (ישעיה מג יד) [גָּלוּ לְעֵילָם שְׁכִינָה עִמָּהֶם שֶׁנֶּאֱמַר וְשַׂמְתִּי
כִסְאִי בְעֵילָם (ירמיה מט לח)] גָּלוּ לֶאֱדוֹם שְׁכִינָה עִמָּהֶם שֶׁנֶּאֱמַר מִי־זֶה

בָּא מֵאֱדוֹם חֲמוּץ בְּגָדִים מִבָּצְרָה (ישעיה סג א) וּכְשֶׁהֵם חוֹזְרִים שְׁכִינָה
חוֹזֶרֶת עִמָּהֶם שֶׁנֶּאֱמַר וְשָׁב ה׳ אֱלֹהֶיךָ אֶת־שְׁבוּתְךָ (דברים ל ג) וְהֵשִׁיב
לֹא נֶאֱמַר אֶלָּא וְשָׁב ה׳ וְאוֹמֵר אִתִּי מִלְּבָנוֹן כַּלָּה אִתִּי מִלְּבָנוֹן תָּבוֹאִי
(שה״ש ד ח). רַבִּי אוֹמֵר כָּאן אַתָּה אוֹמֵר קוּמָה ה׳ וְכָאן אַתָּה אוֹמֵר
שׁוּבָה ה׳ כֵּיצַד יִתְקַיְּמוּ שְׁנֵי כְתוּבִים הַלָּלוּ מַגִּיד הַכָּתוּב כְּשֶׁהָיוּ יִשְׂרָאֵל
נוֹסְעִים הָיָה עַמּוּד הֶעָנָן מְקוּפָּל [וְעוֹמֵד וְלֹא הָיָה מְהַלֵּךְ עַד שֶׁמֹּשֶׁה אָמַר
לוֹ קוּמָה ה׳ וּכְשֶׁהֵם חוֹנִין הָיָה עַמּוּד עָנָן מְקוּפָּל וְעוֹמֵד] וְלֹא הָיָה פוֹרֵס עַד
שֶׁהָיָה אוֹמֵר שׁוּבָה ה׳ נִמְצֵיתָ מְקַיֵּים קוּמָה ה׳ וְנִמְצֵיתָ מְקַיֵּים שׁוּבָה ה׳.

וּבְנֻחֹה יֹאמַר שׁוּבָה ה׳ רִבְבוֹת אַלְפֵי יִשְׂרָאֵל, מַגִּיד הַכָּתוּב כְּשֶׁהָיוּ
יִשְׂרָאֵל נוֹסְעִים אֲלָפִים וְחוֹנִים רְבָבוֹת כִּבְיָכוֹל אָמַר מֹשֶׁה לִפְנֵי הַמָּקוֹם
אֵינֶנִּי מֵנִיחַ אֶת הַשְּׁכִינָה [לָשׁרוֹת] עַד שֶׁתַּעֲשֶׂה לְיִשְׂרָאֵל אֲלָפִים וּרְבָבוֹת
שֶׁמִּתְּשׁוּבָה שֶׁאָמַר אַתָּה יוֹדֵעַ מָה אָמַר לָהֶם ה׳ אֱלֹהֵי אֲבוֹתֵיכֶם יֹסֵף
עֲלֵיכֶם כָּכֶם אֶלֶף פְּעָמִים (דברים א יא) אָמְרוּ לוֹ מֹשֶׁה רַבֵּינוּ הֲרֵי אָנוּ
מוּבְטָחִים בִּבְרָכוֹת הַרְבֵּה [שֶׁכָּךְ הִבְטִיחָנוּ כְּכוֹכְבֵי הַשָּׁמַיִם וּכְחוֹל הַיָּם
וּכְצִמְחֵי אֲדָמָה] וְאַתָּה נוֹתֵן קִצְבָה לְבִרְכוֹתֵינוּ אָמַר לָהֶם אֲנִי בָּשָׂר וָדָם
יֵשׁ קִצְבָה לְבִרְכוֹתַי זוֹ מִשֶּׁלִּי אֲבָל הוּא יְבָרֵךְ אֶתְכֶם כַּאֲשֶׁר דִּבֶּר לָכֶם
כְּחוֹל יַמִּים וּכְצִמְחֵי אֲדָמָה וְכִדְגֵי הַיָּם וּכְכוֹכְבֵי הַשָּׁמַיִם לָרוֹב: וּבְנֻחֹה
יֹאמַר, מַגִּיד הַכָּתוּב שֶׁאֵין שְׁכִינָה שׁוֹרָה לְמַעֲלָה אֶלָּא בָּאֲלָפִים וּרְבָבוֹת
שֶׁנֶּאֱמַר רֶכֶב אֱלֹהִים רִבּוֹתַיִם אַלְפֵי שִׁנְאָן (תהלים סח יח) וּכְשֵׁם שֶׁאֵין
שְׁכִינָה שׁוֹרָה לְמַעֲלָה אֶלָּא בָּאֲלָפִים וּבִרְבָבוֹת כָּךְ אֵין שְׁכִינָה שׁוֹרָה
לְמַטָּה אֶלָּא בָּאֲלָפִים וּרְבָבוֹת

## CHAPTER 3: GENESIS RABBAH 70

כח כ) וַיִּדַּר יַעֲקֹב נֶדֶר לֵאמֹר וגו׳ אֲשֶׁר פָּצוּ שְׂפָתַי וְדִבֶּר־פִּי בַּצַּר

לִי (תהלים סו יד) אָמַר ר׳ יִצְחָק הַבַּבְלִי מַן דְּנָדַר מִצְוָה, מָהוּ לֵאמֹר לֵאמֹר

לְדוֹרוֹת כְּדֵי שֶׁיִּהְיוּ נוֹדְרִין בְּעֵת צָרָתָן, יַעֲקֹב פָּתַח בְּנֶדֶר תְּחִילָה. לְפִיכָךְ

כָּל מִי שֶׁנּוֹדֵר לֹא יְהֵא תוֹלֶה אֶת הַנֶּדֶר אֶלָּא בּוֹ, אָמַר ר׳ אַבָּהוּ כְּתִיב

אֲשֶׁר נִשְׁבַּע לַיְיָ נָדַר לַאֲבִיר יַעֲקֹב (שם קלב ב) לַאֲבִיר אַבְרָהָם וְלַאֲבִיר

יִצְחָק אֵינוֹ אוֹמֵר כֵּן אֶלָּא לַאֲבִיר יַעֲקֹב תָּלָה הַנֶּדֶר בְּמִי שֶׁפָּתַח בּוֹ תְחִילָה,

ר׳ יוּדָן בְּשֵׁם ר׳ אִידִי כָּתוּב וַיִּשְׂמַח הָעָם עַל הִתְנַדְּבָם וגו׳ (דה״א כט ט)

וּלְפִי שֶׁהָיוּ עֲסוּקִין בְּמִצְוַת נְדָבָה וְעָלָה בְּיָדָן לְפִיכָךְ שָׂמְחוּ, מָהוּ אוֹמֵר

וַיְבָרֶךְ דָּוִד אֶת־יְיָ לְעֵינֵי כָּל הַקָּהָל וַיֹּאמֶר דָּוִד בָּרוּךְ אַתָּה יְיָ אֱלֹהֵי

יִשְׂרָאֵל אָבִינוּ (שם שם י) אֱלֹהֵי אַבְרָהָם וְיִצְחָק וְיִשְׂרָאֵל אֵינוֹ אוֹמֵר אֶלָּא

אֱלֹהֵי יִשְׂרָאֵל אֵינוֹ תוֹלֶה הַנֶּדֶר אֶלָּא בְּמִי שֶׁפָּתַח בּוֹ תְחִילָה. אָמַר ר׳ יוּדָן

עוֹד מִן אַתְרָא לֵית הִיא חֲסִירָא וַיִּדְּרוּ יִשְׂרָאֵל (במדבר כא ב) אֵינוֹ אוֹמֵר

אֶלָּא וַיִּדַּר יִשְׂרָאֵל יִשְׂרָאֵל סָבָא [וַיִּדַּר יַעֲקֹב נֶדֶר וגו׳]:

[וַיִּדַּר יַעֲקֹב נֶדֶר וגו׳] אַרְבָּעָה הֵם שֶׁנָּדְרוּ שְׁנַיִם נָדְרוּ וְהִפְסִידוּ

וּשְׁנַיִם נָדְרוּ וְנִשְׂתַּכְּרוּ, יִשְׂרָאֵל וְחַנָּה נִשְׂתַּכְּרוּ, יִפְתָּח נָדַר וְהִפְסִיד יַעֲקֹב

נָדַר וְהִפְסִיד: ר׳ אַיְיבוּ וְר׳ יוֹנָתָן חַד אָמַר מְסוֹרְסָה הִיא הַפָּרָשָׁה וַחֲרָנָה

אָמַר עַל הַסֵּדֶר נֶאֶמְרָה, מַאן דַּאֲמַר מְסוֹרֶסֶת הִיא הִנֵּה אָנֹכִי עִמָּךְ

(בראשית כח טו) אִם־יִהְיֶה אֱלֹהִים עִמָּדִי אֶתְמְהָא מַאן דַּאֲמַר עַל הַסֵּדֶר

נֶאֶמְרָה מַה מְּקַיֵּם אִם יִהְיֶה אֱלֹהִים עִמָּדִי, אֶלָּא שֶׁאִם יִהְיֶה לִי שֶׁנִּתְקַיְימוּ

כָּל הַתְּנָאִין שֶׁהִתְנָה עִמִּי: ר׳ אַבָּהוּ וְרַבָּנִין ר׳ אַבָּהוּ אָמַר אִם־יִהְיֶה

אֱלֹהִים עִמָּדִי וּשְׁמָרַנִי בַּדֶּרֶךְ הַזֶּה מִלְּשׁוֹן הָרַע כְּמָה דְאַתְּ אָמַר וַיַּדְרְכוּ

אֶת־לְשׁוֹנָם קַשְׁתָּם שֶׁקֶר (ירמיה ט ב), וְנָתַן־לִי לֶחֶם לֶאֱכֹל מִגִּילּוּי עֲרָיוֹת

כְּמָה דְאַתְּ אָמַר וְלֹא־חָשַׂךְ מִמֶּנִּי מְאוּמָה כִּי אִם־הַלֶּחֶם אֲשֶׁר־הוּא אוֹכֵל

(בראשית לט ט) לָשׁוֹן נָקִי, וְשַׁבְתִּי בְשָׁלוֹם אֶל בֵּית אָבִי מִשְּׁפִיכוּת דָּמִים,

וְהָיָה יְיָ לִי לֵאלֹהִים מֵעֲבוֹדָה זָרָה, רַבָּנִין פָּתְרִין לַהּ בְּכָל עִנְיָינָא

אִם־יִהְיֶה אֱלֹהִים עִמָּדִי וּשְׁמָרַנִי בַּדֶּרֶךְ הַזֶּה אֲשֶׁר אָנֹכִי הוֹלֵךְ מֵעֲבוֹדָה זָרָה מִגִּלּוּי עֲרָיוֹת וּמִשְּׁפִיכוּת דָּמִים וּמִלָּשׁוֹן הָרָע, אֵין דֶּרֶךְ אֶלָּא עֲבוֹדָה זָרָה בְּמָה דְאַתְּ אָמַר הַנִּשְׁבָּעִים בְּאַשְׁמַת שׁוֹמְרוֹן וְאָמְרוּ חֵי אֱלֹהֶיךָ דָן וְחֵי דֶּרֶךְ בְּאֵר־שָׁבַע וגו' (עמוס ח יד) אֵין דֶּרֶךְ אֶלָּא גִּלּוּי עֲרָיוֹת כֵּן דֶּרֶךְ אִשָּׁה מְנָאָפֶת (משלי ל כ), אֵין דֶּרֶךְ אֶלָּא שְׁפִיכוּת דָּמִים שנ' בְּנִי אַל־תֵּלֵךְ בְּדֶרֶךְ אִתָּם וגו' כִּי רַגְלֵיהֶם לָרַע יָרוּצוּ וִימַהֲרוּ לִשְׁפָּךְ־דָּם (שם א מו מז), אֵין דֶּרֶךְ אֶלָּא לָשׁוֹן הָרָע שנ' וַיִּשְׁמַע אֶת־דִּבְרֵי בְנֵי לָבָן וגו' (בראשית לא א):

ה) וְנָתַן לִי לֶחֶם לֶאֱכֹל וּבֶגֶד לִלְבּשׁ עֲקִילַס הַגֵּר נִכְנַס אֵצֶל ר' אֱלִיעֶזֶר אָמַר לוֹ הֲרֵי כָל שְׁבָחוֹ שֶׁלַּגֵּר שנ' וְאוֹהֵב גֵּר לָתֶת לוֹ לֶחֶם וְשִׂמְלָה (דברים י יח), אָמַר לוֹ וְכִי קַלָּה הִיא בְעֵינֶיךָ דָּבָר שֶׁנִּתְחַבֵּט בּוֹ זָקֵן וְנָתַן־לִי לֶחֶם לֶאֱכֹל וגו' וּבָא וְהוֹשִׁיטָה לּוֹ בְקִנְאָה, נִכְנַס אֵצֶל ר' יְהוֹשֻׁעַ הִתְחִיל מְנַחֲמוֹ בִּדְבָרִים לֶחֶם זוֹ הַתּוֹרָה שנ' לְכוּ לַחֲמוּ בְלַחְמִי (משלי ט ה), שִׂמְלָה זוֹ טַלִּית, זָכָה אָדָם לַתּוֹרָה זָכָה לְמִצְוָה, וְלֹא עוֹד אֶלָּא שֶׁמַּשִּׂיאִין מִבְּנוֹתֵיהֶן לַכְּהוּנָּה וְהָיוּ בְנֵי בְנֵיהֶם מַקְרִיבִים עוֹלוֹת עַל גַּבֵּי הַמִּזְבֵּחַ, לֶחֶם זוֹ לֶחֶם הַפָּנִים, שִׂמְלָה אֵלּוּ בִגְדֵי כְהוּנָּה, הֲרֵי בַּמִּקְדָּשׁ, בַּגְּבוּלִין מִנַּיִן לֶחֶם זוֹ חַלָּה, שִׂמְלָה זוֹ רֵאשִׁית הַגֵּז:

כא) וְשַׁבְתִּי בְשָׁלוֹם אֶל־בֵּית אָבִי וְהָיָה יְ"יָ לִי לֵאלֹהִים ר' יְהוֹשֻׁעַ דְּסִכְנִין בְּשֵׁם ר' לֵוִי גָּמַל הַקָּדוֹשׁ בָּרוּךְ הוּא סִיחָתָן שֶׁלָּאָבוֹת וַעֲשָׂאָהּ מַפְתֵּחַ לִגְאוּלָתָן שֶׁלַבָּנִים, אָמַר לוֹ הַקָּדוֹשׁ בָּרוּךְ הוּא לְיַעֲקֹב אַתָּה אָמַרְתָּ וְהָיָה יְ"יָ לִי לֵאלֹהִים חַיֶּיךָ כָּל טוֹבוֹת וּבְרָכוֹת וְנֶחָמוֹת שֶׁאֲנִי נוֹתֵן לְבָנֶיךָ אֵינִי נוֹתְנָן אֶלָּא בַּלָּשׁוֹן הַזֶּה וְהָיָה בַיּוֹם הַהוּא יֵצְאוּ מַיִם־חַיִּים מִירוּשָׁלַיִם (זכריה יד ח), וְהָיָה בַיּוֹם הַהוּא יְחַיֶּה־אִישׁ עֶגְלַת בָּקָר (ישעיה ז כא), וְהָיָה בַּיּוֹם הַהוּא יוֹסִיף יְ"יָ שֵׁנִית (שם יא יא), וְהָיָה בַיּוֹם הַהוּא יִטְּפוּ הֶהָרִים עָסִיס (יואל ד יח). וְהָיָה בַיּוֹם הַהוּא יִתָּקַע בְּשׁוֹפָר גָּדוֹל (ישעיה כז יג):

כב) וְהָאֶבֶן הַזֹּאת וגו' [וְכֹל אֲשֶׁר תִּתֶּן־לִי עַשֵּׂר אֲעַשְּׂרֶנּוּ לָךְ] חַד אֲמָם שָׁאַל לר' מֵאִיר פֶּטֶר חֲמוֹר בַּמֶּה הוּא נִפְדֶּה, אָמַר לוֹ בְּשֶׂה דִכְתִיב

וּפֶטֶר חֲמוֹר תִּפְדֶּה בְשֶׂה (שמות לד כ), אָמַר לוֹ אֵין לוֹ שֶׂה, אָמַר לוֹ בְּגָדִי,

אָמַר לוֹ מֵאַיִן, מִן־הַכְּבָשִׂים וּמִן־הָעִזִּים תִּקָּחוּ (שם יב ה), אָמַר לוֹ אֵלּוּ

לְפֶסַח, אָמַר לוֹ אַף גְּדִי נִקְרָא שֶׂה, מִן הֵן, וְזֹאת הַבְּהֵמָה אֲשֶׁר תֹּאכֵלוּ

שׁוֹר שֶׂה כְשָׂבִים וְשֵׂה עִזִּים (דברים יד ד), עָמַד וּנְשָׁקוֹ עַל רֹאשׁוֹ: ר' יְהוֹשֻׁעַ

דְּסִיכְנִין בְּשֵׁם ר' לֵוִי כּוּתִי אֶחָד שָׁאַל אֶת ר' מֵאִיר אָמַר לוֹ אֵין אַתֶּם

אוֹמְרִים יַעֲקֹב אֲמִיתִּי הָיָה, אָמַר לוֹ הֵן, אָמַר לוֹ לֹא כָךְ אָמַר וְכֹל אֲשֶׁר

תִּתֶּן־לִי עַשֵּׂר אֲעַשְּׂרֶנּוּ לָךְ, הֵן וְהִפְרִישׁ שֵׁבֶט לֵוִי [אֶחָד מֵעֲשָׂרָה], וְלָמָּה

לֹא הִפְרִישׁ מִשְּׁנֵי שְׁבָטִים, אָמַר לוֹ וְכִי שְׁנֵים עָשָׂר שְׁבָטִים הָיוּ וַהֲלֹא י''ד

הָיוּ שְׁנֵ' אֶפְרַיִם וּמְנַשֶּׁה כִּרְאוּבֵן וְשִׁמְעוֹן יִהְיוּ־לִי (בראשית מח ח), אָמַר

לֵיהּ כָּל דְּכֵן, אוֹסַפְתָּ מַיִם אוֹסִיף קֶמַח, אָמַר לוֹ אֵין אַתְּ מוֹדֶה לִי שֶׁהֵן

ד' אִמָּהוֹת, אָמַר לוֹ הֵן, אָמַר לוֹ צֵא מֵהֶן ד' בְּכוֹרוֹת לד' אִמָּהוֹת,

הַבְּכוֹר קוֹדֶשׁ וְאֵין קוֹדֶשׁ מוֹצִיא קוֹדֶשׁ, אָמַר לוֹ אַשְׁרֵי אוּמָּתְךָ מַה בְּתוֹכָהּ:

כט א) וַיִּשָּׂא יַעֲקֹב רַגְלָיו אָמַר ר' אַחָא חַיֵּי בְשָׂרִים לֵב מַרְפֵּא

(משלי יד ל) כֵּיוָן שֶׁנִּתְבַּשֵּׂר בְּשׂוֹרָה טוֹבָה טָעִין לִיבֵּיהּ רַגְלוֹהִי הֲדָא אָמַר

כְּרֵסֵהּ טָעֲנָא רַגְלַיָּא:

ב ג) וַיַּרְא וְהִנֵּה בְאֵר בַּשָּׂדֶה וגו' ר' חָמָא בַּר' חֲנִינָא פָּתַר בֵּהּ שֵׁת

שִׁיטִין וַיַּרְא וְהִנֵּה בְאֵר בַּשָּׂדֶה זוֹ הַבְּאֵר, וְהִנֵּה שָׁם שְׁלֹשָׁה עֶדְרֵי־צֹאן

רוֹבְצִים עָלֶיהָ מֹשֶׁה אַהֲרֹן וּמִרְיָם, כִּי מִן־הַבְּאֵר הַהִיא יַשְׁקוּ הָעֲדָרִים

שֶׁמִּשָּׁם הָיָה כָּל אֶחָד וְאֶחָד מוֹשֵׁךְ לְדִגְלוֹ וּלְשִׁבְטוֹ וּלְמִשְׁפַּחְתּוֹ, וְהָאֶבֶן

גְּדֹלָה עַל־פִּי הַבְּאֵר אָמַר ר' חֲנִינָא כִּמְלוֹא פִּי כְבָרָה קְטַנָּה הָיָה בָהּ,

וְנֶאֶסְפוּ־שָׁמָּה כָל־הָעֲדָרִים בִּשְׁעַת הַמַּחֲנוֹת, וְגָלֲלוּ אֶת־הָאֶבֶן מֵעַל פִּי

הַבְּאֵר וְהִשְׁקוּ אֶת־הַצֹּאן שֶׁמִּשָּׁם הָיָה כָּל אֶחָד וְאֶחָד מוֹשֵׁךְ לְדִגְלוֹ לְשִׁבְטוֹ

וּלְמִשְׁפַּחְתּוֹ, וְהֵשִׁיבוּ אֶת־הָאֶבֶן עַל־פִּי הַבְּאֵר לִמְקוֹמָהּ בִּשְׁעַת הַמַּסָּעוֹת:

דָּבָר אַחֵר וַיַּרְא וְהִנֵּה בְאֵר בַּשָּׂדֶה זוֹ צִיּוֹן, וְהִנֵּה־שָׁם שְׁלֹשָׁה עֶדְרֵי־צֹאן

אֵלּוּ שָׁלֹשׁ רְגָלִים, כִּי מִן־הַבְּאֵר הַהִיא יַשְׁקוּ שֶׁמִּשָּׁם הָיוּ שׁוֹאֲבִין רוּחַ

הַקּוֹדֶשׁ, וְהָאֶבֶן גְּדֹלָה זוֹ שִׂמְחַת בֵּית הַשּׁוֹאֵבָה, אָמַר ר' הוֹשַׁעְיָא לָמָּה

הָיוּ קוֹרִין אוֹתָהּ שִׂמְחַת בֵּית הַשּׁוֹאֵבָה שֶׁמִּשָּׁם הָיוּ שׁוֹאֲבִין רוּחַ הַקֹּדֶשׁ,
וְנֶאֶסְפוּ־שָׁמָּה כָל־הָעֲדָרִים בָּאִים מִלְּבוֹא חֲמָת עַד נַחַל מִצְרַיִם, וְגָלְלוּ
אֶת־הָאֶבֶן מֵעַל פִּי הַבְּאֵר וְהִשְׁקוּ אֶת־הַצֹּאן שֶׁמִּשָּׁם הָיוּ שׁוֹאֲבִין רוּחַ
הַקֹּדֶשׁ, וְהֵשִׁיבוּ אֶת־הָאֶבֶן עַל־פִּי הַבְּאֵר לִמְקוֹמָהּ מוּנָח לָרֶגֶל הַבָּא:
דָּבָר אַחֵר וַיַּרְא וְהִנֵּה בְאֵר בַּשָּׂדֶה זֶה צִיּוֹן, וְהִנֵּה־שָׁם שְׁלֹשָׁה עֶדְרֵי־צֹאן
אֵלּוּ ג' בָּתֵּי דִינִין דִּתְנִינַן שְׁלֹשָׁה בָּתֵּי דִינִין הָיוּ שָׁם אֶחָד בְּפֶתַח הַר
הַבַּיִת אֶחָד בְּפֶתַח הָעֲזָרָה וְאֶחָד בְּלִשְׁכַּת הַגָּזִית, כִּי מִן־הַבְּאֵר הַהִיא וְגוֹ'
שֶׁמִּשָּׁם הָיוּ שׁוֹמְעִין אֶת הַדִּין, וְהָאֶבֶן גְּדוֹלָה זֶה בֵּית דִּין הַגָּדוֹל שֶׁבְּלִשְׁכַּת
הַגָּזִית, וְנֶאֶסְפוּ־שָׁמָּה כָל־הָעֲדָרִים אֵלּוּ בָּתֵּי דִינִין שֶׁבְּאֶרֶץ יִשְׂרָאֵל,
וְגָלְלוּ אֶת־הָאֶבֶן שֶׁמִּשָּׁם הָיוּ שׁוֹמְעִין אֶת הַדִּין, וְהֵשִׁיבוּ אֶת־הָאֶבֶן שֶׁהָיוּ
נוֹשְׂאִין וְנוֹתְנִין עַד שֶׁמּוֹצִיאִין אֶת הַדִּין עַל בּוֹרְיוֹ: דָּבָר אַחֵר וַיַּרְא וְהִנֵּה
בְאֵר בַּשָּׂדֶה זֶה צִיּוֹן, וְהִנֵּה שָׁם שְׁלֹשָׁה עֶדְרֵי־צֹאן אֵלּוּ ג' מַלְכֻיּוֹת
הָרִאשׁוֹנוֹת, כִּי מִן־הַבְּאֵר הַהִיא וְגוֹ' שֶׁהֶעֱשִׁירוּ מִן הַהֶקְדֵּישׁוֹת הַצְּפוּנוֹת
בַּלְּשָׁכוֹת, וְהָאֶבֶן גְּדוֹלָה זוֹ זְכוּת אָבוֹת, וְנֶאֶסְפוּ־שָׁמָּה כָל־הָעֲדָרִים זוֹ
מַלְכוּת הָרְשָׁעָה שֶׁמַּכְתֶּבֶת טִירוֹנְיָה מִכָּל אוּמּוֹת הָעוֹלָם, וְגָלְלוּ אֶת־הָאֶבֶן
שֶׁהֶעֱשִׁירוּ מִן הַהֶקְדֵּישׁוֹת הַצְּפוּנוֹת בַּלְּשָׁכוֹת וְהֵשִׁיבוּ אֶת־הָאֶבֶן לֶעָתִיד
לָבוֹא זְכוּת אָבוֹת עוֹמֶדֶת: דָּבָר אַחֵר וַיַּרְא וְהִנֵּה בְאֵר זוֹ סַנְהֶדְרִין,
וְהִנֵּה־שָׁם שְׁלֹשָׁה עֶדְרֵי־צֹאן אֵלּוּ ג' שׁוּרוֹת שֶׁלְתַלְמִידֵי חֲכָמִים שֶׁהָיוּ
יוֹשְׁבִין לִפְנֵיהֶם כִּי מִן־הַבְּאֵר וְגוֹ' שֶׁמִּשָּׁם הָיוּ שׁוֹמְעִין אֶת הַהֲלָכָה,
וְהָאֶבֶן גְּדוֹלָה זֶה מוּפְלָא בֵּית דִּין שֶׁמְּסַיֵּים אֶת הַהֲלָכָה, וְנֶאֶסְפוּ־שָׁמָּה
כָל־הָעֲדָרִים אֵלּוּ הַתַּלְמִידִין שֶׁבְּאֶרֶץ יִשְׂרָאֵל וְגָלְלוּ אֶת הָאֶבֶן שֶׁמִּשָּׁם
הָיוּ שׁוֹמְעִין הַהֲלָכָה, וְהֵשִׁיבוּ אֶת־הָאֶבֶן שֶׁהָיוּ נוֹשְׂאִים וְנוֹתְנִין בַּהֲלָכָה
עַד שֶׁמַּעֲמִידִין אוֹתָהּ עַל בּוֹרְיָהּ: דָּבָר אַחֵר וַיַּרְא וְהִנֵּה בְאֵר זוֹ בֵּית
הַכְּנֶסֶת, וְהִנֵּה־שָׁם שְׁלֹשָׁה עֶדְרֵי־צֹאן אֵלּוּ שְׁלֹשָׁה קְרוּיִים, כִּי מִן־הַבְּאֵר
הַהִיא וְגוֹ' שֶׁמִּשָּׁם הָיוּ שׁוֹמְעִין אֶת הַתּוֹרָה, וְהָאֶבֶן גְּדוֹלָה זֶה יֵצֶר הָרָע,
וְנֶאֶסְפוּ־שָׁמָּה כָל־הָעֲדָרִים זֶה הַצִּבּוּר, וְגָלְלוּ אֶת הָאֶבֶן שֶׁמִּשָּׁם הָיוּ

שׁוֹמְעִין הַתּוֹרָה, וְהֵשִׁיבוּ אֶת־הָאֶבֶן שֶׁכֵּיוָן שֶׁיּוֹצְאִים יֵצֶר הָרַע חוֹזֵר
לִמְקוֹמוֹ: ר' יוֹחָנָן פָּתַר לֵהּ בְּסִינַי וַיֵּרָא וְהִנֵּה בְאֵר בַּשָּׂדֶה זֶה סִינַי,
וְהִנֵּה־שָׁם שְׁלֹשָׁה עֶדְרֵי־צֹאן כֹּהֲנִים לְוִיִּים וְיִשְׂרְאֵלִים, כִּי מִן־הַבְּאֵר
הַהִיא וְגו' שֶׁמִּשָּׁם שָׁמְעוּ עֲשֶׂרֶת הַדִּבְּרוֹת וְהָאֶבֶן גְּדוֹלָה זוֹ שְׁכִינָה,
וְנֶאֶסְפוּ־שָׁמָּה כָל־הָעֲדָרִים ר' שִׁמְעוֹן בֶּן יְהוּדָה אִישׁ כְּפַר עַכּוֹס מִשּׁ' ר'
שִׁמְעוֹן שֶׁאִילוּ הָיוּ שָׁם יִשְׂרָאֵל חֲסֵירִים עַד אֶחָד לֹא הָיוּ כְּדַיי לְקַבֵּל אֶת
הַתּוֹרָה, וְגָלְלוּ אֶת הָאֶבֶן שֶׁמִּשָּׁם שָׁמְעוּ עֲשֶׂרֶת הַדִּבְּרוֹת, וְהֵשִׁיבוּ
אֶת־הָאֶבֶן, אַתֶּם רְאִיתֶם כִּי מִן־הַשָּׁמַיִם דִּבַּרְתִּי עִמָּכֶם (שמות ב כב):

ד־ו) וַיֹּאמֶר לָהֶם יַעֲקֹב אַחַי מֵאַיִן אַתֶּם וַיֹּאמְרוּ מֵחָרָן אֲנָחְנוּ
ר' יוֹסֵי בַּר' חֲנִינָה פָּתַר קַרְיָיה בַּגָּלוּת וַיֹּאמֶר לָהֶם יַעֲקֹב וְגו' וַיֹּאמְרוּ
מֵחָרָן אֲנָחְנוּ מֵחֲרוֹנוֹ שֶׁלְּהַקָּדוֹשׁ בָּרוּךְ הוּא אָנוּ בוֹרְחִים, וַיֹּאמֶר לָהֶם
הַיְדַעְתֶּם אֶת־לָבָן בֶּן־נָחוֹר הַיְדַעְתֶּם אֶת מִי שֶׁעָתִיד לְלַבֵּן עֲווֹנוֹתֵיכֶם
כַּשֶּׁלֶג, וַיֹּאמֶר לָהֶם הֲשָׁלוֹם לוֹ וַיֹּאמְרוּ שָׁלוֹם, בְּאֵי זוֹ זְכוּת וְהִנֵּה רָחֵל
בִּתּוֹ בָּאָה עִם הַצֹּאן הָדָא הִיא דִכְתִיב כֹּה אָמַר י"י קוֹל בְּרָמָה נִשְׁמָע
נְהִי בְּכִי תַמְרוּרִים רָחֵל מְבַכָּה עַל־בָּנֶיהָ וְגו' מִנְעִי קוֹלֵךְ מִבֶּכִי וְגו' כִּי
יֵשׁ שָׂכָר לִפְעוּלָּתֵךְ וְגו' (ירמיה לא מו טז): וַיֹּאמֶר לָהֶם הֲשָׁלוֹם בֵּינֵיכֶם
לְבֵינוֹ, וַיֹּאמְרוּ שָׁלוֹם, וְאֵין פְּטָטִין אַתְּ בָּעֵי וְהִנֵּה רָחֵל בָּאָה עִם הַצֹּאן
הָדָא אָמַר שֶׁהַדִּיבּוּר מָצוּי בַּנָּשִׁים:

ז) וַיֹּאמֶר הֵן עוֹד וְגו' אָמַר לָהֶם אִם שׁוֹמְרֵי שָׂכָר אַתֶּם הֵן עוֹד הַיּוֹם
גָּדוֹל, אִם שֶׁלְּכֶם אַתֶּם רוֹעִים לֹא־עֵת הֵאָסֵף הַמִּקְנֶה וְגו':

ח ט) וַיֹּאמְרוּ לֹא נוּכַל וְגו' עוֹדֶנּוּ מְדַבֵּר עִמָּם וְרָחֵל בָּאָה אָמַר
רַבָּן שִׁמְעוֹן בֶּן גַּמְלִיאֵל בּוֹא וּרְאֵה כַּמָּה בֵּין שְׁכִינוֹת לִשְׁכִינוֹת, לְהַלָּן
שֶׁבַע הָיוּ וּבִקְּשׁוּ הָרוֹעִים לְהִזְדַּוֵּוג לָהֶם הָדָא הִיא דִכְתִיב וַיָּבֹאוּ הָרוֹעִים
וַיְגָרְשׁוּם (שמות ב יז), בְּרַם הָכָא אַחַת הָיְיתָה וְלֹא נָגַע בָּהּ בְּרִיָּיה עַל שֵׁם
חוֹנֶה מַלְאַךְ־י"י סָבִיב לִירֵאָיו וַיְחַלְּצֵם (תהלים לד ח) לְסְבִיבִים לִירֵאָיו:

י) וַיְהִי כַּאֲשֶׁר רָאָה יַעֲקֹב אֶת־רָחֵל וְגו' וַיָּגֶל אֶת־הָאֶבֶן אָמַר

ר' יוֹחָנָן בָּזֶה שֶׁמַּעֲבִיר אֶת הַפֶּקַק מֵעַל גַּבֵּי צְלוֹחִית:

יא) וַיִּשַּׁק יַעֲקֹב לְרָחֵל כָּל נְשִׁיקָה שֶׁלְּתִיפְלוּת בַּר מִן ג', נְשִׁיקָה שֶׁלַּגְּדוּלָּה וּנְשִׁיקָה שֶׁלַּפְּרָקִים וּנְשִׁיקָה שֶׁלַּפְּרִישׁוּת, נְשִׁיקָה שֶׁלַּגְּדוּלָּה וַיִּקַּח שְׁמוּאֵל אֶת־פַּךְ הַשֶּׁמֶן וַיִּצֹק עַל־רֹאשׁוֹ וַיִּשָּׁקֵהוּ (ש"א יא), נְשִׁיקָה שֶׁלַּפְּרָקִים וַיֵּלֶךְ וַיִּפְגְּשֵׁהוּ בְּהַר הָאֱלֹהִים וַיִּשַּׁק־לוֹ (שמות ד כז), נְשִׁיקָה שֶׁלַּפְּרִישׁוּת וַתִּשַּׁק עָרְפָּה לַחֲמוֹתָהּ (רות א יד) ר' תַּנְחוּמָ' אָמַר אַף נְשִׁיקָה שֶׁלַּקְּרִיבוּת וַיִּשַּׁק יַעֲקֹב לְרָחֵל שֶׁהָיְתָה קְרוֹבָתוֹ:

וַיִּשָּׂא אֶת־קוֹלוֹ וַיֵּבְךְּ לָמָּה בָכָה, אָמַר אֱלִיעֶזֶר עֶבֶד אַבְרָהָם בְּשָׁעָה שֶׁהָלַךְ לְהָבִיא אֶת רִבְקָה מַה כָּתוּב בּוֹ וַיִּקַּח הָעֶבֶד עֲשָׂרָה גְמַלִּים וְגוֹ' (בראשית כד י) וַאֲנִי לֹא נֶזֶם אֶחָד וְלֹא צָמִיד אֶחָד, דָּבָר אַחֵר לָמָּה בָכָה שֶׁרָאָה שֶׁאֵינָהּ נִכְנֶסֶת עִמּוֹ לַקְּבוּרָה הֲדָא דְהִיא אָמְרָה לָהּ לָכֵן יִשְׁכַּב עִמָּךְ הַלַּיְלָה (שם ל טו), אָמְרָה לָהּ עִימָּךְ הוּא דְמִיךְ, לֵית הוּא דְמִיךְ עִימִי, דָּבָר אַחֵר לָמָּה בָכָה שֶׁרָאָה שֶׁאֲנָשִׁים מְלַחֲשִׁים אֵילוּ לְאֵילוּ, אָמְרוּ מַה בָּא זֶה לְחַדֵּשׁ לָנוּ דָּבָר שֶׁלְּעֶרְוָה, שֶׁמִּשָּׁעָה שֶׁלָּקָה הָעוֹלָם בְּדוֹר הַמַּבּוּל עָמְדוּ אוּמּוֹת הָעוֹלָם וְגָדְרוּ עַצְמָן מִן הָעֶרְוָה וְהָדָא אָמְרָה שֶׁאַנְשֵׁי מִזְרָח גְּדוּרִים מִן הָעֶרְוָה:

יב) וַיַּגֵּד יַעֲקֹב לְרָחֵל כִּי אֲחִי אָבִיהָ וְגוֹ' אִם לְרַמָּאוּת כִּי אֲחִי אָבִיהָ הוּא, וְאִם לְצֶדֶק כִּי בֶן־רִבְקָה הוּא:

וַתָּרָץ וַתַּגֵּד לְאָבִיהָ אָמַר ר' יוֹחָנָן אֵין הָאִשָּׁה לְעוֹלָם רְגִילָה אֶלָּא לְבֵית אִמָּהּ, אֲתִיבוּן וְהָכְּתִיב וַתָּרָץ וַתַּגֵּד לְאָבִיהָ, אָמַר לָהֶן שֶׁמֵּתָה אִמָּהּ, וּלְמִי הָיָה לָהּ לְהַגִּיד, לֹא לְאָבִיהָ:

יג) וַיְהִי כִשְׁמֹעַ לָבָן וְגוֹ' אָמַר אֱלִיעֶזֶר פְּסוּל הַבַּיִת הָיָה וּכְתִיב בֵּיהּ וַיִּקַּח הָעֶבֶד עֲשָׂרָה גְמַלִּים (בראשית כד י), זֶה שֶׁהוּא אֲהוּבוֹ שֶׁלַּבַּיִת עַל אַחַת כַּמָּה וְכַמָּה, וְכֵיוָן דְּלָא חֲמָא אֲפִיסְטַקְיתֵיהּ וַיְחַבֶּק־לוֹ אָמַר דִּילְמָא דִּינָרִין אִינּוּן וִיהִיבִין בְּחַרְצֵיהּ, כֵּיוָן דְּלָא אַשְׁכַּח כְּלוּם וַיְנַשֶּׁק־לוֹ אָמַר דִּילְמָא מַרְגָּלְיָן אִינּוּן וִיהִיבִין בְּפוּמֵיהּ, אָמַר לֵיהּ מָה אַתְּ סָבוּר מָמוֹן אָתִית

טְעִין, לֹא אֲחֵית טְעִין אֶלָּא מִלִּין וַיַּגֵּד לְלָבָן אֵת כָּל־הַדְּבָרִים הָאֵלֶּה:

יד) וַיֹּאמֶר לוֹ לָבָן אַךְ עַצְמִי וּבְשָׂרִי אָתָּה אָמַר לֵיהּ מֶלֶךְ הָיִיתִי סָבוּר לַעֲשׂוֹתְךָ עָלַי, כֵּיוָן דְּלֵית גַּבָּךְ כְּלוּם אַךְ עַצְמִי וּבְשָׂרִי אָתָּה כְּהַדֵּין גַּרְמָא אֲנָא מְהַדַּק לָךְ:

וַיֵּשֶׁב עִמּוֹ חֹדֶשׁ יָמִים אָמַר ר' אַסִּי לִימְּדָתְךָ הַתּוֹרָה דֶּרֶךְ אֶרֶץ עַד אֵיכָן אָדָם צָרִיךְ לִיטַּפֵּל בִּקְרוֹבוֹ עַד חֹדֶשׁ יָמִים:

טו) וַיֹּאמֶר לָבָן לְיַעֲקֹב הֲכִי־אָחִי אַתָּה וַעֲבַדְתַּנִי חִנָּם אִיפְשַׁר כֵּן, אֶלָּא אִם הֲוָה פָּעֲלֵהּ בַּעֲשָׂרָה פוֹלָרִין הֲוָה יָהַב לֵיהּ חַמְשָׁה, וְאִי הֲוָת מוֹבַלְתֵּיהּ בְּשִׁיתָּה פוֹלָרִין הֲוָה יָהִיב לֵיהּ בִּתְלָתָא פוֹלָרִין, אָמַר לֵיהּ מָה אַתְּ סָבוּר מָמוֹן אֲחֵית בָּעֵי, לֹא אֲחֵית אֶלָּא מִן בְּגִין תַּרְתֵּין טַלְיָיתָא:

טז) וּלְלָבָן שְׁתֵּי בָנוֹת כִּשְׁתֵּי קוֹרוֹת מְפוּלָשׁוֹת מִסּוֹף הָעוֹלָם וְעַד סוֹפוֹ, זוֹ הֶעֱמִידָה אַלּוּפִים וְזוֹ הֶעֱמִידָה אַלּוּפִים, זוֹ הֶעֱמִידָה מְלָכִים וְזוֹ הֶעֱמִידָה מְלָכִים, מִזּוֹ עָמְדוּ הוֹרְגֵי אֲרָיוֹת וּמִזּוֹ עָמְדוּ הוֹרְגֵי אֲרָיוֹת, מִזּוֹ מְכַבְּשֵׁי אֲרָצוֹת וּמִזּוֹ מְכַבְּשֵׁי אֲרָצוֹת, מִזּוֹ מְחַלְּקֵי אֲרָצוֹת וּמִזּוֹ מְחַלְּקֵי אֲרָצוֹת, קׇרְבַּן בְּנֵי שֶׁלָּזוֹ דּוֹחֶה אֶת הַשַּׁבָּת וְקׇרְבַּן בֶּן זוֹ דּוֹחֶה אֶת הַשַּׁבָּת, מִלְחֶמֶת בֶּן זוֹ דּוֹחָה אֶת הַשַּׁבָּת וּמִלְחֶמֶת בֶּן זוֹ דּוֹחָה אֶת הַשַּׁבָּת, לָזוֹ נִתַּן שְׁנֵי לֵילוֹת וּלְזוֹ לֵילוֹת שְׁנַיִם, לֵילוֹ שֶׁלְּפַרְעֹה וְלֵילוֹ שֶׁלְּסַנְחֵרִיב לְלֵאָה, לֵילוֹ שֶׁלְּגִדְעוֹן לְרָחֵל לֵילוֹ שֶׁלְּמָרְדְּכַי לְרָחֵל שֶׁנֶּ' בַּלַּיְלָה הַהוּא נָדְדָה שְׁנַת הַמֶּלֶךְ (אסתר ו א):

שֵׁם הַגְּדוֹלָה לֵאָה גְּדוֹלָה בְּמַתְּנוֹתֶיהָ, כְּהוּנָּה לְעוֹלָם וּמַלְכוּת לְעוֹלָם, וְשֵׁם הַקְּטַנָּה רָחֵל קְטַנָּה בְּמַתְּנוֹתֶיהָ, יוֹסֵף לְשָׁעָה וְשָׁאוּל לְשָׁעָה:

יז יח) וְעֵינֵי לֵאָה רַכּוֹת אֲמוֹרָא דְּר' יוֹחָנָן תַּרְגֵּם קַדְמוֹהִי עֵינַיָא דְּלֵאָה הֲווֹ רַכִּיכִין, אָמַר לֵיהּ עֵינַיָא דְּאִמָּךְ הֲווֹ רַכִּיכִין, זוֹ מַהוּ רַכּוֹת, רַכּוֹת מִבְּכִיָּה שֶׁכָּךְ הָיוּ הַתְּנָאִין שֶׁיְּהֵא גָּדוֹל לַגְּדוֹלָה וְקָטָן לַקְּטַנָּה, וְהָיְתָה בּוֹכָה וְאוֹמֶרֶת יְהִי רָצוֹן שֶׁלֹּא תִּפּוֹל בְּחֶלְק עֵשָׂו הָרָשָׁע, אָמַר ר' הוּנָה גְּדוֹלָה תְּפִילָּה שֶׁבִּטְּלָה הַגְּזֵירָה וְלֹא עוֹד אֶלָּא שֶׁקָּדְמָה לַאֲחוֹתָהּ:

וְרָחֵל הָיְתָה יְפַת־תֹּאַר וגו' וַיֶּאֱהַב יַעֲקֹב אֶת־רָחֵל וַיֹּאמֶר וגו'
אָמַר לֵיהּ בְּגִין דַּאֲנָא יָדַע שֶׁאַנְשֵׁי מְקוֹמְךָ רַמָּאִין לְפִיכָךְ אֲנָא מְבָרֵר
עִסְקִי מִמְּךָ, וַיֹּאמֶר אֶעֱבָדְךָ שֶׁבַע שָׁנִים בְּרָחֵל בִּתְּךָ הַקְּטַנָּה, [בְּרָחֵל]
וְלֹא בְלֵאָה, בִּתְּךָ שֶׁלֹּא תָּבִיא אַחֶרֶת מִן הַשּׁוּק וּשְׁמָהּ רָחֵל, הַקְּטַנָּה שֶׁלֹּא
תַּחֲלִיף שְׁמוֹתָן זוֹ בָזוֹ, אֲפִילוּ אַתְּ נוֹתֵן אֶת הָרָשָׁע בַּחֲמוֹר שֶׁלְּחָרָשִׁים
אֵין אַתְּ מוֹעִיל מִמֶּנּוּ כְלוּם:

יט כ) וַיֹּאמֶר־לָבָן טוֹב תִּתִּי וגו' וַיִּהְיוּ בְעֵינָיו כְּיָמִים אֲחָדִים וגו'
אָמַר רַ' חֲנִינָה בֶן פָּזִי נֶאֱמַר כָּאן אֲחָדִים וְנֶאֱמַר לְהַלָּן וְיָשַׁבְתָּ עִמּוֹ יָמִים
אֲחָדִים (בראשית כז מד) מַה כָּאן שֶׁבַע שָׁנִים אַף לְהַלָּן שֶׁבַע שָׁנִים:

כא) וַיֹּאמֶר יַעֲקֹב אֶל־לָבָן הָבָה אֶת־אִשְׁתִּי כִּי מָלְאוּ יָמָי וְאָבוֹאָה
אֵלֶיהָ אָמַר רַ' אַיִּבוּ אֲפִילוּ אָדָם פָּרוּץ אֵינוֹ אוֹמֵר כַּלָּשׁוֹן הַזֶּה, אֶלָּא אָמַר
כָּךְ גָּזַר עָלַי הַקָּדוֹשׁ בָּרוּךְ הוּא שֶׁאֲנִי מַעֲמִיד י"ב שְׁבָטִים, עַכְשָׁיו הֲרֵינִי
בֶן פ"ד שָׁנָה וְאִם אֵין אֲנִי מַעֲמִידָן עַכְשָׁיו אֵימָתַי אֲנִי מַעֲמִידָן, לְפִיכָךְ
צָרַךְ הַכָּתוּב לוֹמַר וַיֹּאמֶר יַעֲקֹב אֶל־לָבָן הָבָה אֶת־אִשְׁתִּי וגו':

כב) וַיֶּאֱסֹף לָבָן אֶת־כָּל אַנְשֵׁי הַמָּקוֹם וַיַּעַשׂ מִשְׁתֶּה כִּנֵּס כָּל אַנְשֵׁי
הַמָּקוֹם, אָמַר לָהֶם יוֹדְעִין אַתֶּם שֶׁהָיִינוּ מְרוּחָקִים לְמַיִם, וְכֵיוָן שֶׁבָּא זֶה
הַצַּדִּיק נִתְבָּרְכוּ הַמַּיִם, אָמְרוּ לֵיהּ מַה דְּהָנֵי לָךְ עֲבִיד, אָמַר לְהוֹן אִם
בָּעֵיִין אַתּוּן אֲנָא מְרַמֵּי בֵיהּ וְיָהַב לֵיהּ לֵאָה, וְהוּא רָחִים לְהָדָא רָחֵל סַגִּי,
וְהוּא עָבַד גַּבְּכוֹן שֶׁבַע שְׁנִין אָחֳרָנִין, אָמְרוּ לֵיהּ עֲבִיד מַה דְּהָנֵי לָךְ, אָמַר
לוֹן הָבוּ לִי מַשְׁכּוֹנִין דְּלֵית חַד מִנְּכוֹן מְפָרֵשׁ לֵיהּ, יָהֲבוּן לֵיהּ מַשְׁכּוֹנִין,
וַאֲזַל אַיְתֵי עֲלֵיהוֹן חֲמַר מְשַׁח וְקוֹפָד, הֱוֵי לְכָךְ נִקְרָא לָבָן הָאֲרַמִּי לְפִי
שְׁרִימָה אֲפִילוּ אַנְשֵׁי מְקוֹמוֹ: כָּל הַהוּא יוֹמָא הֲווֹן מְכַלְּלִין בֵּהּ, כֵּיוָן דְּעַל
בְּרַמְשָׁא אָמַר לְהוֹן מַהוּ כְדֵין, אָמְרוּ לֵיהּ אַתְּ גָּמַלְתָּ חֶסֶד בְּזָכוּתָךְ, הֲווֹן
מְקַלְּסִין קֳדָמֵיהּ וְאָמְרִין הִי לֵאָה הִי לֵאָה, בְּרַמְשָׁא אָתוֹן מַעֲלָתָא וְטַפּוֹן
בּוּצִינַיָּא, אָמַר לְהוֹן מַהוּ כְדֵין, אָמְרוּ לֵיהּ מָה אַתְּ צָבֵי דַּאֲנַן דִּבְזִיּוֹן
דְּכַוְונָתְכוֹן, כָּל הַהוּא לֵילְיָא הֲוָה צָוַח לַהּ רָחֵל וְהִיא מְעַנְיָא לֵיהּ, בְּצַפְרָא

וְהִנֵּה־הִיא לֵאָה, אָמַר מָה רַמָּיְיתָא בַת רַמַּאי, אָמְרָה לֵיה וְאִית סָפַר

דְּלֵית לֵיה תַּלְמִידִין, לָא כָךְ הֲוָה אֲבוּךְ צָוַח לָךְ עֵשָׂו וְאַתְּ עָנֵי לֵיה אַף אַתְּ

קָרֵית לִי וַאֲנָא עֲנֵיתִי לָךְ:

כה־כז) וַיֹּאמֶר אֶל־לָבָן מַה־זֹּאת וגו' וַיֹּאמֶר לָבָן לֹא־יֵעָשֶׂה כֵן וגו'

מַלֵּא שְׁבֻעַ זֹאת וגו' אָמַר ר' יַעֲקֹב בְּר' אַחָא מִיכַּן שֶׁאֵין מְעָרְבִין

שִׂמְחָה בְּשִׂמְחָה:

ל) וַיָּבֹא גַם אֶל־רָחֵל וגו' וַיַּעֲבֹד עִמּוֹ עוֹד שֶׁבַע שָׁנִים אֲחֵרוֹת אָמַר

ר' יוּדָה בְּר' סִימוֹן בְּנוֹהֵג הָעוֹלָם פּוֹעֵל עוֹשֶׂה עִם בַּעַל הַבַּיִת שְׁתַּיִם

שָׁלֹשׁ שָׁעוֹת בֶּאֱמוּנָה וּבַסּוֹף הוּא מִתְעַצֵּל בִּמְלַאכְתּוֹ, בְּרַם הָכָא מָה

רִאשׁוֹנוֹת שְׁלֵימוֹת אַף אַחֲרוֹנוֹת שְׁלֵמוֹת, מָה רִאשׁוֹנוֹת בֶּאֱמָנָה אַף

אַחֲרוֹנוֹת בֶּאֱמָנָה: אָמַר ר' יוֹחָנָן כָּתוּב וַיִּבְרַח יַעֲקֹב שְׂדֵה אֲרָם וַיַּעֲבֹד

יִשְׂרָאֵל בְּאִשָּׁה וּבְאִשָּׁה שָׁמָר (הושע יב יג) אָמַר לָהֶם דִּיגְמָה שֶׁלָּכֶם דּוֹמָה

לְיַעֲקֹב, מַה יַּעֲקֹב עַד שֶׁלֹּא נָשָׂא אִשָּׁה נִשְׁתַּעֲבֵּד מִשֶּׁנָּשָׂא אִשָּׁה

נִשְׁתַּעֲבֵּד אַף אַתֶּם עַד שֶׁלֹּא נוֹלַד גּוֹאֵל נִשְׁתַּעֲבַּדְתֶּם מִשֶּׁנּוֹלַד גּוֹאֵל אַתֶּם

נִשְׁתַּעֲבַּדְתֶּם:

## CHAPTER 4: LEVITICUS RABBAH 27

א) שׁוֹר אוֹ־כֶשֶׂב (ויקרא כב, כז). צִדְקָתְךָ כְּהַרְרֵי־אֵל וגו׳ (תהלים לו, ז).
ר׳ יִשְׁמָעֵאל וְר׳ עֲקִיבָה. ר׳ יִשְׁמָעֵאל אוֹמֵר הַצַּדִיקִין שֶׁהֵן עוֹשִׂין אֶת
הַתּוֹרָה שֶׁנִּתְּנָה מֵהַרְרֵי אֵל הַקָּדוֹשׁ בָּרוּךְ הוּא עוֹשֶׂה עִמָּהֶן צְדָקָה כְּהַרְרֵי
אֵל, אֲבָל הָרְשָׁעִים שֶׁאֵינָן עוֹשִׂין אֶת הַתּוֹרָה שֶׁנִּתְּנָה מֵהַרְרֵי אֵל הַקָּדוֹשׁ
בָּרוּךְ הוּא מְדַקְדֵּק עִמָּהֶן עַד תְּהוֹם רַבָּה, הֲדָא הִיא דִכְתִיב וּמִשְׁפָּטֶיךָ
תְּהוֹם רַבָּה (שם). ר׳ עֲקִיבָה אוֹמֵר אֶחָד אִילּוּ וְאֶחָד אִילּוּ הַקָּדוֹשׁ בָּרוּךְ
הוּא מְדַקְדֵּק עִמָּהֶן אֶת הַדִּין. מְדַקְדֵּק עִם הַצַּדִיקִים וְגוֹבֶה מֵהֶן מְעַט
מַעֲשִׂים רָעִים שֶׁעָשׂוּ בָּעוֹלָם הַזֶּה כְּדֵי לְשַׁלֵּם לָהֶם שָׂכָר טוֹב לֶעָתִיד
לָבוֹא, וּמַשְׁפִּיעַ שַׁלְוָה לָרְשָׁעִים וְנוֹתֵן לָהֶן שָׂכָר מִצְוֹת קַלּוֹת שֶׁעָשׂוּ
בָּעוֹלָם הַזֶּה כְּדֵי לִיפָּרַע מֵהֶם מִשְׁלָם לֶעָתִיד לָבוֹא. ר׳ מֵאִיר אוֹמֵר מְשַׁל
אֶת הַצַּדִיקִים בְּדִירָתָן וּמְשַׁל אֶת הָרְשָׁעִים בְּדִירָתָן. מְשַׁל אֶת הַצַּדִיקִים
בְּדִירָתָן, בְּמִרְעֶה־טוֹב אֶרְעֶה אוֹתָם וגו׳ (יחזקאל לד, יד). וּמְשַׁל אֶת
הָרְשָׁעִים בְּדִירָתָן, בְּיוֹם רִדְתּוֹ שְׁאוֹלָה וגו׳ (יחזקאל לא, טו). ר׳ יְהוּדָה
בְּר׳ אוֹמֵר הֶאֱבַלְתִּי (שם), הוֹבַלְתִּי כָּתוּב, תֵּדַע שֶׁאֵין עוֹשִׂין כִּסּוּי לְגִיגִית
לֹא שֶׁלַכֶּסֶף וְלֹא שֶׁלַזָּהָב לֹא שֶׁלַנְּחֹשֶׁת וְלֹא שֶׁלַבַּרְזֶל וְלֹא שֶׁלַבְּדִיל וְלֹא
שֶׁלָעוֹפֶרֶת אֶלָּא שֶׁלַחֶרֶס, מִפְּנֵי שֶׁהוּא מִמִּינוֹ, כָּךְ אָמַר הַקָּדוֹשׁ בָּרוּךְ הוּא
גֵּיהִנָּם חֹשֶׁךְ וּרְשָׁעִים חֹשֶׁךְ וּתְהוֹם חֹשֶׁךְ יָבָא חֹשֶׁךְ וִיכַסֶּה אֶת חֹשֶׁךְ בְּתוֹךְ
חֹשֶׁךְ, שֶׁנֶּאֱמַר כִּי בַהֶבֶל בָּא וּבַחֹשֶׁךְ יֵלֵךְ וּבַחֹשֶׁךְ שְׁמוֹ יְכֻסֶּה (קהלת ו, ד).
ר׳ יוֹנָתָן בְּשֵׁ׳ ר׳ יֹאשִׁיָּה הָיָה מְסָרֵס הַדִּין קַרְיָיא, צִדְקָתְךָ עַל מִשְׁפָּטֶיךָ
כְּהַרְרֵי אֵל עַל תְּהוֹם רַבָּה. מָה הָרִים הַלָּלוּ כּוֹבְשִׁין עַל תְּהוֹם שֶׁלֹּא יַעֲלֶה
וְיָצִיף אֶת הָעוֹלָם כָּךְ מַעֲשֵׂיהֶם שֶׁלַצַּדִיקִים כּוֹבְשִׁין עַל הַפּוּרְעָנוּת שֶׁלֹּא
תָבֹא לָעוֹלָם. מָה הָרִים הַלָּלוּ אֵין לָהֶן סוֹף כָּךְ אֵין סוֹף לְמַתַּן שְׂכָרָן
שֶׁלַצַּדִיקִים לֶעָתִיד לָבוֹא. מִשְׁפָּטֶיךָ תְּהוֹם רַבָּה, מַה הַתְּהוֹם הַזֶּה אֵין לוֹ
חֵקֶר כָּךְ אֵין חֵקֶר לְפוּרְעָנוּתָן שֶׁלָרְשָׁעִים לֶעָתִיד לָבוֹא. דָּבָר אַחֵר צִדְקָתְךָ
כְּהַרְרֵי־אֵל, מָה הָרִים הַלָּלוּ נִזְרָעִין וְעוֹשִׂין פֵּירוֹת כָּךְ מַעֲשֵׂיהֶן שֶׁלַצַּדִיקִין

עוֹשִׂין פֵּירוֹת, הָדָא הִיא דִכְתִיב אִמְרוּ צַדִּיק כִּי־טוֹב כִּי־פְרִי מַעַלְלֵיהֶם
יֹאכֵלוּ (ישעיה ג, י). מִשְׁפָּטֶיךָ תְּהוֹם רַבָּה, מַה הַתְּהוֹם הַזֶּה לֹא נִזְרַע וְלֹא
עוֹשֶׂה פֵּירוֹת כָּךְ מַעֲשֵׂיהֶן שֶׁלָּרְשָׁעִים אֵינָן עוֹשִׂין פֵּירוֹת, הָדָא הִיא
דִכְתִיב אוֹי לְרָשָׁע רָע כִּי־גְמוּל יָדָיו יֵעָשֶׂה לוֹ (שם יא). דָּבָר אַחֵר צִדְקָתְךָ
כְּהַרְרֵי־אֵל, מָה הָרִים הַלָּלוּ גְּלוּיִם כָּךְ מַעֲשֵׂיהֶן שֶׁלַּצַּדִּיקִים גְּלוּיִים, הָדָא
הִיא דִכְתִיב יִירָאוּךָ עִם־שָׁמֶשׁ (תהלים עב, ה). מִשְׁפָּטֶיךָ תְּהוֹם רַבָּה, מַה
הַתְּהוֹם הַזֶּה טָמוּן כָּךְ מַעֲשֵׂיהֶן שֶׁלָּרְשָׁעִים טְמוּנִין. הָדָא הִיא דִכְתִיב
וְהָיָה בְמַחְשָׁךְ מַעֲשֵׂיהֶם (ישעיה כט, טו). דָּבָר אַחֵר צִדְקָתְךָ כְּהַרְרֵי־אֵל,
אָמַר ר' יְהוּדָה בְר סִימוֹן צְדָקָה שֶׁעָשִׂיתָה עִם נֹחַ בַּתֵּיבָה, כְּהַרְרֵי־אֵל,
הָדָא הִיא דִכְתִיב וַתָּנַח הַתֵּיבָה וגו' עַל הָרֵי אֲרָרָט (בראשית ח, ד). מִשְׁפָּטֶיךָ
תְּהוֹם רַבָּה, מִשְׁפָּטִים שֶׁעָשִׂיתָ עִם דּוֹרוֹ דְּקִדַּקְתָ עִמָּהֶם עַד תְּהוֹם רַבָּה,
הָדָא הִיא דִכְתִיב בַּיּוֹם הַזֶּה נִבְקְעוּ כָּל־מַעְיְנוֹת תְּהוֹם רַבָּה (שם ז, יא).
וְלֹא עוֹד אֶלָּא כְּשֶׁזְּכַרְתּוֹ לֹא לְבַדּוֹ זָכַרְתָּ, אֶלָּא לוֹ וּלְכָל מִי שֶׁהָיָה עִמּוֹ
בַּתֵּיבָה, הָדָא הִיא דִכְתִיב וַיִּזְכֹּר אֱלֹהִים אֶת־נֹחַ וְאֵת כָּל־הַחַיָּה (שם ח, א).

דָּבָר אַחֵר צִדְקָתְךָ כְּהַרְרֵי־אֵל, ר' יְהוֹשֻׁעַ בֶּן חֲנַנְיָה אֲזַל לְרוֹמִי
וְרָאָה שָׁם עַמּוּדִים שֶׁלְּשַׁיִשׁ לְקָרְתָּא דְּמִתְקְרִי קַרְתְּגִינָא וְיַלְפִּית עֵצָה
מִן נְשַׁיָּא. עַל לִמְדִינָה אוֹחֲרִי וּשְׁמָהּ אַפְרִיקִי. נְפַקוּן וְקַדְּמוּנֵיהּ בְּחִיזוּרִין
דְּדַהַב וּבְרֵימוֹנִין דְּדַהַב וּבְלֶחֶם דְּדַהַב. אֲמַר דֵּין דְּמִתְאֲכַל בְּאַרְעֲכוֹן, אָמְרִין
לֵיהּ וְלָא הֲנָה לָךְ כֵּן לְאַרְעָךְ דַּאֲתֵית לָךְ לְהָכָא. אֲמַר לְהוֹן עוֹתַרְכוֹן לָא
אֲתֵית לְמִיחֲמֵי, דִּינְכוֹן אֲתֵית לְמִיחֲמֵי. עַד דְּאִינּוּן קָיְימִין תַּמָּן אֲתוֹן
תְּרֵין גֻּבְרִין מְכוֹרְכִין בְּקִיטָאוֹת מְשׁוּפָעוֹת, בְּשֶׁרָב שֶׁלֹּא יִפְקְעוּ וּבְצִינָה
שֶׁלֹּא יִקְרְשׁוּ, כֵּיוָן שֶׁיָּצָא פְּגַע בְּעָנִי אֶחָד, מַחֲצֶלֶת קָנִים תַּחְתָּיו וּמַחֲצֶלֶת
קָנִים מֵעַל גַּבָּיו, עַל הָעַמּוּדִים קָרָא צִדְקָתְךָ כְּהַרְרֵי־אֵל, אָמַר הָן דְּאַתְּ
יָהִיב אַתְּ יָהִיב וּמַשְׁפַּע, עַל הֶעָנִי קָרָא מִשְׁפָּטֶיךָ תְּהוֹם רַבָּה, הָן דְּאַתְּ
מָחֵי אַתְּ מְדַקְדֵּק.

מַעֲשֶׂה. אֲלֶכְסַנְדְּרוֹס מַקְדּוֹן אֲזַל לְגַבֵּי מַלְכָּא קַצִּיאָה אֲחוֹרֵי הָרֵי

חֹשֶׁךְ. עַל לַחְדָּא מְדִינָה וּשְׁמַהּ קַרְתְּגִינָה וַהֲוָה כּוּלָהּ דִּנְשִׁין. נָפְקִין קַדְמוֹי
וְאָמְרִין לֵיהּ אִין אַתְּ עָבֵיד קְרָבָא עִמָּן וְנָצַח לָן, שְׁמָךְ נָפִיק בְּעַלְמָא
דְּמָחוֹזָא דִנְשַׁיָּא חֲרַבְתְּ, וְאִין אֲנַן עָבְדִין עִימָּךְ קְרָבָא וְנָצְחִין לָךְ, שְׁמָךְ
נָפִיק בְּעַלְמָא דַּעֲבַדְתְּ קְרָבָא עִם נְשַׁיָּא וְנָצְחוּנָךְ, וְתוּב לֵית אַתְּ קָאִים
קֳדָם מַלְכוּ, בְּהַהִיא עָנְתָא אַמָּךְ אַפוֹי וּנְפַק לֵיהּ. מִי נָפֵק לֵיהּ כְּתַב עַל
תְּרַע פּוֹלִי וַאֲמַר אֲנָא אֲלֶכְסַנְדְּרוֹס מַקְדּוֹן מֶלֶךְ שָׁטֵי הֲוֵינָא עַד דְּעָלֵית
קֳדָם מַלְכָּא לְדִינָא. דִּין הֲוָה רָחִיק מִן גְּזֵילָה וְדִין הֲוָה רָחִיק מִן גְּזֵילָה חַד
מִינְּהוֹן אָמַר, חַרְבָּא זַבְנִית מִן הָדֵין גַּבְרָא חֲפָרִית בְּגַוַּהּ וְאַשְׁכְּחִית בֵּהּ
סִימָא וְאַמְרִית לֵיהּ סַב סִימְתָךְ, חַרְבָּא זַבְנִית סִימָא לָא זַבְנִית. וַחֲרָנָא
אָמַר כַּד זַבְנִית חוּרְבְּתָא לְהָדֵין גַּבְרָא הִיא וְכָל מַה דְּאִית בַּהּ זַבְנִית לֵיהּ.
קְרָא מַלְכָּא לְחַד מִנְּהוֹן וַאֲמַר לֵיהּ אִית לָךְ בַּר דְּכַר, אֲמַר לֵיהּ אִין. קְרָא
מַלְכָּא לָחֳרָנָא אֲמַר לֵיהּ אִית לָךְ בְּרָא, אֲמַר לֵיהּ אִין. אֲמַר לְהוֹן אַסְּבוּן
דֵּין לְדֵין וְיֵיכְלוּן סִימְתָא תְּרֵיהוֹן. שָׁרֵי אֲלֶכְסַנְדְּרוֹס מַקְדּוֹן תָּמִיהַּ. אֲמַר
לֵיהּ וּמַה לָךְ תְּמִיהַּ לָא דָּנִית טָבוּת, אֲמַר לֵיהּ אִין. אֲמַר לֵיהּ אִילוּ אִילוּ הֲוָה
הָדֵין דִּינָא בְּאַרְעֲכוֹן הֵיךְ הֲוֵיתוּן דָּיְינִין לֵיהּ, אֲמַר לֵיהּ הֲוֵינָן מְרִימִין
רֵישֵׁיהּ דְּדֵין וּמְרִימִין רֵישֵׁיהּ דְּדֵין וְסִימְתָא סָלְקָא לְמַלְכוּתָא. אֲמַר לֵיהּ
מִטְרָא נָחֵית עֲלֵיכוֹן, אֲמַר לֵיהּ אִין. וְשִׁמְשָׁא דָנְחָא עֲלֵיכוֹן, אֲמַר לֵיהּ
אִין. אֲמַר לֵיהּ אִית בְּאַרְעֲכוֹן בְּעִיר דַּקִּיק, אֲמַר לֵיהּ אִין. תִּיפַּח רוּחֵיהּ
דְּהַהוּא גַּבְרָא דְּבִזְכוּתָא דְּבִעִירָא דַּקִּיקָא אַתּוּן מִשְׁתְּזְבִין. הָדָא הִיא דִכְתִיב
אָדָם וּבְהֵמָה תוֹשִׁיעַ יְיָ (תהלים לו, ז), אָדָם בִּזְכוּת בְּהֵמָה תוֹשִׁיעַ יְיָ,
אָדָם מִפְּנֵי בְהֵמָה תוֹשִׁיעַ יְיָ. כָּךְ אָמְרוּ יִשְׂרָאֵל לִפְנֵי הַקָּדוֹשׁ בָּרוּךְ הוּא
רִבּוֹנוֹ שֶׁלָּעוֹלָם אָדָם אֲנַחְנוּ כִּבְהֵמָה תוֹשִׁיעֵנוּ לְפִי שֶׁאָנוּ נִמְשָׁכִין אַחֲרֶיךָ,
הָדָא הִיא דִכְתִיב מָשְׁכֵנִי אַחֲרֶיךָ נָּרוּצָה (שיה״ש א, ד) וּלְהֵיכָן אָנוּ נִמְשָׁכִין
אַחֲרֶיךָ, לְגַן עֵדֶן, דִּכְתִיב יִרְוְיוּן מִדֶּשֶׁן בֵּיתֶךָ וְנַחַל עֲדָנֶיךָ תַשְׁקֵם
(תהלים לו, ט). אָמַר ר׳ לָעֹזָר בַּר מְנַחֵם עֲדָנָךְ אֵין כְּתִיב כָּאן, אֶלָּא עֲדָנֶיךָ,
מִיכָּן שֶׁכָּל צַדִּיק וְצַדִּיק יֵשׁ לוֹ עֵדֶן בִּפְנֵי עַצְמוֹ. אָמַר ר׳ יִצְחָק כְּתִיב

מִשְׁפַּט אָדָם וּמִשְׁפַּט בְּהֵמָה, מִשְׁפַּט אָדָם וּבַיּוֹם הַשְּׁמִינִי יִמּוֹל (ויקרא יב, ג),
וּמִשְׁפַּט בְּהֵמָה וּמִיּוֹם הַשְּׁמִינִי וָהָלְאָה יֵרָצֶה לְקָרְבַּן אִשֶּׁה (שם כב, כז).

ב) מִי הִקְדִּימַנִי וַאֲשַׁלֵּם (איוב מא, ג). ר' תַּנְחוּמָא פְּתַר קַרְיָא בְּרַוָּוק
שֶׁהוּא שָׁרוּי בִּמְדִינָה וְנוֹתֵן שְׂכַר סוֹפְרִים וּמַשְׁנִים, אָמַר הַקָּדוֹשׁ בָּרוּךְ
הוּא עָלַי לְשַׁלֵּם לוֹ גְּמוּלוֹ וְלִיתֶּן לוֹ בֵּן זָכָר, הָדָא הִיא דִכְתִיב וּגְמֻלוֹ
יְשַׁלֶּם-לוֹ (משלי יט, יז). אָמַר ר' יִרְמְיָה בֶּן אֶלְעָזָר עֲתִידָה בַּת קוֹל לִהְיוֹת
מְפוֹצֶצֶת בְּרָאשֵׁי הֶהָרִים וְאוֹמֶרֶת מִי פָעַל עִם אֵל, כָּל מִי שֶׁפָּעַל עִם אֵל
יָבֹא וְיִטּוֹל שְׂכָרוֹ, הָדָא הִיא דִכְתִיב כָּעֵת יֵאָמֵר לְיַעֲקֹב וּלְיִשְׂרָאֵל מַה-פָּעַל
אֵל (במדבר כג, כג). עַכְשָׁיו יָבֹא וְיִטּוֹל שְׂכָרוֹ. וְרוּחַ הַקּוֹדֶשׁ אוֹמֶרֶת מִי
הִקְדִּימַנִי וַאֲשַׁלֵּם, מִי קִילֵּס לְפָנַי עַד שֶׁלֹּא נָתַתִּי לוֹ נְשָׁמָה, מִי מָל לִשְׁמִי
עַד שֶׁלֹּא נָתַתִּי לוֹ בֵּן זָכָר, מִי עָשָׂה לִי מַעֲקֶה עַד שֶׁלֹּא נָתַתִּי לוֹ גַג,
מִי עָשָׂה לִי מְזוּזָה עַד שֶׁלֹּא נָתַתִּי לוֹ בַיִת, מִי עָשָׂה לִי סוּכָּה עַד שֶׁלֹּא
נָתַתִּי לוֹ מָקוֹם, מִי עָשָׂה לִי לוּלָב עַד שֶׁלֹּא נָתַתִּי לוֹ דָמִים, מִי עָשָׂה לִי
צִיצִית עַד שֶׁלֹּא נָתַתִּי לוֹ טַלֵּת, מִי הִפְרִישׁ לִי פֵּאָה עַד שֶׁלֹּא נָתַתִּי לוֹ
שָׂדֶה, מִי הִפְרִישׁ לִי תְרוּמָה וּמַעֲשֵׂר עַד שֶׁלֹּא נָתַתִּי לוֹ גּוֹרֶן, מִי הִפְרִישׁ
לִי חַלָּה עַד שֶׁלֹּא נָתַתִּי לוֹ עִיסָה, מִי הִפְרִישׁ לְפָנַי קָרְבַּן עַד שֶׁלֹּא נָתַתִּי
לוֹ בְהֵמָה, שׁוֹר אוֹ כֶשֶׂב אוֹ-עֵז.

ג) ר' יַעֲקֹב בַּר זַבְדִּי בְּשׁ' ר' אַבָּהוּ פָּתַח וְלֹא יִהְיֶה-עוֹד לְבֵית יִשְׂרָאֵל
לְמִבְטָח מַזְכִּיר עָוֹן (יחזקאל כט, טז). כְּתִיב שְׂרָפִים עוֹמְדִים מִמַּעַל לוֹ וְגוֹ'
(ישעיה ו, ב). בִּשְׁתַּיִם יְעוֹפֵף (שם), בְּקִילּוּס. וּבִשְׁתַּיִם יְכַסֶּה פָנָיו (שם),
שֶׁלֹּא יַבִּיט בַּשְּׁכִינָה. וּבִשְׁתַּיִם יְכַסֶּה רַגְלָיו (שם), שֶׁלֹּא יִרְאוּ פְּנֵי שְׁכִינָה,
דִכְתִיב וְכַף רַגְלֵיהֶם כְּכַף רֶגֶל עֵגֶל (יחזקאל א, ז), וּכְתִיב עָשׂוּ לָהֶם עֵגֶל
מַסֵּכָה (שמות לב, ח), עַל שׁוּם וְלֹא יִהְיֶה עוֹד לְבֵית יִשְׂרָאֵל לְמִבְטָח מַזְכִּיר
עָוֹן. תַּמָּן תְּנִינָן כָּל הַשּׁוֹפָרוֹת כּוּלָּן כְּשֵׁירִין חוּץ מִשֶּׁלַּפָּרָה. וְלָמָה חוּץ
מִשֶּׁלַּפָּרָה, מִפְּנֵי שֶׁהוּא קֶרֶן שֶׁלָּעֵגֶל, וּכְתִיב עָשׂוּ לָהֶם עֵגֶל מַסֵּכָה, עַל
שׁוּם וְלֹא יִהְיֶה עוֹד לְבֵית יִשְׂרָאֵל לְמִבְטָח מַזְכִּיר עָוֹן. תְּנֵי מִפְּנֵי מָה אֵין

שׁוֹטָה שׁוֹתֶה בְּכוֹס שֶׁלַּחֲבֶרְתָּה, שֶׁלֹּא יֹאמְרוּ בְּכוֹס זֶה שָׁתָה חֲבֶרְתָּה
וּמֵתָה, עַל שׁוּם וְלֹא יִהְיֶה עוֹד לְבֵית יִשְׂרָאֵל לְמִבְטָח מַזְכִּיר עָוֹן. תְּנִינָן
וְהָרַגְתָּ אֶת־הָאִשָּׁה וְאֶת־הַבְּהֵמָה (ויקרא כ, טז), אִם אָדָם חָטָא בְּהֵמָה מַה
חַטָּאת, אֶלָּא לְפִי שֶׁבָּאת לְאָדָם תַּקָּלָה עַל יָדָהּ אָמְרָה תוֹרָה תִּסָּקֵל. דָּבָר
אַחֵר שֶׁלֹּא תְהֵא בְּהֵמָה עוֹבֶרֶת בַּשּׁוּק וְיִהְיוּ אוֹמְרִין זוֹ הִיא הַבְּהֵמָה שֶׁנִּסְקַל
פְּלוֹנִי עַל יָדֶיהָ, עַל שׁוּם וְלֹא יִהְיֶה עוֹד לְבֵית יִשְׂרָאֵל לְמִבְטָח מַזְכִּיר עָוֹן.
וְאַף כָּאן אוֹ שׁוֹר אוֹ כֶשֶׂב אוֹ עֵז כִּי יִוָּלֵד, שׁוֹר נוֹלַד וְלֹא עֵגֶל נוֹלַד, אֶלָּא
מִשּׁוּם שֶׁנֶּאֱמַר עָשׂוּ לָהֶם עֵגֶל מַסֵּכָה, לְפִיכָךְ קְרָאוֹ הַכָּתוּב שׁוֹר וְלֹא
קְרָאוֹ עֵגֶל, שׁוֹר אוֹ־כֶשֶׂב אוֹ־עֵז.

ד) מַה־שֶּׁהָיָה כְּבָר הוּא (קהלת ג, טו). ר' יְהוּדָה וְר' נְחֶמְיָה. ר' יְהוּדָה
אוֹמֵר אִם יֹאמַר לְךָ אָדָם שֶׁאִילּוּ לֹא חָטָא אָדָם הָרִאשׁוֹן וְאָכַל מֵאוֹתוֹ הָעֵץ
הָיָה חַי וְקַיָּם עַד עַכְשָׁיו, אֱמוֹר לוֹ כְּבָר הוּא, אֵלִיָּהוּ חַי וְקַיָּם לְעוֹלָם.
וַאֲשֶׁר לִהְיוֹת כְּבָר הָיָה (שם), אִם יֹאמַר לְךָ אָדָם שֶׁהַקָּדוֹשׁ בָּרוּךְ
הוּא עָתִיד לְהַחֲיוֹת אֶת הַמֵּתִים, אֱמוֹר לוֹ כְּבָר הָיָה, כְּבָר הֶחֱיָה מֵתִים עַל
יְדֵי אֵלִיָּהוּ וְעַל יְדֵי אֱלִישָׁע וְעַל יְדֵי יְחֶזְקֵאל בְּבִקְעַת דּוּרָא. ר' נְחֶמְיָה
אוֹמֵר אִם יֹאמַר לְךָ אָדָם אִיפְשָׁר שֶׁמִּתְּחִלָּה הָיָה הָעוֹלָם כּוּלּוֹ מַיִם בְּמַיִם,
אֱמוֹר לוֹ כְּבָר הוּא, אוֹקְיָאנוּס מָלֵא מַיִם. וַאֲשֶׁר לִהְיוֹת כְּבָר הָיָה, אִם
יֹאמַר לְךָ אָדָם אִיפְשָׁר שֶׁהַקָּדוֹשׁ בָּרוּךְ הוּא עָתִיד לְיַבְּשׁוֹ, אֱמוֹר לוֹ כְּבָר
הָיָה, וּבְנֵי יִשְׂרָאֵל הָלְכוּ בַיַּבָּשָׁה בְּתוֹךְ הַיָּם (שמות טו, יט). ר' אַחָא בְּשֵׁם
ר' שִׁמְעוֹן בֶּן חֲלַפְתָּא כָּל מַה שֶׁהַקָּדוֹשׁ בָּרוּךְ הוּא עָתִיד לַעֲשׂוֹת בָּעוֹלָם
הַבָּא כְּבָר הֶרְאָה לָהֶם בָּעוֹלָם הַזֶּה. שֶׁהוּא מְחַיֶּה מֵתִים, כְּבָר הֶחֱיָה מֵתִים
עַל יְדֵי אֵלִיָּהוּ וְעַל יְדֵי אֱלִישָׁע וְעַל יְדֵי יְחֶזְקֵאל. שֶׁהוּא מַעֲבִיר בַּמַּיִם
בַּיַּבָּשָׁה, כִּי־תַעֲבוֹר בַּמַּיִם אִתְּךָ־אָנִי (ישעיה מג, ב). כְּבָר הֶעֱבִיר אֶת יִשְׂרָאֵל
עַל יְדֵי מֹשֶׁה, וּבְנֵי יִשְׂרָאֵל הָלְכוּ בַיַּבָּשָׁה בְּתוֹךְ הַיָּם (שמות יד, כט).
וּבַנְּהָרוֹת לֹא יִשְׁטְפוּךְ (ישעיה שם), כְּבָר עָשָׂה עַל יְדֵי יְהוֹשֻׁעַ, שֶׁנֶּאֱמַר
בַּיַּבָּשָׁה עָבַר יִשְׂרָאֵל אֶת־הַיַּרְדֵּן (יהושע ד, כב). כִּי־תֵלֵךְ בְּמוֹ־אֵשׁ לֹא

תִּכְוֶה (ישעיה שם), כְּבָר עָשָׂה עַל יְדֵי חֲנַנְיָה מִישָׁאֵל וַעֲזַרְיָה. וְלֶהָבָה לֹא
תְבַעֵר־בָּךְ (שם), כְּבָר עָשָׂה כָּךְ, וְרֵיחַ נוּר לָא עֲדָת בְּהוֹן (דניאל ג, כז).
שֶׁהוּא מַמְתִּיק אֶת הַמָּרִים, כְּבָר עָשָׂה עַל יְדֵי מֹשֶׁה, וַיּוֹרֵהוּ יְיָ עֵץ
וַיַּשְׁלֵךְ אֶל־הַמַּיִם וַיִּמְתְּקוּ הַמָּיִם (שמות טו כה). שֶׁהוּא מַמְתִּיק אֶת הַמַּר
בְּמָר, כְּבָר עָשָׂה עַל יְדֵי אֱלִישָׁע, שֶׁנֶּאֱמַר וַיַּשְׁלֵךְ־שָׁם מֶלַח וַיֹּאמֶר
כֹּה־אָמַר יְיָ רִפִּאתִי לַמַּיִם הָאֵלֶּה (מ״ב ב, כא). שֶׁהוּא מְבָרֵךְ אֶת הַמּוּעָט
כְּבָר עָשָׂה עַל יְדֵי אֵלִיָּהוּ וֶאֱלִישָׁע, כִּי כֹה אָמַר יְיָ אֱלֹהֵי יִשְׂרָאֵל כַּד
הַקֶּמַח לֹא תִכְלָה וְצַפַּחַת הַשֶּׁמֶן לֹא תֶחְסָר (מ״א יז, יד) שֶׁהוּא פוֹקֵד
עֲקָרוֹת, כְּבָר עָשָׂה עַל יְדֵי שָׂרָה רִבְקָה רָחֵל וְחַנָּה. זְאֵב וְטָלֶה יִרְעוּ כְאֶחָד
(ישעיה סה, כה), כְּבָר עָשָׂה עַל יְדֵי חִזְקִיָּהוּ, וְגָר זְאֵב עִם־כֶּבֶשׂ וְגו׳
(שם יא, ו). וְהָיוּ מְלָכִים אֹמְנַיִךְ (שם מט, כג), כְּבָר עָשָׂה עַל יְדֵי דָנִיֵּאל,
בֵּאדַיִן מַלְכָּא נְבוּכַדְנֶאצַּר נְפַל עַל־אַנְפּוֹהִי וּלְדָנִיֵּאל סְגִד (דניאל ב, מו).

ה) וְהָאֱלֹהִים יְבַקֵּשׁ אֶת־נִרְדָּף (קהלת ג, טו). ר׳ הוּנָא בְּשֵׁם ר׳ יוֹסֵף
אָמַר לְעוֹלָם וְהָאֱלֹהִים יְבַקֵּשׁ אֶת־נִרְדָּף. אַתָּה מוֹצֵא צַדִּיק רוֹדֵף צַדִּיק,
וְהָאֱלֹהִים יְבַקֵּשׁ אֶת נִרְדָּף. רָשָׁע רוֹדֵף רָשָׁע, וְהָאֱלֹהִים יְבַקֵּשׁ אֶת־נִרְדָּף.
וְכָל שֶׁכֵּן רָשָׁע רוֹדֵף צַדִּיק, וְהָאֱלֹהִים יְבַקֵּשׁ אֶת־נִרְדָּף. עַד שֶׁאַתָּה חוֹזֵר
וְאוֹמֵר אֲפִילוּ צַדִּיק רוֹדֵף רָשָׁע, וְהָאֱלֹהִים יְבַקֵּשׁ אֶת־נִרְדָּף. ר׳ יוֹסֵי בְּרַ׳
יוּדָן בְּשֵׁם ר׳ יוֹסֵי בַּר נְהוֹרַאי אוֹמֵר לְעוֹלָם הַקָּדוֹשׁ בָּרוּךְ הוּא תּוֹבֵעַ דָּמָן
שֶׁל נִרְדָּפִים מִיַּד רוֹדְפִים. הֶבֶל נִרְדָּף מִפְּנֵי קַיִן, וְהָאֱלֹהִים יְבַקֵּשׁ אֶת־נִרְדָּף
וַיִּשַׁע יְיָ אֶל־הֶבֶל וְאֶל־מִנְחָתוֹ (בראשית ד, ד). נֹחַ נִרְדָּף מִפְּנֵי דוֹרוֹ,
וְהָאֱלֹהִים יְבַקֵּשׁ אֶת־נִרְדָּף, בֹּא־אַתָּה וְכָל־בֵּיתְךָ אֶל־הַתֵּבָה (בראשית ז, א).
וְאוֹמֵר כִּי מֵי נֹחַ זֹאת לִי אֲשֶׁר נִשְׁבַּעְתִּי (ישעיה נד, ט). אַבְרָהָם נִרְדָּף מִפְּנֵי
נִמְרוֹד, וְהָאֱלֹהִים יְבַקֵּשׁ אֶת נִרְדָּף, אַתָּה־הוּא יְיָ הָאֱלֹהִים אֲשֶׁר בָּחַרְתָּ
בְּאַבְרָם וְהוֹצֵאתוֹ מֵאוּר כַּשְׂדִּים (נחמיה ט, ז). יִצְחָק נִרְדָּף מִפְּנֵי יִשְׁמָעֵאל,
וְהָאֱלֹהִים יְבַקֵּשׁ אֶת־נִרְדָּף, כִּי בְיִצְחָק יִקָּרֵא לְךָ זָרַע (בראשית כא, יב).
יַעֲקֹב נִרְדָּף מִפְּנֵי עֵשָׂו, וְהָאֱלֹהִים יְבַקֵּשׁ אֶת־נִרְדָּף, כִּי־יַעֲקֹב בָּחַר לוֹ

יָה יִשְׂרָאֵל לִסְגֻלָּתוֹ (תהלים קלה, ד). מֹשֶׁה נִרְדָּף מִפְּנֵי פַרְעֹה, וְהָאֱלֹהִים
יְבַקֵּשׁ אֶת־נִרְדָּף, לוּלֵי מֹשֶׁה בְחִירוֹ עָמַד בַּפֶּרֶץ לְפָנָיו (שם קו, כג). דָּוִד נִרְדָּף
מִפְּנֵי שָׁאוּל, וְהָאֱלֹהִים יְבַקֵּשׁ אֶת־נִרְדָּף, וַיִּבְחַר בְּדָוִד עַבְדּוֹ (שם עח, ע).
יִשְׂרָאֵל נִרְדָּפִים מִפְּנֵי הָאֻמּוֹת, וְהָאֱלֹהִים יְבַקֵּשׁ אֶת־נִרְדָּף, וּבְךָ בָּחַר י״י
לִהְיוֹת לוֹ לְעָם (דברים יד, ב). וְאַף בַּקָּרְבָּנוֹת כֵּן, שׁוֹר נִרְדָּף מִפְּנֵי אֲרִי,
כֶּבֶשׂ נִרְדָּף מִפְּנֵי זְאֵב, עֵז נִרְדָּף מִפְּנֵי נָמֵר, לְפִיכָךְ אָמַר הַקָּדוֹשׁ בָּרוּךְ
הוּא אַל תַּקְרִיבוּ לְפָנַי מִן הָרוֹדְפִים אֶלָּא מִן הַנִּרְדָּפִים. שׁוֹר אוֹ־כֶשֶׂב
אוֹ־עֵז כִּי יִוָּלֵד.

ו) עַמִּי מֶה־עָשִׂיתִי לְךָ וּמָה הֶלְאֵיתִיךָ עֲנֵה בִי (מיכה ו, ג). אָמַר
ר׳ אַחָא עֲנֵה בִי וְקַבֵּל שָׂכָר וְאַל תַּעֲנֶה בְרֶעֲךָ וּתְקַבֵּל עָלָיו דִּין וְחֶשְׁבּוֹן
לֶעָתִיד לָבוֹא. אָמַר ר׳ שְׁמוּאֵל בַּר נַחְמָן בִּשְׁלשָׁה מְקוֹמוֹת בָּא הַקָּדוֹשׁ
בָּרוּךְ הוּא לְהִתְוַכֵּחַ עִם יִשְׂרָאֵל וְשָׂמְחוּ אֻמּוֹת הָעוֹלָם וְאָמְרוּ כְלוּם אֵ֫ילוּ
יְכוֹלִין לְהִתְוַכֵּחַ עִם בּוֹרְאָן, עַכְשָׁיו הוּא מְכַלָּן מִן הָעוֹלָם. בְּשָׁעָה שֶׁאָמַר
לָהֶן לְכוּ־נָא וְנִוָּכְחָה יֹאמַר י״י (ישעיה א, יח). כֵּיוָן שֶׁרָאָה הַקָּדוֹשׁ בָּרוּךְ
הוּא שֶׁאֻמּוֹת הָעוֹלָם שְׂמֵחִין הָפְכָהּ לָהֶן לְטוֹבָה, אִם־יִהְיוּ חֲטָאֵיכֶם כַּשָּׁנִים
כַּשֶּׁלֶג יַלְבִּינוּ (שם). בְּאוֹתָהּ שָׁעָה תָּמְהוּ אֻמּוֹת הָעוֹלָם וְאָמְרוּ זוֹ תְשׁוּבָה
וְזוֹ תוֹכֵחָה, לָא אֲתָא אֶלָּא מִתְפוֹגְגָא עִם בְּנוֹי. וּבְשָׁעָה שֶׁאָמַר לָהֶן שִׁמְעוּ
הָרִים אֶת־רִיב י״י (מיכה ו, ב) שָׂמְחוּ אֻמּוֹת הָעוֹלָם וְאָמְרוּ הֵיאַךְ אֵ֫ילוּ
יְכוֹלִין לְהִתְוַכֵּחַ עִם בּוֹרְאָן, עַכְשָׁיו הוּא מְכַלֶּה אוֹתָן מִן הָעוֹלָם. כֵּיוָן
שֶׁרָאָה הַקָּדוֹשׁ בָּרוּךְ הוּא שֶׁאֻמּוֹת הָעוֹלָם שְׂמֵחִין הָפְכָהּ לָהֶן לְטוֹבָה,
עַמִּי מֶה־עָשִׂיתִי לְךָ וּמָה הֶלְאֵיתִיךָ עֲנֵה בִי (שם ג). זְכָר־נָא מַה־יָּעַץ בָּלָק
מֶלֶךְ מוֹאָב (שם ה). תָּמְהוּ אֻמּוֹת הָעוֹלָם וְאָמְרוּ זוֹ תְשׁוּבָה וְזוֹ תוֹכֵחָה,
זוֹ אַחַר זוֹ, לָא אֲתָא אֶלָּא לְמִתְפַּגְּגָא עִם בְּנוֹי. וּבְשָׁעָה שֶׁאָמַר לָהֶן וְרִיב
לַי״י עִם־יְהוּדָה וְלִפְקֹד עַל־יַעֲקֹב כִּדְרָכָיו (הושע יב, ג) שָׂמְחוּ אֻמּוֹת
הָעוֹלָם וְאָמְרוּ הֵיאַךְ אֵ֫ילוּ יְכוֹלִין לְהִתְוַכֵּחַ עִם בּוֹרְאָן, עַכְשָׁיו הוּא מְכַלֶּה
אוֹתָן מִן הָעוֹלָם. כֵּיוָן שֶׁרָאָה הַקָּדוֹשׁ בָּרוּךְ הוּא שֶׁאֻמּוֹת הָעוֹלָם שְׂמֵחִין

מִיָּד הֲפָכָהּ לָהֶן לְטוֹבָה, הָדָא הִיא דִכְתִיב בַּבֶּטֶן עָקַב אֶת־אָחִיו (שם ד).

אָמַר ר׳ יוּדָן בְּר׳ שִׁמְעוֹן לְאִשָּׁה אַלְמָנָה שֶׁהָיְתָה קוֹבֶלֶת עַל בְּנָהּ לַדַּיָּין,

כֵּיוָן דַּחֲמַת דַּיָּינָא דַּהֲוָא יָתֵיב וְדָאֵין בְּנוּר וּבְזֶפֶת וּבְמַגְלָבִין אָמְרַת אִין

אֲנָא מוֹדַעֲנָא סוּרְחָנָא דִּבְרִי לְהָדֵין דַּיָּינָא כְּדוֹן הוּא קָטֵיל לֵיהּ. אָרְכַת

עַד דַּחֲסַל. כֵּיוָן דַּחֲסַל אֲמַר לַהּ אַיְטֵי הָדֵין בְּרִיךְ מַה סָּרַח עֲלָיִךְ, אָמְרָה

לֵיהּ מָרִי כַד הֲוָה בִּמְעַיי הֲוָה מְבַעֵט בִּי. אֲמַר לַהּ כְּדוֹן הוּא עָבֵד לָךְ כְּלוּם,

אָמְרָה לֵיהּ לָא. אֲמַר לַהּ זִיל לִיךְ דְּלֵית לֵיהּ בְּהָדָא מִילְתָא סוּרְחָן כְּלוּם.

כָּךְ כֵּיוָן שֶׁרָאָה הַקָּדוֹשׁ בָּרוּךְ הוּא שֶׁאֻמּוֹת הָעוֹלָם שְׂמֵחִין הֲפָכָהּ לָהֶן

לְטוֹבָה, בַּבֶּטֶן עָקַב אֶת־אָחִיו. מִיָּד תָּמְהוּ אוּמּוֹת הָעוֹלָם וְאָמְרוּ זוֹ תְשׁוּבָה

וְזוֹ תוֹכֵחָה, זוֹ אַחַר זוֹ, לָא אֲתָא אֶלָּא לְמִתְפּוּגְגָה עִם בְּנוֹי. וּמָה הֶלְאֵיתִיךָ

(מיכה ו, ג). אָמַר ר׳ בְּרֶכְיָה לְמֶלֶךְ שֶׁשָּׁלַח שְׁלֹשָׁה שְׁלוּחִין לִמְדִינָה

וְעָמְדוּ בְּנֵי הַמְּדִינָה לִפְנֵיהֶם וְשִׁמְּשׁוּ אוֹתָן בְּאֵימָה בְּיִרְאָה בִּרְתֵת וּבְזִיעַ.

כָּךְ אָמַר לָהֶן הַקָּדוֹשׁ בָּרוּךְ הוּא לְיִשְׂרָאֵל שְׁלֹשָׁה שְׁלוּחִים שָׁלַחְתִּי לָכֶם,

מֹשֶׁה אַהֲרֹן וּמִרְיָם, שֶׁמָּא אֲכָלוּ מִכֶּם, שֶׁמָּא שָׁתוּ מִכֶּם, שֶׁמָּא הִטְרִיחוּ

עֲלֵיכֶם כְּלוּם, לֹא בִזְכוּתָן אַתֶּם מִתְפַּרְנְסִין, הַמָּן בִּזְכוּת מֹשֶׁה, הַבְּאֵר

בִּזְכוּת מִרְיָם, עַנְנֵי כָבוֹד בִּזְכוּת אַהֲרֹן. אָמַר ר׳ יִצְחָק לְמֶלֶךְ שֶׁשָּׁלַח

פְּרוֹסְדּוֹגְמָא שֶׁלּוֹ לַמְּדִינָה, מֶה עָשׂוּ בְּנֵי הַמְּדִינָה, עָמְדוּ עַל רַגְלֵיהֶן וּפָרְעוּ

רָאשֵׁיהֶן וְקָרְאוּ אוֹתוֹ בְּאֵימָה וּבְיִרְאָה בִּרְתֵת וּבְזִיעַ. כָּךְ אָמַר הַקָּדוֹשׁ בָּרוּךְ

הוּא לְיִשְׂרָאֵל הָדָא קְרִיַת שְׁמַע וּפְרוֹסְדִּיגְמָא שֶׁלִּי, לֹא הִטְרַחְתִּי עֲלֵיכֶם

וְלֹא אָמַרְתִּי לָכֶם שֶׁתְּהוּ קוֹרִין אוֹתָהּ לֹא עוֹמְדִין עַל רַגְלֵיכֶן וְלֹא פּוֹרְעִין

רָאשֵׁיכֶן, אֶלָּא בְּשִׁבְתְּךָ בְּבֵיתֶךָ וּבְלֶכְתְּךָ בַדֶּרֶךְ (דברים ו, ז). אָמַר ר׳ יְהוּדָה

בְּר׳ סִימוֹן אָמַר הַקָּדוֹשׁ בָּרוּךְ הוּא אֲשֶׁר עֶשֶׂר בְּהֵמוֹת מָסַרְתִּי לָךְ, שָׁלֹשׁ

בִּרְשׁוּתְךָ וְשֶׁבַע אֵינָן בִּרְשׁוּתְךָ. שָׁלֹשׁ שֶׁהֵן בִּרְשׁוּתְךָ, שׁוֹר שֵׂה כְשָׂבִים

וְשֵׂה עִזִּים (דברים יד, ד). וְשֶׁבַע אֵינָן בִּרְשׁוּתְךָ. אַיָּל וּצְבִי וְיַחְמוּר וְאַקּוֹ

וְדִישֹׁן וּתְאוֹ וָזָמֶר (שם ה). לֹא הִטְרַחְתִּי עֲלֵיכֶם וְלֹא אָמַרְתִּי לָכֶם לַעֲלוֹת

בֶּהָרִים וּלְהִתְיַגֵּעַ בַּשָּׂדוֹת וּלְהָבִיא לְפָנַי קָרְבָּן מֵאֵילוּ שֶׁאֵינָן בִּרְשׁוּתְךָ,

אֶלָּא מִמַּה שֶּׁבִּרְשׁוּתָךְ, מִן הַגָּדֵל עַל אֲבוּסֶךָ, שׁוֹר אוֹ־כֶשֶׂב אוֹ־עֵז.

ז) ר׳ לֵוִי פָּתַח הֵן־אַתֶּם מֵאַיִן וּפָעָלְכֶם מֵאָפַע וְגוֹ׳ (ישעיה מא, כד).
מֵאַיִן, מָלֵא כְּלוּם וּמְלֵחָה סְרוּחָה. מֵאָפַע, מִמֵּאָה פְּעִיּוֹת שֶׁהָאִשָּׁה פּוֹעָה
בְּשָׁעָה שֶׁהִיא יוֹשֶׁבֶת עַל הַמַּשְׁבֵּר תִּשְׁעִים וְתִשְׁעָה לְמִיתָה וְאֶחָד לְחַיִּים.
תְּנֵי שָׁלֹשׁ שֵׁמוֹת נִקְרְאוּ לָהּ. חַיִּיתָא מְחַבַּלְתָּא מַתְבְּרָא. חַיִּיתָא דַּהֲוַת
מֵתָה וְחָיִית. מְחַבַּלְתָּא דַּהֲוַת מְמַשְׁכְּנָא לְמִיתָה, הֵיךְ מָה דְאַתְּ אָמַר
אִם־חָבוֹל תַּחְבּוֹל שַׂלְמַת רֵעֶךָ (שמות כב, כה). מַתְבְּרָא דַּהֲוַת תְּבִירָא
לְמִיתָה. תּוֹעֵבָה יִבְחַר בָּכֶם (ישעיה שם), אַף־עַל־פִּי שֶׁהַתִּינוֹק הַזֶּה יוֹצֵא
מִמְּעֵי אִמּוֹ מְלוּכְלָךְ וּמְטוּנָּף מָלֵא רִירִין וְדָם הַכֹּל מְחַבְּקִין וּמְנַשְּׁקִין אוֹתוֹ.
דָּבָר אַחֵר הֵן־אַתֶּם מֵאַיִן, אָמַר ר׳ בֶּרֶכְיָה הֵן לָשׁוֹן יְוָנִי הוּא, הֵינָא,
אֶחָד. אָמַר הַקָּדוֹשׁ בָּרוּךְ הוּא אוּמָּה אַחַת אַתֶּם לִי מֵאוּמּוֹת הָעוֹלָם.
מֵאַיִן, מֵאוֹתָן שֶׁכְּתִיב בָּהֶן כָּל הַגּוֹיִם כְּאַיִן נֶגְדּוֹ (שם מ, יז). וּפָעָלְכֶם מֵאָפַע,
אָמַר ר׳ לֵוִי כָּל פְּעוּלוֹת טוֹבוֹת וְנֶחָמוֹת שֶׁהַקָּדוֹשׁ בָּרוּךְ הוּא עָתִיד לַעֲשׂוֹת
עִם יִשְׂרָאֵל אֵינָן אֶלָּא בִּשְׁבִיל פְּעִיָּה אַחַת שֶׁפִּעִיתֶם לְפָנַי בְּסִינַי וַאֲמַרְתֶּם
כָּל אֲשֶׁר־דִּבֶּר יְ״י נַעֲשֶׂה וְנִשְׁמָע (שמות כד, ז). תּוֹעֵבָה יִבְחַר בָּכֶם, אוֹתָהּ
הַתּוֹעֵבָה שֶׁכְּתִיב בָּהּ עָשׂוּ לָהֶם עֵגֶל מַסֵּכָה, מֵאוֹתָהּ הַתּוֹעֵבָה הֵבִיאוּ
לְפָנַי קָרְבָּן, שׁוֹר אוֹ־כֶשֶׂב אוֹ־עֵז.

ח) בְּרָעָתָם יְשַׂמְּחוּ־מֶלֶךְ (הושע ז, ג). וְכִי מָה רָאָה שׁוֹר לְהֵעָשׂוֹת
רֹאשׁ לְכָל הַקָּרְבָּנוֹת אָמַר ר׳ לֵוִי לְמַטְרוֹנָה שֶׁיָּצָא עָלֶיהָ שֵׁם רַע עִם אֶחָד
מִגְּדוֹלֵי מַלְכוּת, וּבָדַק הַמֶּלֶךְ בַּדְּבָרִים וְלֹא מָצָא בָּהֶן מַמָּשׁ, מֶה עָשָׂה
הַמֶּלֶךְ, עָשָׂה סְעוּדָה וְהוֹשִׁיב אוֹתוֹ הָאִישׁ בְּרֹאשָׁן שֶׁלַּמְסוּבִּין, כָּל כָּךְ
לָמָּה שֶׁבָּדַק הַמֶּלֶךְ בַּדְּבָרִים וְלֹא מָצָא בָּהֶן מַמָּשׁ. כָּךְ אוּמּוֹת הָעוֹלָם מוֹנִין
לָהֶן לְיִשְׂרָאֵל וְאוֹמְרִין לָהֶן עֲשִׂיתֶן אֶת הָעֵגֶל, וּבָדַק הַקָּדוֹשׁ בָּרוּךְ הוּא
בַּדְּבָרִים וְלֹא מָצָא בָּהֶן מַמָּשׁ, לְפִיכָךְ נַעֲשָׂה שׁוֹר רֹאשׁ לְכָל הַקּוֹרְבָּנוֹת,
שׁוֹר אוֹ־כֶשֶׂב אוֹ־עֵז. רַב הוּנָא וְרַב אִידִי בְּשֵׁם ר׳ שְׁמוּאֵל בַּר נַחְמָן מוּצָּלִין
הָיוּ יִשְׂרָאֵל מֵאוֹתוֹ מַעֲשֶׂה, שֶׁאִילּוּ עָשׂוּ יִשְׂרָאֵל אֶת הָעֵגֶל הָיָה לָהֶן

לוֹמַר אֵלֶּה אֱלֹהֶינוּ יִשְׂרָאֵל, אֶלָּא הַגֵּרִים שֶׁעָלוּ עִם יִשְׂרָאֵל מִמִּצְרַיִם, וְגַם עֵרֶב רַב עָלָה אִתָּם (שמות יב, לח), הֵם עָשׂוּ אֶת הָעֵגֶל, וְהָיוּ מוֹנִין לָהֶן וְאוֹמְרִין לָהֶן אֵלֶּה אֱלֹהֶיךָ יִשְׂרָאֵל (שם לב, ח). אָמַר ר׳ יְהוּדָה בַּר׳ סִימוֹן כְּתִיב יָדַע שׁוֹר קֹנֵהוּ וַחֲמוֹר אֵבוּס בְּעָלָיו יִשְׂרָאֵל לֹא יָדַע (ישעיה א, ג), וְלֹא הָיוּ יוֹדְעִין אֶלָּא שֶׁדָּשׁוּ בְּעָקֵב. וְדַכְוָותָהּ כִּי אֱוִיל עַמִּי אוֹתִי לֹא יָדָעוּ (ירמיה ד, כב), וְלֹא הָיוּ יוֹדְעִין, אֶלָּא שֶׁדָּשׁוּ בְּעָקֵב. וְדַכְוָותָהּ וְהִיא לֹא יָדְעָה וגו׳ (הושע ב, י), וְלֹא הֲוַת יָדְעָה, אֶלָּא שֶׁדָּשָׁה בְּעָקֵב.

ט) שׁוֹר אוֹ־כֶשֶׂב. שׁוֹר בִּזְכוּת אַבְרָהָם, שֶׁנֶּאֱמַר וְאֶל־הַבָּקָר רָץ אַבְרָהָם (בראשית יח, ז). כֶּשֶׂב בִּזְכוּתוֹ שֶׁל־יִצְחָק, דִּכְתִיב וַיַּרְא וְהִנֵּה אַיִל (שם כב, יג). עֵז בִּזְכוּתוֹ שֶׁל־יַעֲקֹב, דִּכְתִיב בֵּיהּ לֶךְ־נָא אֶל־הַצֹּאן וְקַח־לִי מִשָּׁם שְׁנֵי גְּדָיֵי עִזִּים טוֹבִים (שם כז, ט). מָהוּ טוֹבִים, ר׳ בֶּרֶכְיָה בְּשֵׁם ר׳ חֶלְבּוֹ טוֹבִים לָךְ וְטוֹבִים לְבָנֶיךָ. טוֹבִים לָךְ שֶׁעַל יְדֵיהֶן אַתְּ מְקַבֵּל סַמָּנֵי בְּרָכוֹת, טוֹבִים לְבָנֶיךָ שֶׁעַל יְדֵיהֶן הוּא מִתְכַּפֵּר לָהֶן בְּיוֹם הַכִּפּוּרִים, כִּי־בַיּוֹם הַזֶּה יְכַפֵּר עֲלֵיכֶם (ויקרא יז, ל).

י) וְהָיָה שִׁבְעַת יָמִים תַּחַת אִמּוֹ (ויקרא כב, כז). וְלָמָּה שִׁבְעַת יָמִים, אֶלָּא כְדֵי שֶׁיִּבָּדֵק שֶׁאִם שֶׁאָם נִגְחַתּוּ אִמּוֹ אוֹ שֶׁנִּמְצָא בּוֹ דְבַר מוּם הֲרֵי זֶה פָּסוּל וְלֹא יִהְיֶה כָשֵׁר לְקָרְבָּן. דִּתְנִינָן תַּמָּן יוֹצֵא דֹפֶן אֵין יוֹשְׁבִין עָלָיו יְמֵי טוּמְאָה וִימֵי טָהֳרָה וְאֵין חַיָּבִין עָלָיו קָרְבָּן. ר׳ שִׁמְעוֹן אוֹמֵר הֲרֵי הוּא כִּילוֹד. דָּבָר אַחֵר וְהָיָה שִׁבְעַת יָמִים תַּחַת אִמּוֹ, וְלָמָּה שִׁבְעַת יָמִים, ר׳ יְהוֹשֻׁעַ דְּסִיכְנִין בְּשֵׁם ר׳ לֵוִי אָמַר לְמֶלֶךְ שֶׁנִּכְנַס לִמְדִינָה וְגָזַר וְאָמַר כָּל אַכְסְנַיִּין שֶׁיֵּשׁ כַּן לֹא יִרְאוּ פָנַי עַד שֶׁיִּרְאוּ פְּנֵי מַטְרוֹנָה תְּחִלָּה. כַּךְ אָמַר הַקָּדוֹשׁ בָּרוּךְ הוּא לֹא תַקְרִיבוּ לְפָנַי קָרְבָּן עַד שֶׁתַּעֲבוֹר עָלָיו שַׁבָּת, שֶׁאֵין שִׁבְעָה בְלֹא שַׁבָּת וְאֵין מִילָה בְלֹא שַׁבָּת, וּמִיּוֹם הַשְּׁמִינִי וָהָלְאָה יֵרָצֶה. אָמַר ר׳ יִצְחָק כְּתִיב מִשְׁפַּט אָדָם וּמִשְׁפַּט בְּהֵמָה, מִשְׁפַּט אָדָם וּבַיּוֹם הַשְּׁמִינִי יִמּוֹל בְּשַׂר עָרְלָתוֹ (ויקרא יב, ג), וּמִשְׁפַּט בְּהֵמָה וּמִיּוֹם הַשְּׁמִינִי וָהָלְאָה (שם כב, כז).

יא) וְשׁוֹר אוֹ־שֶׂה וְגו' (ויקרא כב, כח). ר' בֶּרֶכְיָה בְּשֵׁם ר' לֵוִי כְּתִיב
יוֹדֵעַ צַדִּיק נֶפֶשׁ בְּהֶמְתּוֹ (משלי יב, י). יוֹדֵעַ צַדִּיק, זֶה הַקָּדוֹשׁ בָּרוּךְ הוּא
שֶׁכָּתוּב בְּתוֹרָתוֹ לֹא־תִקַּח הָאֵם עַל־הַבָּנִים (דברים כב, ו). וְרַחֲמֵי רְשָׁעִים
אַכְזָרִי (משלי שם), זֶה סַנְחֵרִיב הָרָשָׁע, שֶׁכָּתִיב בּוֹ אֵם עַל־בָּנִים רֻטָּשָׁה
(הושע י, יד). דָּבָר אַחֵר יוֹדֵעַ צַדִּיק נֶפֶשׁ בְּהֶמְתּוֹ, זֶה הַקָּדוֹשׁ בָּרוּךְ הוּא,
שֶׁכָּתוּב בְּתוֹרָתוֹ וְשׁוֹר אוֹ־שֶׂה אוֹתוֹ וְאֶת בְּנוֹ לֹא תִשְׁחֲטוּ בְּיוֹם אֶחָד.
וְרַחֲמֵי רְשָׁעִים אַכְזָרִי, זֶה הָמָן הָרָשָׁע, דִּכְתִיב בֵּיהּ לְהַשְׁמִיד לַהֲרֹג
וּלְאַבֵּד וְגו' (אסתר ג, יג). אָמַר ר' לֵוִי אוֹי לָהֶם לָרְשָׁעִים שֶׁהֵן מִתְנַמְּקִין
בְּעֵיצוֹת עַל יִשְׂרָאֵל וְכָל אֶחָד וְאֶחָד אוֹמֵר עֲצָתִי יָפָה מֵעֲצָתְךָ. עֵשָׂו אָמַר
שׁוֹטֶה הָיָה קַיִן שֶׁהָרַג אֶת אָחִיו בְּחַיֵּי אָבִיו, לֹא הָיָה יוֹדֵעַ שֶׁאָבִיו פָּרֶה
וְרָבֶה, אֲנִי אֵינִי עוֹשֶׂה כֵן אֶלָּא יִקְרְבוּ יְמֵי אֵבֶל אָבִי וְאַהֲרֹגָה אֶת־יַעֲקֹב
אָחִי (בראשית כז, מא). פַּרְעֹה אָמַר שׁוֹטֶה הָיָה עֵשָׂו שֶׁאָמַר יִקְרְבוּ יְמֵי
אֵבֶל אָבִי, לֹא הָיָה יוֹדֵעַ שֶׁאָחִיו פָּרֶה וְרָבֶה בְּחַיֵּי אָבִיו, אֲנִי אֵינִי עוֹשֶׂה כֵן,
אֶלָּא עַד דְּאִינּוּן דַּקִּיקִין תְּחוֹת כּוּרְסֵי אִמְּהוֹן אֲנָא מְחַנֵּק לְהוֹן, הֲדָא הִיא
דִּכְתִיב כָּל־הַבֵּן הַיִּלּוֹד הַיְאֹרָה תַּשְׁלִיכֻהוּ (שמות א, כב). הָמָן אָמַר שׁוֹטֶה
הָיָה פַּרְעֹה שֶׁאָמַר כָּל־הַבֵּן הַיִּלּוֹד, לֹא הָיָה יוֹדֵעַ שֶׁהַבָּנוֹת נִשָּׂאוֹת
לַאֲנָשִׁים וּפָרוֹת וְרָבוֹת מֵהֶם, אֲנִי אֵינִי עוֹשֶׂה כֵן, אֶלָּא לְהַשְׁמִיד לַהֲרֹג
וּלְאַבֵּד. אָמַר ר' לֵוִי אַף גּוֹג לֶעָתִיד לָבוֹא עָתִיד לוֹמַר כֵּן שׁוֹטִים הָיוּ
הָרִאשׁוֹנִים שֶׁהָיוּ מִתְנַמְּקִין בְּעֵצוֹת עַל יִשְׂרָאֵל וְלֹא הָיוּ יוֹדְעִין שֶׁיֵּשׁ לָהֶן
פַּטְרוֹן בַּשָּׁמַיִם, אֲנִי אֵינִי עוֹשֶׂה כֵן, אֶלָּא בַּתְּחִלָּה אֲנִי מִזְדַּוֵּיג לְפַטְרוֹנָן
וְאַחַרְכָּךְ אֲנִי מִזְדַּוֵּיג לָהֶן, הֲדָא הִיא דִּכְתִיב יִתְיַצְּבוּ מַלְכֵי אֶרֶץ וְרוֹזְנִים
נוֹסְדוּ־יָחַד עַל־י״י וְעַל־מְשִׁיחוֹ (תהלים ב, ב). אָמַר לוֹ הַקָּדוֹשׁ בָּרוּךְ הוּא
רָשָׁע, לִי בָּאתָה לְהִזְדַּוֵּיג, חַיֶּיךָ שֶׁאֲנִי עוֹשֶׂה עִמְּךָ מִלְחָמָה, הֲדָא הִיא
דִּכְתִיב י״י כַּגִּבּוֹר יֵצֵא וְגו' (ישעיה מב, יג). וְיָצָא י״י וְנִלְחַם בַּגּוֹיִם הָהֵם
(זכריה יד, ג). וּמַה כְּתִיב תַּמָּן, וְהָיָה י״י לְמֶלֶךְ עַל־כָּל־הָאָרֶץ (שם ט).

יב) וְכִי־תִזְבְּחוּ זֶבַח־תּוֹדָה (ויקרא כב, כט). ר' פִּינְחָס וְר' לֵוִי

וְר׳ יוֹחָנָן בְּשֵׁם ר׳ מְנַחֵם דְּגַלְיָא. לֶעָתִיד לָבוֹא כָל הַקָּרְבָּנוֹת בְּטֵילִין

וְקָרְבַּן תּוֹדָה אֵינוֹ בָטֵל לְעוֹלָם. כָּל הַהוֹדָיוֹת בְּטֵילִין וְהוֹדָיַית תּוֹדָה אֵינָה

בְּטֵלָה לְעוֹלָם. הָדָא הִיא דִכְתִיב קוֹל שָׂשׂוֹן וְקוֹל שִׂמְחָה קוֹל חָתָן וְקוֹל

כַּלָּה קוֹל אוֹמְרִים הוֹדוּ אֶת־יְ״י צְבָאוֹת כִּי־טוֹב (ירמיה לג, יא), אֵילוּ

הַהוֹדָיוֹת. מְבִיאִים תּוֹדָה בֵּית יְ״י (שם), זֶה קָרְבַּן תּוֹדָה. וְכֵן דָּוִד אָמַר

עָלַי אֱלֹהִים נְדָרֶיךָ אֲשַׁלֵּם תּוֹדוֹת לָךְ (תהלים נו, יג), תּוֹדָה אֵין כְּתִיב כָּאן,

אֶלָּא תּוֹדוֹת, הַהוֹדָיָיה וְקָרְבַּן תּוֹדָה.

## CHAPTER 5: PESIQTA DE RAB KAHANA: 19

א) חֶרְפָּה שָׁבְרָה לִבִּי וָאָנוּשָׁה וָאֲקַוֶּה לָנוּד וָאַיִן וְלַמְנַחֲמִים וְלֹא מָצָאתִי (תהלים סט, כא) חֶרְפָּה שֶׁחֵרְפוּ אוֹתָנוּ עַמּוֹנִים וּמוֹאָבִים. אַתְּ מוֹצֵא כֵּיוָן שֶׁגָּרְמוּ הָעֲוֹנוֹת וְנִכְנְסוּ גוֹיִם לִירוּשָׁלַם נִכְנְסוּ עִמָּהֶם עַמּוֹנִים וּמוֹאָבִים, וְנִכְנְסוּ לְבֵית קוֹדֶשׁ הַקֳּדָשִׁים וְנָטְלוּ אֶת הַכְּרוּבִים וּנְתָנוּן בְּכְלִיבָה, וְהָיוּ מְחַזְּרִין אֹתָם בְּכָל חוּצוֹת יְרוּשָׁלַם וְהָיוּ אֹמְרִין, לֹא הָיוּ יִשְׂרָאֵל אוֹמְרִין שֶׁאֵין אָנוּ עוֹבְדִין עֲבוֹדָה זָרָה, רְאוּ מַה הָיוּ עוֹשִׂים, הֲדָא הִיא דִכְתִיב יַעַן אָמֹר מוֹאָב וְשֵׂעִיר הִנֵּה כְּכָל־הַגּוֹיִם וְגֹ' (יחזקאל כה, ח) וּמַה הֲווֹן אָמְרִין, וַוי וַוי כּוּלָּן כַּחֲדָה. מֵאוֹתָהּ שָׁעָה אָמַר הַקָּדוֹשׁ בָּרוּךְ הוּא, שָׁמַעְתִּי חֶרְפַּת מוֹאָב וְגִידוּפֵי בְּנֵי עַמּוֹן אֲשֶׁר חֵרְפוּ אֶת־עַמִּי בְּנֵי יִשְׂרָאֵל וַיַּגְדִּילוּ עַל־גְּבוּלָם וְגֹ', לָכֵן חַי־אָנִי נְאֻם יְיָ צְבָאוֹת אֱלֹהֵי יִשְׂרָאֵל כִּי־מוֹאָב כִּסְדֹם תִּהְיֶה וּבְנֵי עַמּוֹן כַּעֲמוֹרָה (צפניה ב, ח ט) וָאָנוּשָׁה (תהלים שם). בָּאַת עָלַי מַכָּה גִבְרָתָנִית וּמַתֶּשֶׁת אוֹתִי. וָאֲקַוֶּה לָנוּד וָאַיִן וְלַמְנַחֲמִים וְלֹא מָצָאתִי (שם), אָמַר הַקָּדוֹשׁ בָּרוּךְ הוּא אָנֹכִי אָנֹכִי הוּא מְנַחֶמְכֶם (ישעיה נא, יב).

ב) שִׁמְעוּ כִּי נֶאֱנָחָה אָנִי אֵין מְנַחֵם לִי (איכה א, כא). ר' יְהוֹשֻׁעַ דְּסִכְנִין בְּשֵׁם ר' לֵוִי פָּתַר קַרְיָיא בְּאַהֲרֹן כֹּהֵן גָּדוֹל. אַתְּ מוֹצֵא כֵּיוָן שֶׁמֵּת אַהֲרֹן כֹּהֵן גָּדוֹל בָּאוּ כְנַעֲנִים וְנִזְדַּוְּוגוּ לְיִשְׂרָאֵל הֲדָא הִיא דִכְתִיב וַיִּשְׁמַע הַכְּנַעֲנִי מֶלֶךְ־עֲרָד יוֹשֵׁב הַנֶּגֶב כִּי בָּא יִשְׂרָאֵל דֶּרֶךְ הָאֲתָרִים (במדבר כא, א). מָהוּ דֶּרֶךְ הָאֲתָרִים, כִּי מֵת אַהֲרֹן הַתַּיָּיר הַגָּדוֹל שֶׁלָּהֶם שֶׁהָיָה תָר לָהֶם אֶת הַדֶּרֶךְ. אֵין מְנַחֵם לִי (איכה שם), מֹשֶׁה הָיָה אָבֵל, אֶלְעָזָר הָיָה אָבֵל. כָּל־אוֹיְבַי שָׁמְעוּ רָעָתִי שָׂשׂוּ (שם), אָמְרוּ הָעֵת לֵילֵךְ לָבֹא עֲלֵיהֶם, הָעֵת לֵילֵךְ וּלְכַלֵּה שֹׂנְאֵיהֶם. וְרַבָּנִין פָּתְרִין קַרְיָיא בְּאוּמוֹת הָעוֹלָם. אַתְּ מוֹצֵא כֵּיוָן שֶׁגָּרְמוּ הָעֲוֹנוֹת וְנִכְנְסוּ גוֹיִם לִירוּשָׁלַם, גָּזְרוּ שֶׁבְּכָל מָקוֹם שֶׁיְּהוּ יִשְׂרָאֵל בּוֹרְחִים יְהוּ מַסְגִּירִים אוֹתָם. בִּקְּשׁוּ לִבְרוֹחַ לַדָּרוֹם וְלֹא הִנִּיחוּ לָהֶם, כֹּה אָמַר יְיָ עַל־שְׁלֹשָׁה פִּשְׁעֵי עַזָּה וְעַל־אַרְבָּעָה לֹא אֲשִׁיבֶנּוּ

(עמוס א, ו). בִּקְּשׁוּ לִבְרוֹחַ לַמִּזְרָח וְלֹא הִנִּיחוּ לָהֶם, כֹּה אָמַר יְיָ
עַל־שְׁלֹשָׁה פִּשְׁעֵי דַמֶּשֶׂק וְעַל־אַרְבָּעָה לֹא אֲשִׁיבֶנּוּ (עמוס שם, ג). בִּקְּשׁוּ
לִבְרוֹחַ לַצָּפוֹן וְלֹא הִנִּיחוּ לָהֶם, כֹּה אָמַר יְיָ עַל־שְׁלֹשָׁה פִּשְׁעֵי־צֹר
וְעַל־אַרְבָּעָה לֹא אֲשִׁיבֶנּוּ (עמוס שם, ט). בִּקְשׁוּ לִבְרוֹחַ לַמַּעֲרָב וְלֹא הִנִּיחוּ
לָהֶם, מַשָּׂא בַּעְרָב (ישעיה כא, יג). אָמַר לָהֶם הַקָּדוֹשׁ בָּרוּךְ הוּא הָא
אֲגִישְׁתּוּן אַפֵּיכוֹן, אָמְרוּ לְפָנָיו רִבּוֹן הָעוֹלָמִים וְלֹא אַתְּ הוּא שֶׁעֲשִׂיתָה.
מָשָׁלוּ מָשָׁל לְמָה הַדָּבָר דּוֹמֶה, לְמֶלֶךְ שֶׁנָּשָׂא לְמַטְרוֹנָא וְהָיָה מְצַוֶּה אוֹתָהּ
וְאוֹמֵר לָהּ אַל תָּשִׂיחִי עִם שְׁכֵינוֹתַיִךְ, וְלֹא תַשְׁאִילִי לָהֶן וְלֹא תִשְׁאֲלִי
מֵהֶן. פַּעַם אַחַת הִקְנִיטָה אוֹתוֹ וּטְרָדָהּ וְהוֹצִיאָהּ מִתּוֹךְ פַּלָטִין שֶׁלּוֹ,
וְהָיְתָה מְחַזֶּרֶת עַל בָּתֵּי שְׁכֵינוֹתֶיהָ וְלֹא הָיְתָה אַחַת מֵהֶן מְקַבֶּלֶת אוֹתָהּ.
אָמַר לָהּ הַמֶּלֶךְ הָא אֲגִישְׁתְּ הָא אַפֵּךְ. אָמְרָה לוֹ אֲדוֹנִי הַמֶּלֶךְ וְלֹא אַתְּ הוּא
שֶׁעֲשִׂיתָ, לֹא כָךְ הָיִיתָ מְצַוֶּה עָלַי וְאוֹמֵר לִי אַל תָּשִׂיחִי עִם שְׁכֵינוֹתַיִךְ
וְאַל תַּשְׁאִילִי לָהֶן וְלֹא תִשְׁאֲלִי מֵהֶן, אִילּוּ שָׁאִילִית מִנְהֵין אוֹ אַשְׁאִילִית
לָהֶן, הַיְדָא מִינְהֵין הֲוַת מְחַמְּיָה יָתִי עֲבֵיר בְּגוֹ בֵּיתָהּ וְלָא הֲוַת, מְקַבְּלָה
יָתִי גַּבָּהּ, הֱוֵי כִּי אַתָּה עָשִׂיתָ (איכה שם). כָּךְ אָמְרוּ יִשְׂרָאֵל לְפִי הַקָּדוֹשׁ
בָּרוּךְ הוּא רִבּוֹן הָעוֹלָמִים וְלֹא אַתְּ הוּא שֶׁעֲשִׂיתָה, וְלֹא כָךְ הִכְתַּבְתָּה
לָנוּ בַּתּוֹרָה, לֹא תִתְחַתֵּן בָּם בִּתְּךָ לֹא־תִתֵּן לִבְנוֹ וּבִתּוֹ לֹא תִקַּח לִבְנֶךָ
(דברים ז, ג). אִילּוּ נְסֵיבְנִין מִינְהֵין אוֹ אַנְסֵיבִינַן לְהֵין, הַיְדָא מִנְהֵין הֲוַת
מְחַמָּא בְּרָא אוֹ בְּרַתָּא קָאִים עַל תַּרְעֵיהּ וְלָא הֲוָה מְקַבֵּל יָתֵיהּ, הֱוֵי כִּי
אַתָּה עָשִׂיתָ (איכה שם). הֲבֵאתָ יוֹם־קָרָאתָ וְיִהְיוּ כָמוֹנִי (שם), כָּמוֹנִי בְּצָרָה
וְלֹא כָמוֹנִי בִּרְוָוחָה. אֵין מְנַחֵם לִי (איכה שם), אָמַר הַקָּדוֹשׁ בָּרוּךְ הוּא
אָנֹכִי אָנֹכִי הוּא מְנַחֶמְכֶם (ישעיה נא, יב).

ג) כְּרַחֵם אָב עַל־בָּנִים רִחַם יְיָ (תהלים קג, יג). כְּאֵיזֶה אָב, תַּנֵּי
ר' חִיָּיא כָּרַחֲמָן שֶׁבָּאָבוֹת. וְאֵיזֶה רַחֲמָן שֶׁבָּאָבוֹת, ר' עֲזַרְיָה בְּשֵׁם ר' אָחָא
זֶה אָבִינוּ אַבְרָהָם. אַתְּ מוֹצֵא קוֹדֶם עַד שֶׁלֹּא הֵבִיא הַקָּדוֹשׁ בָּרוּךְ הוּא
מַבּוּל עַל הַסְּדוֹמִיִּים אָמַר אָבִינוּ אַבְרָהָם לִפְנֵי הַקָּדוֹשׁ בָּרוּךְ הוּא, רִבּוֹן

הָעוֹלָמִים נִשְׁבַּעְתָּ שֶׁאֵין אַתָּה מֵבִיא מַבּוּל לָעוֹלָם, וּמַה טַּעֲמָא כִּי מֵי
נֹחַ זֹאת לִי אֲשֶׁר נִשְׁבַּעְתִּי וְגוֹ' (ישעיה נד, ט), מַבּוּל שֶׁל מַיִם אֵין אַתָּה מֵבִיא
שֶׁמָּא מַבּוּל שֶׁל אֵשׁ אַתָּה מֵבִיא, וּמָה אַתָּה מֵעֲרִים עַל הַשְּׁבוּעָה, חָלִילָה
לְךָ מֵעֲשׂוֹת כַּדָּבָר הַזֶּה וְגוֹ' (בראשית יח, כה). אָמַר ר' לֵוִי הֲשׁוֹפֵט כָּל־הָאָרֶץ
לֹא יַעֲשֶׂה מִשְׁפָּט (שם שם, כו), אִם מִשְׁפָּט אַתָּה מְבַקֵּשׁ אֵין עוֹלָם, וְאִם עוֹלָם
אַתָּה מְבַקֵּשׁ אֵין מִשְׁפָּט, מָה אַתָּה מֵיצֵיר חַבְלָא בִּתְרֵין רֵאשׁוֹי, בָּעֵי עַלְמָא
וּבָעֵי דִּינָא דְקוּשְׁטָא, אִין לֵית אַתְּ מְוַותֵּר צִיבְחַד לֵית עַלְמָא יָכִיל קָאִים.
ר' יְהוֹשֻׁעַ בַּר נְחֶמְיָה פְּתַר קַרְיָא בְּאָבִינוּ יַעֲקֹב, וְהוּא עָבַר לִפְנֵיהֶם
וַיִּשְׁתַּחוּ וְגוֹ' (שם לג, ג). מָהוּ וְהוּא עוֹד הוּא הֲוָה בְעָקָא. אָמַר מוּטָב שֶׁיִּפָּגַע
בִּי וְלֹא בְבָנַיי. מֶה עָשָׂה, זַיְּינָם מִבִּפְנִים וְהִלְבִּישָׁם בְּגָדִים לְבָנִים מִבַּחוּץ
וְהִתְקִין עַצְמוֹ לִשְׁלֹשָׁה דְבָרִים, לִתְפִילָה וּלְדוֹרוֹן וּלְמִלְחָמָה. לִתְפִילָה,
הַצִּילֵנִי נָא מִיַּד אָחִי (שם לב, יב). לְדוֹרוֹן, וַתַּעֲבֹר הַמִּנְחָה עַל־פָּנָיו
(שם שם כב). לְמִלְחָמָה, וַיֹּאמֶר אִם־יָבֹא עֵשָׂו אֶל־הַמַּחֲנֶה הָאַחַת־וְהִכָּהוּ
(שם שם ט), מִיכָּא וּלְהָלָא אֲנַן עָבְדִין קַרְבָא עִמֵּיהּ. אָמַר ר' שְׁמוּאֵל דַּרְכּוֹ
שֶׁל אָב לְרַחֵם, כְּרַחֵם אָב עַל־בָּנִים (תהלים קג, יג). וְדַרְכָּהּ שֶׁל אֵם לְנַחֵם,
כְּאִישׁ אֲשֶׁר אִמּוֹ תְּנַחֲמֶנּוּ (ישעיה מו, יג). אָמַר הַקָּדוֹשׁ בָּרוּךְ הוּא אֲנָא עָבֵיד
דִּידְאַב אֲנָא עָבֵד דִּידְאָם. אֲנָא עָבֵיד דִּידְאַב, כְּרַחֵם אָב עַל־בָּנִים
(תהלים שם). אֲנָא עָבֵיד דִּידְאָם, כְּאִישׁ אֲשֶׁר אִמּוֹ תְּנַחֲמֶנּוּ (ישעיה סו, יג).
אָמַר הַקָּדוֹשׁ בָּרוּךְ הוּא אָנֹכִי אָנֹכִי הוּא מְנַחֶמְכֶם (ישעיה נא, יב).

ד) ר' אַבָּא בַּר כַּהֲנָא בְשֵׁם ר' יוֹחָנָן לְמֶלֶךְ שֶׁקִּידֵּשׁ לְמַטְרוֹנָא וְכָתַב
לָהּ כְּתוּבָּה מְרוּבָּה, כָּךְ וְכָךְ חוּפּוֹת אֲנִי אֲעֶשֶׂה לִיךְ, כָּךְ וְכָךְ תַּכְשִׁיטִין
אֲנִי נוֹתֵן לִיךְ, כָּךְ וְכָךְ טִיסְבָּרִיּוֹת אֲנִי נוֹתֵן לִיךְ. הֵנִיחָהּ וְהָלַךְ לוֹ לִמְדִינַת
הַיָּם, וְשָׁהָא שָׁם שָׁנִים הַרְבֵּה, וְהָיוּ חַבְרוֹתֶיהָ מוֹנוֹת אֹתָהּ וְאוֹמְרוֹת לָהּ,
עַד אֵימָתַי אַתְּ יְתִיבָה, סַב לִיךְ בַּעַל עַד דְּאַתְּ טַלְיָיה עַד דְּחַיְילִיךְ עֲלָיךְ,
וְהָיְתָה נִכְנֶסֶת בְּתוֹךְ בֵּיתָהּ וְנוֹטֶלֶת כְּתוּבָּתָהּ וְקוֹרְא בָהּ וּמִתְנַחֶמֶת. לְאַחַר
יָמִים בָּא הַמֶּלֶךְ מִמְּדִינַת הַיָּם אָמַר לָהּ, בִּתִּי תָּמֵהַּ אֲנִי הֵיאַךְ הִמְתַּנְתְּ לִי

כָּל הַשָּׁנִים הַלָּלוּ, אָמְרָה לוֹ אֲדוֹנִי הַמֶּלֶךְ אִילוּלֵי כְּתוּבָה מְרוּבָּה שֶׁכָּתַבְתָּ
לִי כְּבָר הָיוּ חֲבֵירוֹתַי מְאַבְּדוֹת אוֹתִי מִמָּךְ. כָּךְ לְפִי שֶׁבָּעוֹלָם הַזֶּה אוּמּוֹת
הָעוֹלָם מוֹנִים לְיִשְׂרָאֵל וְאוֹמְרִין לָהֶם עַד מָתַי אַתֶּם מוּמָתִים עַל אֱלֹהֵיכֶם
וְנוֹתְנִין נַפְשׁוֹתֵיכֶם עָלָיו וְנֶהֱרָגִים עָלָיו, כַּמָּה־צַעַר הוּא מֵבִיא עֲלֵיכֶם
כַּמָּה בּוּזִים הוּא מֵבִיא עֲלֵיכֶם כַּמָּה יִיסּוּרִים הוּא מֵבִיא עֲלֵיכֶם, בּוֹאוּ
לָכֶם אֶצְלֵינוּ וְעוֹשִׂין אֶנוּ אֶתְכֶם דּוּכְּסִין וְאֶפַּרְכִין וְאִיסְטְרַטְלִיטִים.
וְיִשְׂרָאֵל נִכְנָסִין לְבָתֵּי כְנֵסִיּוֹת וּלְבָתֵּי מִדְרָשׁוֹת וְנוֹטְלִין סֵפֶר תּוֹרָה וְקוֹרִין
בּוֹ וְהִתְהַלַּכְתִּי בְּתוֹכְכֶם וְהִפְרֵיתִי אֶתְכֶם וְהִרְבֵּיתִי אֶתְכֶם וַהֲקִימוֹתִי
אֶת־בְּרִיתִי אִתְּכֶם (ויקרא כו, ט) וּמִתְנַחֲמִים. כְּשֶׁיַּגִּיעַ הַקֵּץ הַקָּדוֹשׁ בָּרוּךְ
הוּא אוֹמֵר לְיִשְׂרָאֵל תְּמֵיהַ אֲנִי הֵיאַךְ הִימְתַּנְתֶּם לִי כָּל הַשָּׁנִים הַלָּלוּ,
וְיִשְׂרָאֵל אוֹמְרִים לִפְנֵי הַקָּדוֹשׁ בָּרוּךְ הוּא רִבּוֹן הָעוֹלָמִים אִילוּלֵי סֵפֶר
תּוֹרָה שֶׁכָּתַבְתָּ לָנוּ כְּבָר הָיוּ אוּמּוֹת הָעוֹלָם מְאַבְּדִין אוֹתָנוּ מִמָּךְ, הָדָא
הִיא דִכְתִיב זֹאת אָשִׁיב אֶל־לִבִּי עַל־כֵּן אוֹחִיל (איכה ג, כא). וְכֵן דָּוִד אוֹמֵר
לוּלֵי תוֹרָתְךָ שַׁעֲשׁוּעָי אָז אָבַדְתִּי בְעָנְיִי (תהלים קיט, צב).

(ה) דָּבָר אַחֵר אָנֹכִי אָנֹכִי הוּא מְנַחֶמְכֶם (ישעיה נא, יב). ר׳ אַבּוּן
בְּשֵׁם רֵישׁ לָקִישׁ לְמֶלֶךְ שֶׁכָּעַס עַל מַטְרוֹנָא וּטְרָדָהּ וְהוֹצִיאָהּ מִבֵּית פַּלָטִין
שֶׁלּוֹ. לְאַחַר יָמִים בִּיקַשׁ לְהַחֲזִירָהּ, אָמְרָה יִכְפּוֹל כְּתוּבָתִי וְאַחַר כָּךְ הוּא
מַחֲזִירֵנִי. כָּךְ אָמַר הַקָּדוֹשׁ בָּרוּךְ הוּא לְיִשְׂרָאֵל בָּנַי בְּסִינַי אָמַרְתִּי לָכֶם
פַּעַם אַחַת אָנֹכִי יְ״י אֱלֹהֶיךָ (שמות כ, ב) וּבִירוּשָׁלַם לֶעָתִיד לָבֹא אֲנִי אוֹמֵר
לָכֶם שְׁנֵי פְעָמִים אָנֹכִי אָנֹכִי הוּא מְנַחֶמְכֶם (ישעיה שם). ר׳ מְנַחֲמָה בְּשֵׁם
ר׳ אַבִּין מֵאוֹתָהּ הַנֶּחָמָה שֶׁנִּחַמְתֶּם לְפָנַי בְּהַר סִינַי וַאֲמַרְתֶּם כֹּל אֲשֶׁר־דִּבֶּר
יְ״י נַעֲשֶׂה וְנִשְׁמָע (שמות כד, ז). מִי־אַתְּ וַתִּירְאִי (ישעיה שם), לֹא אַתְּ הִיא
שֶׁאָמַרְתְּ לִי בַיָּם מִי־כָמֹכָה (שמות טו, יא). וַתִּירְאִי מֵאֱנוֹשׁ יָמוּת (ישעיה שם),
אוֹ אֶלָּא וּמִבֶּן־אָדָם חָצִיר יִנָּתֵן (שם). ר׳ בְּרֶכְיָה בְּשֵׁם ר׳ חֶלְבּוֹ ר׳ שְׁמוּאֵל
בַּר נַחֲמָן בְּשֵׁם ר׳ יוֹנָתָן, רְאוּיִין הָיוּ יִשְׂרָאֵל כְּלָיָיה בִּימֵי הָמָן, אִילוּלֵי
נִסְמְכוּ עַל דַּעְתּוֹ שֶׁל זָקֵן וְאָמְרוּ מָה אִם אָבִינוּ יַעֲקֹב שֶׁהִבְטִיחוֹ הַקָּדוֹשׁ

בָּרוּךְ הוּא וְאָמַר לוֹ הִנֵּה אָנֹכִי עִמָּךְ וּשְׁמַרְתִּיךָ בְּכֹל אֲשֶׁר־תֵּלֵךְ
(בראשית כח, טו), נְתִיָּרֵא, אָנוּ עַל אַחַת כַּמָּה וְכַמָּה. הוּא שֶׁהַנָּבִיא מְקַנְטְרָן
וְאוֹמֵר לָהֶם וַתִּשְׁכַּח יְיָ עוֹשֶׂךָ נוֹטֶה שָׁמַיִם וְיוֹסֵד אָרֶץ (ישעיה נא, יג),
אַנְשִׁיתוּן מַה דְּאָמְרֶת לְכוֹן אִם־יִמַּדּוּ שָׁמַיִם מִלְמַעְלָה וְיֵחָקְרוּ מוֹסְדֵי־אָרֶץ
לְמָטָּה גַּם־אֲנִי אֶמְאַס בְּכָל־זֶרַע יִשְׂרָאֵל עַל־אֲשֶׁר עָשׂוּ נְאֻם־יְיָ
(ירמיה לא, לו), רְאִיתֶם שָׁמַיִם שֶׁנִּיּמַדּוּ וְהָאָרֶץ שֶׁנִּיּתְמוֹטְטָה, מִנְטַיִּית שָׁמַיִם
וָאָרֶץ הָיָה לָכֶם לִלְמֹד, אֶלָּא וַתִּפַחֵד תָּמִיד כָּל־הַיּוֹם מִפְּנֵי חֲמַת הַמֵּצִיק
(ישעיה נא, יג), אָמַר ר' יִצְחָק שֶׁהָיוּ צָרוֹת מְצִיקוֹת זוֹ אַחַר זוֹ. וְאַיֵּה חֲמַת
הַמֵּצִיק (שם), הוּא הָמָן וּשְׁנָווּלְיוֹתָיו[א] אֲשֶׁר כּוֹנֵן לְהַשְׁחִית (שם), בַּחֹדֶשׁ
הָרִאשׁוֹן הוּא־חֹדֶשׁ נִיסָן (אסתר ג, ז). מִיהַר צוֹעֶה לְהִפָּתֵחַ לֹא־יָמוּת
לַשַּׁחַת וְג' (ישעיה נא, יד), אָמַר ר' אַבָּהוּ זֶה אֶחָד מִשִּׁשָּׁה דְּבָרִים סִימָן
יָפֶה לְחוֹלֶה, עִיטּוּשׁ זֵיעָה שֵׁינָה קֶרִי חֲלוֹם הִילּוּךְ מֵעַיִם בְּדֶרֶךְ הָאָרֶץ.
עִיטּוּשׁ מִנַּיִן, עֲטִישׁוֹתָיו תָּהֶל אוֹר (איוב מא, י). זֵיעָה מִנַּיִן, בְּזֵיעַת אַפְּךָ
תֹּאכַל לֶחֶם (בראשית ג, יט). קֶרִי מִנַּיִן, יִרְאֶה זֶרַע וְיַאֲרִיךְ יָמִים
(ישעיה נג, י). שֵׁינָה מִנַּיִן, יָשַׁנְתִּי אָז יָנוּחַ לִי (איוב ג, יג). חֲלוֹם מִנַּיִן
וְתַחֲלִימֵנִי וְהַחֲיֵינִי (ישעיה לח, טז). הִילּוּךְ מֵעַיִם בְּדֶרֶךְ הָאָרֶץ מִנַּיִן, מִהַר
צֹעֶה לְהִפָּתֵחַ לֹא־יָמוּת לַשַּׁחַת (שם נא, יד). אָמַר ר' חַגַּי וּבִלְבַד שֶׁלֹּא
יֵחָסֵר לַחְמוֹ.

ו) וְאָנֹכִי יְיָ אֱלֹהֶיךָ רֹגַע הַיָּם וַיֶּהֱמוּ גַּלָּיו יְיָ צְבָאוֹת שְׁמוֹ (שם נא, טו).
וְכִי מָה רָאָה הַיָּם וּבָרַח, ר' יוּדָה וְר' נְחֶמְיָה. ר' יוּדָה אָמַר מַקְלוֹ שֶׁל
מֹשֶׁה רָאָה וּבָרַח. וְר' נְחֶמְיָה אָמַר שֵׁם הַמְּפוֹרָשׁ הָיָה חָקוּק עָלָיו, יְיָ
צְבָאוֹת שְׁמוֹ, רָאָה אוֹתוֹ וּבָרַח. וָאָשִׂים דְּבָרַי בְּפִיךָ וּבְצֵל יָדִי כִּסִּיתִיךָ וְג'
(שם שם, טז). תַּמָּן תְּנִינָן שִׁמְעוֹן הַצַּדִּיק הָיָה מִשְּׁיָרֵי בִכְנֶסֶת הַגְּדוֹלָה כָּל
הִילְכָתָה. ר' הוּנָא בְּשֵׁם ר' אַחָא עוֹבְדֵי הַיָּם פֵּירְשׁוּ אוֹתוֹ, נָחִיתָ
בְחַסְדְּךָ עַם־זוּ גָּאָלְתָּ (שמות טו, יג), זוֹ גְמִילוּת חֲסָדִים. נֵהַלְתָּ בְעָזְּךָ
אֶל־נְוֵה קָדְשֶׁךָ (שם שם, יד), זוֹ תוֹרָה, יְיָ עוֹז לְעַמּוֹ יִתֵּן יְיָ יְבָרֵךְ וְג'

(תהלים כט, יא). וַעֲדַיִין הָעוֹלָם מִתְמוֹטֵט, וְאֵימָתַי נִתְבַּסֵּס הָעוֹלָם, מִשֶּׁבָּאוּ
לִנְוֵה קָדְשֶׁךָ. תַּמָּן תְּנִינָן רַבָּן שִׁמְעוֹן בֶּן גַּמְלִיאֵל אוֹמֵר עַל שְׁלֹשָׁה דְבָרִים
הָעוֹלָם קַיָּים, וּשְׁלֹשְׁתָּן בְּפָסוּק אֶחָד, אֵלֶּה הַדְּבָרִים אֲשֶׁר תַּעֲשׂוּ דַּבְּרוּ
אֱמֶת אִישׁ אֶת־רֵעֵהוּ אֱמֶת וּמִשְׁפַּט שָׁלוֹם שִׁפְטוּ בְּשַׁעֲרֵיכֶם (זכריה ח, מז),
וּשְׁלֹשְׁתָּן דָּבָר אֶחָד, נַעֲשָׂה הַדִּין נַעֲשָׂה אֱמֶת נַעֲשָׂה שָׁלוֹם. ר' יְהוֹשֻׁעַ
דְּסִכְנִין בְּשֵׁם ר' לֵוִי וָאָשִׂים דְּבָרַי בְּפִיךָ (ישעיה נא, טז), אֵלּוּ דִבְרֵי תוֹרָה.
וּבְצֵל יָדִי כִּסִּיתִיךָ (שם), זוֹ גְמִילוּת חֲסָדִים, לְלַמֶּדְךָ שֶׁכָּל מִי שֶׁהוּא עוֹסֵק
בַּתּוֹרָה וּבִגְמִילוּת חֲסָדִים זוֹכֶה לַחֲסוֹת בְּצִילוֹ שֶׁל הַקָּדוֹשׁ בָּרוּךְ הוּא
הֲדָא הִיא דִכְתִיב מַה־יָּקָר חַסְדְּךָ וּבְנֵי אָדָם בְּצֵל כְּנָפֶיךָ וג' (תהלים לו, ח).
לִנְטוֹעַ שָׁמַיִם וְלִיסוֹד אָרֶץ (ישעיה נא, טז), אֵלּוּ הַקָּרְבָּנוֹת. וְלֵאמֹר לְצִיּוֹן
עַמִּי אָתָּה (שם), אָמַר ר' חֲנִינָא בַּר פַּפָּא חִזַּרְנוּ עַל כָּל הַמִּקְרָא וְלֹא
מָצִינוּ מָקוֹם שֶׁנִּקְרְאוּ יִשְׂרָאֵל צִיּוֹן, וּבְאֵיכָן מָצִינוּ כֵן, וְלֵאמֹר לְצִיּוֹן
עַמִּי אָתָּה (שם).

## CHAPTER 6: ABOT DE RABBI NATHAN
### I:VIII.1–I:XVIII.3

אֵיזֶהוּ סְיָיג שֶׁעָשָׂה אָדָם הָרִאשׁוֹן לִדְבָרָיו הֲרֵי הוּא אוֹמֵר וַיְצַו
ה' אֱלֹהִים עַל־הָאָדָם לֵאמֹר מִכֹּל עֵץ־הַגָּן אָכֹל תֹּאכֵל וּמֵעֵץ הַדַּעַת טוֹב
וָרָע לֹא תֹאכַל מִמֶּנּוּ כִּי בְּיוֹם אֲכָלְךָ מִמֶּנּוּ מוֹת תָּמוּת (בראשית ב׳ י״ז) לֹא
רָצָה אָדָם הָרִאשׁוֹן לוֹמַר לְחַוָּה כַּדֶּרֶךְ שֶׁאָמַר לוֹ הַקָּדוֹשׁ בָּרוּךְ הוּא אֶלָּא
כָּךְ אָמַר לָהּ וּמִפְּרִי הָעֵץ אֲשֶׁר בְּתוֹךְ הַגָּן אָמַר אֱלֹהִים לֹא תֹאכְלוּ מִמֶּנּוּ
וְלֹא תִגְּעוּ בּוֹ פֶּן־תְּמוּתוּן (שם ג׳ ג׳). בְּאוֹתָהּ שָׁעָה הָיָה נָחָשׁ הָרָשָׁע נוֹטֵל
עֵצָה בְּלִבּוֹ אָמַר הוֹאִיל וְאֵינִי יָכוֹל לְהַכְשִׁיל אֶת הָאָדָם אֵלֵךְ וְאַכְשִׁיל אֶת
חַוָּה הָלַךְ וְיָשַׁב אֶצְלָהּ וְהִרְבָּה שִׂיחָה עִמָּהּ אָמַר לָהּ אִם לִנְגִיעָה אַתְּ
אוֹמֶרֶת צִוָּה עָלֵינוּ הַקָּדוֹשׁ בָּרוּךְ הוּא הֲרֵינִי נוֹגֵעַ בּוֹ וְאֵינִי מֵת אַף אַתְּ
אִם תִּגְּעִי בּוֹ אִי אַתְּ מֵתָה. מֶה עָשָׂה הַנָּחָשׁ הָרָשָׁע בְּאוֹתָהּ שָׁעָה עָמַד
וְנָגַע בָּאִילָן בְּיָדָיו וּבְרַגְלָיו וְהִרְתִּיעוֹ עַד שֶׁנָּשְׁרוּ פֵּירוֹתָיו לָאָרֶץ, וְיֵשׁ
אוֹמְרִים לֹא נָגַע בּוֹ כָּל עִיקָּר אֶלָּא כֵּיוָן שֶׁרְאָהוּ אוֹתוֹ אִילָן הָיָה צוֹוֵחַ
עָלָיו וְאָמַר לוֹ רָשָׁע רָשָׁע אַל תִּיגַּע בִּי שֶׁנֶּאֱמַר אַל תְּבוֹאֵנִי רֶגֶל גַּאֲוָה
וְיַד־רְשָׁעִים אַל־תְּנִדֵנִי (תהלים ל״ו י״ב): ד״א אַל תְּבוֹאֵנִי רֶגֶל גַּאֲוָה זֶה
טִיטוֹס הָרָשָׁע שֶׁנִּשְׁחֲקוּ עַצְמוֹתָיו שֶׁהָיָה מוֹרָה בְּיָדוֹ וְהָיָה מַכֶּה עַל גַּבֵּי
הַמִּזְבֵּחַ וְאוֹמֵר לָקוֹס לָקוֹס אַתָּה מֶלֶךְ וַאֲנִי מֶלֶךְ בּוֹא וַעֲשֵׂה עִמִּי מִלְחָמָה
כַּמָּה שְׁוָוְרִים נִשְׁחֲטוּ עָלֶיךָ כַּמָּה עוֹפוֹת נִמְלְקוּ עָלֶיךָ כַּמָּה יֵינוֹת נִסְכּוּ
עָלֶיךָ כַּמָּה כַּמָּה בְּשָׂמִים קְטָרוּ עָלֶיךָ אַתָּה הוּא שֶׁמַּחֲרִיב אֶת כָּל הָעוֹלָם [כֻּלּוֹ]
שֶׁנֶּאֱמַר הוֹי אֲרִיאֵל אֲרִיאֵל קִרְיַת חָנָה דָוִד סְפוּ שָׁנָה עַל־שָׁנָה חַגִּים
יִנְקֹפוּ (ישעיה כ״ט א׳) וְשׁוּב אָמַר לָהּ אִם לַאֲכִילָה אַתְּ אוֹמֶרֶת צִוָּה עָלֵינוּ
הַקָּדוֹשׁ בָּרוּךְ הוּא הֲרֵינִי אוֹכֵל מִמֶּנּוּ וְאֵינִי מֵת וְאַף אַתְּ תֹּאכְלִי מִמֶּנּוּ
וְאִי אַתְּ מֵתָה. מָה אָמְרָה חַוָּה בְּדַעְתָּהּ כָּל הַדְּבָרִים שֶׁפְּקָדַנִי רַבִּי מִתְּחִלָּה
שֶׁקֶר הֵם. לְפִי שֶׁאֵין חַוָּה קוֹרְאָה לָאָדָם הָרִאשׁוֹן מִתְּחִלָּה אֶלָּא רַבִּי. מִיָּד
נָטְלָה וְאָכְלָה וְנָתְנָה לְאָדָם וְאָכַל שֶׁנֶּאֱמַר וַתֵּרֶא הָאִשָּׁה כִּי טוֹב הָעֵץ

לְמַאֲכָל וְכִי תַאֲנָה הוּא לָעֵינַיִם וגו׳ (בראשית ג׳ ו׳): עֶשֶׂר קְלָלוֹת נִתְקַלְלָה
חַוָּה בְּאוֹתָהּ שָׁעָה שֶׁנֶּאֱמַר אֶל־הָאִשָּׁה אָמַר הַרְבָּה אַרְבֶּה עִצְּבוֹנֵךְ
וְהֵרֹנֵךְ בְּעֶצֶב תֵּלְדִי בָנִים וְאֶל־אִישֵׁךְ תְּשׁוּקָתֵךְ וְהוּא יִמְשָׁל בָּךְ (שם י״ז).
אֵלּוּ שְׁתֵּי רְבִיּוֹת דָּם אַחַת דַּם צַעַר נִדָּה וְאַחַת דַּם צַעַר בְּתוּלִים. וְהֵרֹנֵךְ
זֶה צַעַר הָעִבּוּר. בְּעֶצֶב תֵּלְדִי בָנִים כְּמַשְׁמָעוֹ. וְאֶל אִישֵׁךְ תְּשׁוּקָתֵךְ מְלַמֵּד
שֶׁהָאִשָּׁה מִשְׁתּוֹקֶקֶת עַל בַּעֲלָהּ בְּשָׁעָה שֶׁהוּא יוֹצֵא לַדֶּרֶךְ. וְהוּא יִמְשָׁל
בָּךְ שֶׁהָאִישׁ תּוֹבֵעַ בַּפֶּה וְהָאִשָּׁה תּוֹבַעַת בַּלֵּב עֲטוּפָה כְּאָבֵל וַחֲבוּשָׁה בְּבֵית
הָאֲסוּרִין וּמְנוּדָּה מִכָּל אָדָם: מִי גָרַם לְנְגִיעָה זוֹ סְיָיג שֶׁסָּג אָדָם הָרִאשׁוֹן
לִדְבָרָיו. מִכָּאן אָמְרוּ אִם סָג אָדָם לִדְבָרָיו אֵין יָכוֹל לַעֲמוֹד בִּדְבָרָיו.
מִכָּאן אָמְרוּ אַל יוֹסִיף אָדָם עַל דְּבָרִים שֶׁשּׁוֹמֵעַ רַ׳ יוֹסֵי אוֹמֵר עֲשָׂרָה
טְפָחִים וְעוֹמֵד מִמֵּאָה אַמָּה וְנוֹפֵל:

מֶה חָשַׁב נָחָשׁ הָרָשָׁע בְּאוֹתָהּ שָׁעָה אֵלֵךְ וְאֶהֱרוֹג אֶת אָדָם וְאֶשָּׂא
אֶת אִשְׁתּוֹ וְאֶהְיֶה מֶלֶךְ עַל כָּל הָעוֹלָם כּוּלּוֹ וְאֵלֵךְ בְּקוֹמָה זְקוּפָה וְאוֹכַל
כָּל מַעֲדַנֵּי עוֹלָם אָמַר לוֹ הקב״ה אַתָּה אָמַרְתָּ אֶהֱרוֹג אֶת אָדָם וְאֶשָּׂא אֶת
חַוָּה לְפִיכָךְ אֵיבָה אָשִׁית (שם י״ד). אַתָּה אָמַרְתָּ אֶהְיֶה מֶלֶךְ עַל כָּל הָעוֹלָם
לְפִיכָךְ אָרוּר אַתָּה מִכָּל הַבְּהֵמָה (שם). אַתָּה אָמַרְתָּ אֵלֵךְ בְּקוֹמָה זְקוּפָה
לְפִיכָךְ עַל גְּחוֹנְךָ תֵלֵךְ (שם). אַתָּה אָמַרְתָּ אוֹכַל כָּל מַעֲדַנֵּי עוֹלָם לְפִיכָךְ
עָפָר תֹאכַל כָּל יְמֵי חַיֶּיךָ (שם נח):

רַ׳ שִׁמְעוֹן בֶּן מְנַסְיָא אוֹמֵר חֲבָל עַל שַׁמָּשׁ גָּדוֹל שֶׁאָבַד מִן הָעוֹלָם
שֶׁאִלְמָלֵא לֹא נִתְקַלְקֵל הַנָּחָשׁ הָיָה לוֹ לְכָל אֶחָד וְאֶחָד מִיִּשְׂרָאֵל ב׳ נְחָשִׁים
בְּתוֹךְ בֵּיתוֹ אֶחָד מְשַׁגְּרוֹ לַמַּעֲרָב וְאֶחָד מְשַׁגְּרוֹ לַמִּזְרָח וּמְבִיאִים לָהֶם
סַנְדָּלְכִים אֲבָנִים טוֹבוֹת וּמַרְגָּלִיּוֹת וְכָל כְּלֵי חֶמֶד טוֹב שֶׁבָּעוֹלָם
וְאֵין כָּל בְּרִיָּה יְכוֹלָה לְהַזִּיק אוֹתָן וְלֹא עוֹד אֶלָּא שֶׁהָיוּ מַכְנִיסִין אוֹתָן
תַּחַת גָּמָל תַּחַת חֲמוֹר תַּחַת פֶּרֶד וּמוֹצִיאִין זְבָלִים לַגַּנּוֹת וְלַפַּרְדֵּסוֹת:

רַ׳ יְהוּדָה בֶּן בְּתֵירָה אוֹמֵר אָדָם הָרִאשׁוֹן הָיָה מֵיסֵב בְּגַן עֵדֶן
וּמַלְאֲכֵי הַשָּׁרֵת עוֹמְדִין לְקְרָאתוֹ וְצוֹלִין לוֹ בָשָׂר וּמְצַנְּנִין לוֹ יַיִן בָּא

נָחָשׁ וְרָאָה אוֹתוֹ וְהִצִּיץ בִּכְבוֹדוֹ וְנִתְקַנֵּא בּוֹ:

כֵּיצַד נִבְרָא אָדָם הָרִאשׁוֹן שָׁעָה רִאשׁוֹנָה הוּצְבַּר עֲפָרוֹ. שְׁנִיָּה נִבְרָא צוּרָתוֹ. שְׁלִישִׁית נַעֲשָׂה גוֹלֶם. רְבִיעִית נִתְקַשְּׁרוּ אֵבָרָיו. חֲמִישִׁית נִתְפַּתְּחוּ נְקָבָיו. שִׁשִּׁית נִתְּנָה בוֹ נְשָׁמָה. שְׁבִיעִית עָמַד עַל רַגְלָיו. שְׁמִינִית נִזְדַּוּוְגָה לוֹ חַוָּה. תְּשִׁיעִית הִכְנִיסוֹ לְגַן עֵדֶן. עֲשִׂירִית צֻוָּהוּ. אַחַד עָשָׂר סָרַח שְׁתֵּים עָשָׂר נִטְרַד וְהָלַךְ לוֹ לְקַיֵּם מַה שֶׁנֶּאֱמַר וְאָדָם בִּיקָר בַּל־יָלִין (תהלים מ״ט כ״ד): יוֹם רִאשׁוֹן מָהוּ אוֹמֵר לה׳ הָאָרֶץ וּמְלוֹאָהּ תֵּבֵל וְיוֹשְׁבֵי בָהּ (שם כ״ד א׳) כִּי הוּא קָנָה וְיִקְנֶה וְהוּא יָדִין אֶת הָעוֹלָם. בְּיוֹם שֵׁנִי מָהוּ אוֹמֵר גָּדוֹל ה׳ וּמְהוּלָּל מְאֹד בְּעִיר אֱלֹהֵינוּ (שם מ״ח ב׳) חִילֵּק אֶת כָּל מַעֲשָׂיו וְנַעֲשָׂה מֶלֶךְ עַל עוֹלָמוֹ. בַּשְּׁלִישִׁי מָהוּ אוֹמֵר אֱלֹהִים נִצָּב בַּעֲדַת־אֵל בְּקֶרֶב אֱלֹהִים יִשְׁפּוֹט (שם פ״ב) בָּרָא אֶת הַיָּם וְאֶת הַיַּבָּשָׁה וְנִכְפְּלָה אֶרֶץ לִמְקוֹמָהּ וְנַעֲשָׂה מָקוֹם לַעֲדָתוֹ. בָּרְבִיעִי מָהוּ אוֹמֵר אֵל נְקָמוֹת ה׳ אֵל־נְקָמוֹת הוֹפִיעַ (שם צד) בָּרָא אֶת הַחַמָּה וְאֶת הַלְּבָנָה וְהַכּוֹכָבִים וְהַמַּזָּלוֹת שֶׁהֵן מְאִירִין בָּעוֹלָם וְעָתִיד לִיפָּרַע מֵעוֹבְדֵיהֶם. בַּחֲמִישִׁי מָהוּ אוֹמֵר הַרְנִינוּ לֵאלֹהִים עוּזֵּנוּ הָרִיעוּ לֵאלֹהֵי יַעֲקֹב (שם פ״א) בָּרָא עוֹפוֹת וְדָגִים וְאֶת הַתַּנִּינִים שֶׁהֵם מְרַנְּנִים בָּעוֹלָם. בַּשִּׁשִּׁי מָהוּ אוֹמֵר ה׳ מָלָךְ גֵּאוּת לָבֵשׁ לָבֵשׁ ה׳ עוֹז הִתְאַזָּר אַף תִּכּוֹן תֵּבֵל בַּל־תִּמּוֹט (שם צ״ג) גָּמַר אֶת כָּל מַעֲשָׂיו וְנִתְעַלָּה וְיָשַׁב בִּמְרוֹמָיו שֶׁל עוֹלָם. בַּשְּׁבִיעִי מָהוּ אוֹמֵר מִזְמוֹר שִׁיר לְיוֹם הַשַּׁבָּת (שם צ״ב) יוֹם שֶׁכּוּלּוֹ שַׁבָּת שֶׁאֵין בּוֹ לֹא אֲכִילָה וְלֹא שְׁתִיָּה וְלֹא מַשָּׂא וּמַתָּן אֶלָּא צַדִּיקִים יוֹשְׁבִין וְעַטְרוֹתֵיהֶן בְּרָאשֵׁיהֶן וְנִזּוֹנִין מִזִּיו הַשְּׁכִינָה שֶׁנֶּאֱמַר וַיֶּחֱזוּ אֶת־הָאֱלֹהִים וַיֹּאכְלוּ וַיִּשְׁתּוּ (שמות כ״ד) כְּמַלְאֲכֵי הַשָּׁרֵת: וְכָל כָּךְ לָמָּה כְּדֵי שֶׁיִּכָּנֵס לִסְעוּדַת שַׁבָּת מִיָּד:

ר׳ שִׁמְעוֹן בֶּן אֶלְעָזָר אוֹמֵר אֶמְשׁוֹל לְךָ מָשָׁל לַמֶּה אָדָם הָרִאשׁוֹן דּוֹמֶה לְאָדָם אֶחָד שֶׁנָּשָׂא אֶת הַגִּיּוֹרֶת הָיָה יוֹשֵׁב מְפַקְּדָהּ אָמַר לָהּ בִּתִּי אַל תֹּאכְלִי פַת בְּשָׁעָה שֶׁיָּדַיִךְ טְמֵאוֹת וְאַל תֹּאכְלִי פֵּירוֹת שֶׁאֵינָן מְעוּשָּׂרִין

אַל תְּחַלְּלִי שַׁבָּתוֹת וְאַל תִּפְרְצִי בִגְדָרִים וְאַל תֵּלְכִי עִם אִישׁ אַחֵר הָא
אִם עָבַרְתְּ עַל אַחַת מֵהֶן הֲרֵי אַתְּ מֵתָה. מֶה עָשָׂה הָאִישׁ הַהוּא עָמַד וְאָכַל
פַּת בְּפָנֶיהָ בְּשָׁעָה שֶׁיָּדָיו טְמֵאוֹת וְאָכַל פֵּירוֹת שֶׁאֵינָן מְעוּשָּׂרִין וְחִלֵּל
שַׁבָּתוֹת וּפָרַץ בִגְדָרִים וְהוֹשִׁיט לָהּ בְּיָדָיו מָה אָמְרָה גִיּוֹרֶת הַהִיא בְלִבָּהּ
כָּל הַדְּבָרִים שֶׁפִּקְּדַנִי בַּעֲלִי מִתְּחִלָּה שֶׁקֶר הֵם מִיָּד עָמְדָה וְעָבְרָה עַל כּוּלָּם
ר' שִׁמְעוֹן בֶּן יוֹחַאי אוֹמֵר אֶמְשׁוֹל לְךָ מָשָׁל לַמֶּה אָדָם הָרִאשׁוֹן דּוֹמֶה
לְאֶחָד שֶׁהָיָה לוֹ אִשָּׁה בְּתוֹךְ בֵּיתוֹ מֶה עָשָׂה אוֹתוֹ הָאִישׁ הָלַךְ וְהֵבִיא אֶת
הֶחָבִית וְהִנִּיחַ בָּהּ תְּאֵנִים בְּמִנְיָן וֶאֱגוֹזִים בְּמִנְיָן וְצָד אֶת הָעַקְרָב וּנְתָנוֹ
עַל פִּי הֶחָבִית וְהִקִּיפָהּ בְּצָמִיד פָּתִיל וְהִנִּיחָהּ בְּקֶרֶן זָוִיּוֹת אָמַר לָהּ בִּתִּי
כָּל שֶׁיֵּשׁ לִי בַּבַּיִת הַזֶּה מָסוּר בְּיָדָךְ חוּץ מֵחָבִית זוֹ שֶׁלֹּא תִגְּעִי בָהּ כָּל
עִיקָר. מֶה עָשְׂתָה הָאִשָּׁה הַהִיא כֵּיוָן שֶׁיָּצָא בַעְלָהּ לַשּׁוּק עָמְדָה וּפָתְחָה
אֶת הֶחָבִית וְהוֹשִׁיטָה יָדָהּ לְתוֹכָהּ וַעֲקַצַּתָּה הָעַקְרָב הָלְכָה לָהּ וְנָפְלָה
עַל הַמִּטָּה. כֵּיוָן שֶׁבָּא בַעְלָהּ מִן הַשּׁוּק אָמַר לָהּ מַה זֶה. אָמְרָה לוֹ יָדִי
הוֹשַׁטְתִּי עַל הֶחָבִית וַעֲקַצַּתְנִי עַקְרָב וַהֲרֵינִי מֵתָה. אָמַר לָהּ לֹא כָךְ
אָמַרְתִּי לָךְ מִתְּחִלָּה כָּל מַה שֶׁיֵּשׁ לִי בְבַיִת זֶה מָסוּר בְּיָדָךְ חוּץ מֵחָבִית
זוֹ שֶׁלֹּא תִגְּעִי בָהּ כָּל עִיקָר. מִיָּד כָּעַס עָלֶיהָ וֶהוֹצִיאָהּ. כָּךְ אָדָם הָרִאשׁוֹן
דּוֹמֶה בְּשָׁעָה שֶׁאָמַר לוֹ הַקָּדוֹשׁ בָּרוּךְ הוּא מִכָּל עֵץ־הַגָּן אָכֹל תֹּאכֵל
וּמֵעֵץ הַדַּעַת טוֹב וָרָע לֹא תֹאכַל מִמֶּנּוּ כִּי בְּיוֹם אֲכָלְךָ מִמֶּנּוּ מוֹת תָּמוּת
(בראשית ב' י"ז) כֵּיוָן שֶׁאָכַל מִמֶּנּוּ נִטְרַד לְקַיֵּים מַה שֶׁנֶּאֱמַר אָדָם בִּיקָר
בַּל־יָלִין נִמְשַׁל כַּבְּהֵמוֹת נִדְמוּ (תהלים מ"ט כ"א):

בּוֹ בַיּוֹם נוֹצַר בּוֹ בַיּוֹם נִבְרָא בּוֹ בַיּוֹם נוֹצְרָה צוּרָתוֹ בּוֹ בַיּוֹם
נַעֲשָׂה גוֹלֶם בּוֹ בַיּוֹם נִתְקַשְּׁרוּ אֵיבָרָיו וְנִתְפַּתְּחוּ נְקָבָיו בּוֹ בַיּוֹם נִתְּנָה
בּוֹ נְשָׁמָה בּוֹ בַיּוֹם עָמַד עַל רַגְלָיו בּוֹ בַיּוֹם נִזְדַּוְוּגָה לוֹ חַוָּה בּוֹ בַיּוֹם קָרָא
שֵׁמוֹת בּוֹ בַיּוֹם הִכְנִיסוֹ לְגַן עֵדֶן בּוֹ בַיּוֹם צִוָּהוּ בּוֹ בַיּוֹם סָרַח בּוֹ בַיּוֹם
נִטְרַד לְקַיֵּים מַה שֶׁנֶּאֱמַר אָדָם בִּיקָר בַּל־יָלִין (שם). בּוֹ בַיּוֹם עָלוּ לְמִטָּה
שְׁנַיִם וְיָרְדוּ אַרְבָּעָה ר' יְהוּדָה בֶּן בְּתֵירָה אוֹמֵר בּוֹ בַיּוֹם עָלוּ לְמִטָּה

שָׁנִים וְיָרְדוּ שִׁבְעָה בּוֹ בַּיּוֹם נִגְזְרוּ עַל אָדָם ג׳ גְּזֵרוֹת שֶׁנֶּאֱמַר וּלְאָדָם אָמַר
כִּי שָׁמַעְתָּ לְקוֹל אִשְׁתֶּךָ וְגו׳ אֲרוּרָה הָאֲדָמָה בַּעֲבוּרֶךָ בְּעִצָּבוֹן תֹּאכֲלֶנָּה
[וְגו׳] וְקוֹץ וְדַרְדַּר תַּצְמִיחַ לָךְ וְאָכַלְתָּ־אֶת־עֵשֶׂב הַשָּׂדֶה (בראשית ג׳ י״ז וי״ח).
כֵּיוָן שֶׁשָּׁמַע אָדָם הָרִאשׁוֹן שֶׁאָמַר לוֹ הקב״ה וְאָכַלְתָּ אֶת עֵשֶׂב הַשָּׂדֶה מִיָּד
נִזְדַּעְזְעוּ אֵבָרָיו אָמַר לְפָנָיו רִבּוֹנוֹ שֶׁלְעוֹלָם אֲנִי וּבְהֶמְתִּי נֹאכַל בְּאֵבוּס אֶחָד
אָמַר לוֹ הַקָּדוֹשׁ בָּרוּךְ הוּא הוֹאִיל וְנִזְדַּעְזְעוּ אֵבָרֶיךָ בְּזֵעַת אַפֶּיךָ תֹּאכַל
לֶחֶם (שם). וּכְשֵׁם שֶׁנִּגְזְרוּ עַל אָדָם הָרִאשׁוֹן כָּךְ נִגְזַר עַל חַוָּה
ג׳ גְּזֵרוֹת שֶׁנֶּאֱמַר אֶל־הָאִשָּׁה אָמַר הַרְבָּה אַרְבֶּה עִצְּבוֹנֵךְ וְהֵרֹנֵךְ בְּעֶצֶב
תֵּלְדִי בָנִים [וְאֶל־אִישֵׁךְ תְּשׁוּקָתֵךְ וְהוּא יִמְשָׁל־בָּךְ (שם ט״ז) הַרְבָּה אַרְבֶּה
עִצְּבוֹנֵךְ וְהֵרֹנֵךְ] הַרְבָּה בַּזְּמַן שֶׁהָאִשָּׁה רוֹאָה דַּם נִדָּתָהּ בַּתְּחִלָּה וְסַתָּהּ קָשֶׁה
לָהּ. אַרְבֶּה בַּזְּמַן שֶׁהָאִשָּׁה נִבְעֶלֶת תְּחִלַּת בְּעִילָתָהּ קָשֶׁה לָהּ. עִצְּבוֹנֵךְ
[וְהֵרֹנֵךְ] בַּזְּמַן שֶׁהָאִשָּׁה מִתְעַבֶּרֶת פָּנֶיהָ מְכֹעָרוֹת וּמוֹרִיקוֹת כָּל ג׳ חֳדָשִׁים
הָרִאשׁוֹנִים: כֵּיוָן שֶׁבָּא לְעֵת עֶרֶב רָאָה אָדָם הָרִאשׁוֹן אֶת הָעוֹלָם שֶׁמַּחֲשִׁיךְ
מַחֲשִׁיךְ עָלַי אֶת הָעוֹלָם וְהוּא אֵינוֹ יוֹדֵעַ שֶׁכֵּן בִּשְׁבִיל שֶׁסָּרַחְתִּי הַקָּדוֹשׁ
בָּרוּךְ הוּא וּבָא לַמַּעֲרָב אָמַר אוֹי לִי דֶּרֶךְ הָעוֹלָם. לַשַּׁחֲרִית כֵּיוָן שֶׁרָאָה
אֶת הָעוֹלָם שֶׁמֵּאִיר וּבָא לַמִּזְרָח שָׂמַח שִׂמְחָה גְדוֹלָה עָמַד וּבָנָה מִזְבְּחוֹת
וְהֵבִיא שׁוֹר שֶׁקַּרְנוֹתָיו קוֹדְמוֹת לְפַרְסוֹתָיו וְהֶעֱלָהוּ עוֹלָה שֶׁנֶּאֱמַר וְתִיטַב
לַה׳ מִשּׁוֹר פָּר מַקְרִן מַפְרִיס (תהלים ס״ט ל״ב): שׁוֹר שֶׁהֶעֱלָה אָדָם הָרִאשׁוֹן
וּפָר שֶׁהֶעֱלָה נֹחַ וְאַיִל שֶׁהֶעֱלָה אַבְרָהָם אָבִינוּ תַּחַת בְּנוֹ עַל גַּבֵּי הַמִּזְבֵּחַ
כּוּלָּם קַרְנוֹתֵיהֶן קוֹדְמוֹת לְפַרְסוֹתֵיהֶן שֶׁנֶּאֱמַר וַיִּשָּׂא אַבְרָהָם אֶת־עֵינָיו
וַיַּרְא וְהִנֵּה־אַיִל אַחַר נֶאֱחָז (בראשית כ״ג י״ג): בְּאוֹתָהּ שָׁעָה יָרְדוּ שָׁלֹשׁ
כִּתּוֹת שֶׁל מַלְאֲכֵי הַשָּׁרֵת וּבִידֵיהֶם כִּנּוֹרוֹת וּנְבָלִים וְכָל כְּלֵי שִׁיר וְהָיוּ
אוֹמְרִים שִׁירָה עִמּוֹ שֶׁנֶּאֱמַר מִזְמוֹר שִׁיר לְיוֹם הַשַּׁבָּת טוֹב לְהֹדוֹת לַה׳
וְגו׳ לְהַגִּיד בַּבֹּקֶר חַסְדֶּךָ וֶאֱמוּנָתְךָ בַּלֵּילוֹת (תהלים צ״ב א׳) לְהַגִּיד בַּבֹּקֶר
חַסְדֶּךָ זֶה הָעוֹלָם הַבָּא שֶׁנִּמְשָׁל כַּבֹּקֶר שֶׁנֶּאֱמַר חֲדָשִׁים לַבְּקָרִים רַבָּה
אֱמוּנָתֶךָ (איכה ג׳ כ״ג) וֶאֱמוּנָתְךָ בַּלֵּילוֹת זֶה הָעוֹלָם הַזֶּה שֶׁנִּמְשָׁל בַּלֵּילוֹת

שֶׁנֶּאֱמַר מַשָּׂא דּוּמָה אֵלַי קֹרֵא מִשֵּׂעִיר שֹׁמֵר מַה־מִלַּיְלָה שֹׁמֵר מַה־מִלֵּיל (ישעיה כ״א י״א):

בְּאוֹתָהּ שָׁעָה אָמַר הַקָּדוֹשׁ בָּרוּךְ הוּא אִם אֵינִי דָן אֶת הַנָּחָשׁ נִמְצֵאתִי מַחֲרִיב אֶת כָּל הָעוֹלָם כּוּלּוֹ וְאָמַר זֶה שֶׁהִמְלַכְתִּי וַעֲשִׂיתִיו מֶלֶךְ עַל כָּל הָעוֹלָם כּוּלּוֹ הֵיאַךְ נִשְׁתַּבֵּשׁ וְאָכַל מִפֵּירוֹת הָאִילָן מִיָּד נִפְנָה אֵלָיו וְקִלְּלוֹ שֶׁנֶּאֱמַר וַיֹּאמֶר ה׳ אֱלֹהִים אֶל־הַנָּחָשׁ וְגו׳ (בראשית ג׳ י״ד). ר׳ יוֹסֵי אוֹמֵר אִלְמָלֵא לֹא נִכְתַּב קִלְלָתוֹ בְסוֹפָן כְּבָר הֶחֱרִיב אֶת כָּל הָעוֹלָם [כולו]:

כְּשֶׁבְּרָאוֹ הַקָּדוֹשׁ בָּרוּךְ הוּא לְאָדָם הָרִאשׁוֹן צָר אוֹתוֹ פָּנִים וְאָחוֹר שֶׁנֶּאֱמַר אָחוֹר וָקֶדֶם צַרְתָּנִי וַתָּשֶׁת עָלַי כַּפֶּךָ (תהלים קל״ט ה׳) וְיָרְדוּ מַלְאֲכֵי הַשָּׁרֵת לְשַׁחֲתוֹ וּנְטָלוֹ הַקָּדוֹשׁ בָּרוּךְ הוּא תַּחַת כְּנָפָיו שֶׁנֶּאֱמַר וַתָּשֶׁת עָלַי כַּפֶּךָ (שם): דָּבָר אַחֵר וַתָּשֶׁת עָלַי כַּפֶּךָ כֵּיוָן שֶׁסָּרַח נָטַל לוֹ הַקָּדוֹשׁ בָּרוּךְ הוּא אַחַת מֵהֶן. מִכָּאן לְאָדָם וְלַמִּקְדָּשׁ כְּשֶׁנִּבְרְאוּ בִּשְׁתֵּי יָדָיו נִבְרְאוּ. מִנַּיִן לְאָדָם שֶׁנִּבְרָא בִּשְׁתֵּי יָדָיו שֶׁנֶּאֱמַר יָדֶיךָ עָשׂוּנִי וַיְכוֹנְנוּנִי (שם קי״ט ע״ג) מִנַּיִן לַמִּקְדָּשׁ שֶׁנִּבְרָא בִּשְׁתֵּי יָדָיו שֶׁנֶּאֱמַר מִקְדָּשׁ אֲדֹנָי כּוֹנְנוּ יָדֶיךָ (שמות ט״ו י״ח) וְאוֹמֵר וַיְבִיאֵם אֶל־גְּבוּל קָדְשׁוֹ הַר־זֶה קָנְתָה יְמִינוֹ (תהלים ע״ח נ״ד) וְאוֹמֵר ה׳ יִמְלוֹךְ לְעוֹלָם וָעֶד (שמות ט״ו י״ט):

# CHAPTER 6: ABOT DE RABBI NATHAN
## IV:V.1–IV:VII

עַל גְּמִילוּת חֲסָדִים כֵּיצַד הֲרֵי הוּא אוֹמֵר כִּי חֶסֶד חָפַצְתִּי וְלֹא־זָבַח
(הושע ו' ו') הָעוֹלָם מִתְּחִלָּה לֹא נִבְרָא אֶלָּא בְּחֶסֶד שֶׁנֶּאֱמַר כִּי־אָמַרְתִּי עוֹלָם
חֶסֶד יִבָּנֶה שָׁמַיִם תָּכִין אֱמוּנָתְךָ בָהֶם (תהלים פ"ט ג'). פַּעַם אַחַת הָיָה רַבָּן
יוֹחָנָן בֶּן זַכַּאי יוֹצֵא מִירוּשָׁלַיִם וְהָיָה ר' יְהוֹשֻׁעַ הוֹלֵךְ אַחֲרָיו וְרָאָה בֵית
הַמִּקְדָּשׁ חָרֵב אָמַר ר' יְהוֹשֻׁעַ אוֹי לָנוּ עַל זֶה שֶׁהוּא חָרֵב מָקוֹם שֶׁמְּכַפְּרִים
בּוֹ עֲוֹנוֹתֵיהֶם שֶׁל יִשְׂרָאֵל. אָמַר לוֹ בְּנִי אַל יֵרַע לְךָ יֵשׁ לָנוּ כַּפָּרָה
אַחַת שֶׁהִיא כְּמוֹתָהּ וְאֵיזֶה זֶה גְּמִילוּת חֲסָדִים שֶׁנֶּאֱמַר כִּי חֶסֶד חָפַצְתִּי
וְלֹא־זָבַח (הושע ו' ו'). שֶׁכֵּן מָצִינוּ בְּדָנִיֵּאל אִישׁ חֲמוּדוֹת שֶׁהָיָה מִתְעַסֵּק
בִּגְמִילוּת חֲסָדִים. וּמַה הֵן גְּמִילוּת חֲסָדִים שֶׁהָיָה דָנִיֵּאל מִתְעַסֵּק בָּהֶם אִם
תֹּאמַר עוֹלוֹת וּזְבָחִים מַקְרִיב בְּבָבֶל וַהֲלֹא כְבָר נֶאֱמַר הִשָּׁמֶר לְךָ
פֶּן־תַּעֲלֶה עוֹלוֹתֶיךָ בְּכָל־מָקוֹם אֲשֶׁר תִּרְאֶה כִּי אִם־בַּמָּקוֹם אֲשֶׁר־יִבְחַר
ה' בְּאַחַד שְׁבָטֶיךָ שָׁם תַּעֲלֶה עוֹלוֹתֶיךָ (דברים י"ב י"ג י"ד) אֶלָּא מַה הֵן
גְּמִילוּת חֲסָדִים שֶׁהָיָה מִתְעַסֵּק בָּהֶן הָיָה מְתַקֵּן אֶת הַכַּלָּה וּמְשַׂמְּחָהּ וּמְלַוֶּוה
אֶת הַמֵּת וְנוֹתֵן פְּרוּטָה לֶעָנִי וּמִתְפַּלֵּל שְׁלֹשָׁה פְעָמִים בְּכָל יוֹם וּתְפִלָּתוֹ
מִתְקַבֶּלֶת בְּרָצוֹן שֶׁנֶּאֱמַר וְדָנִיֵּאל כְּדִי יְדַע דִּי־רְשִׁים כְּתָבָא עַל לְבַיְתֵהּ
וְכַוִּין פְּתִיחָן לֵיהּ בְּעִלִּיתֵהּ נֶגֶד יְרוּשְׁלֵם וְזִמְנִין תְּלָתָא בְיוֹמָא הוּא בָּרֵךְ
עַל־בִּרְכוֹהִי וּמְצַלֵּא וּמוֹדֵא קֳדָם אֱלָהֵהּ כָּל־קֳבֵל דִּי הֲוָא עָבֵד מִן־קַדְמַת
דְּנָא (דניאל ו' י"א א):

וּכְשֶׁבָּא אַסְפַּסְיָנוֹס לְהַחֲרִיב אֶת יְרוּשָׁלַיִם אָמַר לָהֶם שׁוֹטִים מִפְּנֵי
מָה אַתֶּם מְבַקְּשִׁים לְהַחֲרִיב אֶת הָעִיר הַזֹּאת וְאַתֶּם מְבַקְּשִׁים לִשְׂרוֹף
אֶת בֵּית הַמִּקְדָּשׁ וְכִי מָה אֲנִי מְבַקֵּשׁ מִכֶּם אֶלָּא שֶׁתְּשַׁגְּרוּ לִי קֶשֶׁת אַחַת
אוֹ חֵץ אַחַת וְאֵלֵךְ לִי מִכֶּם. אָמְרוּ לוֹ כְּשֵׁם שֶׁיָּצָאנוּ עַל שְׁנַיִם רִאשׁוֹנִים
שֶׁהֵם לְפָנֶיךָ וַהֲרַגְנוּם כָּךְ גֵּצֵא לְפָנֶיךָ וְנַהֲרָגֵךְ. כֵּיוָן שֶׁשָּׁמַע רַבָּן יוֹחָנָן בֶּן
זַכַּאי שָׁלַח וְקָרָא לְאַנְשֵׁי יְרוּשְׁלַיִם וְאָמַר לָהֶם בָּנַי מִפְּנֵי מָה אַתֶּם

מַחֲרִיבִין אֶת הָעִיר הַזֹּאת וְאַתֶּם מְבַקְשִׁים לִשְׂרוֹף אֶת בֵּית הַמִּקְדָּשׁ וְכִי
מָהוּ מְבַקֵּשׁ מִכֶּם הָא אֵינוֹ מְבַקֵּשׁ מִכֶּם אֶלָּא קֶשֶׁת אַחַת אוֹ חֵץ אַחַת וְיֵלֵךְ
לוֹ מִכֶּם. אָמְרוּ לוֹ כְּשֵׁם שֶׁיָּצְאוּ עַל שְׁנַיִם שֶׁלְּפָנָיו וַהֲרָגְנוּם כָּךְ נֵצֵא
עָלָיו וְנַהַרְגֵהוּ. הָיוּ לְאִסְפַּסְיָינוֹס אֲנָשִׁים שְׁרוּיִין כְּנֶגֶד חוֹמוֹתֶיהָ שֶׁל
יְרוּשָׁלַיִם וְכָל דָּבָר וְדָבָר שֶׁהָיוּ שׁוֹמְעִין הָיוּ כוֹתְבִין עַל הַחֵצִי וְזוֹרְקִין
חוּץ לַחוֹמָה לוֹמַר שֶׁרַבָּן יוֹחָנָן בֶּן זַכַּאי מֵאוֹהֲבֵי קֵיסָר הוּא. וְכֵיוָן שֶׁאָמַר
לָהֶם רַבָּן יוֹחָנָן בֶּן זַכַּאי יוֹם אֶחָד וּשְׁנַיִם וּשְׁלֹשָׁה וְלֹא קִבְּלוּ מִמֶּנּוּ שָׁלַח
וְקָרָא לְתַלְמִידָיו לְרַבִּי אֱלִיעֶזֶר וְרַבִּי יְהוֹשֻׁעַ אָמַר לָהֶם בָּנַי עִמְדוּ
וְהוֹצִיאוּנִי מִכָּאן עֲשׂוּ לִי אָרוֹן וְאִישַׁן בְּתוֹכוֹ. רַבִּי אֱלִיעֶזֶר אָחַז בְּרֹאשׁוֹ
רַבִּי יְהוֹשֻׁעַ אָחַז בְּרַגְלָיו וְהָיוּ מוֹלִיכִין אוֹתוֹ עַד שְׁקִיעַת הַחַמָּה עַד
שֶׁהִגִּיעוּ אֵצֶל שַׁעֲרֵי יְרוּשָׁלַיִם. אָמְרוּ לָהֶם הַשּׁוֹעֲרִים מִי הוּא זֶה. אָמְרוּ
לָהֶן מֵת הוּא וְכִי אֵין אַתֶּם יוֹדְעִין שֶׁאֵין מְלִינִים אֶת הַמֵּת בִּירוּשָׁלַיִם.
אָמְרוּ לָהֶן אִם מֵת הוּא הוֹצִיאוּהוּ. וְהוֹצִיאוּהוּ וְהָיוּ מוֹלִיכִין אוֹתוֹ (עַד
שְׁקִיעַת הַחַמָּה) עַד שֶׁהִגִּיעוּ אֵצֶל אַסְפַּסְיָינוֹס. פָּתְחוּ הָאָרוֹן וְעָמַד לְפָנָיו.
אָמַר לוֹ אַתָּה הוּא רַבָּן יוֹחָנָן בֶּן זַכַּאי שְׁאַל מָה אֶתֶּן לָךְ. אָמַר לוֹ אֵינִי
מְבַקֵּשׁ מִמְּךָ אֶלָּא יַבְנֶה שֶׁאֵלֵךְ וְאֶשְׁנֶה בָּהּ לְתַלְמִידַי וְאֶקְבַּע בָּהּ תְּפִלָּה
וְאֶעֱשֶׂה בָּהּ כָּל מִצְוֹת. אָמַר לוֹ לֵךְ וְכָל מַה שֶׁאַתָּה רוֹצֶה לַעֲשׂוֹת עֲשֵׂה.
אָמַר לוֹ רְצוֹנְךָ שֶׁאוֹמַר לְפָנֶיךָ דָּבָר אֶחָד. אָמַר לוֹ אֱמוֹר. אָמַר לוֹ הֲרֵי
אַתְּ עוֹמֵד בַּמַּלְכוּת. אָמַר לוֹ מִנַּיִן אַתָּה יוֹדֵעַ. אָמַר לוֹ כָּךְ מָסוּר לָנוּ שֶׁאֵין
בֵּית הַמִּקְדָּשׁ נִמְסָר בְּיַד הֶדְיוֹט אֶלָּא בְּיַד מֶלֶךְ שֶׁנֶּאֱמַר וְנִקַּף סָבְכֵי הַיַּעַר
בַּבַּרְזֶל וְהַלְּבָנוֹן בְּאַדִּיר יִפּוֹל (ישעי׳ י׳ ל״ד). אָמְרוּ לֹא הָיָה יוֹם אֶחָד שְׁנַיִם
וּשְׁלֹשָׁה יָמִים עַד שֶׁבָּא אֵלָיו דְּיוּפְלָא מֵעִירוֹ שֶׁמֵּת קֵיסָר וְנִמְנוּ עָלָיו
לַעֲמוֹד בַּמַּלְכוּת. הֵבִיאוּ לוֹ קֶשֶׁת שֶׁל זֵירִים כְּנֶגֶד הַחוֹמָה שֶׁל יְרוּשָׁלַיִם.
הֵבִיאוּ לוֹ נְסָרִים שֶׁל אֶרֶז וְנָתַן לְתוֹךְ קֶשֶׁת שֶׁל זֵירִים וְהָיָה מַכֶּה בָהֶן
עַל הַחוֹמָה עַד שֶׁפָּרַץ בָּהּ פִּירְצָה. הֵבִיאוּ רֹאשׁ חֲזִיר וְנָתְנוּ לְתוֹךְ קֶשֶׁת
שֶׁל זֵירִים וְהָיָה מַשְׁלִיךְ אוֹתוֹ כְּלַפֵּי אֵבָרִים שֶׁעַל גַּבֵּי הַמִּזְבֵּחַ. בְּאוֹתָהּ

שָׁעָה נִלְכְּדָה יְרוּשָׁלַיִם וְהָיָה רַבָּן יוֹחָנָן בֶּן זַכַּאי יוֹשֵׁב וּמְצַפֶּה וְחָרֵד
כְּדֶרֶךְ שֶׁהָיָה עֵלִי יוֹשֵׁב וּמְצַפֶּה שֶׁנֶּאֱמַר וְהִנֵּה עֵלִי יוֹשֵׁב עַל־הַכִּסֵּא יַד
דֶּרֶךְ מְצַפֶּה כִּי־הָיָה לִבּוֹ חָרֵד עַל אֲרוֹן הָאֱלֹהִים (שמואל א׳ ד׳ י״ג). כֵּיוָן
שֶׁשָּׁמַע רַבָּן יוֹחָנָן בֶּן זַכַּאי שֶׁהֶחֱרִיב אֶת יְרוּשָׁלַיִם וְשָׂרַף אֶת בֵּית הַמִּקְדָּשׁ
בָּאֵשׁ קָרַע בְּגָדָיו וְקָרְעוּ תַלְמִידָיו אֶת בִּגְדֵיהֶם וְהָיוּ בוֹכִין וְצוֹעֲקִין
וְסוֹפְדִין: וְאוֹמֵר פְּתַח לְבָנוֹן דְּלָתֶיךָ וְתֹאכַל אֵשׁ בַּאֲרָזֶיךָ (זכרי׳ י״א א׳)
אֵלוּ כֹּהֲנִים גְּדוֹלִים שֶׁהָיוּ בַמִּקְדָּשׁ שֶׁהָיוּ נוֹטְלִים מַפְתְּחוֹתֵיהֶם בְּיָדָן
וְזוֹרְקִין כְּלַפֵּי מַעֲלָה וְאוֹמְרִים לִפְנֵי הַקָּדוֹשׁ בָּרוּךְ הוּא רִבּוֹנוֹ שֶׁל עוֹלָם
הֵילָךְ מַפְתְּחוֹתֶיךָ שֶׁמָּסַרְתָּ לָנוּ הוֹאִיל וְלֹא הָיִינוּ גִזְבָּרִין נֶאֱמָנִין לַעֲשׂוֹת
מְלֶאכֶת הַמֶּלֶךְ וּלֶאֱכוֹל מִשֻּׁלְחָן הַמֶּלֶךְ. אַבְרָהָם יִצְחָק וְיַעֲקֹב וּשְׁנֵים עָשָׂר
שְׁבָטִים הָיוּ בוֹכִין וְצוֹעֲקִין וְסוֹפְדִין: וְאוֹמֵר הֵילֵל בְּרוֹשׁ כִּי נָפַל אֶרֶז
אֲשֶׁר אַדִּירִים שֻׁדָּדוּ [הֵילִילוּ אַלּוֹנֵי בָשָׁן כִּי יָרַד יַעַר הַבָּצִיר] (שם שם ב׳).
הֵילֵל בְּרוֹשׁ כִּי־נָפַל אֶרֶז זֶה אֶרֶז זֶה בֵּית הַמִּקְדָּשׁ. אֲשֶׁר אַדִּירִים שֻׁדָּדוּ זֶה
אַבְרָהָם יִצְחָק וְיַעֲקֹב וִי״ב שְׁבָטִים. הֵילִילוּ אַלּוֹנֵי בָשָׁן זֶה מֹשֶׁה אַהֲרֹן
וּמִרְיָם. כִּי יָרַד יַעַר הַבָּצִיר זֶה בֵּית הַמִּקְדָּשׁ. קוֹל יִלְלַת הָרוֹעִים כִּי
שֻׁדְּדָה אַדַּרְתָּם (שם ג׳) זֶה דָּוִד וּשְׁלֹמֹה בְנוֹ. קוֹל שַׁאֲגַת כְּפִירִים כִּי שֻׁדַּד
גְּאוֹן הַיַּרְדֵּן (שם) זֶה אֵלִיָּהוּ וֶאֱלִישָׁע:

## CHAPTER 6: ABOT DE RABBI NATHAN
### VIII:VI.1-2

כְּשֵׁם שֶׁהַצַּדִּיקִים הָרִאשׁוֹנִים הָיוּ חֲסִידִים כָּךְ בְּהֶמְתָּן הָיוּ חֲסִידוֹת.

אָמְרוּ גְּמַלָּיו שֶׁל אַבְרָהָם אָבִינוּ לֹא נִכְנְסוּ לְבַיִת שֶׁיֵּשׁ בּוֹ עֲבוֹדַת אֱלִילִים

שֶׁנֶּאֱמַר וְאָנֹכִי פִּנִּיתִי הַבַּיִת וּמָקוֹם לַגְּמַלִּים (בראשית כ״ד ל״א): וְאָנֹכִי

פִּנִּיתִי אֶת הַבַּיִת מִתְּרָפִים. וּמַה תַּלְמוּד לוֹמַר וּמָקוֹם לַגְּמַלִּים מְלַמֵּד שֶׁלֹּא

נִכְנְסוּ לְבֵית לָבָן הָאֲרַמִּי עַד שֶׁפִּנּוּ כָל הָעֲבוֹדַת אֱלִילִים מִפְּנֵיהֶם:

מַעֲשֶׂה בַּחֲמוֹרוֹ שֶׁל רַבִּי חֲנִינָא בֶּן דּוֹסָא שֶׁגְּנָבוּהוּ לִסְטִים וְחָבְשׁוּ אֶת

הַחֲמוֹר בֶּחָצֵר וְהִנִּיחוּ לוֹ תֶּבֶן וּשְׂעוֹרִים וּמַיִם וְלֹא הָיָה אוֹכֵל וְשׁוֹתֶה.

אָמְרוּ לָמָּה אָנוּ מְנִיחִין אוֹתוֹ שֶׁיָּמוּת וְיַבְאִישׁ לָנוּ אֶת הֶחָצֵר. עָמְדוּ וּפָתְחוּ

לָהּ אֶת הַדֶּלֶת וְהוֹצִיאוּהָ וְהָיְתָה מְנַהֶקֶת וְהוֹלֶכֶת עַד שֶׁהִגִּיעָה אֵצֶל רַבִּי

חֲנִינָא בֶּן דּוֹסָא. כֵּיוָן שֶׁהִגִּיעָה אֶצְלוֹ שָׁמַע בְּנוֹ קוֹלָהּ אָמַר לוֹ אַבָּא דּוֹמֶה

קוֹלָהּ לְקוֹל בְּהֶמְתֵּנוּ אָמַר לוֹ בְּנִי פְּתַח לָהּ אֶת הַדֶּלֶת שֶׁכְּבָר מֵתָה בְרָעָב.

עָמַד וּפָתַח [אֶת] הַדֶּלֶת וְהִנִּיחַ לָהּ תֶּבֶן וּשְׂעוֹרִים וּמַיִם וְהָיְתָה אוֹכֶלֶת

וְשׁוֹתָה. לְפִיכָךְ אָמְרוּ כְּשֵׁם שֶׁהַצַּדִּיקִים הָרִאשׁוֹנִים הָיוּ חֲסִידִים כָּךְ

בְּהֶמְתָּן חֲסִידוֹת כְּמוֹתָן:

# CHAPTER 6: ABOT DE RABBI NATHAN
## XII:1.5–XII:11.5

בְּאוֹתָה שָׁעָה בִקֵשׁ מֹשֶׁה מִיתָה כְּמִיתָתוֹ [שֶׁל] אַהֲרֹן מִפְּנֵי שֶׁרָאָה
מִטָּתוֹ מוּצַעַת בְּכָבוֹד גָּדוֹל וְכִתּוֹת כִּתּוֹת שֶׁל מַלְאֲכֵי הַשָּׁרֵת סוֹפְדוֹת
אוֹתוֹ. וְכִי בֵינוֹ לְבֵין אָדָם שָׁאַל וַהֲלֹא בֵינוֹ לְבֵין עַצְמוֹ שָׁאַל וְשָׁמַע
הַקָּדוֹשׁ בָּרוּךְ הוּא לְחִישָׁתוֹ. [וּמִנַּיִן שֶׁבִּקֵשׁ מֹשֶׁה מִיתָתוֹ כְּמִיתָתוֹ שֶׁל
אַהֲרֹן וְשָׁמַע לְחִישָׁתוֹ] שֶׁנֶּאֱמַר מוּת בָּהָר אֲשֶׁר אַתָּה עוֹלֶה שָׁמָּה וְהֵאָסֵף
אֶל־עַמֶּךָ כַּאֲשֶׁר־מֵת אַהֲרֹן אָחִיךָ בְּהֹר הָהָר (דברים ל״ב ג״א) הָא לָמַדְתָּ
שֶׁבִּקֵשׁ [מֹשֶׁה] מִיתָה כְּמִיתָתוֹ שֶׁל אַהֲרֹן: בְּאוֹתָה שָׁעָה אָמַר לוֹ לְמַלְאַךְ
הַמָּוֶת לֵךְ הָבֵא לִי נִשְׁמָתוֹ שֶׁל מֹשֶׁה. הָלַךְ מַלְאַךְ הַמָּוֶת וְעָמַד לְפָנָיו אָמַר
לוֹ מֹשֶׁה תֵּן לִי נִשְׁמָתְךָ. גָּעַר בּוֹ אָמַר לוֹ בַּמָּקוֹם שֶׁאֲנִי יוֹשֵׁב אֵין נוֹתְנִין
לְךָ רְשׁוּת לַעֲמוֹד וְאַתָּה אָמַרְתָּ תֵּן לִי נִשְׁמָתְךָ גָּעַר בּוֹ וְהוֹצִיאוֹ בִּנְזִיפָה.
עַד שֶׁאָמַר לוֹ הַקָּדוֹשׁ בָּרוּךְ הוּא לְמֹשֶׁה מֹשֶׁה דַּיֶּיךָ הָעוֹלָם הַזֶּה שֶׁהֲרֵי
הָעוֹלָם הַבָּא שָׁמוּר לְךָ [שֶׁכְּבָר הַמָּקוֹם מְתוּקָן לְךָ] מִשֵּׁשֶׁת יְמֵי בְרֵאשִׁית
שֶׁנֶּאֱמַר וַיֹּאמֶר ח' הִנֵּה מָקוֹם אִתִּי וְנִצַּבְתָּ עַל־הַצּוּר (שמות ל״ג ב״ב) נְטָלָה
הַקָּדוֹשׁ בָּרוּךְ הוּא לְנִשְׁמָתוֹ שֶׁל מֹשֶׁה וּגְנָזָהּ תַּחַת כִּסֵּא הַכָּבוֹד. וּכְשֶׁנְּטָלָהּ
לֹא נְטָלָהּ אֶלָּא בִנְשִׁיקָה שֶׁנֶּאֱמַר עַל פִּי ה' (דברים ל״ד ה'): לֹא נִשְׁמָתוֹ
שֶׁל מֹשֶׁה בִּלְבַד גְּנוּזָה תַּחַת כִּסֵּא הַכָּבוֹד אֶלָּא [כָּל] נִשְׁמָתָן שֶׁל צַדִּיקִים
גְּנוּזוֹת תַּחַת כִּסֵּא הַכָּבוֹד שֶׁנֶּאֱמַר וְהָיְתָה נֶפֶשׁ אֲדֹנִי צְרוּרָה בִּצְרוֹר
הַחַיִּים (שמואל א' כ״ה כ״ט). יָכוֹל אַף שֶׁל רְשָׁעִים כֵּן תַּלְמוּד לוֹמַר וְאֵת
נֶפֶשׁ אוֹיְבֶיךָ יְקַלְּעֶנָּה בְּכַף הַקָּלַע (שם שם) אַף עַל פִּי שֶׁזּוֹרֵק מִמָּקוֹם
לְמָקוֹם אֵינוֹ יוֹדֵעַ עַל מַה שֶׁתִּסָּמֵךְ. אַף כֵּן נִשְׁמָתָן שֶׁל רְשָׁעִים זוֹמְמוֹת
וְהוֹלְכוֹת וְשׁוֹטְטוֹת בָּעוֹלָם וְאֵינָן יוֹדְעוֹת עַל מַה שֶׁיִּסָּמֵכוּ: שׁוּב אָמַר
לוֹ [הַקָּדוֹשׁ בָּרוּךְ הוּא] לְמַלְאַךְ הַמָּוֶת לֵךְ וְהָבֵא לִי נִשְׁמָתוֹ שֶׁל מֹשֶׁה הָלַךְ
לִמְקוֹמוֹ בִּקְשׁוֹ וְלֹא מְצָאוֹ. הָלַךְ אֵצֶל הַיָּם הַגָּדוֹל אָמַר לוֹ מֹשֶׁה בָּא לְכָאן.
אָמַר לוֹ מִיּוֹם שֶׁעָבְרוּ יִשְׂרָאֵל בְּתוֹכִי שׁוּב לֹא רְאִיתִיו. הָלַךְ אֵצֶל הָרִים

וּגְבָעוֹת וְאָמַר לָהֶם מֹשֶׁה בָּא לְכָאן אָמְרוּ לוֹ מִיּוֹם שֶׁקִּבְּלוּ יִשְׂרָאֵל אֶת
הַתּוֹרָה בְּהַר סִינַי שׁוּב לֹא רְאִינוּהוּ. [הָלַךְ] אֵצֶל שְׁאוֹל וַאֲבַדּוֹן אָמַר לָהֶם
מֹשֶׁה בָּא לְכָאן. אָמְרוּ לוֹ שְׁמוֹ שָׁמַעְנוּ וְאוֹתוֹ לֹא רָאִינוּ. [הָלַךְ] אֵצֶל
מַלְאֲכֵי הַשָּׁרֵת אָמַר לָהֶם מֹשֶׁה בָּא לְכָאן. אָמַר לוֹ אֱלֹהִים הֵבִין דַּרְכּוֹ
וְהוּא יָדַע אֶת־מְקוֹמוֹ אֱלֹהִים גְּנָזוֹ לְחַיֵּי הָעוֹלָם הַבָּא וְאֵין כָּל בְּרִיָּה יוֹדַעַת
שֶׁנֶּאֱמַר וְהַחָכְמָה מֵאַיִן תִּמָּצֵא וְאֵיזֶה מְקוֹם בִּינָה לֹא־יָדַע אֱנוֹשׁ עֶרְכָּהּ
וְלֹא תִמָּצֵא בְּאֶרֶץ הַחַיִּים תְּהוֹם אָמַר לֹא בִי־הִיא וְיָם אָמַר אֵין עִמָּדִי
(איוב כ״ח י״ג י״ד ט״ו) אֲבַדּוֹן וָמָוֶת אָמְרוּ בְּאָזְנֵינוּ שָׁמַעְנוּ שִׁמְעָהּ
(שם שם כ״ב), אַף יְהוֹשֻׁעַ הָיָה יוֹשֵׁב וּמִצְטַעֵר עַל מֹשֶׁה עַד שֶׁאָמַר לוֹ
הַקָּדוֹשׁ בָּרוּךְ הוּא יְהוֹשֻׁעַ לָמָּה אַתָּה מִצְטַעֵר עַל מֹשֶׁה מֹשֶׁה עַבְדִּי מֵת:

## CHAPTER 6: ABOT DE RABBI NATHAN
### XVII:11.1-2

הַתְקֵן עַצְמְךָ לִלְמוֹד תּוֹרָה שֶׁאֵינָהּ יְרוּשָׁה לָךְ כֵּיצַד בְּשָׁעָה שֶׁרָאָה
מֹשֶׁה רַבֵּינוּ [אֶת בָּנָיו] שֶׁאֵין בָּהֶן תּוֹרָה שֶׁיַּעַמְדוּ בִנְשִׂיאוּת אַחֲרָיו
נִתְעַטֵּף וְעָמַד בִּתְפִלָּה. אָמַר לְפָנָיו רִבּוֹנוֹ שֶׁל עוֹלָם הוֹדִיעֵנִי אֶת מִי
יִכָּנֵס אֶת מִי יֵצֵא בְּרֹאשׁ כָּל הָעָם הַזֶּה שֶׁנֶּאֱמַר וַיְדַבֵּר מֹשֶׁה אֶל־ה' לֵאמֹר
יִפְקֹד ה' אֱלֹהֵי הָרוּחוֹת לְכָל־בָּשָׂר אִישׁ עַל־הָעֵדָה אֲשֶׁר־יֵצֵא לִפְנֵיהֶם
וַאֲשֶׁר יָבֹא לִפְנֵיהֶם (במדבר כ״ז ט״ז ט״ז וי״ז). אָמַר לוֹ הַקָּדוֹשׁ בָּרוּךְ הוּא
לְמֹשֶׁה מֹשֶׁה קַח־לְךָ אֶת־יְהוֹשֻׁעַ (שם שם י״ח). [אָמַר לוֹ הַקָּדוֹשׁ בָּרוּךְ הוּא
לְמֹשֶׁה] לֵךְ וַעֲמֹד לוֹ תּוּרְגְּמָן וְיִדְרוֹשׁ לְפָנֶיךָ בְּרֹאשׁ גְּדוֹלֵי יִשְׂרָאֵל.
בְּאוֹתָהּ שָׁעָה אָמַר לוֹ מֹשֶׁה לִיהוֹשֻׁעַ יְהוֹשֻׁעַ עַם זֶה שֶׁאֲנִי מוֹסֵר לָךְ.
אֵינִי מוֹסֵר לָךְ תְּיָישִׁים אֶלָּא גְדָיִים. וּכְבָשִׂים אֵינִי מוֹסֵר לָךְ אֶלָּא טְלָאִים.
שֶׁעֲדַיִין לֹא נִתְעַסְּקוּ בַּמִּצְוֹת וַעֲדַיִין לֹא הִגִּיעוּ לִתְיָישִׁים וּכְבָשִׂים שֶׁנֶּאֱמַר
אִם־לֹא תֵדְעִי לָךְ הַיָּפָה בַּנָּשִׁים צְאִי־לָךְ בְּעִקְבֵי הַצֹּאן וּרְעִי אֶת־גְּדִיֹּתַיִךְ
עַל מִשְׁכְּנוֹת הָרוֹעִים:

# General Index

# Index to Biblical and Talmudic References

### MISHNAH